KT-486-963

Show Me Microsoft® Windows XP, Second Edition

Steve Johnson

Perspection, Inc.

Que Publishing
800 East 96th Street
Indianapolis, IN 46240 USA

Show Me Microsoft® Windows XP, Second Edition

Copyright © 2004 by Perspection, Inc.
All rights reserved. No part of this book shall be reproduced, stored in a retrieval system, or transmitted by any means, electronic, mechanical, photo-copying, recording, or otherwise, without written permission from the pub-lisher. No patent liability is assumed with respect to the use of the informa-tion contained herein. Although every precaution has been taken in the preparation of this book, the publisher and author assume no responsibility for errors or omissions. Nor is any liability assumed for damages resulting from the use of the information contained herein.

International Standard Book Number: 0-7897-3336-6

Library of Congress Catalog Card Number: 2004111746

Printed in the United States of America

First Printing: September 2004

08 07 06   9 8 7 6

Que Publishing offers excellent discounts on this book when ordered in quantity for bulk purchases or special sales. For information, please contact:

U.S. Corporate and Government Sales

1-800-382-3419

corpsales@pearsontechgroup.com

For sales outside the U.S., please contact:

International Sales

International@pearsoned.com

Trademarks

All terms mentioned in this book that are known to be trademarks or service marks have been appropriately capitalized. Que cannot attest to the accuracy of this information. Use of a term in this book should not be regarded as affecting the validity of any trademark or service mark.

Microsoft is a registered trademark of Microsoft Corporation. Windows is a registered trademark of Microsoft Corporation. Bluetooth is a trademark owned by the Bluetooth SIG, Inc.

Warning and Disclaimer

Every effort has been made to make this book as complete and as accurate as possible, but no warranty or fitness is implied. The authors and the pub-lishers shall have neither liability nor responsibility to any person or entity with respect to any loss or damage arising from the information contained in this book.

Publisher
Paul Boger

Associate Publisher
Greg Wiegand

Managing Editor
Steve Johnson

Author
Steve Johnson

Project Editor
Elise Bishop

Technical Editor
Nicholas Chu

Production Editor
Beth Teyler

Page Layout
Beth Teyler
Kate Lyerla
Joe Kalsbeek
Josh Kalsbeek

Interior Designers
Steve Johnson
Marian Hartsough

Indexer
Katherine Stimson

Proofreader
Holly Johnson

Team Coordinators
Sharry Lee Gregory

Acknowledgements

a

Perspection, Inc.

Show Me Microsoft Windows XP, Second Edition has been created by the professional trainers and writers at Perspection, Inc. to the standards you've come to expect from Que publishing. Together, we are pleased to present this training book.

Perspection, Inc. is a software training company committed to providing information and training to help people use software more effectively in order to communicate, make decisions, and solve problems. Perspection writes and produces software training books, and develops multimedia and Web-based training. Since 1991, we have written more than 70 computer books, with several bestsellers to our credit, and sold over 4.7 million books.

This book incorporates Perspection's training expertise to ensure that you'll receive the maximum return on your time. You'll focus on the tasks and skills that increase productivity while working at your own pace and convenience.

We invite you to visit the Perspection Web site at:

www.perspection.com

Acknowledgements

The task of creating any book requires the talents of many hard-working people pulling together to meet impossible deadlines and untold stresses. We'd like to thank the outstanding team responsible for making this book possible: the writer, Steve Johnson; the editor, Elise Bishop; the technical editor, Nicholas Chu; the production team, Beth Teyler, Kate Lyerla, Joe Kalsbeek, and Josh Kalsbeek; and the indexer, Katherine Stimson.

At Que publishing, we'd like to thank Greg Wiegand for the opportunity to undertake this project, Sharry Gregory for administrative support, and Sandra Schroeder for your production expertise and support.

Perspection

Dedication

Most importantly, I would like to thank my wife Holly, and my three children, JP, Brett, and Hannah, for their support and encouragement during the project.

About The Author

Steve Johnson has written more than thirty-five books on a variety of computer software, including Microsoft Office 2003 and XP, Microsoft Windows XP, Apple Mac OS X Panther, Macromedia Flash MX 2004, Macromedia Director MX 2004, Macromedia Fireworks, Adobe Photoshop CS, and Web publishing. In 1991, after working for Apple Computer and Microsoft, Steve founded Perspection, Inc., which writes and produces software training. When he is not staying up late writing, he enjoys playing golf, gardening, and spending time with his wife, Holly, and three children, JP, Brett, and Hannah. When time permits, he likes to travel to such places as New Hampshire in October, and Hawaii. Steve and his family live in Pleasanton, California, but can also be found visiting family all over the western United States.

Upgrade

Introduction

Welcome to *Show Me Microsoft Windows XP, Second Edition*, a visual quick reference book that shows you how to work efficiently with Microsoft Windows XP. This book has been completely revised to include coverage on Service Pack 2 (also abbreviated as SP2), a major new release of Windows XP.

Find the Best Place to Start

You don't have to read this book in any particular order. We've designed the book so that you can jump in, get the information you need, and jump out. However, the book does follow a logical progression from simple tasks to more complex ones. Each task is no more than two pages long. To find the information that you need, just look up the task in the table of contents, index, or troubleshooting guide, and turn to the page listed. Read the task introduction, follow the step-by-step instructions along with the illustration, and you're done.

What's New

If you're searching for what's new in Windows XP, just look for the icons: New! (new for Windows XP, First Edition) or NewSP2 (new for Service Pack 2). The new icons appear in the table of contents and throughout this book so you can quickly and easily identify a new or improved feature in Windows XP. An overview and page location of the new features appear on page 4-5.

How This Book Works

Each task is presented on no more than two facing pages, with step-by-step instructions in the left column and screen illustrations in the right column. This arrangement lets you focus on a single task without having to turn the page.

How You'll Learn

Find the Best Place to Start

What's New

How This Book Works

Step-by-Step Instructions

Real World Examples

Troubleshooting Guide

Show Me Live Software

Step-by-Step Instructions

This book provides concise step-by-step instructions that show you "how" to accomplish a task. Each set of instructions include illustrations that directly correspond to the easy-to-read steps. Also included in the text are timesavers, tables, and sidebars to help you work more efficiently or to teach you more in-depth information. A "Did You Know?" provides tips and techniques to help you work smarter, while a "See Also" leads you to other parts of the book containing related information about the task.

Real World Examples

This book uses real world examples to help convey "why" you would want to perform a task. The examples give you a context in which to use the task. You'll observe how *Home Sense, Inc.*, a fictional home improvement business, uses Windows XP to get jobs done.

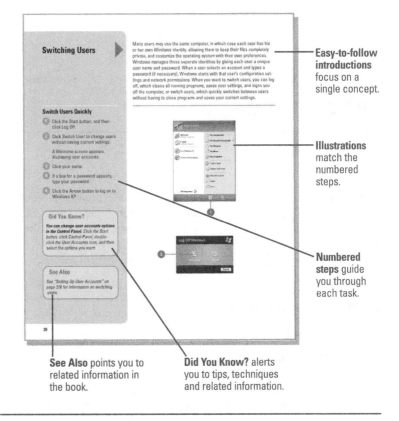

Easy-to-follow introductions focus on a single concept.

Illustrations match the numbered steps.

Numbered steps guide you through each task.

See Also points you to related information in the book.

Did You Know? alerts you to tips, techniques and related information.

Real world examples help you apply what you've learned to other tasks.

Troubleshooting Guide

This book offers quick and easy ways to diagnose and solve common Windows XP problems that you might encounter. The troubleshooting guide helps you determine and fix a problem using the task information you find. The problems are posed in question form and are grouped into categories that are presented alphabetically.

Troubleshooting points you to information in the book to help you fix your problems.

Show Me Live Software

In addition, this book offers companion software that shows you how to perform most tasks using the live program. The easy-to-use VCR-type controls allow you to start, pause, and stop the action. As you observe how to accomplish each task, Show Me Live highlights each step and talks you through the process. The Show Me Live software is available free at *www.perspection.com or www.quepublishing.com/showme.*

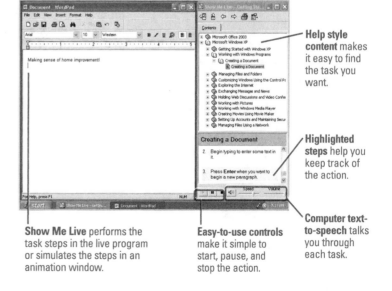

Help style content makes it easy to find the task you want.

Highlighted steps help you keep track of the action.

Computer text-to-speech talks you through each task.

Show Me Live performs the task steps in the live program or simulates the steps in an animation window.

Easy-to-use controls make it simple to start, pause, and stop the action.

We Want To Hear From You!

As the reader of this book, *you* are our most important critic and commentator. We value your opinion and want to know what we're doing right, what we could do better, what areas you'd like to see us publish in, and any other words of wisdom you're willing to pass our way.

As an associate publisher for Que, I welcome your comments. You can email or write me directly to let me know what you did or didn't like about this book—as well as what we can do to make our books better.

Please note that I cannot help you with technical problems related to the *topic* of this book. We do have a User Services group, however, where I will forward specific technical questions related to the book.

When you write, please be sure to include this book's title and author as well as your name, email address, and phone number. I will carefully review your comments and share them with the author and editors who worked on the book.

Email: feedback@quepublishing.com

Mail: Greg Wiegand
         Que Publishing
         800 East 96th Street
         Indianapolis, IN 46240 USA

For more information about this book or another Que title, visit our Web site at www.quepublishing.com. Type the ISBN (excluding hyphens) or the title of a book in the Search field to find the page you're looking for.

Contents

C

Getting Started with Windows XP

1

Introduction

Microsoft Windows XP Home or Professional is an **operating system**, a computer program that controls the basic operation of your computer and the programs you run. A **program**, also known as an **application**, is task-oriented software you use to accomplish a specific task, such as word processing, managing files on your computer, or performing calculations. Windows XP displays programs in rectangular frames on your screen, called windows (thus the name of the operating system). A **window** can contain the contents of a file and the application in which it was created, **icons** (picture representations of a program or a file), or other usable data. A **file** is a collection of information (such as a letter or list of addresses) that has a unique name, distinguishing it from other files. This use of windows and icons is called a **graphical user interface** (**GUI**, pronounced "gooey"), meaning that you ("user") interact ("interface") with the computer through the use of graphics: icons and other meaningful words, symbols, and windows.

Before you get started with Windows XP, check out the new features for the first edition and the newly revised second edition, which provides complete coverage of Windows XP Service Pack 2.

Using Windows XP Home or Professional

Windows XP comes in five editions: the Home Edition for consumers; the Professional Edition for business and power users; the Media Center Edition for Media Center PCs with a focus on home entertainment; the Tablet Edition for Tablet PCs; and a 64-bit version for Intel Itanium processor-based systems, called Windows XP 64-Bit Edition. The Home Edition and the Media Center Edition are a subset of the Professional Edition. In other words, the Home and Media Center Editions contain all the same features contained in the Professional Edition. However, the Professional Edition contains additional features that are geared toward the business world. The Windows XP Tablet PC Edition expands on Windows XP Professional, providing additional capabilities for notebook computers. Each edition allows users to install either an upgrade version for those who already have Windows 98 or later installed on their computers, or a full version for those who have Windows 95 or Windows NT 3.51 or earlier, or no operating system installed on their computers.

Windows XP Professional features not found in the Home Edition

Slightly different user interface

Windows XP Professional comes with a few user interface default settings that are different from those in Windows XP Home.

Accesses a remote desktop

You can access a Windows XP Professional remote desktop from any operating system that supports a Terminal Services client, such as Windows 98 or Me, and Windows XP Home.

Connects to large networks

Most larger networks (typically more than five computers) are domain-based. Windows XP Professional allows you to access, join, and be managed by a Windows domain-based network (typically maintained by a system administrator), while Windows XP Home only allows you to access resources in a domain.

Provides Backup and system recovery

With the Backup utility program, you can back up files to a disk or tape and create an Automated System Recovery disk to help you recover a system from a serious error, such as a system crash.

Protects sensitive data

You can use the Encrypting File System (EFS) to protect your important data against theft or hackers. If you encrypt a file with EFS, only you can open the file and work with it. This is especially useful on your laptop because if it is lost or stolen no one else can access the files on your hard drive.

Supports more than one microprocessor

Windows XP Professional supports up to two microprocessors, while Windows XP Home supports only one. This allows you to perform simultaneous tasks, such as printing large documents and calculating large amounts of numbers, more quickly.

Supports multiple languages

You can create, read, and edit documents in many languages with the English version of Windows XP Professional. With the Multilingual User Interface Pack, an add-on pack, you can change the user interface language for each user.

Supports Internet Information Services

You can set up a personal web server using the Internet Information Services web server software to publish web pages.

Provides dynamic disk management

If you have more than one hard drive, you can set them up as a single drive.

Programs available in the Professional version

Printers and Other Hardware in the Home version

User Interface Differences		
User Interface Item	Windows XP Home	Windows XP Professional
Start menu	Printers and Other Hardware (not available unless enabled)	Printers and Faxes; My Recent Documents
Fax functionality	Not available unless you install it	Available
Guest account	Activated	Deactivated
Check box option on Screen Saver tab in the Display Properties dialog box	On resume, display Welcome screen	On resume, password protect

Identifying New Features in Windows XP

Windows XP comes with new features that make your computer significantly easier and faster to use than earlier versions of Windows. Windows XP makes it easier to open files and programs, find information, and accomplish other common tasks, such as send and receive secure e-mail, browse the Internet securely, scan and view pictures, play music and videos, and change settings.

Windows XP, First Edition

Welcome screen and Fast User Switching (p. 6, 20) With the Welcome screen, you can share the same computer with family and friends and still maintain privacy and control over your personal files with customized user accounts. You can use Fast User Switching to switch between users without having to close each other's programs.

Enhanced Start menu and taskbar grouping (p. 12, 100-103) The two-column Start menu organizes frequently-used programs and tasks. If you open many files, programs, and windows, the taskbar groups together similar windows according to program type to save space.

Task-focused design (p. 16, 52-55) Windows, such as My Computer and My Documents, display a task pane with commands and options associated with your current task or selection. The Control Panel also displays options by category in addition to the Classic view.

Help and Support Center (p. 18) The Help and Support Center allows you to search multiple sources, including the Microsoft Knowledge Base on the Internet, print from the online documentation, and access frequently used topics.

Search Companion (p. 60) The Search Companion helps you search for and retrieve relevant information.

CD burning (p. 78) With a CD recording device installed on your computer, you can create your own CDs.

Windows Messenger (p. 175-198) Windows Messenger offers an easy way to communicate with your friends and co-workers in real time using text, voice, and video.

Scanner and Camera Wizard (p. 204-211) The wizard walks you through scanning a single image, a collection of images, and multi-page documents.

Enhanced My Pictures and My Music folders (p. 212, 243) With My Pictures, you can order prints, view pictures, publish pictures to the Internet, and compress pictures. With My Music, you can view a list of music files, play music files, and shop for music online.

Enhanced Windows Media Player (p. 223-242) You can play DVDs or VCDs, create your own music CDs, and export videos to portable devices.

Home Networking (p. 318) You can set up a home network and share an Internet connection and other computer resources, such as a printer or fax.

Remote Assistance (p. 338) Remote Assistance gives a friend permission to connect to your computer over the Internet, observe your screen, and control your computer.

System Restore (p. 392) System Restore allows you to restore your computer to a previous version of the system.

Windows XP, Service Pack 2

Windows Firewall security (p. 115) Windows Firewall protects your computer from Internet or network intruders.

The Security Center (p. 294) Use the Security Center to check current security settings, including Windows Firewall, Automatic Updates, and antivirus software.

Automatic Updates (p. 390) Microsoft regularly releases small fixes, patches, and updates to Windows. With AutoUpdate and an Internet connection, Windows can check the Microsoft web site for updates, and download and install the components you need in the background.

Enhanced Internet Explorer and Outlook Express security (p. 306-309) Enhanced security settings to warn you about viruses and other threats that spread using web sites or e-mail. Internet Explorer also manages add-ons programs, blocks annoying pop-up windows and drive-by downloads, and provides information to help you keep your computer more secure.

Data Execution Prevention This security feature works with your computer processor to help prevent unauthorized programs from running on your computer.

Wireless network setup (p. 328) The Wireless Network Wizard makes it easy to configure a secure wireless connection, including Bluetooth.

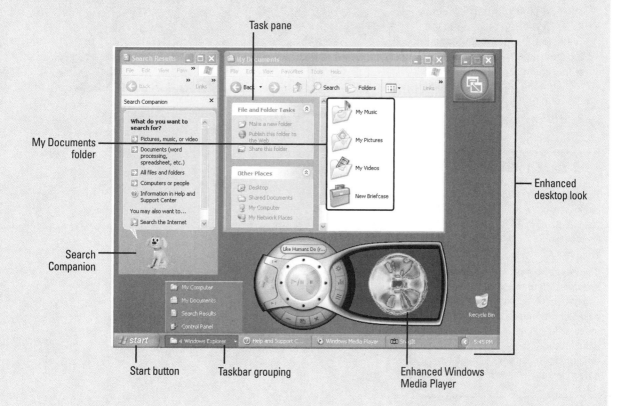

Task pane

My Documents folder

Search Companion

Enhanced desktop look

Start button   Taskbar grouping   Enhanced Windows Media Player

Starting Windows XP ▶

Windows XP automatically starts when you turn on your computer. When you first start Windows XP, you see a Welcome screen (**New!**), or a Log On dialog box depending on your installation. The Welcome screen identifies you on a shared or workgroup computer (a network), while the Log On dialog box identifies you on a domain network. After you enter a user name, password, and in some cases a domain name (for large network purposes), you see the Windows XP desktop.

Start Windows XP Using the Welcome Screen

① Turn on your computer, and wait while Windows XP loads and displays the Welcome screen.

② Click your user name.

③ Type your password. Be sure to use the correct capitalization.

④ Click the green arrow, or press Enter.

The first time you start Windows XP, a ScreenTip pointing to the Windows XP Tour icon on the taskbar appears, asking if you want to take a tour of Windows XP. Click the ScreenTip to take the tour, or click the Close button.

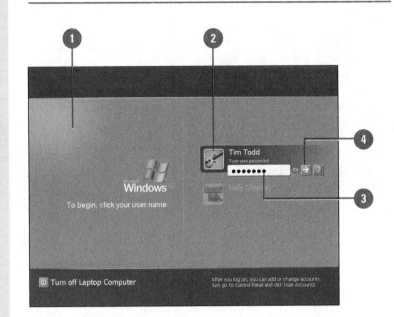

Did You Know?

You can start the Windows XP tour later. Click the Start button on the taskbar, point to All Programs, point to Accessories, and then click Tour Windows XP.

The Windows password is case-sensitive. Windows makes a distinction between uppercase and lowercase letters. Your password should be at least seven characters long, the optimal length for encryption, which is the process of logically scrambling data to keep a password secure.

Start Windows XP Using a Network Log On Dialog Box

1. Turn on your computer and wait while Windows XP loads and opens the Welcome to Windows dialog box, if option set.

2. Press and then release the Ctrl, Alt, and Delete keys at the same time, if necessary.

   The Log On to Windows dialog box opens.

3. Type the name that your network administrator assigned you, and then press Tab.

4. Type your password. Be sure to use the correct capitalization.

5. Select a domain from the list arrow, or type the network domain. If you're logging on locally, select the computer name.

6. Click OK.

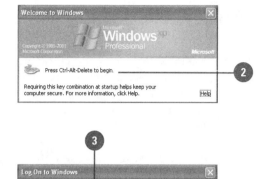

Did You Know?

A domain network and a workgroup are different. A domain network is a group of computers connected together to share and manage resources by an administrator from a central computer called a domain controller. A workgroup is a network of computers connected together to share resources, but each computer is maintained and shared separately.

Starting Windows XP

What you see at start up	Means you have a
Desktop	Nonshared (single user) computer; no user name and password required
Welcome screen	Shared (multiple users) or workgroup computer; user name and password required
Log On dialog box	Networked (connected to a computer on a domain network) computer; user name and password required

Exploring the Windows Desktop

When you first start Windows XP (New), you see the Windows desktop, or a Welcome/logon screen (a way to identify yourself on the computer), depending on your installation. The **desktop** is an on-screen version of an actual desk, containing windows, icons, files, and programs. You can use the desktop to access, store, organize, modify, share, and explore information (such as a letter, the news, or a list of addresses), whether it resides on your computer, a network, or the Internet. The bar at the bottom of your screen is called the **taskbar**; it allows you to start programs and switch among currently running programs. At the left

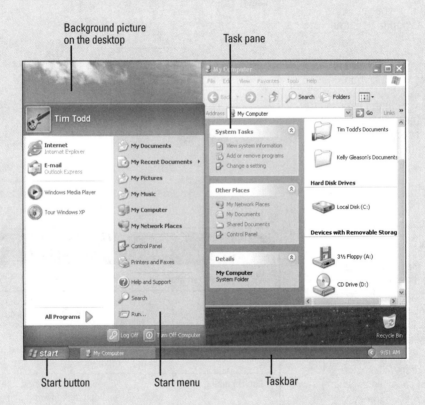

Background picture on the desktop

Task pane

Start button   Start menu   Taskbar

end of the taskbar is the **Start button**, which you use to start programs, find and open files, access the Windows Help and Support Center, and much more. At the right end of the taskbar is the **notification area**, which displays the time, the date, and program related icons. If you upgraded your computer to Windows XP from a previous version of Windows, your desktop might contain additional desktop icons and toolbars, such as the Quick Launch toolbar, which contains buttons you use to quickly start your Internet browser and media player and to show the desktop.

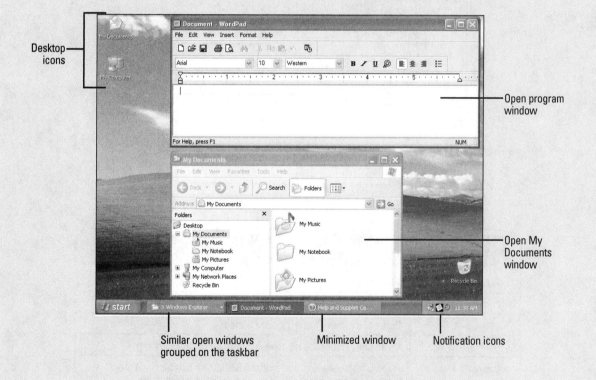

Desktop icons

Open program window

Open My Documents window

Similar open windows grouped on the taskbar

Minimized window

Notification icons

Using the Mouse

A **mouse** is a handheld input device you roll across a flat surface (such as a desk or a mouse pad) to position the **mouse pointer**, the small symbol that indicates the pointer's relative position on the desktop. When you move the mouse, the mouse pointer on the screen moves in the same direction. The shape of the mouse pointer changes to indicate different activities. Once you move the mouse pointer to a desired position on the screen, you use the mouse buttons, right or left, to tell your computer what you want it to do.

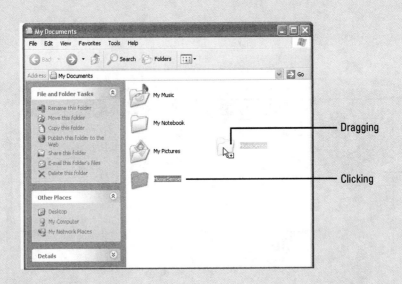

Dragging

Clicking

Basic Mouse Techniques

Task	What to do
Pointing	Move the mouse to position it over an item on the desktop.
Clicking	Press and release the left mouse button.
Double-clicking	Press and release the left mouse button twice quickly.
Dragging	Point to an item, press and hold the left mouse button, move the mouse to a new location, and then release the mouse button.
Right-clicking	Point to an item, and then press and release the right mouse button.

Using the Mouse for Quick Results

A typical mouse has two mouse buttons. You use the left one to click buttons, select text, and drag items around the screen. When you click an item with the right button, such as an icon, text, or graphic, a shortcut menu appears with a list of commands related to the selected item. For example, when you right-click a file icon, a shortcut menu appears with a list of file commands, such as Open, Explore, Search, Delete, and Rename. Instead of searching for commands on the main menus, you can save time and get quick results by using a shortcut menu.

Use the Shortcut Menu Command

1. Right-click an item.

2. Click a command from the shortcut menu.

Did You Know?

You can swap the functions of the right and left mouse buttons. Click the Start button on the taskbar, click Control Panel, double-click the Mouse icon, click the Buttons tab, select the Switch Primary And Secondary Buttons check box, and then click OK.

A mouse wheel can make scrolling fast and easy. If your mouse has a wheel between the two mouse buttons, you can roll it to quickly scroll a few lines or an entire screen at a time.

See Also

See "Changing Mouse Settings" on page 404 for information on changing the way the mouse works.

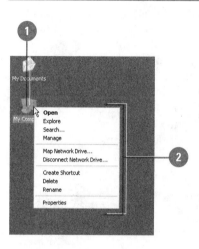

For Your Information

Using the Mouse with the Web Style

Windows XP integrates the use of the Internet with its other functions. You can choose to extend the way you click on the Internet with the rest of your computer by single-clicking (known as the Web style) icons to open them, or stay with the default by double-clicking (known as the Classic style). To change from one style to the other, click the Start button, click Control Panel, click Switch To Classic View (if necessary), double-click the Folder Options icon, click the Single-Click To Open An Item (Point To Select), or Double-Click To Open An Item (Single-Click To Select) option, and then click OK. The steps in this book assume you are using Windows Classic style.

Using the Start Menu

The key to getting started with the Windows desktop is learning how to use the Start button on the taskbar. Clicking the Start button on the taskbar displays the Start menu, a list of commands that allow you to start a program, open a document, change a Windows setting, find a file, or display support information. The top of the Start menu indicates who is currently using the computer. The left column of the Start menu is separated into two lists (**New!**): pinned items above the separator line and most frequently used items below. The **pinned** items remain on the Start menu, like a push pin holds paper on a bulletin board. The most frequently used items change as you use programs: Windows keeps track of which programs you use and displays them on the Start menu for easy access. The right column of the Start menu provides easy access to folders, Windows settings, help information, and search functionality. An arrow next to a menu item indicates a **cascading menu**, or **submenu**, which is a list of commands for that menu item. Pointing at the arrow displays a submenu from which you can choose additional commands. As you become more familiar with Windows, you might want to customize the Start menu to include additional items that you use most often and change Windows settings in the Control Panel to customize your Windows desktop.

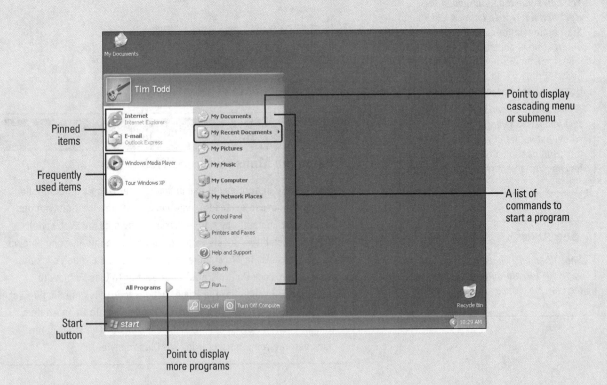

Pinned items

Frequently used items

Start button

Point to display more programs

Point to display cascading menu or submenu

A list of commands to start a program

Start Menu Commands

Command	Description
Internet	Starts your Internet browser; by default, Internet Explorer
E-Mail	Starts your e-mail program; by default, Outlook Express
All Programs	Opens a list of all the programs included on the Start menu
My Documents	Opens the My Documents folder, where you store and manage files
My Recent Documents	Opens a list of the most recently opened and saved documents
My Pictures	Opens the My Pictures folder, where you store and manage photos, images, and graphic files
My Music	Opens the My Music folder, where you store and manage sound and audio files
My Computer	Opens the My Computer window, where you access information about disk drives and other hardware devices
My Network Places	Opens the My Network Places window, where you can connect to a network
Control Panel	Provides options to customize the appearance and functionality of the computer
Printers and Faxes	Displays installed printers, fax printers, and a wizard to help you install additional devices; available only with Windows XP Professional
Printers and Other Hardware	Displays installed printers, other, hardware and a wizard to help you install other devices; available only with Windows XP Home
Help and Support	Displays Windows Help topics, tutorials, troubleshooting, support options, and tools
Search	Allows you to locate programs, files, folders, or computers on your computer network, or find information or people on the Internet
Run	Opens a program or file based on a location and file name that you type or select
Log Off	Allows you to log off the system and log on as a different user
Turn Off Computer or Shut Down	Provides options to turn off the computer, restart the computer, or set the computer in stand by or hibernate mode

Managing Windows

One of the powerful things about Windows is that you can open more than one window or program at once. This means, however, that the desktop can get cluttered with many open windows for the various programs you are using. A button appears on the taskbar for each open window. If there isn't enough room on the taskbar to display a button for each open window, Windows XP groups similar types of windows under one button (New!). You can identify a window by its name on the title bar at the top of the window. To organize your desktop, you must sometimes change the size of a window or move it to a different location. Each window is surrounded by a border that you can use to move or resize the window. Each window has resize buttons in the upper-right corner.

Switch Among Open Windows

1. On the taskbar, click a button.

2. If windows are grouped, a menu appears.

3. Click the window you want from the menu.

> ### Did You Know?
>
> **You can tile all open windows side by side.** Right-click a blank area on the taskbar, and then click Tile Windows Horizontally or Tile Windows Vertically.

Move a Window

1. Point to the window's title bar.

2. Drag the window to a new location, and then release the mouse button.

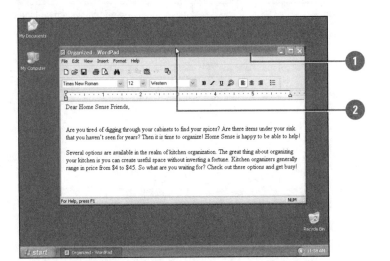

Use Buttons to Resize and Close a Window

All windows contain the same sizing and close buttons:

◆ **Maximize button.** Click to make a window fill the entire screen.

◆ **Restore Down button.** Click to reduce a maximized window.

◆ **Minimize button.** Click to shrink a window to a taskbar button.

◆ **Close button.** Click to close the window.

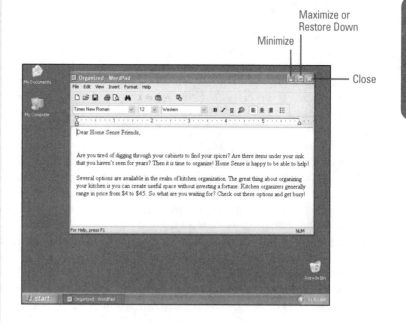

Maximize or Restore Down

Minimize

Close

Use the Mouse to Resize a Window

 If the window is maximized, click the Restore Down button.

2 Move the mouse over one of the borders of the window until the mouse pointer changes into a two-headed arrow.

The directions of the arrowheads show you the directions in which you can resize the window.

3 Drag the window border until the window is the size you want.

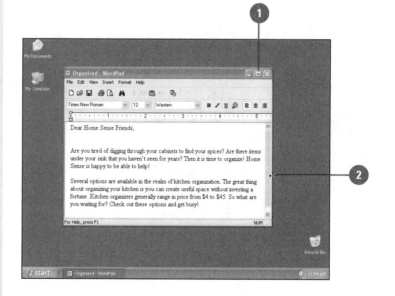

Using Menus, Toolbars, and Panes

A **menu** is a list of commands that you use to accomplish certain tasks, such as when you use the Start menu to open the Control Panel. A **command** is a directive that provides access to a program's features. Each Windows program has its own set of menus, which are on the menu bar along the top of the program window. The **menu bar** organizes commands into groups of related operations. Each group is listed under the name of the menu, such as File or Help. To access the commands in a menu, you click the name of the menu. If a command on a menu includes a keyboard reference, known as a **keyboard shortcut**, you can perform the action by pressing the first key, then pressing the second key to perform the command quickly. You can also carry out some of the most frequently used commands on a menu by clicking a button on a toolbar. A **toolbar** contains buttons that are convenient shortcuts for menu commands. A **pane** is a frame within a window where you can quickly access commands and navigation controls (New!). You can use menus, toolbar buttons, and commands in a pane to change how the Control Panel window's contents appear. On a menu, a **check mark** identifies a currently selected feature, meaning that the feature is enabled, or turned on. To disable, or turn off the feature, you click the command again to remove the check mark. A **bullet mark** also indicates that an option is enabled. To disable a command with a bullet mark next to it, however, you must select another command (within the menu section, separated by gray lines) in its place.

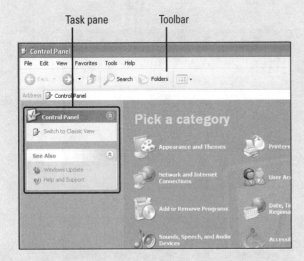

Task pane   Toolbar   Menu   Check mark

Bullet mark

16

Choosing Dialog Box Options

A **dialog box** is a window that opens when you choose a menu command followed by an ellipsis (. . .). The ellipsis indicates that you must supply more information before the program can carry out the command you selected. Dialog boxes open in other situations as well, such as when you open a program in the Control Panel. In a dialog box, you choose various options and provide information for completing the command.

Choose Dialog Box Options

All dialog boxes contain the same types of options, including the following:

- ◆ **Tabs.** Click a tab to display its options. Each tab groups a related set of options.

- ◆ **Option buttons.** Click an option button to select it. You can usually select only one.

- ◆ **Up and down arrows.** Click the up or down arrow to increase or decrease the number, or type a number in the box.

- ◆ **Check box.** Click the box to turn on or off the option. A checked box means the option is selected; a cleared box means it's not.

- ◆ **List box.** Click the list arrow to display a list of options, and then click the option you want.

- ◆ **Text box.** Click in the box and type the requested information.

- ◆ **Button.** Click a button to perform a specific action or command. A button name followed by an ellipsis (...) opens another dialog box.

- ◆ **Preview box.** Many dialog boxes show an image that reflects the options you select.

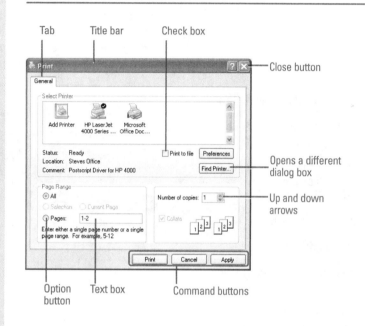

Tab   Title bar   Check box   — Close button   Opens a different dialog box   Up and down arrows   Option button   Text box   Command buttons

---

For Your Information

Navigating a Dialog Box

Rather than clicking to move around a dialog box, you can press the Tab key to move from one box or button to the next. You can also use Shift+Tab to move backward, or Ctrl+Tab and Ctrl+Shift+Tab to move between dialog box tabs.

Using Windows Help and Support

When you have a question about how to do something in Windows XP, you can usually find the answer with a few clicks of your mouse. The Microsoft Help and Support Center (**New!**) is a resource of information, training, and support to help you learn and use Windows XP. Help and Support is like a book stored on your computer with additional links to the Internet, complete with a search feature, and an index to make finding information easier. If you have an Internet connection, you can get online help from a support professional at Microsoft or from other users on the Windows newsgroup (an electronic form where people share information), or you can invite a friend to chat with you, view your screen, and work on your computer to provide remote support.

Use the Help and Support Center

1. Click the Start button, and then click Help And Support.

2. Click a link to the main topic of interest. Click a link to a subtopic, if necessary.

3. Click the item of interest.

4. Read the information.

5. If you can't find the information you need:

   ◆ Click the Search text box, type a word or phrase, and then press Enter.

   ◆ Click the Index button, and then use keywords.

   ◆ Click the Support button to access resources on the Internet.

6. Click the Close button.

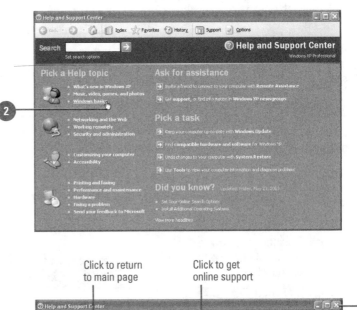

Click to return to main page

Click to get online support

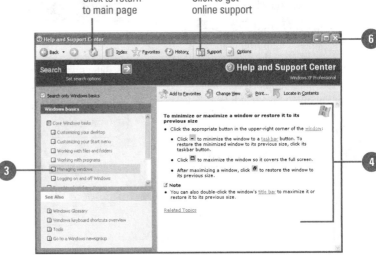

Use Dialog Box Help

1 In a dialog box, click the Help button.

2 Click the item you want information about.

3 Read the Help information.

4 Click anywhere to close Help.

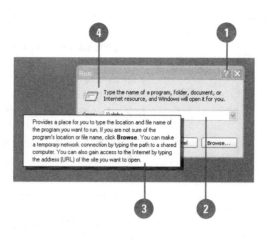

Use Program Help

1 Click the program's Help menu, and then click Help Topics to open the Help program.

2 Click the Contents tab, click the main topic of interest. Click a subtopic, if necessary.

3 Read the Help information.

4 If you can't find the information you need, click the Index tab or the Search tab, and get Help information using keywords.

5 Click the Close button.

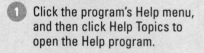
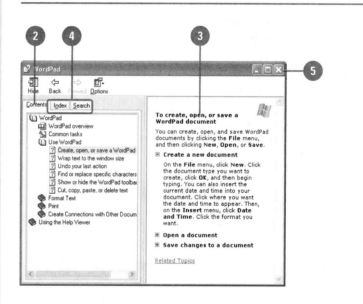

Switching Users

Many users can use the same computer. Their individual Windows identities allow them to keep their files completely private and to customize the operating system with their own preferences. Windows manages these separate identities, or accounts, by giving each user a unique user name and password. When a user selects an account and types a password (if necessary), Windows starts with that user's configuration settings and network permissions. When you want to change users, you can log off, which closes all running programs, saves your settings, and signs you off the computer, or switch users, which quickly switches between users without having to close programs and saves your current settings (**New!**).

Switch Users Quickly

1. Click the Start button, and then click Log Off.

2. Click Switch User to change users without saving current settings.

   A Welcome screen appears, displaying user accounts.

3. Click your name.

4. If a box for a password appears, type your password.

5. Click the Arrow button to log on to Windows XP.

Did You Know?

You can change user account options in the Control Panel. Click the Start button, click Control Panel, double-click the User Accounts icon, and then select the options you want.

See Also

See "Adding and Deleting User Accounts" on page 280 for information on switching users.

Log Off Your Computer

Click the Start button, and then click Log Off.

Click Log Off to close all your programs, save your settings, and sign yourself off the computer.

A Welcome screen appears, displaying user accounts.

③ Click your name.

④ If a box for a password appears, type your password.

⑤ Click the Arrow button to log on to Windows XP.

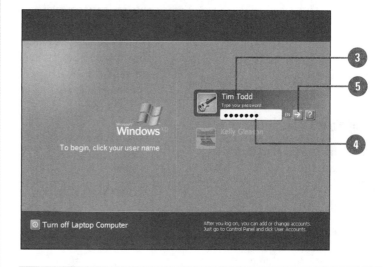

Log Off and Log On a Network Computer

① Click the Start button, and then click Log Off.

② Click Log Off to close all your programs, save your settings, and sign yourself off the computer.

③ Press and then release the Ctrl, Alt, and Delete keys at the same time.

④ Type your assigned user name.

⑤ Type your assigned password.

⑥ Select or type a network domain name to access a network or the computer name to access the local computer.

⑦ Click OK.

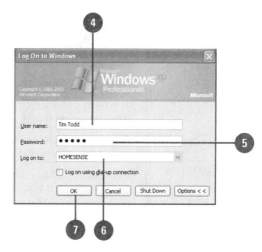

Turning Off Your Computer

When you finish working on your computer, you need to make sure to turn off, or shut down, your computer properly. This involves several steps: saving and closing all open files, closing all open windows, exiting all running programs, shutting down Windows itself, and, finally, turning off the computer. However, if you shut down your computer before or while installing Windows updates (download must be complete), Windows will automatically complete the install before shutting down (NewSP2), so you don't have to wait around. Shutting down your computer makes sure Windows and all its related programs are properly closed; this avoids potential problems starting and working with Windows in the future. If you turn off the computer by pushing the power switch while Windows or other programs are running, you could lose important data.

Turn Off Your Computer

1 Click the Start button, and then click Turn Off Computer or Shut Down.

2 Click the option you want:

◆ **Turn Off** or **Shut down.** Exits Windows XP and prepares the computer to be turned off

◆ **Restart.** Exits Windows XP and restarts the computer

◆ **Stand By.** Switches the computer to low-power mode and maintains your session

◆ **Hibernate.** Saves your session, exits Windows XP, and then restores your session the next time you start Windows

IMPORTANT *Options vary depending on Windows settings.*

See Also

See "Updating Windows" on page 390 for information on automatically updating Windows.

Button changes to Hibernate when the option is available.

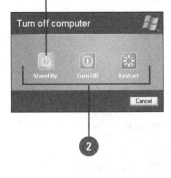

Shut Down Options	
Option	**When to use it**
Turn Off or Shut Down	When you finish working with Windows and you want to shut off your computer
Restart	When you want to restart the computer and begin working with Windows again
Hibernate	When you want to stop working with Windows for a while and safely turn off power; restores your session to start working again later; available when the Power Options (in the Control Panel) are turned on
Stand By	When you want to stop working with Windows for a few moments and conserve power (ideal for a laptop or portable computer); available when a power scheme is selected in Power Options (in the Control Panel)

Working with Windows Programs

Introduction

Now that you know how to work with the graphical elements that make Windows work, you're ready to work with programs. A **program** is software you use to accomplish a specific task, such as word processing or managing files on your computer. This shows you how to access your Windows programs (and to customize this access). It also shows you how to create and edit files in your programs, share information between programs, and what to do when a program is not responding. Windows comes with several small programs, called **Accessories**, that are extremely useful for completing basic tasks, such as creating a written document or performing basic calculations. Windows XP also provides a number of ways for you to resolve some common problems. For example, you can use older programs (designed to run on previous versions of Windows) on your Windows XP computer by changing specific settings using the Accessories menu. You can run commands from a text-based interface (called a command line), and Windows provides an interface for quitting a program that has stopped responding without turning off your computer and losing information in other programs. In addition, this chapter covers the fun stuff: Games. You can play games on your computer, or with other people over the internet.

Starting and Exiting a Program

The most common way to start a Windows program is to use the Start menu, which provides easy access to programs installed on your computer. Clicking the Start button on the taskbar displays the Start menu, which lists common and recently used programs and the All Programs submenu (**New!**). The All Programs submenu is the master list of every program on your computer. If you start a program, such as your e-mail program, every time you start Windows, you can save some time by adding the program to the Startup folder. When you're done working with a program, you should exit, or close it, to conserve your computer's resources.

Start a Program from the Start Menu

Windows XP provides several ways to start a program:

◆ Click the Start button, and then click a program.

◆ Click the Start button, point to All Programs, point to a program group if necessary, and then click a program.

◆ Click the Start button, click My Computer or My Documents, navigate to the folder with the program or file associated with the program you want, and then double-click the icon.

◆ Click the Start button, click Run, type the full path and file name of the program, and then click OK.

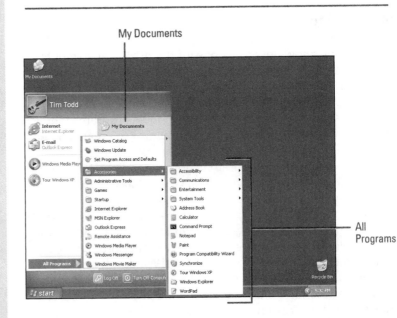

My Documents

All Programs

Did You Know?

You can double-click a program's file icon to start it. Double-click the icon on the desktop or click the Start button, click My Computer, locate the file icon, and then double-click it.

Exit a Program

Windows XP provides several ways to exit a program:

◆ Click the File menu, and then click Exit.

◆ Click the Close button on the program's title bar.

◆ Double-click the Control-menu on the program's title bar.

◆ Right-click the program's taskbar button, and then click Close.

Did You Know?

You can display the Programs list in a single column. Right-click the Start button, click Properties, click Customize, click the Advanced tab, select the Scroll Programs check box, and then click OK twice. Point to the black triangle arrows at the top and bottom to scroll through the list.

See Also

See "Using Windows Accessories" on page 27 for information on using Windows built-in programs.

Control menu

Close button

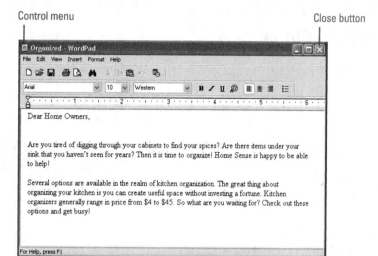

2

Changing the Way a Program Starts

If you start a program, such as your e-mail program, every time you start Windows, you can save some time by adding the program to the Startup folder. The contents of the Startup folder appear on the Startup submenu on the All Programs menu. Every time you start Windows, the programs in the Startup folder automatically start. Sometimes a program installs a program to the Startup folder. If you don't want the program automatically starting with Windows, you can remove it from the Startup folder.

Add a Program to the Startup Submenu

1. Click the Start button, and then locate the program you want to add to the Startup submenu.

2. Hold down the Ctrl key, and then drag the program on top of the Startup item on the All Programs submenu.

   Using the Ctrl key copies the program to the Startup submenu.

3. When the Startup submenu opens, drag the program onto the submenu, and then release the mouse button and the Ctrl key.

   The next time Windows XP starts, the program will start.

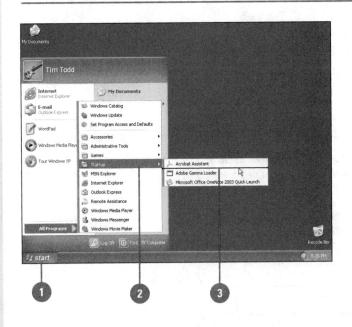

Remove a Program from the Startup Submenu

1. Click the Start button, point to All Programs, and then point to Startup.

2. Right-click the program you want to remove on the Startup submenu.

3. Click Delete, and then click Yes to confirm the deletion.

   Windows deletes the program from the Startup submenu, not from your computer.

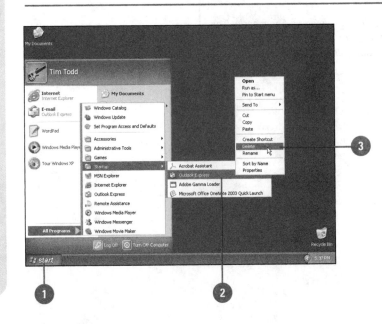

Using Windows Accessories

Windows comes with several accessories, built-in programs that, while not as feature-rich as many programs sold separately, are extremely useful for completing basic tasks.

One of the most useful features Windows offers is the ability to use data created in one file in another file, even if the two files were created in different Windows programs. To work with more than one program or file at a time, you simply need to open them on your desktop. A program button on the taskbar represents any window that is open on the desktop. When you want to switch from one open window to another, click the program button on the taskbar. If you tile, or arrange open windows on the desktop so that they are visible, you can switch among them simply by clicking in the window in which you want to work.

Frequently Used Windows Accessories	
Program	**Description**
Address Book	Stores names, addresses, and other contact information
Calculator	Performs arithmetic calculations
Character Map	Inserts special characters from installed fonts
Internet Explorer	Displays Web (HTML) pages
Magnifier	Magnifies parts of the screen
MSN Explorer	Provides Internet Explorer, Windows Messenger, Windows Media Player, and Hotmail (Web e-mail) functionality all in one program
Narrator	Reads aloud the screen contents
Notepad	Creates, edits, and displays text only documents
On-Screen Keyboard	Allows keyboard input using the mouse or other pointing device
Outlook Express	Provides e-mail, newsgroup, and directory services
Paint	Creates and edits bitmap pictures
Sound Recorder	Creates and plays digital sound files
Windows Media Player	Plays sound, music, and video
Windows Messenger	Sends and receives instant messages to online contacts
Windows Movie Maker	Creates movies using audio and video files
WordPad	Creates, edits, and displays text, Rich Text Format, and Word documents

2

Creating a Document

A **document** is a file you create using a word processing program, such as a letter, memo, or resume. When you start WordPad, a blank document appears in the work area, known as the document window. You can enter information to create a new document and save the result in a file, or you can open an existing file and save the document with changes. As you type, text moves, or **wraps**, to a new line when the previous one is full.

Create a Document

1. Click the Start button, point to All Programs, point to Accessories, and then click WordPad.

   If WordPad is already open, click the New button on the toolbar, click Rich Text Document, and then click OK.

2. Type your text.

3. Press Enter when you want to start a new paragraph.

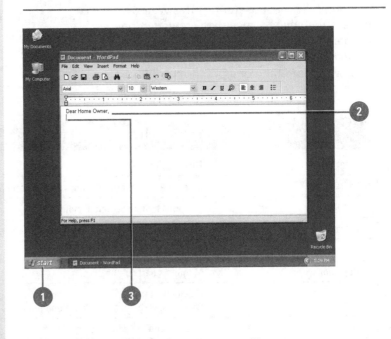

Change the Page Setup

1. Click the File menu, and then click Page Setup.

2. Specify the paper size and source.

3. Specify the page orientation, either portrait or landscape.

4. Specify the page margins.

5. Click OK.

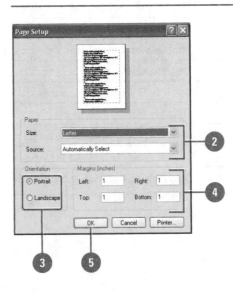

28

Open an Existing Document from Within a Program

1. Click the Open button on the toolbar.

2. Click the Files Of Type list arrow, and then click the file type you want to open.

3. Click an icon on the Places bar to open a frequently used folder.

4. If desired, click the Look In list arrow, and then click the drive or folder from where you want to open the file.

5. Double-click the folder from which you want to open the file.

6. Click the document you want to open.

7. Click Open.

Open a Recent Document from the Start Menu

1. Click the Start button.

2. Point to My Recent Documents.

3. Click the recently opened document you want to re-open.

Did You Know?

You can remove all recently used documents from the My Recent Documents submenu. Right-click the Start button, click Properties, click Customize, click the Advanced tab in the Customize Start Menu dialog box, and then click Clear List.

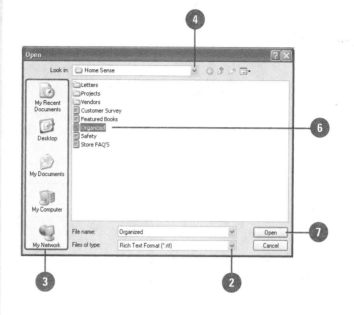

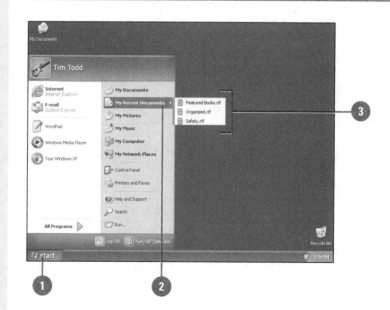

Editing Text

One of the advantages of using a word processing program is that you can edit a document or change the contents without re-creating it. In the WordPad work area, the mouse pointer changes to the I-beam pointer, which you can use to reposition the insertion point (called navigating) and insert, delete, or select text. Before you can edit text, you need to highlight, or select, the text you want to modify. Then you can delete, replace, move (cut), or copy text within one document or between documents even if they're different programs. When you cut or copy an item, it's placed on the Clipboard, which stores only a single piece of information at a time. You can also move or copy selected text without storing it on the Clipboard by using drag-and-drop editing.

Select and Edit Text

1 Move the I-beam pointer to the left or right of the text you want to select.

2 Drag the pointer to highlight the text.

> **TIMESAVER** *Double-click a word to select it; triple-click a paragraph to select it.*

3 Perform one of the following editing commands:

- ◆ To replace text, type your text.

- ◆ To delete text, press the Backspace key or the Delete key.

Insert and Delete Text

1 Click in the document to place the insertion point where you want to make the change.

- ◆ To insert text, type your text.

- ◆ To delete text, press the Backspace key or the Delete key.

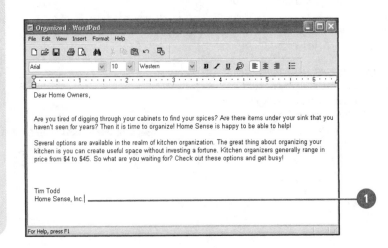

Move or Copy Text

1. Select the text you want to move or copy.

2. Click the Cut button or Copy button on the toolbar.

3. Click where you want to insert the text.

4. Click the Paste button on the toolbar.

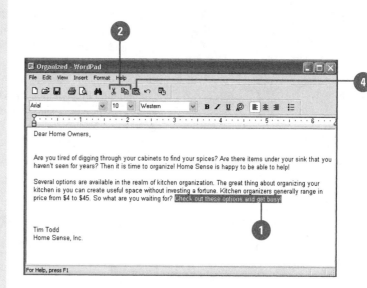

Move or Copy Text Using Drag and Drop

1. Select the text you want to move or copy.

2. Point to the selected text, and then click and hold the mouse button.

   If you want to copy the text to a new location, also press and hold the Ctrl key. A plus sign (+) appears in the pointer box, indicating that you are dragging a copy of the selected text.

3. Drag the selected text to the new location, and then release the mouse button (and the Ctrl key, if necessary).

4. Click anywhere in the document to deselect the text.

Dear Home Owners,

Are you tired of digging through your cabinets to find your spices? Are there items under your sink that you haven't seen for years? Then it is time to organize! Home Sense is happy to be able to help!

Several options are available in the realm of kitchen organization. The great thing about organizing your kitchen is you can create useful space without investing a fortune. Kitchen organizers generally range in price from $4 to $45. So what are you waiting for? Check out these options and get busy!

Tim Todd
Home Sense, Inc.

Dear Home Owners,

Are you tired of digging through your cabinets to find your spices? Are there items under your sink that you haven't seen for years? Then it is time to organize! Home Sense is happy to be able to help!

Several options are available in the realm of kitchen organization. The great thing about organizing your kitchen is you can create useful space without investing a fortune. Kitchen organizers generally range in price from $4 to $45. So what are you waiting for?

Check out these options and get busy!

Tim Todd
Home Sense, Inc.

Formatting Text

You can change the format or the appearance of text and graphics in a document so that the document is easier to read or more attractive. A quick and powerful way to add emphasis to parts of a document is to format text using bold, italics, underline, or color. For special emphasis, you can combine formats, such as bold and italics. In addition, you can change the font style and size. A **font** is a set of characters with the same typeface or design that you can increase or decrease in size, such as Arial or Times New Roman. Font size is measured in points; one point is 1/72 of an inch high.

Format Text

1. Select the text or click in the paragraph you want to format.

2. Use any of the formatting tools to style text:

   ◆ Font list arrow

   ◆ Font Size list arrow

   ◆ Font Script list arrow; a language type

   ◆ Bold button

   ◆ Italic button

   ◆ Underline button

   ◆ Color button

3. Use any of the formatting tools to adjust text spacing:

   ◆ Alignment buttons

   ◆ Bullet button

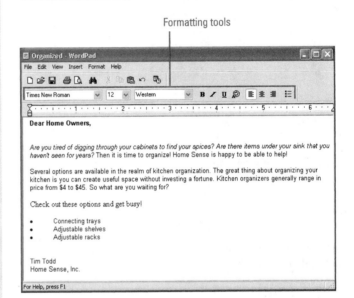

Formatting tools

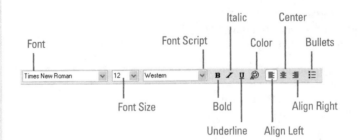

Setting Paragraph Tabs

Tabs set text or numerical data alignment in relation to the edges of a document. A **tab stop** is a predefined stopping point along the document's typing line. Default tab stops are set every half-inch on the ruler, but you can set multiple tabs per paragraph at any location. Each paragraph in a document contains its own set of tab stops. The default tab stops do not appear on the ruler, but the manual tab stops you set do appear. Once you place a tab stop, you can drag the tab stop to position it where you want. If you want to add or adjust tab stops in multiple paragraphs, simply select the paragraphs first.

Create and Clear a Tab Stop

1. Select the text or click in the paragraph you want to format.

2. Click the ruler where you want to set the tab stop.

3. To move a tab, drag the tab stop to position it where you want.

4. To clear a tab stop, drag it off the ruler.

See Also

See "Setting Paragraph Indents" on page 34 for information on changing the text alignment.

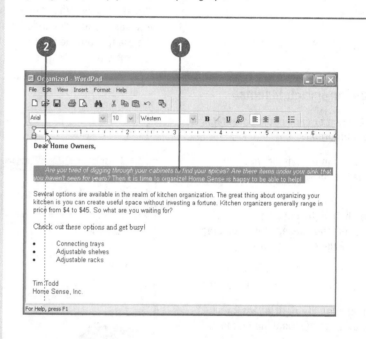

For Your Information

Changing the Word Wrap Display

As you type a complete line of text, it wraps to the next line. Depending on your preference, you can change the Document window to display text wrapped to the window or ruler. To change word wrap options, click the View menu, click Options, click the tab with your text format, click the word wrap option you want, and then click OK. In the Options dialog box, you can set different word wrap options for each of the text formats in which you can save documents, such as Text, Rich Text, Word, and Write. The wrapping options affect only how text appears on your screen. When printed, the document uses the margin settings specified in Page Setup.

Setting Paragraph Indents

When you indent a paragraph, you move its edge in from the left or right margin. You can indent the entire left or right edge of a paragraph or just the first line. The markers on the ruler control the indentation of the current paragraph. The left side of the ruler has three markers. The top triangle, called the **first-line indent marker**, controls where the first line of the paragraph begins. The bottom triangle, called the **hanging indent marker**, controls where the remaining lines of the paragraph begin. The small square under the bottom triangle, called the **left indent marker**, allows you to move the first-line Indent marker and the left indent marker simultaneously. When you move the left indent marker, the distance between the hanging indent and the first-line indent remains the same. The triangle on the right side of the ruler, called the **right indent marker**, controls where the right edge of the paragraph ends.

Change Paragraph Indents

Select the text or click in the paragraph you want to format.

- To change the left indent of the first line, drag the First-Line Indent marker.

- To change the indent of the second and subsequent lines, drag the Hanging Indent marker.

- To change the left indent for all lines, drag the Left Indent marker.

- To change the right indent for all lines, drag the Right Indent marker.

As you drag a marker, the dotted guideline helps you position the indent accurately.

See Also

See "Setting Paragraph Tabs" on page 33 for information on changing the text alignment.

Hanging Indent marker

Left Indent marker

First-Line Indent marker

Right Indent marker

Previewing and Printing a Document

Before printing, you should verify that the page looks the way you want. You save time, money, and paper by avoiding duplicate printing. Print Preview shows you the exact placement of your text on each printed page. Printing a paper copy is a common way to review and share a document. You can use the Print button on the toolbar to print a copy of your document using the current settings, or you can open the Print dialog box and specify the print options you want.

Preview a Document

1. Click the Print Preview button on the toolbar.

2. Use the toolbar buttons to preview the document:

   ◆ To change the view size, click Zoom In or Zoom Out.

   ◆ To view other pages, click Next Page or Prev Page.

   ◆ To view two pages at a time, click Two Pages.

   ◆ To print the document, click Print.

3. When you're done, click Close.

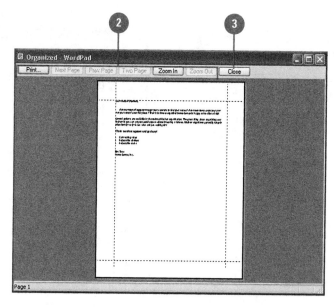

Print All or Part of a Document

1. Click the File menu, and then click Print.

2. Click a printer.

3. Specify the range of pages you want to print.

4. Specify the number of copies you want to print.

5. Click Print.

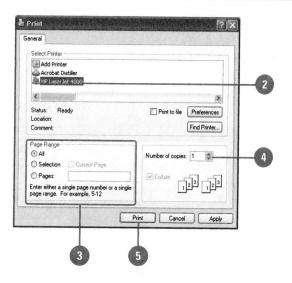

Saving and Closing a Document

Saving your files frequently ensures that you don't lose work during an unexpected power loss. The first time you save, specify a file name and folder in the Save As dialog box. The next time you save, the program saves the file with the same name in the same folder. If you want to change a file's name or location, you can use the Save As dialog box again to create a copy of the original file. To conserve your computer's resources, close any file you are not working on.

Save a Document

1. Click the File menu, and then click Save As.

2. Click an icon on the Places bar to open a frequently used folder.

3. If desired, click the Save In list arrow, and then click the drive or folder where you want to save the file.

4. Double-click the folder in which you want to save the file.

5. Type a name for the file, or use the suggested one.

6. To change the format of a file, click the Save As Type list arrow, and then click a file format.

7. Click Save.

> **Did You Know?**
>
> **You can save a file in a new folder.** In the Save As dialog box, click the Create New Folder button, type the new folder name, click Open, and then click Save.

Close a Document

1. Click the Close button.

2. If necessary, click Yes to save your changes.

Sharing Information Among Programs

Windows XP makes it easy to insert a file or part of a file created in one program into a file created in a different program. The ability to share files and information among different programs is called **object linking and embedding (OLE)**. With OLE, you can work with a document in WordPad and at the same time take advantage of the specialized tools in another program, such as Paint or Microsoft Excel. By using OLE, you'll be able to access features from other programs, edit data easily, update to the latest information, and save space.

Information shared between two programs is an **object**, which can be a picture from a graphics program, a chart from a spreadsheet program, a video clip, text, or almost anything else you can create on a computer. The program that creates the object is called the

source program; the program that creates the file into which you want to insert the object is called the **destination program**. Likewise, the file that originally contained the object is the **source file**, and the file where you want to insert the object is the **destination file**. Both embedding and linking involve inserting an object into a destination file; they differ in where they store their respective objects. With **embedding**, a copy of the object becomes part of the destination file. If you want to edit the object, you make changes in the destination file, and the original file remains intact. With **linking**, a representation of the object appears in the destination file, but the object is stored in the source file. If you want to edit the linked object, you make changes in the source file or its representation in the destination file, and the other file will reflect the changes the next time you open it.

Source program   Destination program

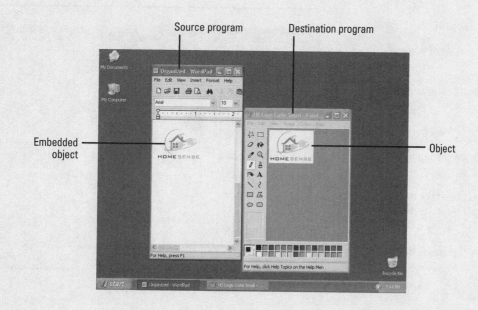

Embedded object

Object

Inserting and Editing Information

Instead of switching back and forth between programs to copy and paste information, you can insert, or embed, the information. Embedding inserts a copy of one document into another. Once you embed data, you can edit it using the menus and toolbars of the source program without leaving the program in which it's embedded (that is, the destination program). For example, you can create a picture in a program, such as Paint, or select an existing picture and insert it into a WordPad document. The inserted picture is an object which you can resize.

Embed an Existing Object

1. Click where you want to embed the object.

2. Click the Insert menu, and then click Object.

3. Click the Create From File option.

4. Click Browse, and then double-click the file with the object you want to embed.

5. Click OK.

Embed a New Object

1. Click where you want to embed the object.

2. Click the Insert menu, and then click Object.

3. Click the Create New option.

4. Double-click the type of object you want to create.

5. Enter information in the new object using the menus and toolbars in the source program.

6. Click outside the object to close the object.

Edit an Object

1 Open the document with the object you want to edit.

2 Double-click the object.

3 Edit the object using the menus and toolbars in the source program.

4 Click outside the object to close the object.

Did You Know?

You can use Paste Special to embed part of a file. Select and copy the information, click where you want to embed the copied information, click the Edit menu, click Paste Special, click the Paste option to embed, select a format, and then click OK.

Resize an Object

1 Click the object to select it.

2 Drag a sizing handle to change the size of the object.

◆ Drag a corner sizing handle to change height and width simultaneously.

◆ Drag the top or bottom middle sizing handle to change height.

◆ Drag the left or right middle sizing handle to change width.

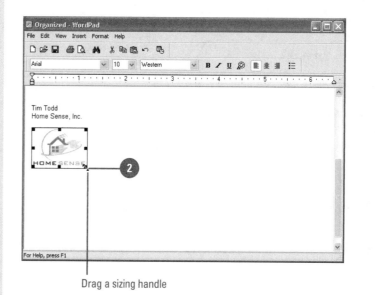

Drag a sizing handle

Linking and Updating Information

When you want to keep source and destination files in sync with each other, you can link the source file that created the object with the destination file that displays the object. Linking displays information stored in one document (the source file) into another (the destination file). You can edit the linked object from either file, although changes are stored in the source file. Only a representation of the object appears in the destination file; any changes made to the object are done in the source file, whether you access it by double-clicking the object in the destination file or by opening it in the source program.

Link an Object Between Programs

1. Click where you want to embed the object.

2. Click the Insert menu, and then click Object.

3. Click the Create From File option.

4. Click Browse, and then double-click the file with the object you want to link.

5. Select the Link check box.

6. Click OK.

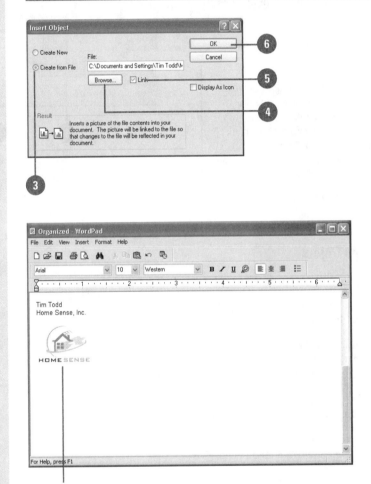

Linked object

Did You Know?

You can use Paste Special to link part of a file. Select and copy the information, click where you want to link the copied information, click the Edit menu, click Paste Special, click the Paste Link option to link, select a format, and then click OK.

Update a Linked File

1 Open the file with the source program.

2 Edit the file using the source program's commands.

3 Click the Save button on the toolbar.

4 Click the Close button to exit the source program.

5 Open the linked file with the destination program.

The object automatically updates.

6 Click the Save button on the toolbar.

7 Click the Close button to exit the destination program.

Did You Know?

You can change a link to update manually. In the destination program, select the object, click the Edit menu, click Links, click the Manual option button, and then click Close.

For Your Information

Finding, Changing, and Breaking a Linked Object

Instead of opening a linked object from the source file to make changes, you can open a linked object from the destination file using the Open Source button in the Links dialog box. The Open Source button finds the source file containing the linked object and opens that file. After making changes, you exit and return to the destination file. The Links dialog box keeps track of the source file location. You can change the linked source to a different file by using the Change Source button. If you want to disregard a link and change it to an embedded object, select the linked object in the destination file, click Edit on the menu bar, click Object Properties, click the Link tab, click Break Link, click Yes in the message box, and then click OK. On the Link tab in the Object Properties dialog box, you can also open or change the source file, change update options, and update the source for the selected object.

Inserting Special Characters

When you need to insert special characters such as ©, ™, or ® that don't appear on your keyboard, you can use a special accessory program called Character Map to do the job. Character Map displays all the characters that are available for each of the fonts on your computer.

Insert a Special Character

1. Click the Start button, point to All Programs, point to Accessories, point to System Tools, and then click Character Map.

2. Click the Font list arrow, and then click a font.

3. Double-click the character you want to insert.

    TIMESAVER *Click a character to see an enlarged view of it.*

4. Click Copy to place the character on the Clipboard.

5. Click the Close button.

6. Click in the document to place the insertion point.

7. Click the Edit menu, and then click Paste.

    TIMESAVER *Press Ctrl+V to quickly paste the contents from the Clipboard.*

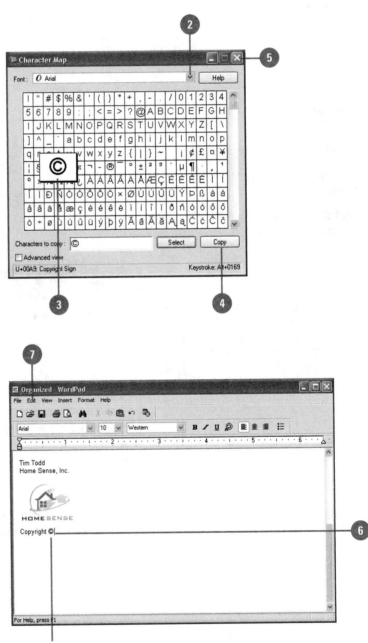

Copyright special character

Calculating Numbers

If you don't have a handheld calculator handy, you can use the Calculator program provided by Windows XP to quickly perform standard calculations or even more complex ones. Calculator performs basic arithmetic, such as addition and subtraction, as well as functions found on a scientific calculator, such as logarithms and factorials.

Use the Calculator

1 Click the Start button, point to All Programs, point to Accessories, and then click Calculator.

2 Click the View menu, and then click Standard or Scientific.

3 Enter a number, or click the number buttons.

4 Click a function button.

5 Enter another number.

6 When you've entered all the numbers you want, click the equals (=) button.

7 Click the Edit menu, and then click Copy to copy the result to the Clipboard to paste in a document.

8 When you're done, click the Close button.

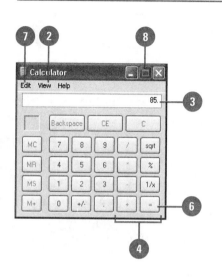

Did You Know?

You can use the numeric keypad on your keyboard with the Calculator. Press the number, +, -, *, /, and Enter keys to quickly enter numbers and use the calculator.

You can find out the purpose of a key. Right-click the key, and then click What's this?

Running Commands

Besides running Windows XP programs, you can also enter commands and run programs written in MS-DOS. **MS-DOS** stands for Microsoft Disk Operating System. MS-DOS, or DOS, employs a **command-line interface** through which you must type commands at a **command prompt** to run different tasks. A character such as a > or $ appears at the beginning of a command prompt. Each DOS command has a strict set of rules called a **command syntax** that you must follow when expressing a command. Many commands allow you to include switches and parameters that give you additional control of the command.

Run a Command

1. Click the Start button, point to All Programs, point to Accessories, and then click Command Prompt.

2. At the prompt, type a command including any parameters, and then press Enter.

3. When you're done, click the Close button, or type **exit**, and then press Enter.

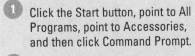

Find a Command

1. Click the Start button, point to All Programs, point to Accessories, and then click Command Prompt.

2. At the prompt, type **help**, and then press Enter.

3. Read the list of commands. Use the scroll bar or scroll arrows to display additional information.

4. When you're done, click the Close button, or type **exit**, and then press Enter.

Get Information About a Command

1 Click the Start button, point to All Programs, point to Accessories, and then click Command Prompt.

2 At the prompt, type a command followed by a space and **/?**, and then press Enter.

3 Read the information about the command. Use the scroll bar or scroll arrows to display additional information.

4 When you're done, click the Close button, or type **exit**, and then press Enter.

Did You Know?

You can use a wildcard character to change more than one file. An asterisk is a wildcard and represents any number of characters. For example, the command *dir at*.doc* matches at back.doc, ati.doc, and atlm.doc.

You can change the appearance of the Command Prompt window. Right-click the Command Prompt window title bar, and then click Properties.

2

2

3

Common DOS Commands

Command	Purpose
cd *foldername*	Changes to the specified folder
cls	Clears the screen
copy	Copies the specified files or folder
dir	Lists the contents of the current folder
c: (where c is a drive)	Switches to the specified drive
exit	Closes the Command Prompt window
rename	Renames the specified file or files
more *filename*	Displays the contents of a file, one screen of output at a time
type *filename.txt*	Displays the contents of the text file

2

Playing Games

If you have some free time, you can play games to pass the time. Windows provides several games you can play against the computer—FreeCell, Hearts, Minesweeper, Pinball, Solitaire, and Spider Solitaire.

Play a Game

1. Click the Start button, point to All Programs, point to Games, and then click the game you want.

2. Play the game.

3. When you're done, click the Game menu, and then click a command to start a new game with the same or different players, or exit the game.

See Also

See "Playing Internet Games" on page 48 for information on playing games over the Internet against other players.

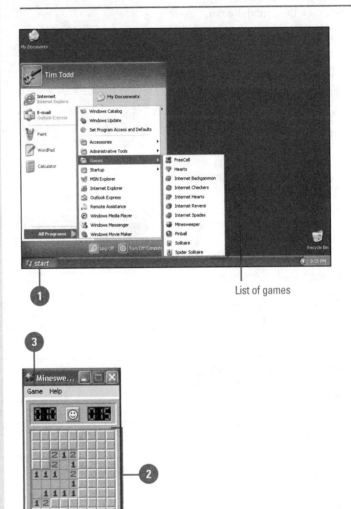

List of games

Did You Know?

You can get more information about playing each game in Help. Start the game, click the Help menu, and then click Contents or Help Topics.

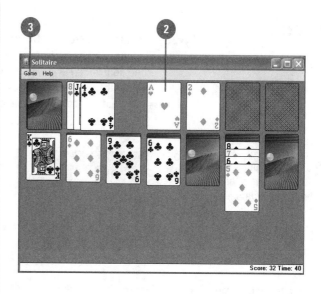

Playing the Game	
Game	**Object is to**
FreeCell	Stack the cards in the cells at the top in descending order, starting from any card, alternating the red and black cards.
Hearts	Score the lowest number of points, one point for each heart and 13 points for the Queen of Spades. You play a card to follow suit or a heart or the Queen of Spades when you can't follow suit.
Minesweeper	Uncover all the squares that don't contain mines in the shortest amount of time. You use the numbers in the uncovered squares to determine which adjacent squares contain mines.
Pinball	Launch a ball and keep it in play as long as possible while you score points. You use the Z and / keys to move the flippers and the Spacebar to shoot the ball in play.
Solitaire	Reveal all the cards that are turned face down by stacking them in descending order (alternating the red and black cards) on the lower piles, and stack them in ascending order from Ace through King by suit in the upper piles. You use the mouse to drag one card on top of another.
Spider Solitaire	Stack the cards by suit in one column in descending order.

Playing Internet Games

Windows XP provides several games you can play against players over the Internet (**New!**)—Backgammon, Checkers, Hearts, Reversi, and Spades. When you start an Internet game, the game server called zone.com finds players matched to your skill level and language from around the world. You can't select the players or locations of your opponents, but you can communicate with them by using the Chat controls.

Play an Internet Game

1 Click the Start button, point to All Programs, point to Games, and then click the Internet game you want.

2 Click Play. If you're not connected to the Internet, connect when prompted.

3 Click a message to send to your opponent.

4 Play the game.

5 When you're done, click the Game menu, and then click a command to start a new game with the same or different players, or exit the game.

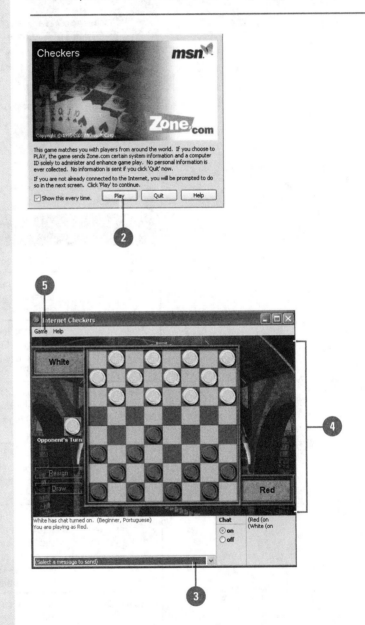

Did You Know?

You can play Internet games using Windows Messenger. In order to play, you and your opponent need to have the game installed on your computers.

See Also

See "Sending and Receiving Instant Messages" on page 184 for information on playing games over the Internet using Windows Messenger.

Running Older Programs

Some older programs are designed to run on earlier versions of Windows and don't work properly on Windows XP. You can set the compatibility of Windows XP to act like an earlier version of Windows to run an older program.

Set Compatibility for an Older Program

1. Click the Start button, and then locate the older program.

2. Right-click the program you want to run, and then click Properties.

3. Click the Compatibility tab.

4. Select the Run This Program In Compatibility Mode For check box.

5. Click the list arrow, and then click the version of Windows in which the program was designed.

6. Select the check boxes for applying the appropriate settings to the display, based on the program's documentation.

7. Click OK.

Did You Know?

You can learn more about program compatibility. On the Compatibility tab of the Properties dialog box, click the Program Compatibility link.

You can test your program using the Program Compatibility Wizard. On the Compatibility tab of the Properties dialog box, click Program Compatibility, to open the Help and Support Center, and then follow the instructions.

Quitting a Program Not Responding

If a program stops responding while you work, Windows provides you with the option to end the task (**New!**). When you end a task, you'll probably lose any unsaved work in the problem program. If the problem persists, you might need to reinstall the program or contact product support to fix the problem.

End a Task Not Responding

1. Right-click the taskbar, and then click Task Manager.

   If Windows doesn't respond when you right-click, press Ctrl+Alt+Delete, and then click Task Manager.

2. Click the Applications tab.

3. Select the program not responding.

4. Click End Task. If you're asked to wait, click End Now.

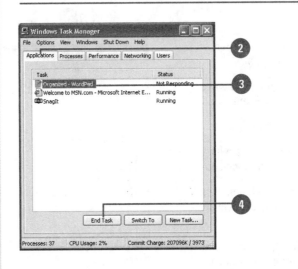

End a Program Not Responding

1. If a program is not responding, click the Close button on the program's title bar. Click several times, if necessary.

2. If you see a dialog box telling you the program is not responding, click End Now.

3. When a message appears, click Send Error Report to send information about the error over the Internet to Microsoft, or click Don't Send to continue.

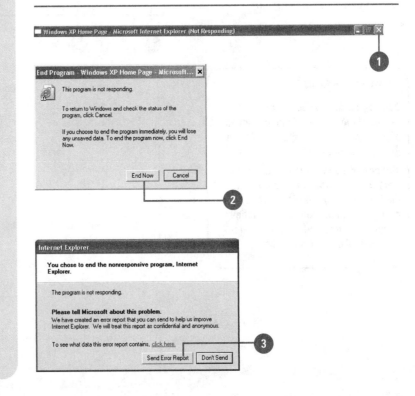

Managing Files and Folders

3

Introduction

File management is organizing and keeping track of files and folders. It helps you stay organized so information is easy to locate and use. A folder is a container for storing programs and files, similar to a folder in a file cabinet. As with a file cabinet, working with poorly managed files is like looking for a needle in a haystack—it is frustrating and time-consuming to search through irrelevant, misnamed, and out-of-date files to find the one you want. Windows allows you to organize folders and files in a file hierarchy, imitating the way you store paper documents in real folders. Just as a file cabinet contains several folders, each containing related documents with dividers grouping related folders together, so the Windows file hierarchy allows you to organize your files in folders, then place folders in other folders. At the top of each hierarchy is the name of the hard drive or main folder. This drive or folder contains several files and folders, and each folder contains related files and folders.

Using the file management tools, you save files in folders with appropriate names for easy identification, quickly and easily create new folders so you can reorganize information, delete files and folders that you no longer need, search for a file when you cannot remember where you stored it, create shortcuts to files and folders for quick and easy access, and compress files and folders to save space.

Opening and Viewing My Computer

The My Computer window is the starting point to access every disk, folder, and file on your computer. You can access the My Computer window from the Start menu (New!). The My Computer window displays several types of local, removable, and network drives. Drives and folders are represented by icons. Each drive is assigned a drive letter, denoted with parentheses and a colon, such as Local Disk (C:), to make it easier to identify. Typically, the floppy is drive A, the hard (also known as local) disk is drive C, and the CD is drive D. If your computer includes additional drives, your computer assigns them letters in alphabetical order. Once you open more than one drive or folder, you can use buttons on the Standard Buttons toolbar to help you move quickly between folders.

Open and View My Computer

1. Click the Start button, and then click My Computer.

2. Click a drive to select it.

3. Review the tasks you can do with the selected drive.

4. Click to display details about the drive.

5. Double-click the drive to open it.

6. Click the Back button or Forward button on the toolbar to return or move to a previously visited window.

   TIMESAVER *You can press the Backspace key to go back to a previous folder you visited.*

7. When you're done, click the Close button.

Did You Know?

You can add the My Computer icon to the desktop. Right-click the desktop in a blank area, click Properties, click the Desktop tab, click Customize Desktop, select the My Computer check box, and then click OK.

You can find Windows system information in My Computer. Click the Start button, click My Computer, click View System Information in the task pane, and then click the General tab.

See Also

See "Changing the Window View" on page 56 for information on changing the display of a folder's contents.

Typical Disk Drives on a Computer

Icon	Type Description
	Local A hard magnetic disk (or hard disk) on which you can store large amounts of data. The Local Disk (C:) stores all the files on your computer.
	Floppy A soft removable magnetic disk that comes in a 3½-inch size, which stores up to 1.44 MB of data. Floppy disks are slower to access than a hard disk, but are portable and much less expensive.
	Removable A removable magnetic disk on which you can store computer data, such as a Zip disk (requires software). Another is a Flash memory card the size of a large stamp that holds128, 256, 512 MB or greater. Flash drives connect directly into a USB plug without software.
	Compact Disc-Read-Only Memory (CD-ROM) An optical disk on which you can stamp, or burn, up to 1 GB (typical size is 650 MB) of data in only one session. The disc cannot be erased or burned again with additional new data.
	Compact Disc-Recordable (CD-R) A type of CD-ROM on which you can burn up to 1 GB of data in multiple sessions. The disc can be burned again with new data, but cannot be erased.
	Compact Disc-Rewritable (CD-RW) A type of CD-ROM on which you can read, write, and erase data, just like a floppy or hard disk.
	Digital Video Disc (DVD) A type of CD-ROM that holds a minimum of 4.7 GB, enough for a full-length movie.

Window Toolbar Buttons

Button	Name	Function
Back	Back	Moves to the previous location you visited
	Forward	Moves forward to the previous location you visited
	Up	Moves up one level in the file hierarchy
Search	Search	Lets you search for folders or files
Folders	Folders	Displays a list of folders on your computer
	Views	Displays the contents of a folder using different views

Opening and Viewing My Documents

With a set of personal folders, Windows makes it easy to manage the personal and business files and folders you work with every day. My Documents is a personal folder that contains additional personal folders, such as My Pictures, My Music, and My Videos (**New!**). Depending on previous installation, devices installed, or other users, your personal folders might differ. You can access your personal My Documents folder from the Start menu. In the My Documents folder, you can view file information, organize files and folders, and open files and folders. Once you open more than one folder, you can use buttons on the Standard Buttons toolbar to help you move quickly between folders.

Open and View My Documents

1. Click the Start button, and then click My Documents.

2. Click a file to select it.

3. Review the tasks you can do with the selected file.

4. Click to display details about the file.

5. Double-click the file to open it.

6. Use the scroll bars to view additional documents. Drag the scroll box, or click the scroll arrows.

7. When you're done, click the Close button.

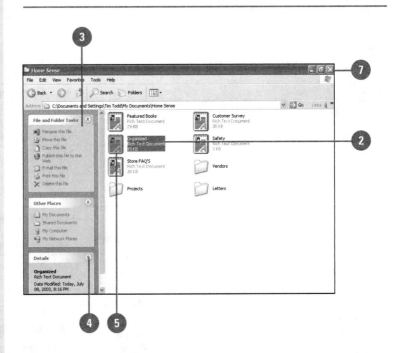

Did You Know?

Windows creates a separate My Documents folder for each user.
When you share a computer, Windows creates a separate My Documents folder and stores personalized settings for each user. Each user's My Documents folder is located in the Documents And Settings folder under the user's name on the local hard disk.

Open Any Folder

1. Click the Start button, and then click My Documents.

2. Click a folder to select it.

3. Review the tasks you can do with the selected folder.

4. Click to display details about the folder.

5. Double-click the folder to open it.

6. Click the Back button or Forward button on the toolbar to return or move to a previously visited window.

7. When you're done, click the Close button.

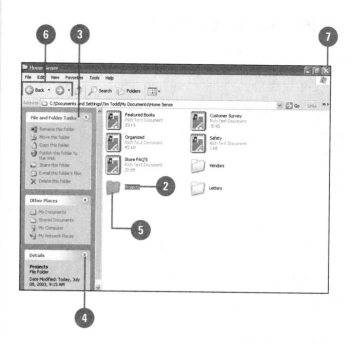

Did You Know?

Windows stores music and picture files in separate folders in My Documents. Windows stores music files in the My Music folder and pictures in the My Pictures folder, which you can access from the Start menu.

See Also

See "Changing the Window View" on page 56 for information on changing the display of a folder's contents.

For Your Information

Opening a Document with a Different Program

Most documents on your desktop are associated with a specific program. For example, if you double-click a document whose file name ends with the three-letter extension ".txt," Windows XP automatically opens the document with Notepad, a text-only editor. There are situations, though, when you need to open a document with a program other than the one Windows chooses, or when you want to choose a different default program. For example, you might want to open a text document in WordPad rather than Notepad so that you can add formatting and graphics. To do this, right-click the document icon you want to open, point to Open With, and then click the application you want to use to open the document, or click Choose Program to access more program options. Once you open a text file using WordPad, this option is automatically added to the Open With menu.

Changing the Window View

Windows displays the contents of a drive or folder in different ways to help you find the information your looking for about a file or folder. The available views include Filmstrip, Thumbnails, Tiles, Icons, List, and Details. You can change the window view from the View menu, or you can click the Views button on the Standard Buttons toolbar.

Filmstrip (New!) view displays pictures in a slide show. An enlarged image of the selected picture appears at the top, and thumbnail views of all the files and subfolders in the folder appear at the bottom. This view is available only in folders customized to display pictures, such as the My Pictures folder.

Thumbnails view displays a miniature representation of the file or folder. A picture file displays a preview of the image, and a customized folder displays one or more pictures. Other files and folders simply display an icon.

Tiles view displays icons, sorted alphabetically into vertical columns, with information about the file next to each icon.

Icons view displays icons, sorted alphabetically in horizontal rows, with the name of the file or folder below each icon.

List view displays small icons, sorted alphabetically into vertical columns, with the name of the file or folder next to each icon.

Details view displays small icons, sorted alphabetically in a single vertical column, with the name of the file or folder and additional information, such as size, type, and date, in columns to the right.

Filmstrip view

Thumbnails view

Tiles view

Icons view

List view

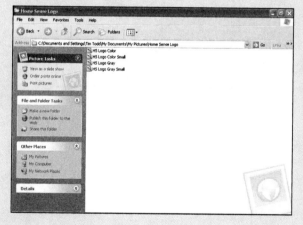

Details view

Viewing the Folders List

Windows XP offers a useful feature for managing files and folders, called the **Folders list** (also known as the **Folders Explorer bar**). The Folders list displays the window in two panes, or frames, which allows you to view information from two different locations. The left pane of the Folders list displays the file hierarchy of all the drives and folders on the computer, and the right pane displays the contents of the selected drive or folder. This arrangement enables you to view the file hierarchy of your computer and the contents of a folder simultaneously making it easy to copy, move, delete, and rename files and folders. Using the plus sign (+) and the minus sign (-) to the left of an icon in the Folders list allows you to display different levels of the drives and folders on your computer without opening and displaying the contents of each folder.

View the Folders List

1 Open any folder window.

2 Click the Folders button on the toolbar.

   TIMESAVER *Press the Windows key+E to open My Computer with the Folders list.*

3 Perform the commands you want to display folder structure and contents:

   ◆ To show the file and folder structure, click the plus sign (+).

   ◆ To hide the file and folder structure, click the minus sign (-).

   ◆ To display the contents of a folder, click the folder icon.

4 When you're done, click the Close button.

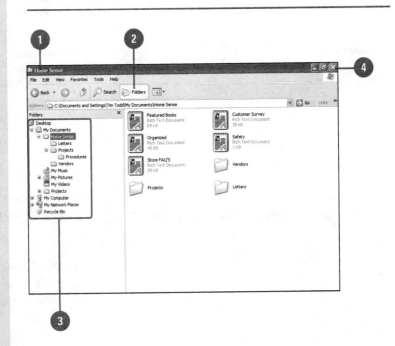

Did You Know?

You can quickly determine if a folder contains folders. When neither plus sign (+) nor minus sign (-) appears next to an icon in the Folders list, the item has no folders in it.

Locating Files Using the History List

Windows keeps a list of your most recently used files, folders, and network computers in the History folder. Instead of navigating through a long list of folders to open a recently used file, you can use the History list to find it quickly. The History list works exactly like the one in a web browser. You can view the History Explorer bar in several ways: by date, by site, by most visited, and by order visited today.

Find a File from the History List

1 Open any folder.

2 Click the View menu, point to Explorer Bar, and then click History.

TIMESAVER *Press Ctrl+H to open the History list.*

3 In the History list, click the View button, and then click the view you want.

4 To open a file, click the file name.

5 When you're done, click the Close button.

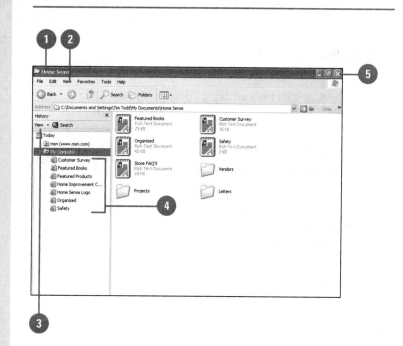

Did You Know?

You can use the Search button to locate files in the History list. In the History Explorer bar, click the Search button, type a keyword, and then click Search Now.

You can resize the Explorer bar. Position the pointer (which changes to a double arrow) on the vertical bar separating the two window panes, and then drag to change the size of the panes.

Searching for Files and Folders

Sometimes remembering precisely where you stored a file is difficult. Windows provides a Search Companion to help you find files or folders. The Search Companion (**New!**) opens in the Explorer bar and gives you the option to find files or folders by name, location, size, type, and the creation or last modification date. You can also narrow your search by selecting categories, listed in the Search Companion. The Search Companion is accessible from the Start menu or any folder window to help you locate files and folders.

Search for Files and Folders

1. Click the Start button, and then click Search, or click the Search button on the toolbar in a folder window.

   TIMESAVER *Press F3 to open the Search Companion from the desktop.*

2. Click the green arrow next to the type of file or folder you want to find. Each type contains different search options.

3. Select or enter as much search criteria as you can.

4. Click Search to retrieve the files or folders that meet the criteria.

5. When you're done, click the Close button.

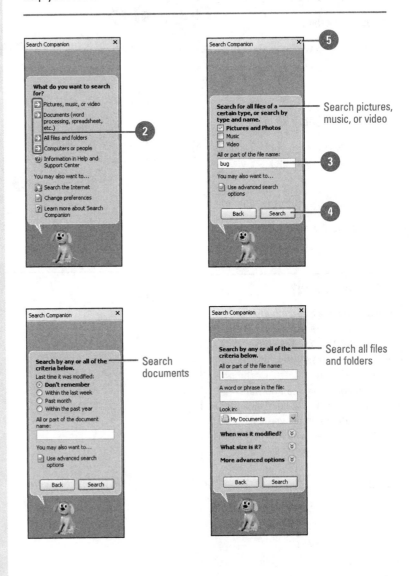

Search pictures, music, or video

Search documents

Search all files and folders

Did You Know?

You can turn off the animated character. In the Search Companion, click Change Preferences, and then click Without An Animated Screen Character.

You can use wildcards to expand a search. Use the * (asterisk) wildcard symbol in a file name when you're unsure of the entire name. For example, type **S*rs** to find all files beginning with "S" and ending with "rs," such as Stars and Sports cars.

Use the Results

◆ **Complete search.** Click Yes, Finished Searching to close the Search Companion.

◆ **Refine this search.** Click the green arrow next to the refinement you want to perform.

◆ **Sort the result by category.** Click the column title in Details view, or click the View menu, point to Arrange Icons By, and then click a category.

◆ **Find out about an item.** Point to a file or folder name or location to display pop-up information.

◆ **Open a file.** Double-click the file icon.

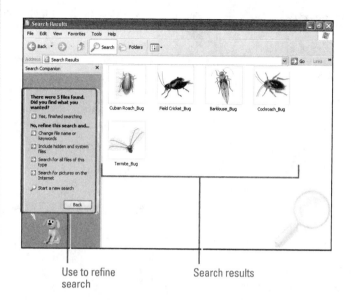

Use to refine search

Search results

Did You Know?

You can get details about a file or folder. Point to the file or folder to display a pop-up description. If you want more information, right-click the file or folder, and then click Properties.

You can widen the column results to see more details. In Details view, drag the dividing line between two column titles at the top of the column.

You can reduce the search time. When you search all your documents for certain words, the search is painfully long. You can use the indexing service to speed it up. In the Search Companion, click Change Preferences, click With Indexing Service, and then click Yes, Enable Indexing Service. The service creates a file that takes a few megabytes on your hard disk.

For Your Information

Saving a Search

If you perform the same search on a regular basis, you can save time by saving the search criteria. After you complete the search you want to save, click the File menu, click Save Search, navigate to the place where you want to save the .fnd file, name the file, and then click Save. To use the search file, double-click the .fnd file. The Search window opens, displaying the search criteria. Click the Search button to perform the search.

Creating and Renaming Files and Folders

The keys to organizing files and folders effectively within a hierarchy are to store related items together and to name folders informatively. Creating a new folder can help you organize and keep track of files and other folders. In order to create a folder, you select the location where you want the new folder, create the folder, and then lastly, name the folder. You should name each folder meaningfully so that just by reading the folder's name you know its contents. After you name a folder or file, you can rename it at any time.

Create a Folder

1 Open the drive or folder where you want to create a folder.

2 Click Make A New Folder in the task pane.

3 With the New Folder name selected, type a new name.

4 Press Enter.

Did You Know?

File names can be up to 255 characters. You can use spaces and underscores in names, but you can't use the following characters: * : < > | ? " \ or /.

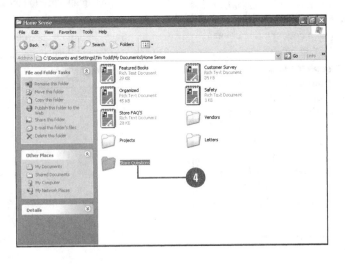

Rename a File or Folder

 Click the file or folder to select it.

2 Click Rename This File or Rename This Folder.

3 With the name selected, type a new name, or click to position the insertion point, and then edit the name.

4 Press Enter.

TIMESAVER *Right-click the file or folder you want to rename, click Rename, type a name, and then press Enter.*

Did You Know?

You can rename a group of files.
Select all the files you want to rename, right-click one of the selected files, click Rename from the shortcut menu, type a name, and then press Enter. The group name appears with numbers in consecutive order.

Copying and Moving Files and Folders ▶

Sometimes you will need to move a file from one folder to another, or copy a file from one folder to another, leaving the file in the first location and placing a copy of it in the second. You can move or copy a file or folder using a variety of methods. If the file or folder and the location where you want to move it are visible in a window or on the desktop, you can simply drag the item from one location to the other. Moving a file or folder on the same disk relocates it whereas dragging it from one disk to another copies it so that it appears in both locations. When the destination folder or drive is not visible, you can use the Cut (to move), Copy, and Paste commands on the Edit menu to move or copy the items.

Copy a File or Folder

1 Open the drive or folder containing the file or folder you want to copy or move.

2 Select the files or folders you want to copy.

3 Click Copy The Selected Items, Copy This File, or Copy This Folder. The commands change depending on the selection.

4 Click the plus sign (+) to display the destination folder, and then click the destination folder.

5 Click Copy.

For Your Information

Sending Files and Folders

When you right-click most objects on the desktop or in My Computer or Windows Explorer, the Send To command, located on the shortcut menu, lets you send, or move, a file or folder to a new location on your computer. For example, you can send a file or folder to a removable disk to make a quick backup copy of the file or folder, to a mail recipient as an electronic message, or to the desktop to create a shortcut. You can also use the Send To command to move a file or folder from one folder to another. To send a file or folder, right-click the file or folder you want to send, point to Send To on the shortcut menu, and then click the destination you want.

Move a File or Folder

1. Open the drive or folder containing the file or folder you want to copy or move.

2. Select the files or folders you want to move.

3. Click Move The Selected Items, Move This File, or Move This Folder. The commands change depending on the selection.

4. Click the plus sign (+) to display the destination folder, and then click the destination folder.

5. Click Move.

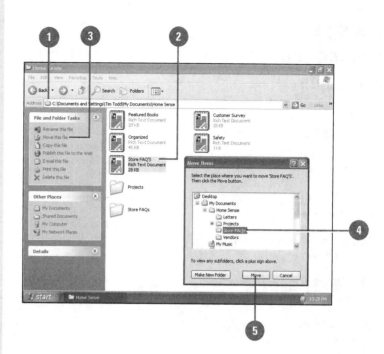

Copy or Move a File or Folder Using Drag and Drop

1. Open the drive or folder containing the file or folder you want to copy or move.

2. Select the files or folders you want to copy or move.

3. Click the Folders button on the toolbar.

4. Click the plus sign (+) to display the destination folder, and then click the destination folder.

5. Right-click the selected files or folders, drag to the destination folder, and then click Copy Here or Move Here.

> **TIMESAVER** *To move the selected items, drag them to the destination folder. To copy the items, hold down the Ctrl key while you drag.*

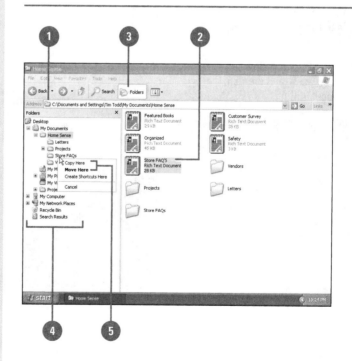

3

Deleting and Restoring Files and Folders

When you organize the contents of a folder, disk, or the desktop, you might find files and folders that you no longer need. You can delete these items or remove them from the disk. If you delete a file or folder from the desktop or from the hard disk, it goes into the Recycle Bin. The **Recycle Bin**, located on your desktop, is a temporary storage area for deleted files. The Recycle Bin stores all the items you delete from your hard disk so that if you accidentally delete an item, you can remove it from the Recycle Bin to restore it. Be aware that if you delete a file from a removable disk, it is permanently deleted, not stored in the Recycle Bin. The files in the Recycle Bin do occupy room on your computer, so you need to empty it to free up space.

Delete Files and Folders

1. Select the files and folders you want to delete.

2. Click Delete This File, Delete This Folder, or Delete Selected Items.

   TIMESAVER *Press the Delete key to delete selected items.*

3. Click Yes to confirm the deletion and place the items in the Recycle Bin.

4. On the desktop, right-click the Recycle Bin icon, and then click Empty Recycle Bin.

   Your computer removes the items.

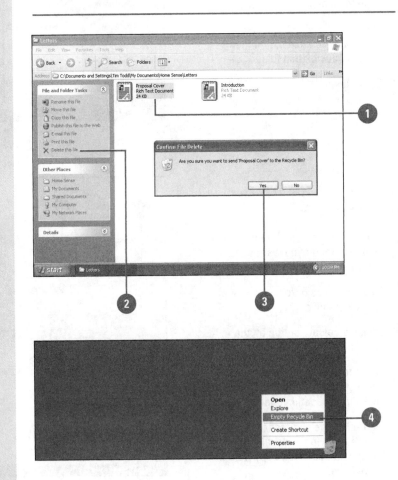

Restore Files and Folders

1 Double-click the Recycle Bin icon on the desktop.

2 Select the item or items you want to restore.

3 Click Restore This Item or Restore All Items.

Did You Know?

You can undo a deletion. If you accidentally delete a file, click the Edit menu, and then click Undo Delete. Windows XP remembers your last three actions.

You can't open a deleted folder and restore selected items. When you've deleted a folder, you have to restore the entire folder.

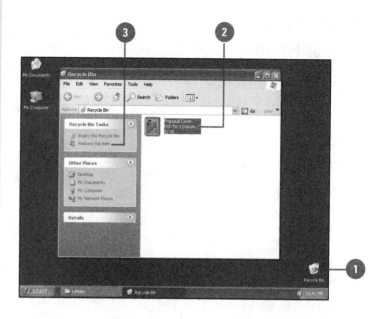

For Your Information

Changing Recycle Bin Properties

You can adjust several Recycle Bin settings by using the Properties option on the Recycle Bin shortcut menu. For example, if you want to delete files immediately rather than place them in the Recycle Bin, right-click the Recycle Bin, click Properties, and then select the Do Not Move Files To The Recycle Bin check box. Also, if you find that the Recycle Bin is full and cannot accept any more files, you can increase the amount of disk space allotted to the Recycle Bin by moving the Maximum size of Recycle Bin slider to the right. The percentage shown represents how much space the contents of the Recycle Bin takes on the drive.

Creating a Shortcut to a File or Folder

It could take you a while to access a file or folder buried several levels down in a file hierarchy. To save some time, you can create shortcuts to the items you use frequently. A **shortcut** is a link that you can place in any location to gain instant access to a particular file, folder, or program on your hard disk or on a network just by double-clicking. The actual file, folder, or program remains stored in its original location, and you place an icon representing the shortcut in a convenient location, such as in a folder or on the desktop.

Create a Shortcut to a File or Folder

1 Open the drive or folder containing the file or folder in which you want to create a shortcut.

2 Right-click the file or folder, and then click Create Shortcut.

3 To change the shortcut's name, right-click the shortcut, click Rename from the shortcut menu, type a new name, and then press Enter.

4 Drag the shortcut to the desired location.

For Your Information

Placing Shortcuts on the Start Menu and Taskbar

You can place shortcuts to frequently used files, folders, and programs on the Start menu or toolbar on the taskbar. To do this, simply drag the shortcut file, folder, or program to the Start button, wait until the Start menu opens, drag to the All Programs submenu, wait until the submenu opens, and then drag the shortcut to the appropriate place on the menu. You can also drag a shortcut to a toolbar on the taskbar using the same method. When you release the mouse, the item appears on the menu or toolbar.

Adding a Folder to the Favorites List

Rather than navigating through a long list of folders to get to the location you want to display, you can use a Favorites list to locate and organize folders. When you view a folder that you want to display at a later time, you can add the folder to your Favorites list. Once you add the folder to the Favorites list, you can return to the folder by opening your Favorites list and selecting the link to the folder you want. In addition to adding folders to the Favorites list, you can also add locations on the Internet. If your list of favorites grows long, you can delete favorites you don't use anymore or move favorites into folders.

Add a Folder to the Favorites List

1. Open the folder you want to add to your Favorites list.

2. Click the Favorites menu, and then click Add To Favorites.

3. Type a name for the favorite, or use the default name supplied.

4. Click Create In, and then select a location on the Favorites menu to place the site.

5. If you want a new folder, click New Folder, type a folder name, and then click OK.

6. Click OK.

   Use the Favorites menu to quickly return to a favorite location.

> ### See Also
>
> *See "Adding a Web Page to the Favorites List" on page 123 for information on working with favorites.*

3

Changing Folder Options

When you work with files and folders, Windows displays folder contents in a standard way, known as the **default**. The default folder view settings are as follows: Tiles view displays files and folders as icons; common task links appear in the left pane; folders open in the same window; and items open when you double-click them. Depending on previous installation or users, your folder view settings might differ. Instead of changing the folder view to your preferred view—Thumbnails, Icons, List, or Details—each time you open a folder, you can change the view permanently to the one you prefer. In addition to the defaults, you can change options such as folder settings to show or hide file extensions for known file types, show or hide hidden files and folders, show the Control Panel in My Computer, and show pop-up descriptions of folders and desktop items.

Change the Way All Folders Work

1. Click the Start button, and then click My Computer.

2. Click the Tools menu, and then click Folder Options.

3. Click the General tab.

4. Select a Tasks option to display frequently used tasks or the contents of the folder.

5. Select a Browse Folders option to display each folder in the same window or its own window.

6. Select a Click Items As Follows option to single-click or double-click items.

7. Click OK.

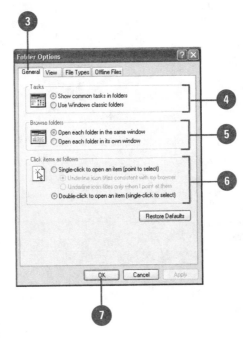

Did You Know?

You can restore all folder options to default Windows settings. On the General tab in the Folder Options dialog box, click Restore Defaults.

Change the Folder View

1 Click the Start button, and then click My Computer.

2 Click the Tools menu, and then click Folder Options.

3 Click the View tab.

4 To set the current view to all folders, click Apply To All Folders.

5 Select the check boxes for the options you want, and clear the check boxes for the ones you don't.

6 Click OK.

Did You Know?

You can reset folder views to original Windows settings. On the View tab in the Folder Options dialog box, click Reset All Folders.

You can quickly learn about each folder in the dialog box. Click the Help button in the Folders View dialog box, and then click the option you want.

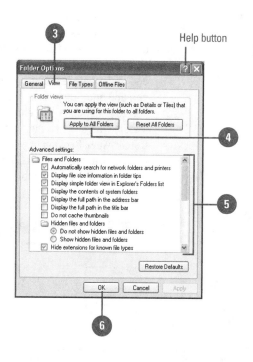

Help button

3

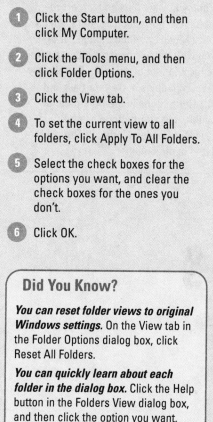

For Your Information

Understanding File Extensions

The program Windows uses to open a document depends on a three-letter extension to the document's file name, called a **file extension**. You might have never seen a document's file extension because your system might be set up to hide it. The file extension for simple text files is ".txt" (pronounced "dot t-x-t"), and many graphic files have the extension ".bmp". This means that the full name for a text file named Memo is Memo.txt. If you double-click a document whose file name ends with the three-letter extension ".txt," Windows automatically opens the document with Notepad, a text-only editor. If you want to display or change file extension settings, click the Start button, click My Documents, click the Tools menu, and then click Folder Options. If you want to display file extensions in dialog boxes and windows, click the View tab, and then clear the Hide Extensions For Known File Types check box in the Advanced settings list box. If you want to change the program Windows automatically starts with a given file extension, click the File Types tab in the Folder Options dialog box to see the list of the file extensions Windows recognizes and the programs associated with each of them, and make changes as appropriate.

Changing File and Folder List Views

You can display files and folders in a variety of different ways, depending on what you want to see and do. When you view files and folders in Details view, a default list of file and folder information appears, which consists of Name, Size, Type, and Date Modified. If the default list of file and folder details doesn't provide you with the information you need, you can add and remove any file and folder information from the Details view (New!). If you need to change the way Windows sorts your files and folders, you can use the column indicator buttons in the right pane of Details view. Clicking one of the column indicator buttons, such as Name, Size, Type, or Date Modified, in Details view sorts the files and folders by the type of information listed in the column.

Change File Details to List

1. Open the folder you want to change.

2. Click the View menu, and then click Choose Details.

3. Select the check boxes with the details you want to include and clear the ones you don't.

4. Click the Move Up or Move Down buttons to change the order of the selected items.

5. Click the Show or Hide button to show or hide the selected items.

6. Specify the width in pixels of the column for the selected items.

7. Click OK.

   TIMESAVER *Right-click a column title in Details view, and then click the detail you want to show or hide.*

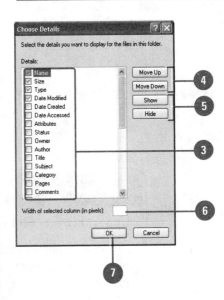

Did You Know?

An ellipsis indicates information is hidden. To show the information, drag the edge of the column indicator button to resize the column.

Arranging Files and Folders

After you select a view to display your files and folders, you can change the way individual files and folders are sorted by using other Arrange Icons options on the View menu. You can sort the files by name, size, file type, or date. After you sort them, you can arrange the sorted list by group according to the sorted view. For example, when you sort files by name and show them in groups, the files are grouped by letter.

Arrange Items in a Window

1. Open the drive or folder you want to arrange.

2. Click the View menu, point to Arrange Icons By.

3. Click the view you want to use: Name, Size, Type, or Modified.

4. Click the View menu, point to Arrange Icons By, and then click an arrangement option.

   ◆ Show In Groups (New!)

   ◆ Auto Arrange

   ◆ Align To Grid (New!)

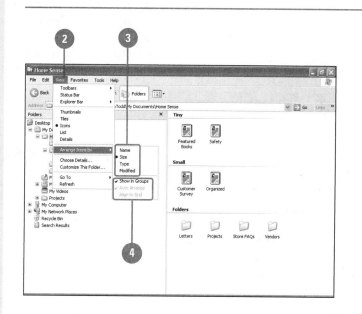

Did You Know?

Not all options are available for all views. The Arrange Icons By submenu changes based on the current view.

See Also

See "Customizing the Taskbar" on page 100 for information on modifying the taskbar.

Options for Arranging Files and Folders

Option	Arranges Files and Folders
Name	Alphabetically
Size	By size, with the largest folder or file listed first
Type	By type, such as all documents created using the WordPad program
Modified	Chronologically by their last modification date, with the latest modification date listed last
Show In Groups	In letter groups by alphabetical order; toggle on and off
Auto Arrange	Automatically in orderly rows and columns; toggle on and off; not available with Show In Groups
Align To Grid	Automatically in rows and columns by invisible grid points; toggle on and off; not available with Show In Groups

3

Customizing Personal Folders

In the My Documents folder, you can create your own folders and customize view options based on the contents (**New!**). In the left pane of the My Pictures, My Music, and My Videos folders, Windows provides links to file management activities specifically related to the contents of the folder and other places on your computer, such as Print Pictures in the My Pictures folder, or Play All in the My Music or My Video folders. When you create a new folder, you can customize it for pictures, music, and videos by applying a folder template, which is a collection of folder task links and viewing options. When you apply a template to a folder, you apply specific features to the folder, such as specialized task links and viewing options for working with pictures, music, and videos.

Change the Folder Look

1 Open the folder you want to change.

2 Click the View menu, and then click Customize This Folder.

3 Click the Customize tab.

4 Select the type of folder you want.

5 Select the Also Apply This Template To All Subfolders check box to apply the option.

6 Click Choose Picture to select a picture for display on the folder in Thumbnails view.

7 Click Change Icon to select a different icon for the folder, and then click OK.

8 Click OK.

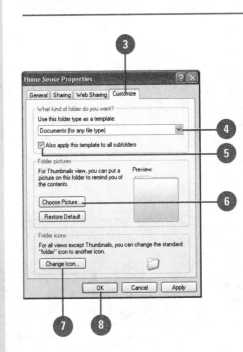

See Also

See "Viewing Pictures" on page 212 for information on using the My Pictures folder and see "Viewing and Playing Music Files" on page 243 for information on using the My Music folder.

Sharing Files or Folders with Others

Windows maintains a set of personal folders and options for everyone on your computer to make sure the contents of each user's personal folders remain private. The contents of your personal folders are private, unless you decide to share the contents with others who use your computer. If you want the other users on your computer to have access to files, you can place those files in a shared folder called the Shared Documents folder (**New!**) that each user can access. If you're connected to a network, the files in the shared folder are available to network users.

Share a File

1. Open the drive or folder containing the files or folders you want to share.

2. Select the files or folders you want to share.

3. Drag the selected items onto the Shared Documents item.

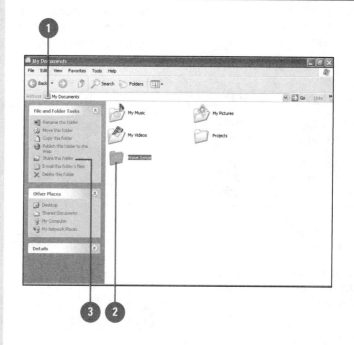

Did You Know?

You can drag files directly to the Shared Documents folder. Click the Folders button on the Standard Buttons toolbar, and then drag the files you want to share onto the Shared Documents folder in the Folders list.

See Also

See "Sharing a Folder over a Network" on page 334 for information on sharing files over a network.

3

Compressing Files and Folders

You can compress files in special folders that use compressing software to decrease the size of the files they contain (**New!**). Compressed folders are useful for reducing the file size of one or more large files, thus freeing disk space and reducing the time it takes to transfer files to another computer over the Internet or network. A compressed folder is denoted by a zippered folder icon. You can compress one or more files in a compressed folder by simply dragging them onto the compressed folder icon. When a file is compressed, a copy is used in the compression, and the original remains intact. You can uncompress, or extract, a file from the compressed folder and open it as you normally would, or you can open a file directly from the compressed folder by double-clicking the Compressed File icon. When you open a file directly, Windows extracts the file when it opens and compresses it again when it closes.

Compress Files and Folders

1. Select the files and folders you want to copy to a compressed folder.

2. Right-click one of the selected items, point to Send To, and then click Compressed (Zipped) Folder.

3. If you want, rename the compressed folder.

4. To copy additional files or folders to the compressed folder, drag the files onto the compressed folder.

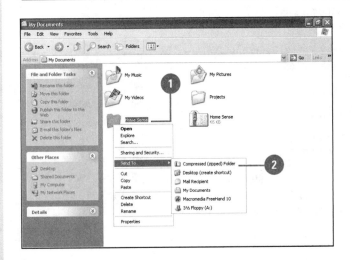

View Compressed Files

1. Double-click the compressed folder to open it.

2. Double-click an item in the folder to open it using its associated program.

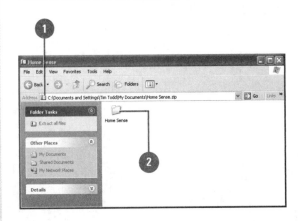

Decompress Files

1 Double-click the compressed folder to open it.

2 Select the files you want to decompress.

3 To decompress a single file, click Copy This File, and then select the destination folder.

4 To decompress all the files, click Extract All Files, and then step through the Extraction Wizard.

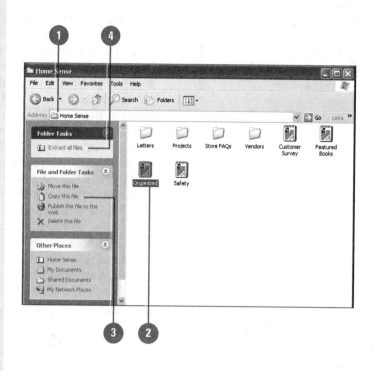

For Your Information

Compressing Files and Folders on an NTFS Drive

If your hard disk is formatted as NTFS, you need to use a different method to compress existing files and folders. NTFS is an advanced file system that provides additional performance, security, and reliability over the standard file system FAT (File Allocation Table) or FAT32. To display the file system, select your hard disk icon in My Computer in the left pane under Details. To compress an existing file or folder on an NTFS drive, right-click the file or folder you want to compress, click Properties, click Advanced on the General tab, select the Compress Contents To Save Disk Space check box, and then click OK twice. In the Confirm Attribute Changes dialog box, select the option you want, and then click OK.

Managing Files Using a CD

The low cost and large storage size of compact discs, or CDs, and the popularity of CD recording hardware make creating and using CDs (New!) an effective approach to some file management tasks. For example, CDs are an effective way to back up information or transfer large amounts of information to another computer without a network. Before you can create a CD, you must have blank CDs and a CD recorder (also known as a writer or burner) installed on your computer. You can copy, or write, files and folders to either a compact disc-recordable (CD-R) or a compact disc rewritable (CD-RW). With CD-Rs, you can write files and folders only once and read them many times, but you can't erase them. With CD-RWs, you can read, write, and erase files and folders many times, just like a floppy or hard disk. When you write to, or burn, a CD, Windows needs disk space on your hard disk to store temporary files that are created during the process, so make sure you have 700 MB of free hard disk space when using a standard CD and 1 gigabyte (GB) for a high-capacity CD. Do not copy more files and folders to the CD than it will hold; anything beyond the limit will not copy to the CD. Standard CDs hold up to 700 megabytes (MB). High-capacity CDs hold up to 850 MB.

Prepare Files and Folders for a CD

1. Select the files and folders you want to copy to a CD.

2. Right-click one of the selected items, point to Send To, and then click CD Drive.

   If balloon help appears, pointing to an icon in the notification area and indicating you have files waiting to be written to the CD, you can click the balloon to open the CD recording drive.

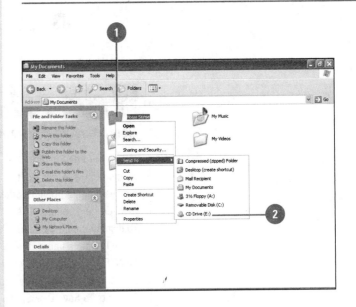

Preview Files and Folders for a CD

1. Click the Start button, and then click My Computer.

2. Double-click the CD Drive.

Did You Know?

You can change CD recording properties. Right-click the CD recording drive icon in My Computer, click Properties, and then click the Recording tab. Select a recording speed or change the Windows space reserve, and then click OK.

Create a CD

1. Click the Start button, click My Computer, and then double-click the CD Drive.

2. With a blank CD in the CD drive, click Write These Files To CD to start the CD Writing Wizard.

3. Type a name for the CD.

4. To close the wizard, select the Close The Wizard After The Files Have Been Written check box.

5. Click Next.

6. To make another copy of the CD, select the Yes, Write These Files To Another CD check box, insert a new blank CD into the CD drive, and then click Next.

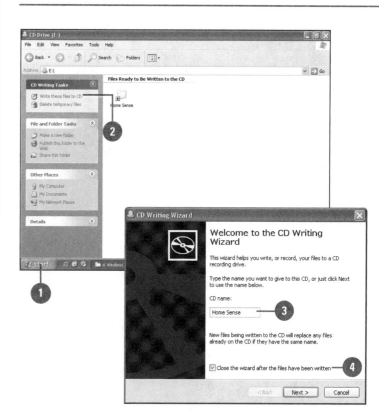

Customizing Windows Using the Control Panel

Introduction

Windows XP gives you the ability to customize your work environment (your computer's desktop and other settings) to suit your personal needs and preferences. You can adjust most Windows features through the Control Panel, a central location for changing Windows settings. From the **Control Panel** you access the individual programs for changing the **properties**, or characteristics, of a specific element of your computer, such as the desktop, the taskbar, or the Start menu. Each icon in the Control Panel represents an aspect of Windows that you can change to fit your own working habits and personal needs. For example, you can use the Display icon to change the background picture or color of the desktop, or the Taskbar and Start Menu icon to customize the taskbar and Start menu. Some Control Panel settings are vital to how you work (such as the Date and Time, or the Language settings) and others are purely aesthetic (such as that background picture, or which screen saver you use).

The Control Panel also includes icons to setup user accounts and maintain security (see Chapter 11), setup and manage local-area, wide-area, and wireless networks (see Chapter 12), access printers and faxes (see Chapter 13), add and remove programs and automatically update Windows (see Chapter 14), and work with hardware, such as a scanner, digital camera, modem, audio and speakers, mouse, and keyboard (see Chapter 15).

Viewing the Control Panel

The Control Panel is a collection of utility programs that determine how Windows looks and works on your computer. The Control Panel displays in Category or Classic view. Category view (**New!**) displays the Control Panel into functional categories based on tasks, while the Classic view displays an icon for each utility program as in previous versions of Windows. You can change views by using the Control Panel task pane.

View the Control Panel in Classic View

1. Click the Start button, and then click Control Panel.

2. Click Switch To Classic View.

> ### See Also
>
> See "Customizing the Start Menu" on page 102 for information on changing the Start menu to directly open Control Panel programs.

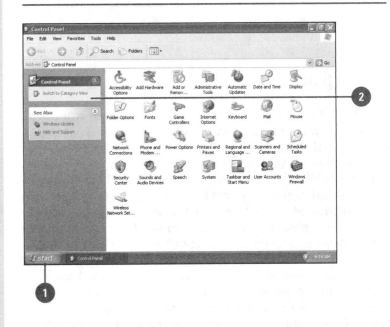

View the Control Panel in Category View

1. Click the Start button, and then click Control Panel.

2. Click Switch To Category View.

3. Click a category link.

4. Click a task or the Control Panel icon link.

5. Click the Back button on the toolbar to return to Category View.

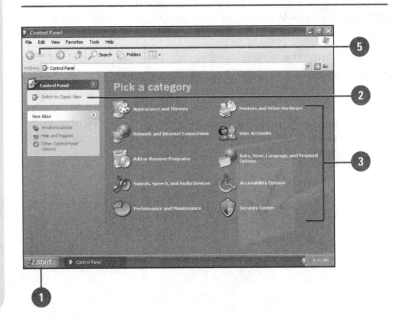

Changing the
Desktop Background

The desktop **background**, or wallpaper, is a picture that serves as your desktop's backdrop, the basic surface on which icons and windows appear. You can select a background picture and change how it looks using the Desktop tab in the Display Properties dialog box. Once you select a background picture, you can display it on the screen three different ways: **Tile** displays the picture consecutively across the screen; **Center** displays the picture in the center of the screen; and **Stretch** enlarges the picture and displays it in the center of the screen. Instead of selecting a background picture, which can sometimes make icons on the desktop difficult to see, you can also change the background to a color.

Use a Background Color

1. Right-click a blank area on the desktop, and then click Properties.

2. Click the Desktop tab.

3. Click None.

4. Click the list arrow, and then click a color.

5. Click OK or Apply.

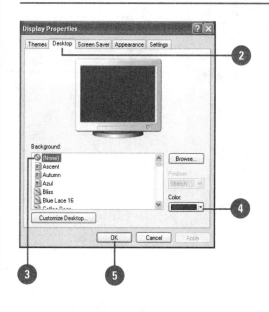

Use a Picture

1. Right-click a blank area on the desktop, and then click Properties.

2. Click the Desktop tab.

3. Click the picture you want.

4. To select another picture, click Browse, locate and select a picture, and then click Open.

5. Click OK or Apply.

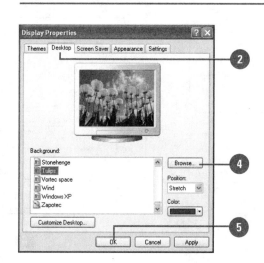

Customizing the Desktop

Because more and more people are using the Internet, Windows allows you to view web content on your desktop as you would in a web browser, such as Internet Explorer, a program specifically designed to view web content on the Internet. **Web items** are elements you can place on the desktop to access or display information from the Internet. For example, you can add a web item to display stock prices or weather information continuously. When you place Web items on the desktop, they are active, which means the web content is updated as the content changes while you're connected to the Internet. In addition, you can also customize the desktop to show or hide the familiar icons My Documents, My Computer, My Network Places, or Internet Explorer.

Display or Hide Desktop Icons

1 Right-click a blank area on the desktop, and then click Properties.

2 Click the Desktop tab.

3 Click Customize Desktop.

4 On the General tab, select or clear the check boxes to show or hide desktop icons.

5 To change the appearance of an icon, select the icon, click Change Icon, select an icon, and then click OK.

6 Click OK.

7 Click OK.

> ### See Also
>
> *See "Cleaning Up the Desktop" on page 86 for information on customizing the desktop.*

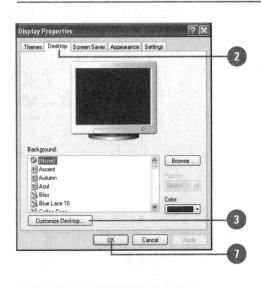

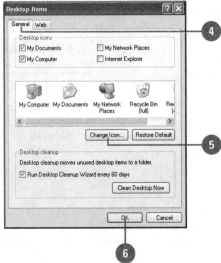

Add Web Content to the Desktop

1. Right-click a blank area on the desktop, and then click Properties.

2. Click the Desktop tab, and then click Customize Desktop.

3. Click the Web tab.

4. Click New.

5. Click Visit Gallery to download free web items, type a Web address to a specific web page, or click Browse to select a picture or HTML document.

6. Click OK, and then click OK again.

Display or Hide Desktop Web Content

1. Right-click a blank area on the desktop, and then click Properties.

2. Click the Desktop tab, and then click Customize Desktop.

3. Click the Web tab.

4. Select or clear the check boxes to show or hide desktop icons.

5. Click OK, and then click OK again.

Did You Know?

You can add web pages as active desktop items. In your browser, locate the page you want to add as an active desktop item, right-click the page, and then click Set As Desktop Item.

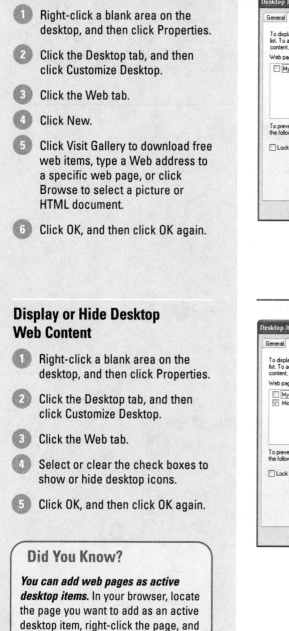

Cleaning Up the Desktop

If your desktop gets cluttered with shortcut icons, you can use the Desktop Cleanup Wizard (**New!**) to move shortcuts that you don't use anymore into a folder. The wizard automatically runs every 60 days, or you can start it at any time. When you run the Desktop Cleanup Wizard, Windows moves the selected shortcuts into the Unused Desktop Shortcuts folder on the desktop, where you can still access or move the icons.

Clean Up the Desktop

1. Right-click a blank area on the desktop, and then click Properties.

2. Click the Desktop tab, and then click Customize Desktop.

3. To have Windows XP run the cleanup wizard every 60 days, select the Run Desktop Cleanup Wizard Every 60 Days check box.

4. Click Clean Desktop Now to start the Desktop Cleanup Wizard, and then click Next.

5. Clear the check boxes for shortcuts you don't want removed from the desktop.

6. Click Next.

7. Review the deletion list of shortcuts.

8. Click Finish.

Did You Know?

You can right-click your way to a clean desktop. Right-click an empty area of the desktop, point to Arrange Icons By, and then click Run Desktop Cleanup Wizard.

Using a Screen Saver

In the past, you needed a screen saver, a continually moving display, to protect your monitor from burn in, which occurs when the same display remains on the screen for extended periods of time and becomes part of the screen. Those days are gone with the emergence of new display technology. Screen savers are more for entertainment than anything else. When you leave your computer idle for a specified wait time, a screen saver displays a continuous scene, such as an aquarium, until you move your mouse to stop it.

Select a Screen Saver

1. Right-click a blank area on the desktop, and then click Properties.

2. Click the Screen Saver tab.

3. Click the list arrow, and then click a screen saver.

4. Click Settings.

5. Select the options you want for the screen saver, and then click OK.

6. Click Preview to see the screen saver in full-screen view, and then move your mouse to end the preview.

7. Specify the time to wait until your computer starts the screen saver.

8. To require a password, select the On Resume, Password Protect check box.

9. Click OK or Apply.

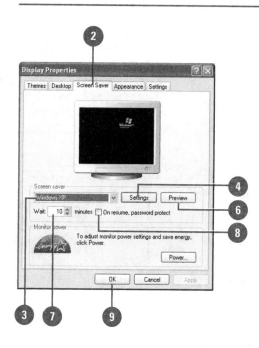

Did You Know?

You can create a screen saver slide show. On the Screen Saver tab, click My Pictures Slideshow from the Screen Saver list arrow, and then click Settings to select pictures.

You can turn off a screen saver. On the Screen Saver tab, click (None) from the Screen Saver list arrow.

Changing the Display ▶

If you find yourself frequently scrolling within windows as you work or squinting to read small text, you might want to change the size of the desktop on your monitor. A monitor displays pictures by dividing the display screen into thousands or millions of dots, or pixels, arranged in rows and columns. The pixels are so close together that they appear connected. The **screen resolution** refers to the number of pixels on the entire screen, which determines the amount of information your monitor displays. A low screen resolution setting, such as 640 by 480 pixels (width by height), displays less information on the screen, but the items on the screen appear relatively large, while a high setting, such as 1024 by 768 pixels, displays more information on the screen, but the items on the screen appear smaller. You can also change the color quality. The higher the color quality, the more colors the computer displays, which requires greater system memory. The most common color quality settings are as follows: 16-bit, which displays 768 colors, and 24-bit and 32-bit, both of which display 16.7 million colors.

Change the Display Size

1. Right-click a blank area on the desktop, and then click Properties.

2. Click the Settings tab.

3. Drag the slide to specify a screen size.

4. Click the list arrow, and then click a color quality.

5. Click OK or Apply.

6. If the Monitor Settings dialog box appears, click Yes or No to accept or decline the new settings.

   Windows reverts to original settings after 15 seconds.

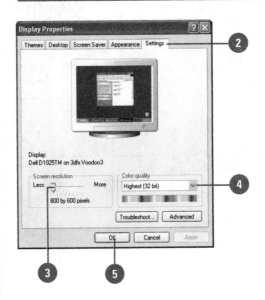

Did You Know?

You can eliminate flicker on your monitor. On the Settings tab, click Advanced, click the Monitor tab, and then increase the screen refresh rate.

Using Multiple Monitors

You can increase the size of your workspace on the desktop and your productivity by adding another monitor to your computer. For example, you can work on a document in WordPad on one monitor and search for web content in your web browser on the other monitor. One monitor is the primary monitor, which displays the dialog boxes that appear when you start your computer and most programs; the other monitor is the secondary monitor, which displays windows, icons, and programs you drag to it from the primary monitor. Before you can use more than one monitor, you need to install another **display adapter**, a hardware device that allows a computer to communicate with its monitor, on your computer that supports multiple monitors. After you install the display adapter according to the manufacturer's instructions and restart the computer, Windows detects the new device and installs the related software. In the Control Panel, double-click the Display icon in Classic View, click the Settings tab, click the monitor icon that represents the secondary monitor that you want to use, select the Extend My Windows Desktop Onto This Monitor check box, and then click Apply to activate the secondary monitor. To arrange multiple monitors, click the monitor icons and drag them in the preview window to the positions you want. You can set different screen resolutions and color settings for each monitor. See

"Adding a Secondary Monitor" on page 414 for more information on using multiple monitors.

If you don't have multiple monitors, you can create a virtual one using the Virtual Desktop Manager, which comes as part of PowerToys for Windows XP. PowerToys are free utility programs you can download from Microsoft at *www.microsoft.com*. The Virtual Desktop Manager is a new taskbar that gives you four side-by-side virtual monitors. Each virtual monitor can have its own background picture and desktop icons and can display its own windows. See *"Having Fun with PowerToys"* on page 464 for information on downloading PowerToys from the web.

4

Changing the Desktop Appearance

You can change the entire appearance of the desktop by using desktop themes. A desktop **theme** changes the desktop background, screen saver, mouse pointers, sounds, icons, and fonts based on a set theme, such as baseball, science, sports, travel, or underwater. You can even change your desktop to the classic Windows look. You can use one of the predefined desktop themes or create your own. If a theme isn't exactly what you want, you can change the appearance of colors, fonts, and sizes used for major window elements such as title bars, icons, menus, borders, and the desktop itself.

Select a Desktop Theme

1. Right-click a blank area on the desktop, and then click Properties.

2. Click the Themes tab.

3. Click the list arrow, and then click a theme.

4. Click OK or Apply.

Customize the Desktop Appearance

1. Right-click a blank area on the desktop, and then click Properties.

2. Click the Appearance tab.

3. Click the Windows And Buttons list arrow, and then click a style.

4. Click the Color Scheme list arrow, and then click a color scheme.

5. Click the Font Size list arrow, and then click a font size.

6. Click Advanced if you want to change the color, size, or font for individual items.

7. Click OK or Apply.

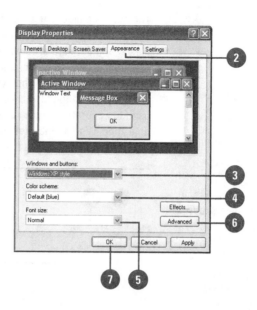

Set Desktop Appearance Effects

1. Right-click a blank area on the desktop, and then click Properties.

2. Click the Appearance tab, and then click Effects.

3. Set one or more of the following effects:

    ◆ Transition effect for menus and toolbars.

    ◆ Smooth edges of screen fonts; use ClearType.

    ◆ Use large icons.

    ◆ Show shadows under menus.

    ◆ Show window contents while dragging.

    ◆ Hide underlined letters for keyboard navigation until I press the Alt key.

4. Click OK, and then click OK or Apply.

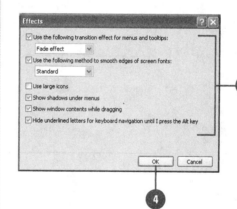

4

Setting the Date and Time

The date and time you set in the Control Panel appear in the lower-right corner of the taskbar. Programs use the date and time to establish when files and folders are created and modified. To change the date and time, you modify settings on the Date & Time tab in the Date and Time Properties dialog box. When you modify the time, it's important to also verify or update the time zone setting on the Time Zone tab, which is used to accurately display creation and modification dates in a different time zone. With an Internet connection, you can set options on the Internet tab to make sure the time is accurate (**New!**).

Change the Date or Time

1. Double-click the time on the taskbar in the notification area.

2. Click the Time Zone tab.

3. Click the list arrow, select a time zone, and then select or clear the Automatically Adjust Clock For Daylight Saving Changes check box.

4. Click the Date & Time tab.

5. Click the list arrows, and then select the month and year.

6. Click a day, and then specify a time.

7. Click OK or Apply.

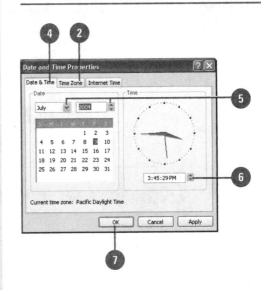

Keep the Time Accurate

1. Double-click the time on the taskbar in the notification area.

2. Click the Internet Time tab.

3. Select the Automatically Synchronize With An Internet Time Server check box.

4. Click the Server list arrow, and then click a time server.

5. Click Update Now, and then wait for the time to update.

6. Click OK or Apply.

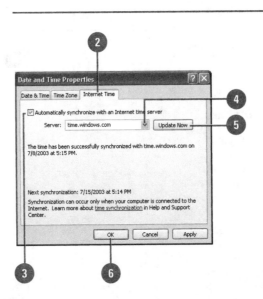

Changing Regional Options

For those who work in international circles, you can change the format of the date, time, currency, and number into almost any form. For example, you can change the decimal symbol and list separator, the format used for negative numbers and leading zeros, and the measurement system (U.S. or metric).

Change the Display for Dates, Times, Currency, and Numbers

1. Click the Start button, click Control Panel, and then double-click the Regional and Language Options icon in Classic view.

2. Click the Regional Options tab.

3. Click the Format list arrow, and then click a locale with the settings you want.

4. Click Customize to change individual settings.

5. Click OK.

6. Click OK.

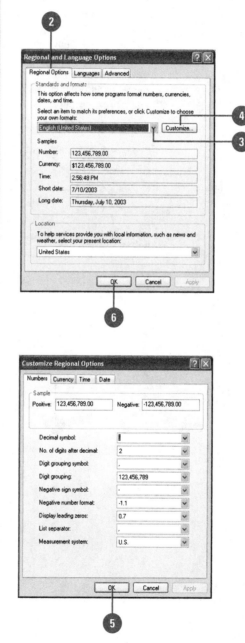

Did You Know?

You can change regional format by language and country. On the Regional Options tab, click the Standards And Formats list arrow, and then click a language.

See Also

See "Changing Language Options" on page 94 for information on working with different languages.

Changing Language Options ▶

You can also install multiple input languages on your computer and easily switch between them. An **input language** is the language in which you enter and display text. When you install additional languages on your computer, the language for the operating system doesn't change, only the characters you type on the screen. Each language uses its own keyboard layout, which rearranges the letters that appear when you press keys. When you install Text services or another language, the Language Bar toolbar appears on your desktop and in the Toolbars menu. Text services are text-related add-on programs for a second keyboard layout, handwriting recognition, speech recognition, and an Input Method Editor (IME), which is a system that lets you input Asian language characters with a standard 101-keyboard. You can switch between different language keyboard layouts using the Language bar or keyboard shortcuts.

Change Text Services and Input Languages

1. Click the Start button, click Control Panel, and then double-click the Regional and Language Options icon in Classic view.

2. Click the Languages tab, and then click Details.

3. Click the Language list arrow, and then click a language to use when you start your computer.

4. Click Add to add an input language.

5. Select an input language, and then click Remove to delete it, or click Properties to modify it.

6. Click Language Bar to change the look and behavior of the Language bar.

7. Click Key Settings to define keyboard shortcuts to switch between input languages.

8. Click OK.

9. Click OK or Apply.

Change the Language Used for Dialog Boxes

1. Click the Start button, click Control Panel, and then double-click the Regional and Language Options icon in Classic view.

2. Click the Advanced tab.

3. Click the Language list arrow, and then click a language with the settings you want.

4. Click OK or Apply.

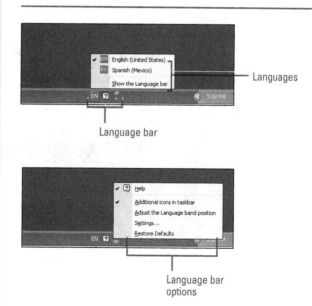

Use the Language Toolbar

◆ To switch languages, click the Language bar, and then click a language.

◆ To change Language bar settings, right-click the Language bar, and then click an option, such as transparency, vertical (orientation), and minimize.

◆ To change Text Services and Input Languages, right-click the Language bar, and then click Settings.

Languages

Language bar

Language bar options

4

Working with Fonts

Everything you type appears in a **font**, or typeface, a particular design set of letters, numbers, and other characters. The height of characters in a font is measured in points, each point being approximately 1/72 inch, while the width is measured by **pitch**, which refers to how many characters can fit in an inch. You might have heard common font names, such as Times New Roman, Arial, Courier, or Symbol. Windows comes with a variety of fonts for displaying text and printing documents. Using the Fonts window, you can view these fonts, compare them to each other, see a sample of how a font appears when printed, and even install new fonts.

Install a Font

1. Click the Start button, click Control Panel, and then double-click the Fonts icon in Classic view.

2. Click the File menu, and then click Install New Font.

3. Navigate to the drive and folder containing the font you want to install.

4. Select the font. To select more than one font, hold down the Ctrl key while you click each font.

5. Click OK.

6. Click the Close button.

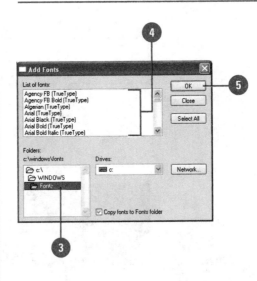

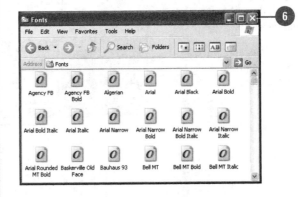

See Also

See "Formatting Text" on page 32 for information on using fonts.

Display Related Fonts

1 Click the Start button, click Control Panel, and then double-click the Fonts icon in Classic view.

2 Click the Similarity button on the toolbar.

3 Click the List Fonts By Similarity To list arrow, and then click the font in which you want to display similar fonts.

4 Double-click the font name to display a sample sheet of the font, and then click Done.

5 Click the Close button.

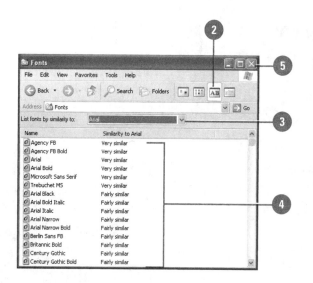

Frequently Asked Questions

What's the Difference Between the Fonts?

Everything you type appears in a font, a particular typeface design and size for letters, numbers, and other characters. Usually, each typeface, such as Times New Roman, is made available in four variations: normal, bold, italic, and bold italic. There are two basic types of fonts: scalable and bitmapped. A **scalable font** (also known as **outline font**) is based on a mathematical equation that creates character outlines to form letters and numbers of any size. The two major scalable fonts are Adobe's Type 1 PostScript and Apple/Microsoft's TrueType or OpenType. Scalable fonts are generated in any point size on the fly and require only four variations for each typeface. A **bitmapped font** consists of a set of dot patterns for each letter and number in a typeface for a specified type size. Bitmapped fonts are created or prepackaged ahead of time and require four variations for each point size used in each typeface. Although a bitmapped font designed for a particular font size will always look the best, scalable fonts eliminate storing hundreds of different sizes of fonts on a disk.

4

Displaying and Arranging Toolbars

Toolbars provide easy access to commonly used tasks. Windows XP comes with a set of toolbars you can use to access programs, folders, documents, and Web pages right from the taskbar. You can rearrange, resize, and move the toolbars to compliment your working style. When you move a toolbar, you can attach, or dock it, to any of the sides on the desktop or you can float it in a window anywhere within the desktop.

Show or Hide a Toolbar

1. Right-click a blank area on the taskbar.

2. Point to Toolbars, and then click a toolbar without a check mark.

   A toolbar with a check mark is already displayed.

Did You Know?

You can display hidden buttons on a toolbar. Click the double-arrow at the end of the toolbar.

You can display buttons on the taskbar. Click the up or down arrow on the taskbar to scroll through the taskbar buttons.

See Also

See "Customizing the Taskbar" on page 100 for information on modifying the taskbar.

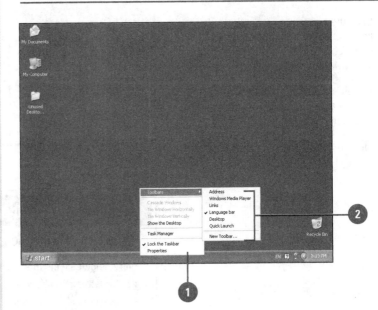

Toolbars on the Taskbar

Toolbar	Description
Address	Opens web pages, network locations, files, and folders using the Address bar from Internet Explorer
Links	Opens links using the Links toolbar from Internet Explorer
Language bar	Switches between languages
Desktop	Opens windows to files, folders, and shortcuts on the desktop
Quick Launch	Starts Internet Explorer, Outlook Express, and Windows Media Player, or minimizes all the windows on the desktop

Unlock or Lock the Taskbar

1. Right-click a blank area on the taskbar.

2. Click Lock The Taskbar.

   ◆ Toolbars on the taskbar are locked when a check mark is displayed.

   ◆ Toolbars on the taskbar are unlocked when a check mark isn't displayed.

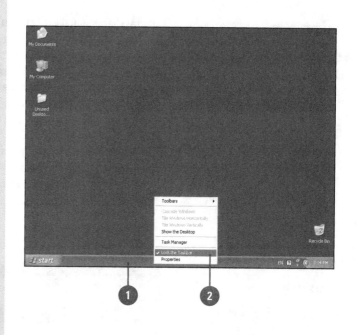

Move a Toolbar

1. Right-click a blank area on the taskbar, and then click Lock The Taskbar to remove the check mark, if necessary.

2. Point to the name of the toolbar, and then drag it to a new location on the desktop docked to the side or floating in the middle.

Did You Know?

You can resize a toolbar. Unlock the taskbar, and then drag the small vertical bar at the beginning of the toolbar.

You can expand or collapse a toolbar. Unlock the taskbar, and then double-click the small vertical bar at the beginning of the toolbar.

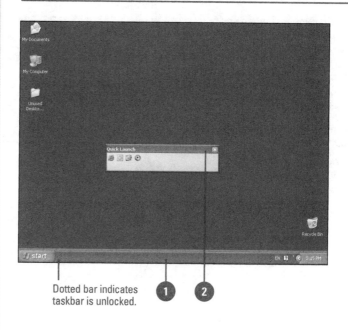

Dotted bar indicates taskbar is unlocked.

4

Customizing the Taskbar

The taskbar is initially located at the bottom of the Windows desktop and is most often used to switch from one program to another. As with other Windows elements, you can customize the taskbar; for example, you can change its size and location, customize its display, or add or remove toolbars to help you perform the tasks you need to do. If you need more room on the screen to display a window, Auto-hide can be used to hide the taskbar when it's not in use. You can also group similar windows (such as several WordPad documents) together on the taskbar to save space (New!). If icons in the notification area (New!) are hidden when you want to see them, you can customize the notification area to always show the icons you want to use.

Customize the Taskbar

1. Right-click a blank area on the taskbar, and then click Properties.

2. Click the Taskbar tab.

3. Select the Auto-hide The Taskbar check box to hide the taskbar when you're not using it.

   The taskbar appears when you move the mouse to where the taskbar would appear.

4. Select the Keep The Taskbar On Top Of Other Windows check box to keep the taskbar available.

5. Select the Group Similar Taskbar Buttons check box to have similar windows grouped together in one button when the taskbar is crowded.

6. Select the Show Quick Launch check box to display the Quick Launch toolbar.

7. Click OK.

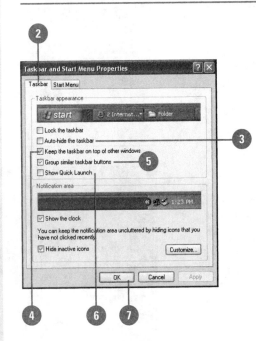

Customize the Notification Area

1. Right-click a blank area on the taskbar, and then click Properties.

2. Click the Taskbar tab.

3. Select the Show The Clock check box to display the clock.

4. Select the Hide Inactive Icons check box to hide seldom-used icons in the notification area.

5. Click Customize.

6. Specify which icons are always displayed, which are never displayed, and which are hidden when inactive.

7. Click OK.

8. Click OK.

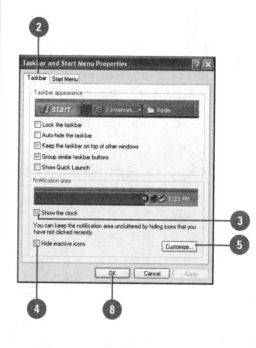

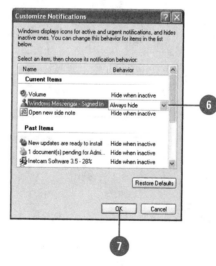

Did You Know?

You can access taskbar and Start menu settings in the Control Panel. Double-click the Taskbar and Start Menu icon in the Control Panel in Classic view.

You can move the taskbar. Unlock the taskbar, and then drag a blank area on the taskbar to a new location on any side of the desktop.

See Also

See "Displaying and Arranging Toolbars" on page 98 for information on working with toolbars on the taskbar.

4

Customizing the Start Menu

The left column of the Start menu is separated into two lists (**New!**): pinned items above the separator line and most frequently used items below. The pinned items remain on the Start menu, like a push pin holds paper on a bulletin board, until you unpin them. The right column of the Start menu provides easy access to folders, Windows settings, help information, and search functionality. You can add shortcuts to programs, files, or folders to the Start menu or customize the way the Start menu looks and functions.

Choose a Start Menu Style

1. Right-click the Start button, and then click Properties.

2. Click the Start menu or Classic Start menu option.

3. Click OK or Apply.

Did You Know?

You can rearrange Start menu items. Click the Start button, point to All Programs, locate the item you want to move, and then drag the item to a new location. A thick, black line indicates the new location of the item.

Pin or Unpin a Program on the Start Menu

1. Click the Start button, and then locate a program.

2. To pin a program, right-click the program, and then click Pin To Start Menu.

3. To unpin a program, right-click a pinned program on the Start menu, and then click Unpin From Start menu.

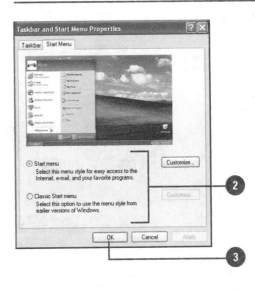

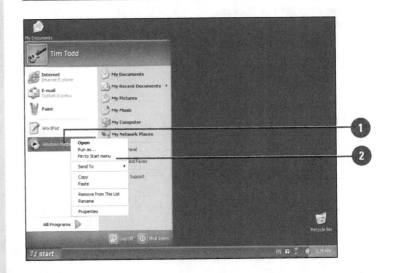

Customize the Start Menu

1. Right-click the Start button, click Properties, and then click Customize.

2. On the General tab, click an icon size option.

3. Click the up or down arrow to specify the number of recently used programs on the Start menu.

4. Click the Advanced tab.

5. Select the Open Submenus When I Pause On Them With My Mouse check box.

6. Select the Highlight Newly Installed Programs check box.

7. Select check boxes and click options to specify the items you want or don't want included on the Start menu.

8. Select the List My Most Recently Opened Documents check box to list them on the My Recent Document submenu.

9. Click OK.

10. Click OK or Apply.

Did You Know?

You can add a shortcut to an item to the Start menu. Right-click the item, point to Send To, and then click Desktop. Drag the shortcut from the Desktop onto the Start button, and then drag it to a new location on the All Programs submenu.

Changing the Way a CD or DVD Starts

When you insert a CD or DVD into your computer, you can specify how you want Windows to respond. You can have Windows detects the type of content on the disc and automatically start, or prompt you each time to choose an action (**New!**). If you have CDs with music files, pictures, video files, or mixed content, you can change the action Windows takes when it detects the content on the disc. You can have Windows play the first file using Windows Media Player, open the first folder to view files using Windows Explorer, or take no action.

Set AutoPlay Options

1. Click the Start button, and then click My Computer.

2. Right-click the CD Drive, and then click Properties.

3. Click the AutoPlay tab.

4. Click the list arrow, and then select a content type.

5. Click the Select An Action To Perform option, and then select an action, or click the Prompt Me Each Time To Choose An Action option.

6. Click OK.

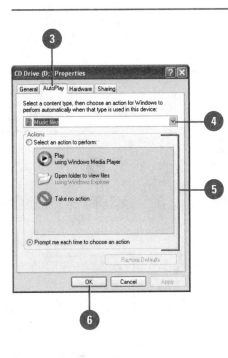

Did You Know?

You can stop Windows from performing an action on a CD or DVD. Hold down the Shift key while you insert the CD or DVD.

You can reset AutoPlay properties. On the AutoPlay tab, click Restore Defaults.

Using Accessibility Tools

If you have difficulty using a mouse or typing, have slightly impaired vision, or are deaf or hard of hearing, you can adjust the appearance and behavior of Windows XP to make your computer easier for you to use. The Accessibility Wizard helps you configure Windows for your vision, hearing, and mobility needs. The Accessibility Wizard also enables you to save your settings in a file that you can use on another computer. To open the Accessibility Wizard, click the Start button on the taskbar, point to All Programs, point to Accessories, point to Accessibility, click Accessibility Wizard, and then follow the steps in the wizard. You can also use the Accessibility tools in the Control Panel to adjust the way your keyboard, display, and mouse function to suit various vision and motor abilities. Some of the accessibility tools available include StickyKeys, FilterKeys, ToggleKeys, Sound-Sentry, ShowSounds, High Contrast, and MouseKeys. You can also set general accessibilities options that automatically turn off accessibility features, provide warning sounds, and determine when to apply the settings. The accessibility tools in Windows are intended to provide a low level of functionality for those with special needs. If these tools do not meet your daily needs, you might need to purchase a more advanced accessibility program.

Accessibility Tools

Option	Description
StickyKeys	Enables simultaneous keystrokes while pressing one key at a time, such as Ctrl+Alt+Del
FilterKeys	Adjusts the response of your keyboard; ignores repeated characters or fast key presses
ToggleKeys	Emits sounds when you press certain locking keys, such as Caps Lock, Num Lock, or Scroll Lock
SoundSentry	Provides visual warnings for system sounds
ShowSounds	Instructs programs to provide captions
High Contrast	Sets the desktop appearance to high contrast
Cursor Blink Rate	Adjusts the speed of the blinking cursor in programs, such as WordPad
Cursor Width	Adjusts the width of the cursor in programs, such as WordPad
MouseKeys	Enables the numeric keypad to perform mouse functions
SerialKey devices	Provides support for alternative input devices

4

Using the Utility Manager

The Utility Manager (**New!**) allows you to check the status of and start or stop the Magnifier, Narrator, and On-Screen Keyboard accessibility programs. Magnifier is a utility that enlarges an area of the screen. Narrator is a text-to-speech utility that gives users who are blind or have impaired vision access to the computer. On-Screen Keyboard is a utility that displays a keyboard on the screen where users with mobility impairments can type using a mouse, joystick, or other pointing device. If you have administrator access to your computer, you can specify how the accessibility programs start when you log on, lock the desktop, or start the Utility Manager.

Use the Utility Manager

1. Press ⊞+U to start the Utility Manager.

   TIMESAVER *The Windows key ⊞ is located in the lower-left corner of the keyboard.*

2. If Narrator starts, click OK, and then click Exit to close the program.

3. Click the program you want to manage.

4. Select or clear the check boxes you want to specify how you want the selected program to start.

5. Click Start or Stop.

6. Click OK.

See Also

See "Listening to the Computer" on page 108 for information on using Narrator.

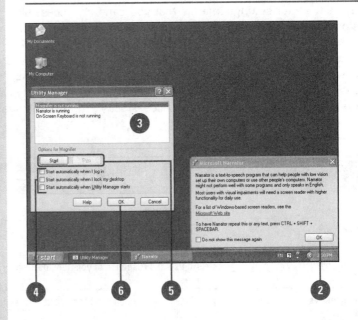

Use the Magnifier

1. Click the Start button, point to All Programs, point to Accessories, point to Accessibility, and then click Magnifier.

2. If an introductory dialog box appears, click OK.

3. Click the Magnification Level list arrow, and then click a level.

4. Select or clear the check boxes with the tracking options to follow the mouse cursor, keyboard focus, or text editing.

5. Select or clear the check boxes with the presentation options to invert colors, start minimized, or show Magnifier.

6. Click the Minimize button to use the Magnifier program, or click Exit to close the program. (Restore the Magnifier window, if necessary.)

Use the On-Screen Keyboard

1. Open the program in which you want to type.

2. Click the Start button, point to All Programs, point to Accessories, point to Accessibility, and then click On-Screen Keyboard.

3. If an introductory dialog box appears, click OK.

4. Position the cursor, if necessary.

5. Type the text you want, or type keyboard commands.

6. When you're done, click the Close button.

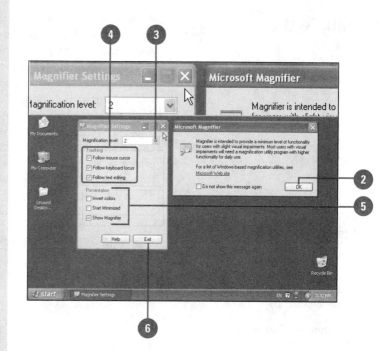

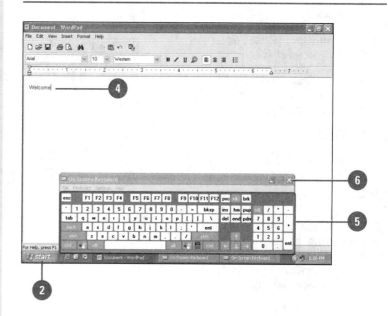

Listening to the Computer

Windows XP comes with an accessibility tool called Narrator (**New!**) that reads aloud what appears on your screen, such as window items, menu options, and typed characters. Windows uses Text-to-Speech (TTS) technology to recognize text and play it back as spoken words using a synthesized voice, which is chosen from several pre-generated voices. Narrator is designed for those who are blind or have impaired vision and works with the Windows desktop and setup, Control Panel, Notepad, WordPad, and Internet Explorer. Narrator supports only the English language and might not read words aloud correctly in other programs. You can adjust the speed, volume, or pitch of the voice in Narrator and change other Text-to-Speech options using Speech properties in the Control Panel.

Use the Narrator

1. Click the Start button, point to All Programs, point to Accessories, point to Accessibility, and then click Narrator.

2. If an introductory dialog box appears, click OK.

3. Select the Announce Events On Screen check box to identify items on the desktop.

4. Select the Read Typed Characters check box.

5. Select the Move Mouse Pointer To The Active Item check box.

6. Select the Start Narrator Minimized check box to minimize the Narrator dialog box.

7. Click Voice.

8. Select a voice and adjust the voice speed, volume, and pitch.

9. Click OK.

10. Click the Minimize button to use the Narrator program or click Exit to close the program. (Restore the Narrator window, if necessary.) Click Yes, if necessary.

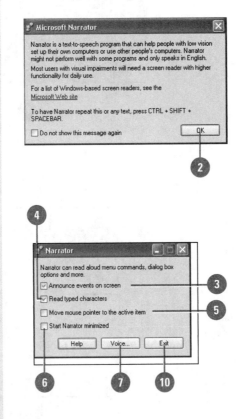

Change Text-To-Speech Options

1. Click the Start button, click Control Panel, and then double-click the Speech icon in Classic view.

2. Click the Text To Speech tab.

3. Click the Voice Selection list arrow, and then select a synthesized voice.

4. Drag the Voice Speed slider to adjust the speed of the voice.

5. Click Preview Voice.

6. Click OK.

See Also

See "Recognizing Your Speech" on page 110 for information on speech capabilities.

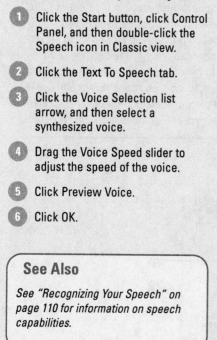

Recognizing Your Speech

If you have a speech-enabled program, you can initialize and customize speech recognition options using Speech properties in the Control Panel. **Speech recognition (New!)** is the ability to convert a spoken voice into electronic text. You can use the speech recognition properties to select a language, create a profile to accommodate your speaking style and environment, and train your computer in as little as ten minutes to recognize and adapt to the sound of your voice, word pronunciation, accent, speaking manner, and new or distinctive words. Some programs use speech differently, so you need to check the speech-enabled program for details.

Train the Computer to Recognize Your Voice

1. Click the Start button, click Control Panel, and then double-click the Speech icon in Classic view.

2. Click the Speech Recognition tab.

3. Click the list arrow, and then select a language.

4. Click New to start the Profile Wizard.

5. Type your name, and then click Next.

6. Follow the wizard instructions to create a profile, adjust the microphone, and train your voice. Click Next to continue after each wizard dialog box.

7. When you're done, click Finish.

8. Click OK.

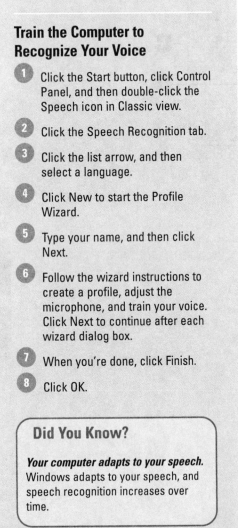

Did You Know?

Your computer adapts to your speech. Windows adapts to your speech, and speech recognition increases over time.

Exploring the Internet

5

Introduction

The **Internet** is a global collection of more than 150 million computers (and growing) linked together to share information. The Internet's physical structure includes telephone lines, cables, satellites, and other telecommunications media. Using the Internet, computer users can share many types of information, including text, graphics, sounds, videos, and computer programs. The **World Wide Web** (also known as the Web or www) is a part of the Internet that consists of Web sites located on different computers around the world.

History of the Internet and the World Wide Web

The Internet has its roots in the Advanced Research Projects Agency Network (ARPANET), which the United States Department of Defense started in 1969. In 1986, the National Science Foundation formed NSFNET, which replaced ARPANET. NSFNET expanded the foundation of the U.S. portion of the Internet with high-speed, long-distance data lines. In 1991, the U.S. Congress expanded the capacity and speed of the Internet further and opened it to commercial use. The Internet is now accessible in almost every country in the world. The World Wide Web was developed in Switzerland in 1991 to make finding documents on the Internet easier. Software programs designed to access the Web, known as Web browsers, use point-and-click interfaces. The first such Web browser, Mosaic, was introduced at the University of Illinois in 1993. Since the release of Mosaic, Microsoft Internet Explorer and Netscape have become the two most popular Web browsers.

Understanding Web Sites and Browsers

A **web site** contains web pages linked together to make searching for information on the Internet easier. **Web pages** are documents that contain highlighted words, phrases, and graphics, called **hyperlinks** (or simply **links**) that open other web pages when you click them. Some web pages contain frames. A frame is a separate window within a web page that lets you see more than one web page at a time. **Web browsers** are software programs that you use to "browse the web," or access and display web pages. Browsers make the web easy to navigate by providing a graphical,

point-and-click environment. Microsoft Internet Explorer 6 is a popular browser from Microsoft that is built-in to Windows XP. Netscape (formally Netscape Navigator and Netscape Communicator) is another popular browser. With a web browser, you can display web pages from all over the world, display web content on the desktop, use links to move from one web page to another, play audio and video clips, search the web for information, make favorite web pages available offline (when you're not connected to the Internet), and print text and graphics on web pages.

Web browser

Web site

Web page

Link

Connecting to the Internet

Universities and large companies are most likely connected to the Internet via high-speed wiring that transmits data very quickly. Home computer owners usually rely on a modem and the phone lines already in place. In a growing number of areas, however, several faster connection options are becoming available and affordable: ISDN (Integrated Services Digital Network); DSL (Digital Subscriber Lines), wires that provide a completely digital connection; and cable modems, which use cable television lines. DSL and cable modems, also known as broadband connections, are continually turned on and connected and use a network setup so you don't need to establish a connection using a dial-up modem. Data travels more slowly over phone wires than over digital lines and cable modems. Whether you use a phone line, an ISDN, DSL line, or a cable modem, Windows can help you establish a connection between your computer and the Internet using the New Connection Wizard. First, you need to select an ISP (Internet Service Provider), which is a company that sets up an Internet account for you and provides Internet access. ISPs maintain servers connected directly to the Internet 24 hours a day. You pay a fee, sometimes by the hour, but more often a flat monthly rate. To connect to the Internet, you need to obtain an Internet account and connection information from your ISP or your system administrator. For details, see "Creating an Internet Connection" on page 114. If you are working on a network, you can also share one Internet connection with everyone. For information on creating an Internet Connection Sharing (ICS), see "Sharing an Internet Connection" on page 340.

Protecting your Computer with a Firewall

When you connect to the Internet, you can access web sites on the Internet, but other users on the Internet can also access information on your computer and potentially infect it with harmful viruses and worms. For more information, see "Avoiding Viruses and Other Harmful Attacks" on page 296.

You can prevent this by activating Windows Firewall (previously called Internet Connection Firewall), another security layer of protection. A **firewall** is a security system that creates a protective barrier between your computer or network and others on the Internet. Windows Firewall (New SP2) monitors all communication between your computer and the Internet and prevents unsolicited inbound traffic from the Internet from entering your computer. Windows Firewall blocks all unsolicited communication from reaching your computer unless you specifically allow it (unblock) to come through, known as an exception. For example, if you run a program, such as Windows Messenger or a multiplayer game that needs to receive information from the Internet or a network, Windows Firewall asks if you want to block or unblock the connection. If you choose to unblock it, Windows Firewall creates an exception so the program can receive information. For details, see "Setting Up Windows Firewall" on page 115. As a troubleshooting tool, you can keep a firewall log of blocked and unblocked connections. The default name for the log is pfirewall.log, and it's located in the Windows folder.

If you send and receive e-mail, Windows Firewall doesn't block spam or unsolicited e-mail or stop you from opening e-mail with harmful attachments. To protect your computer from these attacks, see "Protecting Against E-Mail Attacks" on page 309. Windows Firewall helps block viruses and worms from reaching your computer, but it doesn't detect or disable them if they are already on your computer or come through e-mail. To protect your computer, you need to install antivirus software.

5

Creating an Internet Connection

Sometimes connecting your computer to the Internet can be the most difficult part of getting started. The New Connection Wizard simplifies the process, whether you want to set up a new connection using an existing account or select an Internet service provider (ISP) to set up a new account. In either case, you will need to obtain connection information from your ISP or your system administrator.

Create a Connection to the Internet

1 Click the Start button, point to All Programs, point to Accessories, point to Communications, and then click New Connection Wizard.

2 Click Next.

3 Click the Connect To The Internet option, and then click Next.

4 Click the Set Up My Connection Manually option or click one of the ISP options, and then click Next.

◆ If you selected one of the ISP options, follow the on-screen instructions.

5 Select the dial-up or broadband option in which you want to sign up, and then click Next.

6 Type a connection name, and then click Next.

7 Type a phone number for a dial-up connection, and then click Next.

8 Click the Anyone's Use option to share the connection, or click the My Use Only option to create a private connection, and then click Next.

9 Type your user name and password, select the connection options you want, and then click Next.

10 Click Finish.

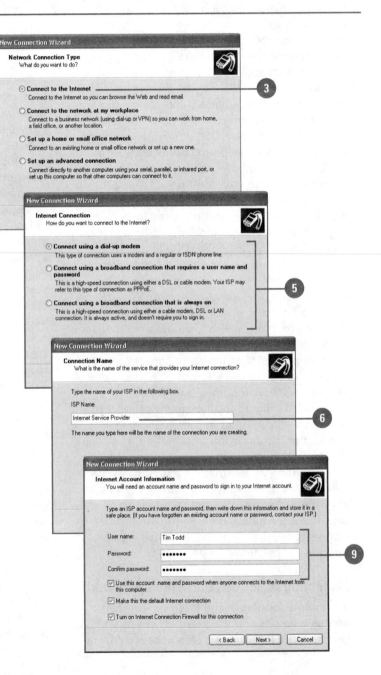

Setting Up Windows Firewall

If your computer is directly connected to the Internet, you need Windows Firewall (NewSP2) to protect your computer from unauthorized access from others on the Internet. For SP2, Windows Firewall is enabled by default for all Internet and network connections. However, some computer manufacturers and network administrators might turn it off, so you need to check it. When Windows Firewall is enabled, you might not be able to use some communication features, such as sending files with a messaging program or playing an Internet game, unless the program is listed on the Exceptions tab in Windows Firewall. If you use multiple Internet and networking connections, you can use the Advanced tab to enable or disable individual connections.

Set Up Windows Firewall

1 Click the Start button, click Control Panel, double-click the Windows Firewall icon in Classic view, and then click the General tab.

IMPORTANT *If you're part of a network, options are grayed out.*

2 Click the On (recommended) option.

3 To set maximum protection, select the Don't Allow Exceptions check box or clear it to make exceptions.

4 To make program exceptions, click the Exceptions tab.

5 Select the check boxes with the exceptions you want; if necessary, click Add Program to add it.

6 Click OK.

See Also

See "Connecting to the Internet" on page 113 for information on firewalls.

Did You Know?

You can restore Windows Firewall default settings. In Windows Firewall, click the Advanced tab, click Restore Defaults, and then click OK.

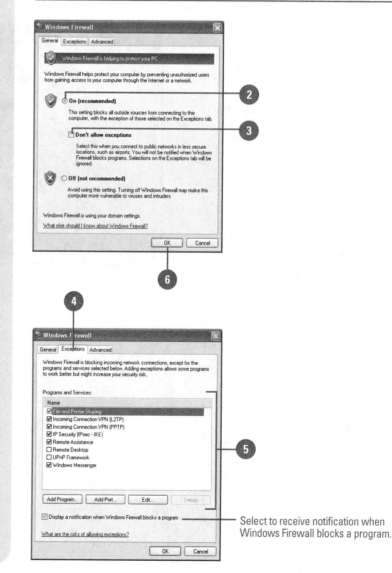

Select to receive notification when Windows Firewall blocks a program.

Starting Internet Explorer

Internet Explorer is a web browser that you use to search the World Wide Web. You can start Internet Explorer using the Start menu, the Internet Explorer icon on the desktop, or the button on the Quick Launch toolbar on the taskbar. After you start Internet Explorer, you might need to connect to the Internet by selecting a dial-up or broadband service and entering a user name and password. The elements of the Internet Explorer window allow you to view, print, and search for information on the Internet. Once you establish a connection to the Internet, you are ready to explore web pages on the Internet.

Start Internet Explorer

1. Click the Start button, and then click Internet.

   TIMESAVER *Click the Launch Internet Explorer button on the Quick Launch toolbar.*

2. If necessary, click Connect to dial your ISP. You might need to type your user name and password before Internet Explorer will connect to the Internet.

   The Internet Explorer window opens.

Did You Know?

You can find Internet Explorer on the All Programs submenu. If Internet Explorer doesn't appear on the left column of the Start menu, it's available on the All Programs submenu.

See Also

See "Displaying and Arranging Toolbars" on page 98 for information on displaying the Quick Launch toolbar.

See "Customizing the Start Menu" on page 102 for information on showing Internet Explorer on the Start menu.

Viewing the Internet Explorer Window

Menu bar
Contains all the commands you need to access and move around web pages, customize Internet Explorer, and get Help

Standard toolbar
Provides buttons to locate and move around web pages, as well as work in Internet Explorer

Title bar
Displays the name of the web page you are viewing

Address bar
Displays the address of the current web page or document you are viewing or trying to access

Links bar
Contains buttons for quick access of favorite web sites

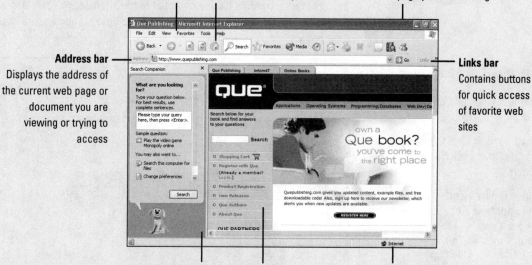

Explorer bar
Displays links to web pages from Search results, Favorites list, and History list. The Explorer bar is only visible when you click the corresponding button on the Standard toolbar.

Browser pane
Displays the current web page, document, or folder contents

Status bar
Indicates the progress of loading a web page, as well as other messages about selected actions

5

Browsing the Web

A **web address** (also known as a URL, which stands for Uniform Resource Locator) is a unique place on the Internet where you can locate a web page. With Internet Explorer, you can browse sites on the web with ease by entering a web address or by clicking a link. Each method is better at different times. For example, you might type an address in the Address bar to start your session. Then you might click a link on that web page to access a new site. With Internet Explorer, you can find Internet addresses faster with AutoComplete. When you type an Internet address in the Address bar, Internet Explorer tries to find a recently visited page that matches what you've typed so far. If Internet Explorer finds a match, it fills in the rest of the address. You can also use **AutoComplete** to fill out forms on the web, including single-line edits, and user names and passwords.

View a Web Page

Use any of the following methods to display a Web page:

◆ In the Address bar, type the web address, and then click Go or press Enter.

If you have recently entered the web page address, AutoComplete remembers it and tries to complete the address for you. The suggested match is highlighted. Click the correct address or continue to type until the address you want appears in the Address list.

◆ Click any link on the web page, such as a picture or colored, underlined text. The mouse pointer changes to a hand when it is over a link.

Type a web address

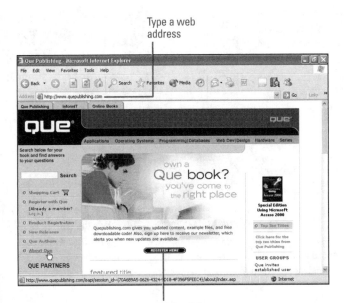

Click a link

> ### Did You Know?
>
> *You can have AutoComplete quickly complete a web address.* In the Address bar, type the name of the web site, such as *perspection*, and then press Ctrl+Enter. AutoComplete adds the "www." and ".com".

Turn Off AutoComplete Options

1. Click the Tools menu, and then click Internet Options.

2. Click the Content tab.

3. Click AutoComplete.

4. Clear the AutoComplete option you want to turn off.

5. To clear current AutoComplete entries, click Clear Forms.

6. Click OK.

7. Click OK.

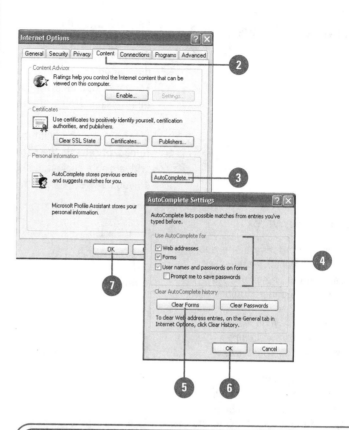

Did You Know?

You can clear AutoComplete entries.
In the AutoComplete Settings dialog box, click Clear Forms.

You can browse folders and run programs from the Address bar. Click anywhere in the Address bar, then type the location of the folder or program. For example, typing **C:\Windows** opens the Windows folder.

For Your Information

Understanding a Web Address

The address for a web page is called a URL. Each web page has a unique URL that is typically composed of four parts: the protocol (a set of rules that allow computers to exchange information), the location of the web site, the name that maintains the web site, and a suffix that identifies the type of site. A URL begins with a protocol, followed by a colon, two slashes, the location of the web site, a dot, the name of the web site, a dot, and a suffix. The web site is the computer where the Web pages are located. At the end of the web site name, another slash may appear, followed by one or more folder names and a file name. For example, in the address, http://*www*.perspection.com/downloads/main.htm, the protocol is *http* (HyperText Transfer Protocol), the location of the web site is *www* (World Wide Web), the name of the web site is *perspection*, and the suffix is *com* (a commercial organization); a folder at that site is called */downloads*; and within the folder is a file called *main.htm*.

Navigating Basics

As you browse the Web or your local hard disk, you may want to retrace your steps and return to a web page, document, or hard disk you've recently visited. You can move backward or forward one location at a time, or you can jump directly to any location from the Back list or Forward list, both of which show locations you've previously visited in this session. After you start to load a web page, you can stop if the page opens too slowly or if you decide not to access it. If a Web page loads incorrectly or you want to update the information it contains, you can reload, or **refresh**, the page. If you get lost on the web, you can start over with a single click of the Home button. You can also resize your toolbars so you can see more of the web address or Links bar.

Move Back or Forward

◆ To move back or forward one web page or document at a time, click the Back button or the Forward button on the Standard toolbar.

   TIMESAVER *To move back, press Alt+left arrow. To move forward, press Alt+right arrow.*

◆ To move back or forward to a specific web page or document, click the Back or Forward list arrow on the Standard toolbar, and then select the web page or document you want to visit.

Back button

Forward button

Forward button list arrow

Stop, Refresh, or Go Home

◆ Click the Stop button on the Standard toolbar.

   TIMESAVER *Press Esc.*

◆ Click the Refresh button on the Standard toolbar.

   TIMESAVER *Press F5.*

◆ Click the Home button on the Standard toolbar.

Stop button

Refresh button

Changing Your Home Page

Your **home page** in Internet Explorer is the page that opens when you start the program. When you first install Internet Explorer, the default home page is the Microsoft Network (MSN) web site. If you want a different page to appear when you start Internet Explorer and whenever you click the Home button, you can change your home page. You can choose one of the millions of web pages available through the Internet, or you can select a particular file on your hard drive.

Change the Home Page

1. Open the web page you want to be the new home page.

2. Click the Tools menu, and then click Internet Options.

3. Click the General tab.

4. Click Use Current.

5. Click OK.

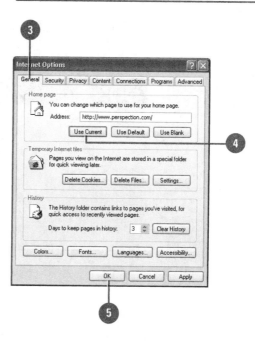

Did You Know?

You can set your home page to MSN. Click the Tools menu, click Internet Options, click Use Default, and then click OK.

You can set your home page to a blank page. Click the Tools menu, click Internet Options, click Use Blank, and then click OK.

5

Modifying the
Links Bar

The Links bar, located to the right of the Address bar, provides easy access buttons to display web pages. The Links bar comes with predefined buttons to Microsoft-related web pages, but you can add or remove buttons, or your can change the web pages associated with the buttons on the Links bar to customize it to meet your needs.

Resize the Links Bar

1. Position the mouse pointer over the word Links, and then click and hold the mouse, which changes to a four-headed arrow.

   TROUBLE? *If the Links bar doesn't move, you need to unlock it. Right-click the Links bar, and then click Lock the Toolbars to deselect it.*

2. Drag the handle to the left to reveal more of the links or down to display the Links bar as a separate bar.

Add a Link Button to the Links Bar

1. Open the web page or display the folder you want to add to the Links bar.

2. Drag the web page in the Address bar to the Links bar.

3. Release the mouse button to position the new item.

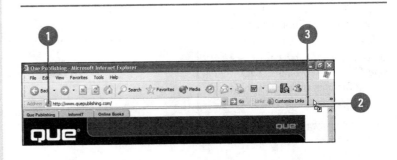

New link button

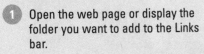

Did You Know?

You can quickly remove a link button from the Links bar. Right-click the button you want to delete, click Delete, and then click Yes to confirm the deletion.

Adding a Web Page to the Favorites List

Rather than memorizing URLs or keeping a handwritten list of web pages you want to visit, you can use a Favorites list to store and organize the addresses. When you display a web page in your document window that you want to display again at a later time, you can add the web page to your Favorites list. You add web pages in the Internet Explorer window to your Favorites list in the same way you add folders in the My Computer or Windows Explorer window to the list. Once you add the web page to the Favorites list, you can return to the page by opening your Favorites list and selecting the link to the page you want.

Create a Favorites List

1 Open the web site you want to add to your Favorites list.

2 Click the Favorites menu, and then click Add To Favorites.

3 Type the name for the site, or use the default name supplied.

4 Click Create In, and then select a location on the Favorites menu to place the site.

5 If you want to create a new folder, click New Folder, type a folder name, and then click OK.

6 Click OK.

Use the Favorites menu to quickly return to a favorite location.

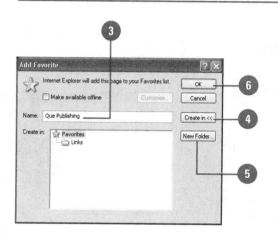

Did You Know?

You can import favorites from another browser. Click the File menu, click Import and Export, and then follow the steps in the Import/Export wizard.

For Your Information

Organizing Favorites

If your list of favorites grows long, you can delete favorites you don't visit anymore or move favorites into folders. Click the Favorites menu, click Organize Favorites, select one or more files from the Favorites list, and then click Delete or Move To Folder. If you want to add a new folder to your Favorites list, click Create Folder, type the new folder name, and then press Enter. If you prefer to use another name for a favorite, you can select the favorite you want to rename, click Rename, type the new name, and then press Enter. When you're done, click Close to exit.

5

Viewing and Maintaining a History List

Sometimes you run across a great web site and simply forget to add it to your Favorites list. With Internet Explorer there's no need to try to remember all the sites you visit. The History feature keeps track of where you've been by date, site, most visited, or order visited today. To view the History list, click the History button on the toolbar, and then click a day or week in the Explorer Bar to expand the list of web sites visited. Because the History list can grow to occupy a large amount of space on your hard drive, it's important to control the length of time you retain web sites in the list. Internet Explorer deletes the History list periodically, based on the settings you specify. You can also delete individual listings in the History folder as needed.

View a Web Site from the History List

1. Click the History button on the Standard toolbar.

2. Click a week or day to expand or compress the list of web sites visited.

3. Click the folder for the web site you want to view, and then click a page within the web site.

4. When you're done, click the Close button.

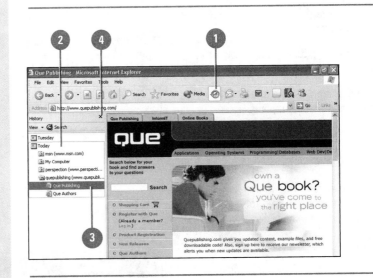

Change the History List View

1. Click the History button on the Standard toolbar.

2. Click the View button, and then click the view option you want.

3. When you're done, click the Close button.

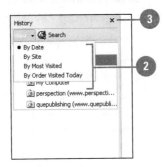

Did You Know?

You can delete an individual history entry. Click the History button, right-click the link you want to delete, click Delete, and then click Yes.

Clear the History List

1. Click the Tools menu, and then click Internet Options.

2. Click the General tab.

3. Click Clear History, and then click Yes to confirm the operation.

4. Click OK.

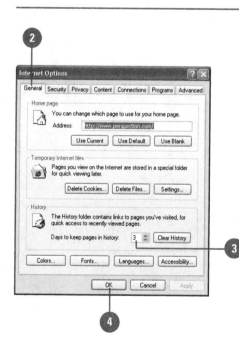

Change the Number of Days Pages Are Saved

1. Click the Tools menu, and then click Internet Options.

2. Click the General tab.

3. Specify the total number of days you want to keep links listed in the History folder.

4. Click OK.

Did You Know?

You can search for a history entry. Click the History button on the Standard toolbar, click Search, type the history entry you want to find, and then click Search Now.

Making a Web Page Available Offline

When you make a web page available offline, you can read its content when your computer is not connected to the Internet or network. For example, you can view web pages on your laptop computer when you have no Internet or network connection. Or, you might want to read web pages at home but not want to tie up a phone line. When you make a web page available offline, you save, or **synchronize**, the latest online version of your web page on your hard disk drive for offline viewing. You can specify how much content you want available, such as an individual web page or a web page and all of its linked web pages. You can also choose how you want to update that content on your computer. When you choose to view a web page and all its linked pages offline, be aware that the additional linked pages take up a lot of hard drive space.

Set Up a Web Site for Offline Viewing

1. Open the web site you want to add.

2. Click the Favorites menu, and then click Add To Favorites.

3. Select the Make Available Offline check box.

4. Click Customize, and then click Next to configure your page.

5. Click the Yes option to allow viewing of the entire web site, or click the No option to restrict your offline viewing to the single page, and then click Next.

6. Choose the synchronization schedule option you want, and then click Next.

   If a web site provides a schedule, you may want to choose this option to receive the most up-to-date information.

7. If the web site requires user authentication, enter your user name and password.

8. Click Finish.

9. Choose a folder to store the page, and then click OK.

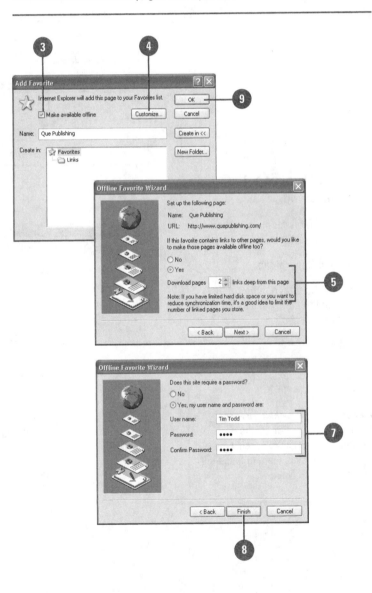

Synchronize Your Offline Web Pages

 Click the Tools menu, and then click Synchronize.

TIMESAVER *Click the Favorites button on the toolbar, right-click the offline web page, and then click Synchronize.*

2 Select the web site(s) you want to synchronize.

3 Click Synchronize.

4 Click Close, if necessary.

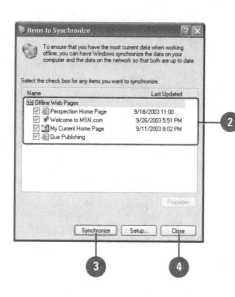

View an Offline Web Page

1 Click the File menu, and then click Work Offline.

2 Click the Favorites menu, and then click a synchronized favorite.

Files not set for offline viewing display a grayed out.

3 Browse the site at high speed from your hard disk.

When the pointer changes to a circle with a line through it, the link is not available offline. You can still click those links, but you will have to reconnect to the Internet to see the content.

Did You Know?

You need to turn on Work Offline again. When you choose to work offline, Internet Explorer starts in offline mode until you click File on the menu bar, and then click Work Offline again to clear the check mark.

5

Managing Offline Pages

If you have added several channels or web pages for offline viewing, you might want to change how often Internet Explorer synchronizes your local copy with the Internet. You may also want to have Internet Explorer send you a mail message letting you know that the content has changed. Maybe you are about to disconnect from the Internet and want to synchronize all your web pages and channels at once for an extended offline session. Or perhaps a site now requires that you supply a user name and password. By managing your offline pages, you can easily make changes to the way Internet Explorer synchronizes with the Internet.

Manage an Offline Page

1 Click the Tools menu, and then click Synchronize.

2 Select the web site you want to modify.

3 Click Properties.

4 To change properties for the selected offline content, click the following:

◆ The Web Document tab to change the availability of the page for offline viewing.

◆ The Schedule tab to change the frequency of synchronization.

◆ The Download tab to limit the amount of hard disk space the local copy uses, specify user name and password options for sites that require them, or enter an e-mail address where to send notification changes.

5 Click OK.

6 Click Close.

Synchronize an Offline Page

1. Click the Tools menu, and then click Synchronize.

2. Click Setup.

3. To change synchronization settings for your selected web pages, click the following:

   ◆ The Logon/Logoff tab to decide what content updates when using different connections to the Internet.

   ◆ The On Idle tab to update content only when your computer is idle because synchronizing may slow down your computer.

   ◆ The Scheduled tab to add new synchronization tasks to your schedule. You can also change or remove any of the existing schedules.

4. Click OK.

5. Click Synchronize or Close.

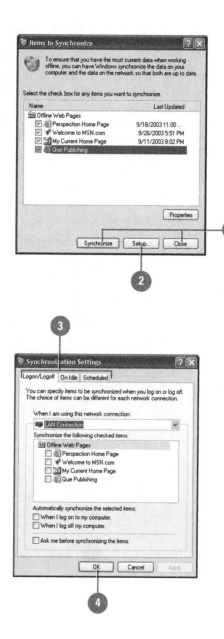

Searching the Web ▶

You can find all kinds of information on the web. The best way to find information is to use a search engine. A **search engine** is a program you access through a web site and use to search through a collection of Internet information to find what you want. Many search engines are available on the web, such as MSN, AltaVista, Google, AOL Search, and Excite. When performing a search, the search engine compares **keywords** with words that if finds on various Internet web sites. Keywords are words or phrases that best describe the information you want to retrieve. If the search engine finds your keywords in the stored database, it lists the matched sites on a web page. These matched sites are sometimes called **hits**. The company that manages the search engine determines what information its database stores, so search results of different search engines vary.

Search for Information

① Click the Start button, and then click Internet Explorer, or open any folder window, such as My Documents.

② Click the Search button on the toolbar.

TIMESAVER *Press Windows key+F to open the Search window.*

③ Click Search The Internet and a category, if necessary.

④ Type the information you want to find.

⑤ Click Search.

⑥ Click a link, and then view the information on the page.

⑦ To perform a new search, click Start A New Search at the bottom of the Search Companion.

⑧ When you're done, click the Close button on the Search Companion.

Change Search Preferences

1. Click the Start button, and then click Internet Explorer, or open any folder window, such as My Documents.

2. Click the Search button on the toolbar.

3. Click Change Preferences.

4. Click Change Internet Search Behavior.

5. Click the With Search Companion or With Classic Internet Search option to select a search type.

6. Select a default search engine.

7. Click OK.

8. When you're done, click the Close button on the Search Companion.

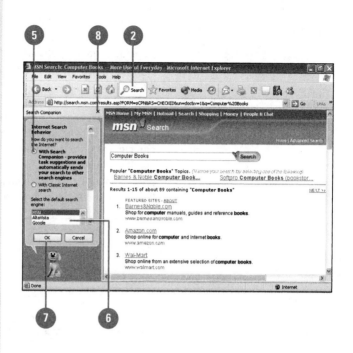

Did You Know?

You can use the Address bar to search for information. In the Address bar, type **go**, **find**, or **?** followed by a space and a word or phrase, and then press Enter. To turn off or change Address bar searches, click the Tools menu, click Internet Options, click the Advanced tab, select options under Search From The Address Bar, and then click OK.

You can find specific text on a web page. Click the Edit menu, click Find (On This Page), type the text you want to find, select find options, and then click Find Next.

You can start an Internet search from the Start menu. Click the Start button, click Search, connect to the Internet if necessary, click Search The Internet, and then perform the search.

For Your Information

Searching for People on the Web

Internet Explorer includes several directory services to help you find people you know who may have access to the Internet. To find a person on the Internet, click the Start button, click Search, click Printers, Computers, Or People, and then click People In Your Address Book to open the Find People dialog box. Click the Look In list arrow and then select a directory service, such as WhoWhere? Type the person's name, and then click Find Now. Each directory service accesses different databases on the Internet, so if you don't find the person using the first service, try a different directory service.

5

Previewing and Printing a Web Page

Web pages are designed for viewing on a computer screen, but you can also print all or part of one. Before you print, you should verify that the page looks the way you want. You save time, money, and paper by avoiding duplicate or wasteful printing. Print Preview shows you exactly how the web page will look on the printed page. This is especially helpful when you have multiple pages to print. When you are ready to print, Internet Explorer provides many options for printing web pages. For web pages with frames, you can print the page just as you see it, or you can elect to print a particular frame or all frames. You can even use special Page Setup options to include the date, time, or window title on the printed page. You can also choose to print the web addresses from the links contained on a web page.

Preview a Web Page

1. Click the File menu, and then click Print Preview.

2. Use the Print Preview toolbar buttons to preview or print the web page:

   ◆ Print the page(s).

   ◆ Set up the page for printing.

   ◆ Switch between pages.

   ◆ Zoom in and out.

   ◆ Specify how to print frames; only available when frames are present.

3. When you're done, click Close.

> ### See Also
>
> See "Previewing and Printing a Document" on page 35 for more information on using the Preview window and the Print dialog box.

Print button

Page setup button

Navigation buttons —— Magnification buttons

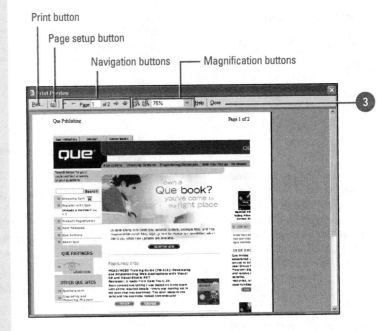

Print a Web Page

1. Click the File menu, and then click Print.

   TIMESAVER *To print the current page with the current print settings, click the Print button on the Standard toolbar.*

2. Click a printer.

3. Specify the range of pages you want to print.

4. Specify the number of copies you want to print.

5. Click Print.

> ### See Also
>
> *See Chapter 10 "Printing and Faxing" on page 343 for information on installing and using a printer.*

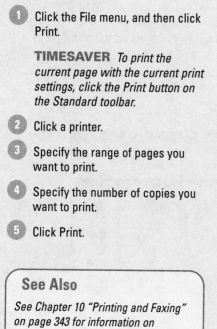

For Your Information

Setting Up the Page Format

When you print a web page, you can use the Page Setup dialog box to control the printing of text and graphics on a page. The Page Setup dialog box specifies the printer properties for page size, orientation, and paper source; in most cases, you won't want to change them. From the Page Setup dialog box, you can also change header and footer information. In the Headers and Footers text boxes, you can type text to appear as a header and footer of a web page you print. In these text boxes, you can also use variables to substitute information about the current page, and you can combine text and codes. For example, if you type **Page &p of &P** in the Header text box, the current page number and the total number of pages print at the top of each printed page. Check Internet Explorer Help for a complete list of header and footer codes.

5

Saving Pictures or Text from a Web Page

If you find information on a web page that you want to save for future reference or share with others, you can copy and paste it to another document or save it on your computer. When you copy information from a web page, make sure you're not violating any copyright laws.

Save a Picture from a Web Page

1. Open the web page with the picture you want to save.

2. Point to the picture you want to save to display a toolbar on the graphic, and then click the Save button.

   If the toolbar doesn't appear, right-click the picture, and then click Save Picture As.

3. Select the drive and folder in which you want to save the file.

4. Type a name for the file, or use the suggested name.

5. To change the format of a file, click the Save As Type list arrow, and then click a file format.

6. Click Save.

Did You Know?

You can save a page or picture without opening it. Right-click the link for the item you want to save, and then click Save Target As.

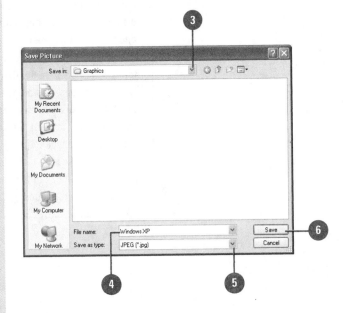

Set a Picture from a Web Page as the Background Picture

1. Open the web page with the picture you want to use.

2. Right-click the picture, and then click Set As Wallpaper or Set As Background.

Copy Text from a Web Page

1. Open the web page with the text you want to copy.

2. Select the text you want to copy.

   TROUBLE? *The I-beam cursor may or may not appear. You can still select the text.*

3. Right-click the selected text, and then click Copy.

4. Switch to where you want to paste the text.

5. Click the Edit menu, and then click Paste.

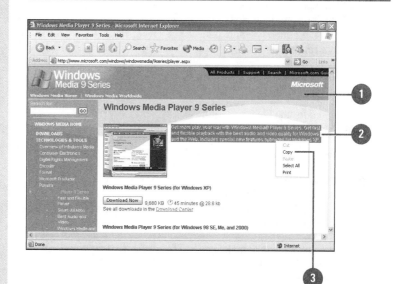

Did You Know?

You can create a desktop shortcut to the current web page. Right-click in the web page, click Create Shortcut, and then click OK.

5

Downloading Files from the Web

There are thousands of sites on the Internet offering all sorts of files you can download to your computer, from trailers to the latest game demos. You can download files from any web site by finding the file you want, right-clicking the link, and telling Internet Explorer where you want to save the file. Some web sites are designed with specific links to make it easier to download files. When you click a download link, a Security Warning dialog box opens, asking you to run or don't run the file from the Internet or save the file to your computer. Internet Explorer checks to see whether there are any irregularities with the file or a potential for harm based on the file type, and provides strong warning and guidance to help you understand more about the file you are downloading (New SP2).

Download a File from a Web Page

1 Open the web page from which you want to download a file.

2 Click the download link, and then click Save, or right-click the link pointing to the actual file, and then click Save Target As.

3 Select the folder in which you want to save the file.

4 Type a name for the file, or use the suggested name.

5 Click Save.

The File Download dialog box displays the estimated time to download the file, along with the estimated transfer time.

6 When the download is complete, click Open or Run to open or run the file, or click Close.

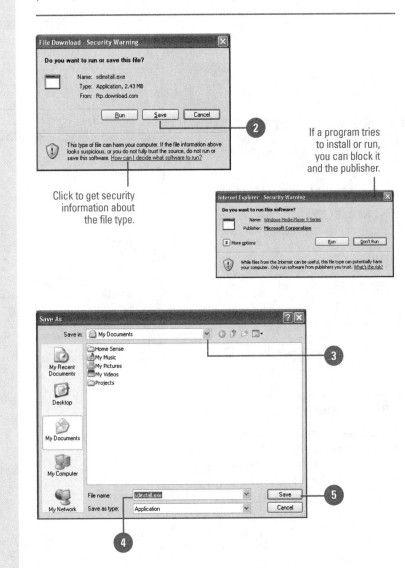

If a program tries to install or run, you can block it and the publisher.

Click to get security information about the file type.

Did You Know?

You can access a site with lots of files to download. Try these sites to find plenty of files to download: *http://www.download.com* and *http://www.shareware.com*

Downloading Files from an FTP Site

Sometimes you'll need to connect directly to a File Transfer Protocol (FTP) site to download or transfer a file to a remote computer. Internet Explorer allows you to easily access and download files from any FTP site, public or private. Public FTP sites allow you to access files without requiring that you have an account on the server. Private FTP sites expect you to enter your user name and password in order to see the folders and files. When you are connected to an FTP site, Internet Explorer's view of the files is the same as looking at a folder on your local hard disk. Within this view you can drag onto your desktop or right-click to copy the file in a particular folder on your computer.

Download a File from an FTP Site

1. In the Address bar, type the address for the FTP site, and then press Enter.

2. If necessary, type your user name and password, and then click OK.

   IMPORTANT *Before you download files, make sure your antivirus software is up-to-date.*

3. Right-click the file you want to download, and then click Copy To Folder.

   TIMESAVER *You can select the items you want to download, and then use the Copy and Paste commands. Select the files, press Ctrl+C, display the destination folder, and then press Ctrl+V.*

4. Select the folder in which you want to save the file.

5. Click OK.

Did You Know?

You can include your user name and password in the address for the ftp site. Type *ftp://username:password @ftp.server/folder.*

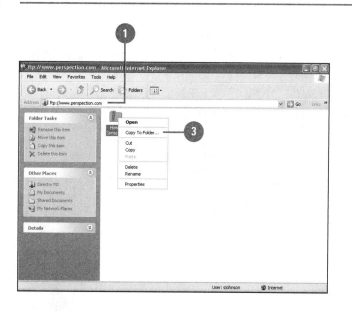

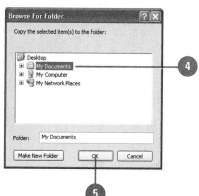

Saving a Web Page

You can save a web page you want to view offline even if you don't need to share it with others or update its content, such as a published article whose content will not change. There are several ways you can save the web page, from saving just the text to saving all of the graphics and text needed to display that page as it appears on the web. When you save a complete web page, Internet Explorer saves all the graphic and text elements in a folder. If you need to send a web page to a friend or co-worker, you can save all the elements of the web page in a single file to make the process easier.

Save a Web Page

1 Click the File menu, and then click Save As.

2 Select the drive and folder in which you want to save the file.

3 Type a name for the file, or use the suggested name.

4 Click the Save As Type list arrow, and then click one of the following:

◆ Web Page, Complete to save the formatted text and layout with all the linked information, such as pictures, in a folder.

◆ Web Archive, Single File to save all the elements of the web page in a single file.

◆ Web Page, HTML Only to save the formatted text and layout without the linked information.

◆ Text File to save only the text.

5 Click Save.

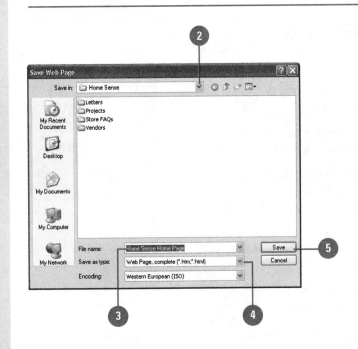

See Also

See "Saving and Closing a Document" on page 36 for more information on using the Save As dialog box.

Browsing with MSN Explorer

MSN Explorer is Internet software you can use to browse the Web, send e-mail and instant messages to friends, listen to music, watch videos, and manage finances online. MSN Explorer combines Microsoft's Internet software technologies, such as Microsoft Internet Explorer, Microsoft Windows Media Player, and MSN Messenger Service, with its leading web services, such as Hotmail and CNBC Money. You don't have to be an MSN member to use MSN Explorer, but you do need to have a Microsoft .NET Passport, which you can obtain when you associate an existing e-mail address with a User Account using the .NET Passport Wizard, or you can sign up for a free Hotmail or MSN e-mail account during the setup process. With MSN Explorer you can search the web and access web sites as in Internet Explorer.

Browse with MSN Explorer

1. Click the Start button, point to All Programs, and then click MSN Explorer.

2. If you're using MSN Explorer for the first time, follow the setup instructions.

3. Use the buttons to display the home page, send and receive e-mail or instant messages, participate in chats and online communities, or link to MSN sites.

4. Use the Address bar, web page links, and the Back and Forward button to navigate.

5. Use the buttons to display and manage your personal content.

6. Click to customize your personal settings.

7. Click the controls to listen to music or other content using Windows Media Player.

8. Click Help & Settings to change your password, customize your home page and MSN Explorer, or change settings for your mail.

9. When you're done, click Sign Out to stay connected, or click the Close button to exit the program.

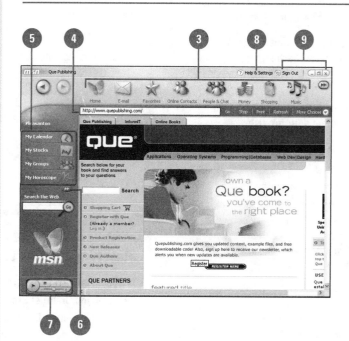

5

Using Another Web Browser

Windows XP comes with Internet Explorer as the default web browser. If you prefer to use another browser, you can remove Internet Explorer from your computer using the Add/Remove Programs utility in the Control Panel, install another browser, and set it as your default Internet program on the left column of the Start menu (New!).

Use Another Web Browser

1. If you want, remove Internet Explorer using the Add/Remove Programs utility in the Control Panel.

2. Install another browser according to the manufacturer instructions.

3. Right-click the Start button, and then click Properties.

4. Click Customize.

5. Click the Internet list arrow, and then select your browser.

6. Click OK, and then click OK again.

See Also

See "Adding or Removing Windows Components" on page 373 for information on adding or removing Windows components.

Did You Know?

You can use the same procedure to use another e-mail program. Windows XP also comes with Outlook Express as the default e-mail program. You can use the same basic procedure to use another e-mail program.

For Your Information

Resetting Internet Explorer Settings

If you installed another web browser after installing Internet Explorer, some of your Internet Explorer settings may have changed. You can reset your Internet Explorer settings to their original defaults, including your home page and search pages, and choice of default browser, without changing your other browser's settings. To reset Internet Explorer settings, click the Tools menu, click Internet Options, click the Programs tab, and then click Reset Web Settings.

Exchanging Messages and News

Introduction

If you're like many people today who are using the Internet to communicate with friends and business associates, you probably have piles of information (names, e-mail addresses, phone numbers, etc) that you need often. Unless this information is in one convenient place, and can be accessed immediately, the information becomes ineffective and you become unproductive. Microsoft Outlook Express solves these problems by integrating management and organization tools into one simple system. Windows XP includes Microsoft Outlook Express 6, a powerful program for managing **electronic mail** (known as e-mail), and contact information like names, and email addresses.

Using Outlook Express with an Internet connection allows you to accomplish several tasks:

- ◆ Create and send e-mail messages
- ◆ Manage multiple e-mail accounts with different Internet service providers
- ◆ Use the Windows Address Book to store and retrieve e-mail addresses
- ◆ Create stationery or add a personal signature to your e-mail messages
- ◆ Attach a file to an e-mail message
- ◆ Find people you know on the web
- ◆ Print e-mail messages
- ◆ Join any number of newsgroups, which are collections of e-mail messages on related topics

What You'll Do

Start Outlook Express

Set Up an Account

View the Outlook Express Start Page

View the Outlook Express Window

Add a Contact to the Address Book

Compose and Send E-Mail

Create E-Mail Stationery

Read and Reply to E-Mail

Send and Retrieve a File

Manage E-Mail Messages

Divert Incoming E-Mail to Folders

Manage Accounts

Select a News Server

Subscribe to a Newsgroup

Read and Filter the News

Post a News Message

Read News and E-Mail Offline

Import and Export Information

Starting Outlook Express

Whether you want to exchange e-mail with colleagues and friends or join newsgroups to trade ideas and information, Outlook Express provides you with the tools you need. When you install Windows XP, a menu item for Outlook Express appears in the left column of the Start menu and the All Programs submenu. The first time you start Outlook Express, you need to set up an e-mail account. The Internet Connection Wizard walks you through the process. You can set Outlook Express as your default e-mail program so that whenever you click an e-mail link on a web page or choose the mail command in your web browser, Outlook Express opens. You can also set Outlook Express as your default news reader so that when you click a newsgroup link on a Web page or choose the news reader command in your Web browser, Outlook Express opens.

Start Outlook Express

 Click the Start button.

 Click Outlook Express.

TROUBLE? *If Outlook Express doesn't appear in the left column of the Start menu, it's available on the All Programs submenu.*

If the Internet Connection Wizard opens, follow the step-by-step instructions to set up your e-mail account.

See Also

See "Setting Up an Account" on page 144 for information on creating an e-mail account.

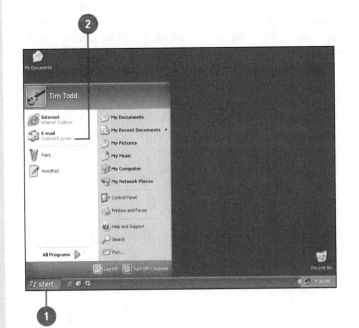

Set Options to Start Outlook Express from Your Web Browser

1. Click the Start button, and then click Internet Explorer.

2. Click the Tools menu, and then click Internet Options.

3. Click the Programs tab.

4. Click either the E-mail or Newsgroup list arrow, and then click Outlook Express.

5. Click OK.

Did You Know?

You can display the Inbox when you start Outlook Express. Click the When Outlook Express Starts, Go Directly To My Inbox check box on the Outlook Express Start Page.

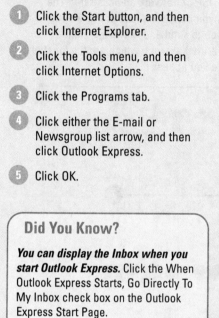

For Your Information

Getting Help in Outlook Express

If you want to connect to the Internet to get mail or learn how to use Outlook Express features, you can get help from several different sources. To get Outlook Express Help, you can use the Help system that comes with the program, or you can view Outlook Express web sites on the Internet. To open Outlook Express Help, click the Help menu, and then click Contents And Index. To learn more about Outlook Express from web sites on the Internet, click the Help menu, point to Microsoft On The Web, and then click Product News. Your browser starts and displays the Outlook Express web site.

Setting Up an Account

Before you can set up an e-mail account, you need your account name, password, e-mail server type, and the names of your incoming and outgoing e-mail servers from your ISP or network administrator. The Internet Connection Wizard helps you connect to one or more e-mail servers. Outlook Express allows you to send and retrieve e-mail messages from different types of **e-mail servers**, which are the locations where your e-mail is stored before you access it.

Set Up an Account from the Internet Connection Wizard

1. Start Outlook Express for the first time, and the Internet Connection Wizard begins.

2. Type your name, and then click Next.

3. Enter your e-mail address, and then click Next.

4. Click the Mail Server list arrow, and then select the incoming mail server you want to use.

5. Enter the name of the incoming mail server.

6. Enter the name of the outgoing mail server, and then click Next.

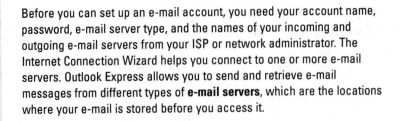

7 Enter your account name and a password, and then click Next.

8 Click Finish.

See Also

See "Managing Accounts" on page 164 for information on how to set up more than one e-mail account.

Internet Connection Wizard

Internet Mail Logon

Type the account name and password your Internet service provider has given you.

Account name: ttodd

Password: •••••••

☑ Remember password

If your Internet service provider requires you to use Secure Password Authentication (SPA) to access your mail account, select the 'Log On Using Secure Password Authentication (SPA)' check box.

☐ Log on using Secure Password Authentication (SPA)

< Back   Next >   Cancel

7

Frequently Asked Questions

How Do I Choose an E-Mail Server?

Outlook Express supports three types of incoming e-mail servers: **POP3** (Post Office Protocol), **IMAP** (Internet Message Access Protocol), and **HTTP** (Hypertext Transfer Protocol). A protocol is a set of rules and standards that control the transmission of content, format, sequencing, and error management for information over the Internet or network much like rules of the road govern the way you drive. POP3 servers allow you to access e-mail messages from a single Inbox folder, while IMAP servers allow you to access multiple folders. HTTP servers are used on web sites, such as Hotmail, and allow you to send and receive e-mail messages in Outlook Express or on a web site. When you use POP3 or IMAP e-mail servers, you also need to provide an outgoing e-mail server. **SMTP** (Simple Mail Transfer Protocol) is generally used to send messages between e-mail servers.

6

Viewing the Outlook Express Start Page

E-Mail

The New Mail message link opens the New Message dialog box, where you can compose and send e-mail messages. The Read Mail link jumps to the Inbox, where you can read and reply to incoming e-mail messages.

Tip of the Day

The Tip Of The Day pane displays an Outlook Express tip; click Next and Previous at the bottom of the pane to move between the tips.

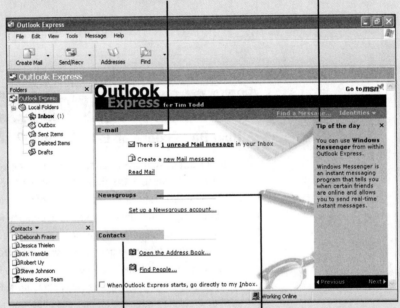

Contacts

The Open The Address Book link opens the Address Book, where you can enter and edit your contacts list. The Find People link opens the Find People dialog box, where you can search for people on the Internet or in your Address Book.

Newsgroup

The Set Up A Newsgroups Account link creates a newsgroup account. The Read News link connects to newsgroups that you can view and subscribe to.

Viewing the Outlook Express Window

Outlook Express start page
Click to return to the Outlook Express start page.

Menu bar
The Menu bar gives you access to all Outlook Express commands.

Toolbar
The Toolbar contains buttons for the most commonly used commands you need to work with mail messages.

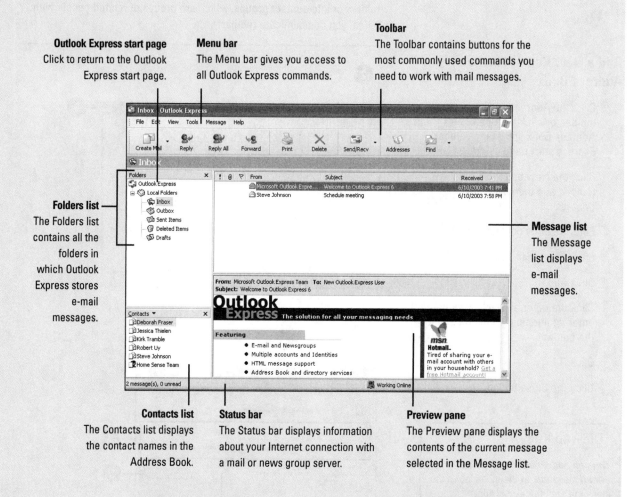

Folders list
The Folders list contains all the folders in which Outlook Express stores e-mail messages.

Message list
The Message list displays e-mail messages.

Contacts list
The Contacts list displays the contact names in the Address Book.

Status bar
The Status bar displays information about your Internet connection with a mail or news group server.

Preview pane
The Preview pane displays the contents of the current message selected in the Message list.

Frequently Asked Questions

How Do You Customize The Layout?

You can use the Layout command on the View menu to customize the Outlook Express window to suit your needs. You can show or hide different parts of the window and customize the Preview pane display.

6

Adding a Contact to the Address Book

A **contact** is a person or company that you communicate with. One contact can often have several mailing addresses, phone numbers, or e-mail addresses. You can store this information in the Address Book along with other detailed information, such as job title, cellular phone number, and web page addresses. You can organize your contacts into folders or into **contact groups**, which are groups of related people with whom you communicate regularly.

Add a New Contact to the Address Book

1. Click the Addresses button on the toolbar, or click the Open The Address Book link on the Outlook Express start page.

2. Click the New button on the toolbar, and then click New Contact.

3. Enter the new contact's name.

4. Enter the e-mail address.

5. Click Add.

6. Click the other available tabs to enter additional information about the contact.

7. Click OK.

8. Click the Close button.

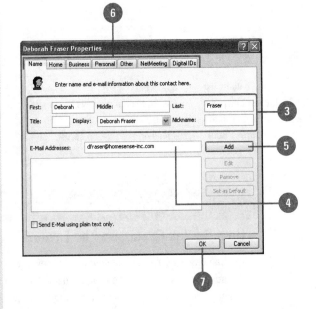

Did You Know?

You can add an address from an e-mail message. In the Inbox, open the message with the e-mail address you want, right-click the address, and then click Add To Address Book.

You can automatically add a reply address to your Address Book. Click the Tools menu, click Options, click the Send tab, select the Automatically Put People I Reply To In My Address Book check box, and then click OK.

Create a Contact Group

1. Click the Addresses button on the toolbar.

2. Click the New button on the toolbar, and then click New Group.

3. Type a name for the new group.

4. Click Select Members to display your current list of contacts.

5. Click the list arrow, and then select the folder in which you want to save the contacts group.

6. Click each member in the list of contacts you want to add, and then click Select.

   Repeat this step to add more contacts.

7. Click OK.

8. To remove a contact from the group, click the contact, and then click Remove.

9. Click OK.

10. When you're done, click the Close button.

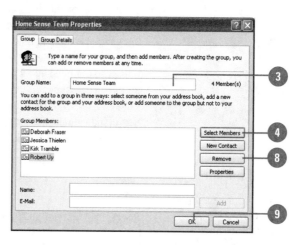

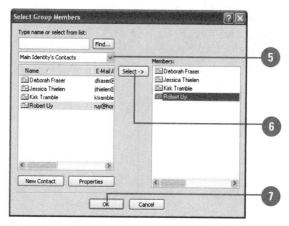

Did You Know?

You can sort your Address Book. Sort your Address Book by name, e-mail address, or phone number by clicking the appropriate column heading. You can switch the sorting method from ascending to descending by clicking the same column heading again.

For Your Information

Printing Contacts from the Address Book

You can print your contact information in a variety of formats, such as Memo, Business Card, and Phone List. The Memo style prints all the information you have for a contact with descriptive titles. The Business Card style prints the contact information without descriptive titles. The Phone List style prints all the phone numbers for a contact or for all your contacts. To print contact information, open the Address Book, select a specific contact (if desired), click the Print button on the toolbar, select a print range, print style, and the number of copies you want to print, and then click Print in the Print dialog box.

6

Composing and Sending E-Mail

E-mail is becoming the primary form of written communication for many people. E-mail messages follow a standard memo format, with fields for the sender, recipient, date, and subject of the message. To send an e-mail, you need to enter the recipient's e-mail address, type a subject, then type the message itself. For a personal touch, you can also create an e-mail message with stationery designs. You can send the same e-mail to more than one individual, to a contact group, or to a combination of individuals and groups. Before you send the e-mail, you can set a priority flag (high, normal, or low) to convey the message's importance.

Compose and Send an E-Mail

1. Click the Create Mail button on the toolbar, or click the Create A New Mail Message link on the Outlook Express start page.

   ◆ To create an e-mail with stationery, click the Create Mail button list arrow, then click a stationery.

2. Click the To button to open the Address Book.

   TIMESAVER *Type the recipient's name in the To box.*

3. Click a recipient or group.

4. Click one of the following:

   ◆ The To button if you want the recipient to receive the message and to see the addresses in the To and Cc fields.

   ◆ The Cc button if you want the recipient to receive a copy of the message and to see the addresses in the To and Cc fields.

   ◆ The Bcc button if you want the recipient to receive a copy of the message but not be listed as a recipient on any other copy of the message.

5. Click OK.

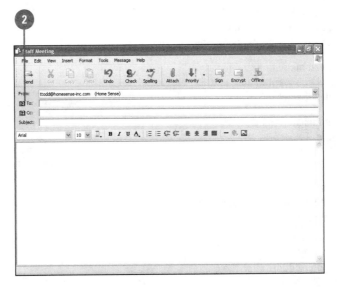

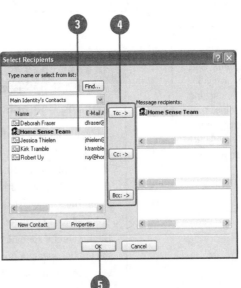

6 Click in the Subject box, and then enter a brief description of your message.

7 Click in the message box, and then type the text of your message.

8 If you want, click the Priority button list arrow on the toolbar, and then select a priority level.

9 If you want, use the commands on the Formatting toolbar to format your message.

10 Click the Send button on the toolbar. Or click the File menu, click Send Later, and then click OK to confirm that the message has been placed in your Outbox folder.

11 If you chose Send Later, click the Send/Recv button on the toolbar to contact the mail server and deliver your message.

TIMESAVER *Press Ctrl+M to send and receive e-mail for all accounts.*

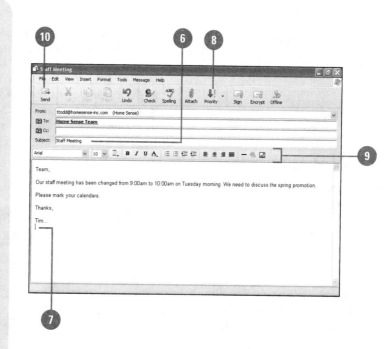

Did You Know?

Outlook Express helps you select contact names. If you have several people with the same first name or similar first names, you can enter that name by itself on the To line. When you click the Send button, Outlook Express will display a list of all contacts that share that name or that part of a name. Click the one you want to send the e-mail message to, and then click OK.

You can send and receive e-mail from a specific account. Click the Send/Recv button list arrow, and then click the account you want.

For Your Information

Checking the Spelling in E-Mail

Before you send an e-mail message, you should spell check the text and read through the content to make sure your spelling is accurate and your content conveys the message you want to the recipient(s). If you have Microsoft Word, Microsoft Excel, or Microsoft PowerPoint installed on your computer, Outlook Express uses the spell check from the Microsoft Office program to check the spelling of your e-mail messages. If you do not have one of these programs installed, the Spelling command is not available, and you need to check spelling manually. To start the spell check, type an e-mail message, click the Tools menu, and then click Spelling. To have Outlook Express spell check all of your e-mail messages before sending them, display the Outlook window, click the Tools menu, click Options, click the Spelling tab in the Options dialog box, select the Always Check Spelling Before Sending check box, and then click OK.

Creating E-Mail Stationery

If you're tired of the typical bland, unexciting look of e-mail, Outlook Express has the answer—Outlook Express stationery. This feature allows you to create e-mail messages with their own colorful background and font styles. You can also customize your messages with a signature or by attaching your business card. A **signature** is any file, text file with your signature, or photo of yourself that you choose. Several stationery styles are included with Outlook Express.

Create a Signature

1. Click the Tools menu, and then click Options.

2. Click the Signatures tab.

3. Click New to create a new signature.

4. Type the information for the signature. If available, select the file that contains your signature.

5. To enter more than one signature, repeat steps 3 and 4.

6. Select the signature you want to use most of the time, and then click Set As Default.

7. If you have multiple accounts, click Advanced, select the check boxes for the accounts you want to use, and then click OK.

8. If you want, select the Add Signatures To All Outgoing Messages check box, or select the Don't Add Signatures To Replies And Forwards check box.

9. Click OK.

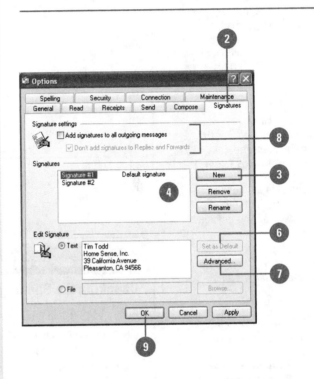

Did You Know?

You can add your signature to e-mail quickly. In an e-mail message, click where you want the signature, click the Insert menu, and then click Signature. If you have more than one signature, point to Signature, and then click the signature you want to use.

Create Stationery Using the Stationery Setup Wizard

1 Click the Tools menu, and then click Options.

2 Click the Compose tab.

3 Click Create New, and then click Next to begin the Stationery Setup Wizard.

4 Select a picture and color, and then click Next.

5 Choose the font, font size, and color, and then click Next.

6 Choose the left and top margin, and then click Next.

7 Type a name for your stationery, and then click Finish.

8 Select the Mail check box to always include stationery with your e-mail messages.

9 Click Select to choose the standard stationery, and then click OK.

10 Click OK.

Did You Know?

You can create a message using other or new stationery. Click the New Mail button list arrow on the toolbar, and then select a stationery, or click Select Stationery to select from other choices or to create a new one.

You can select a stationery for every new message. Click the Tools menu, click Options, click the Compose tab, select the Mail check box, click Select, click a stationery file, click OK, click the Send tab, click the HTML option, and then click OK.

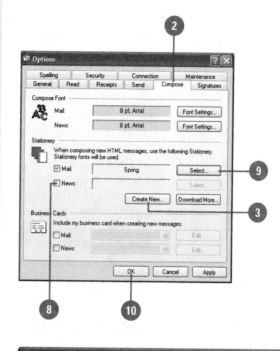

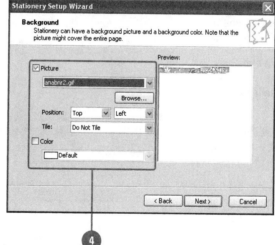

6

Reading and Replying to E-Mail

You can receive e-mail anytime—even when your computer is turned off. You can retrieve your e-mail manually or set Outlook Express to do so automatically. When you start Outlook Express, the program checks for new e-mail. It continues to check periodically while the program is open. New messages appear in boldface in the Inbox along with any messages you haven't moved or deleted. Message flags may appear next to a message, which indicate a certain priority, the need for follow up, or an attachment. Outlook Express blocks images and other potentially harmful content from automatically downloading in an e-mail message from unknown people (NewSP2). Blocked items are replaced with a red "x". You can use the Information Bar or modify the e-mail to view the blocked content. You can respond to a message in two ways: reply to it, which creates a new message addressed to the sender(s) and other recipients; or forward it, which creates a new message you can send to someone else. In either case, the original message appears in the response.

Open and Read an E-Mail

1. Click the Inbox icon in the folder list for the mail account you want.

2. Open an e-mail message.

   ◆ Click an e-mail message to read it in the Preview pane.

   ◆ Double-click an e-mail message or press Enter for a selected message to open it in its own window.

3. To download blocked pictures and other content, click the Information Bar at the top of the message.

4. Click the Previous or Next button on the Message toolbar to read additional e-mail messages.

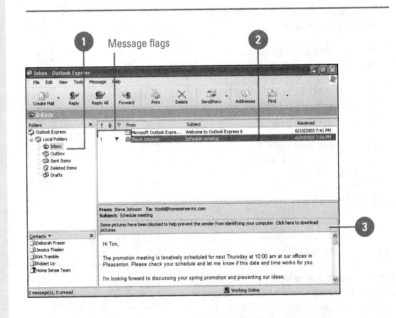

Message flags

See Also

See "Avoiding Viruses and Other Harmful Attacks" on page 296 for information on viruses.

See "Protecting Against E-mail Attacks" on page 309 for information on how to protect your computer against viruses from an e-mail.

See "Avoiding Viruses and Other Harmful Attacks" on page 296 for information on viruses.

See "Protecting Against E-mail Attacks" on page 309 for information on how to protect your computer against viruses from an e-mail.

For Your Information

Reading E-Mail in Plain Text To Avoid Viruses

If you're unsure of the source of an e-mail, yet still want to protect your computer from viruses, you can securely view the e-mail in plain text, instead of HTML which can contain potentially harmful content, such as viruses and worms. To read all e-mail in plain text, click the Tools menu, click Options, click the Read tab, select the Read All Messages In Plain Text check box, then click OK.

Reply to an E-Mail

1. Open the e-mail message you want to reply to.

2. Click the Reply button to respond to the sender only, or click the Reply All button to respond to the sender and to all other recipients.

   TIMESAVER *Press Ctrl+R to reply to the message author.*

3. Add or delete names from the To or the Cc box.

4. Type your message.

5. Attach any files to send.

6. Click the Send button on the toolbar.

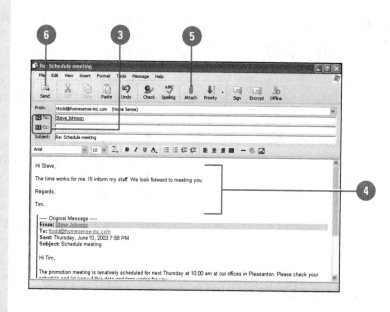

Forward an E-Mail

1. Open the e-mail message you want to forward.

2. Click the Forward button on the toolbar.

3. Type the name(s) of the recipient(s), or click the To button, and then select the recipient(s).

4. Type your message.

5. Attach any files to send.

6. Click the Send button on the toolbar.

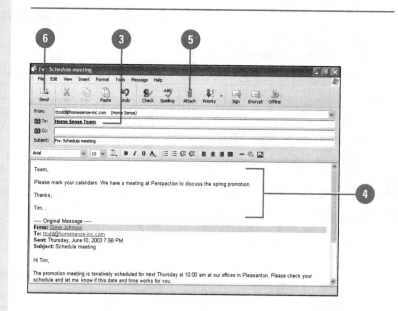

Did You Know?

Attachments aren't sent on replies.
When you reply to a message that had an attachment, the attachment isn't returned to the original sender. You can forward the message to the original sender if you need to send the attachment back.

Sending and Retrieving a File

You can use e-mail to easily share a file, such as a picture or a document by attaching it to an e-mail. Upon receiving the e-mail, the recipient can open the file in the program that created it or save it. Make sure you know and trust the sender before you open it, because it might contain a virus or other security threat. It's important to keep your antivirus software up-to-date. The Attachment Manager (NewSP2) provides security information to help you understand more about the file you are downloading. If an attachment is considered safe, Outlook Express makes it completely available to you. Examples of safe attachments are text files (.txt) and graphic files, such as JPEGs (.jpg) and GIFs (.gif). If an attachment is potentially unsafe, such as an executable program (.exe), screensavers (.scr) or script files (including .vbs), Outlook Express displays a notice on the Information Bar and blocks it so you will not be able to open it without taking explicit action. If Outlook Express can't determine the safety of an attachment, it displays a security warning (when you try to move, save, open, or print the file) with information about the file.

Send a File in an E-Mail

1. Compose a new message or reply to an existing message.

   IMPORTANT *Some ISPs have trouble sending attachments over 3 MB; check with your ISP.*

2. Click the Attach button on the toolbar.

3. Select the drive and folder that contains the file you want to attach.

4. Click to select the file.

5. Click Attach.

6. Click the Send button on the toolbar.

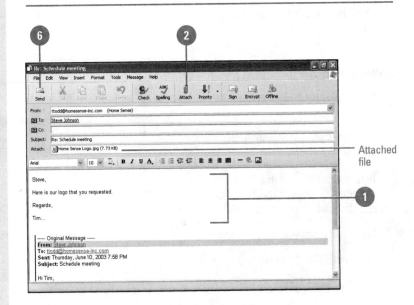

Attached file

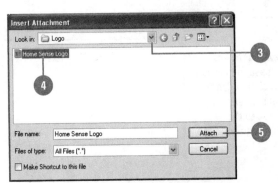

Did You Know?

You can open an attachment from an e-mail message. Select the e-mail message in the Inbox, click the Attachment icon on the Preview pane, and then click the name of the file.

Open a File in an E-Mail

1. Select the message with the attached file.

   IMPORTANT *If you're not sure of the source of an attachment, don't open it, because it might contain a virus or worm. Be sure to use anti-virus software.*

2. Click the Attachment icon, and then click the file name.

3. Click Open.

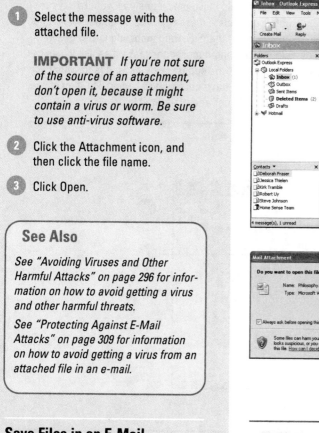

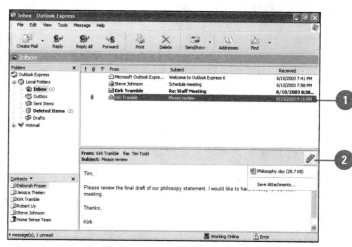

See Also

See "Avoiding Viruses and Other Harmful Attacks" on page 296 for information on how to avoid getting a virus and other harmful threats.

See "Protecting Against E-Mail Attacks" on page 309 for information on how to avoid getting a virus from an attached file in an e-mail.

Save Files in an E-Mail

1. Select the message with the attached file.

2. Click the Attachment icon, and then click Save Attachments.

3. Select the attached file you want to save or click Select All to select all the attached files.

4. Click Browse, select the drive and folder where you want to save the file, and then click Open.

5. Click Save.

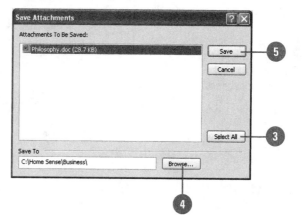

6

Managing E-Mail

A common problem with using e-mail is an overcrowded Inbox. To keep your Inbox organized, you should move messages you want to save to other folders and subfolders, delete messages you no longer want, and create new folders as you need them. Storing incoming messages in other folders and deleting unwanted messages make it easier to see the new messages you receive and to keep track of messages to which you have already responded. If you have not finished composing a message, you can save it in the Drafts folder and work on it later.

Create a New Folder

1. Click the File menu, point to New, and then click New Folder.

2. Type a name for the new folder.

3. Click the folder in which you want to place the new folder.

   - Click Local Folders to place the folder in the folder list.

   - Click one of the other folders in the list to make the new folder a subfolder.

4. Click OK.

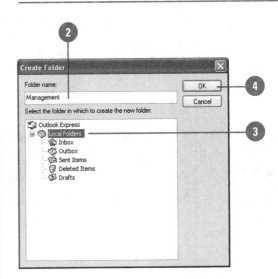

Organize E-Mail in Folders

1. Select the e-mail message you want to move. If necessary, press and hold the Ctrl key, and click to select multiple e-mail messages.

2. Drag the e-mail message(s) to the new folder.

Work on a Draft E-Mail

1. Open a new or a reply to an existing e-mail message, and then type a message.

2. Click the File menu, and then click Save, and then click OK.

3. Close the e-mail message.

4. Click the Drafts folder in the folder list.

5. Double-click the e-mail message to view it.

6. When you're done with the message, click the Send button.

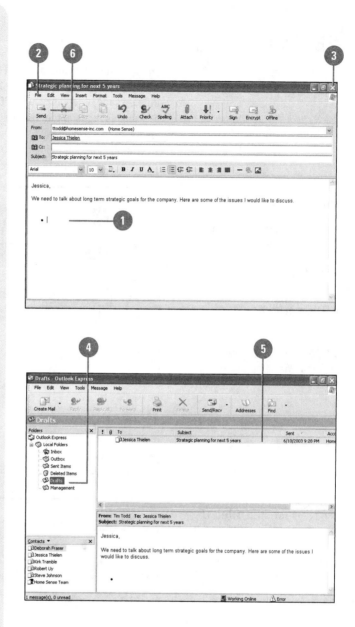

Did You Know?

You can flag an important message that need attention later. Select the e-mail message, click the Message menu, and then click Flag Message.

You can sort messages quickly. To sort messages by sender, subject, date, priority or flag, click a header in the Preview pane.

See Also

See "Deleting E-Mail" on page 160 for information on working with the Deleted Items folder.

Deleting E-Mail

When you delete an e-mail message, Outlook Express simply moves it into the Deleted Items folder. If you want to recover a deleted message, you just have to retrieve it from the Deleted Items folder. To get rid of a message permanently, you need to open the Deleted Items folder, select the message, and click Delete. Outlook Express automatically places e-mail messages in the Sent Items folder every time you send them. You will want to periodically open the Sent Items folder and delete messages so your mail account doesn't get too large. You can also use maintenance options to help you clean up.

Delete Unwanted E-Mail

1. Click a folder icon in the folder list with the e-mail you want to delete.

2. Click the e-mail you want to delete.

3. Click the Delete button on the toolbar.

   TIMESAVER *Press Delete or Ctrl+D to delete the selected message(s).*

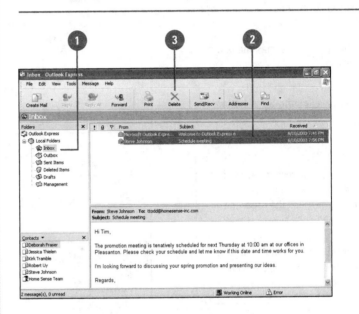

Recover E-Mail from the Deleted Items Folder

1. Click the Deleted Items folder in the folder list to open the folder.

2. Select the e-mail message you want to retrieve.

3. Drag the e-mail message to another folder.

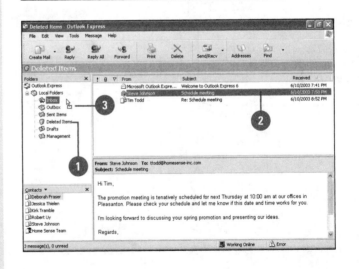

Change E-Mail Maintenance Options

1. Click the Tools menu, and then click Options.

2. Click the Maintenance tab.

3. Select the maintenance options you want.

   ◆ Delete messages on exit or after a certain number of days.

   ◆ Compact messages to save space.

4. Click OK.

Diverting Incoming E-Mail to Folders

Outlook Express can direct incoming messages that meet criteria to other folders in the Folders list rather than to your Inbox. For example, your friend loves sending you funny e-mail, but you often don't have time to read it right away. You can set message rules to store any messages you receive from your friend in a different folder so they won't clutter your Inbox. When you are ready to read the messages, you simply open the folder and access the messages just as you would messages in the Inbox. If you receive unwanted e-mail from a specific address, you can block all messages from that sender.

Set Rules for Incoming E-Mail

1. Click the Tools menu, point to Message Rules, and then click Mail.

   If no rules are set, skip to step 3.

2. Click New to create a new rule, or select a rule and click Modify to edit an existing one.

3. Click the appropriate conditions for your rule.

4. Click the appropriate actions for your rule.

5. Click a link to enter the underlying information for that condition or action.

6. Specify the criteria for your rule in the Selection dialog box that appears, and then click OK.

7. Repeat steps 5 and 6 for each condition and action you have set.

8. Type a name for this rule.

9. Click OK.

10. Click OK.

See Also

See "Managing E-Mail " on page 158 for information on creating custom folders for storing messages.

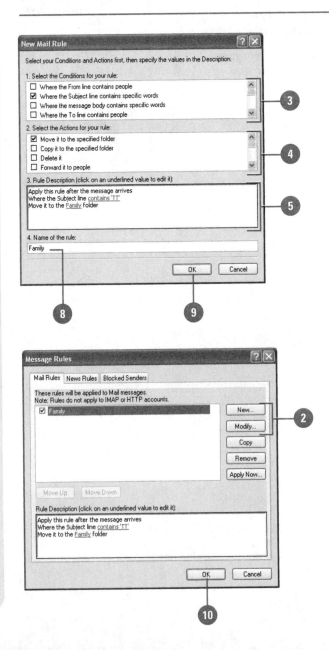

Block Junk E-Mail from a Sender

1. Select the e-mail you want to block.

2. Click the Message menu, and then click Block Sender.

   Outlook adds the sender to your blocked senders list.

3. Click Yes or No to remove all messages from this sender from the current folder.

Did You Know?

You can block an instant message. In the Contacts pane, double-click the on-line contact you want to block. In the Instant Message window, click Block.

Change Junk E-Mail Options

1. Click the Tools menu, point to Message Rules, and then click Blocked Senders List.

2. To unblock a sender, clear the Mail check box; you cannot clear both check boxes.

3. To remove a blocked sender, select the sender, and then click Remove.

4. Click OK, and then click OK again.

Did You Know?

You can apply rules right now. Click the Tools menu, point to Message Rules, and then click Mail. Click Apply Now. Select the rule(s) you want to apply and the folder that contains the messages, and then click Apply Now.

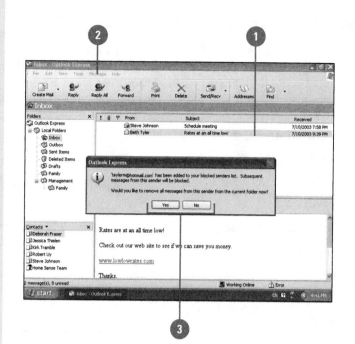

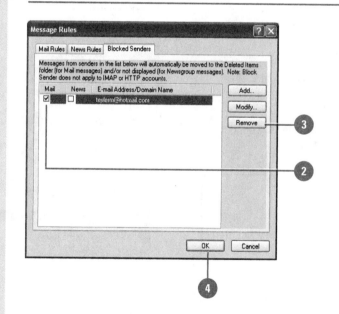

6

Managing Accounts

You can set up Outlook Express to receive e-mail from different accounts, or if several people share an e-mail account, you can set up folders for each person, and then route incoming mail messages to each individual's folder. If multiple users share the same computer, Outlook Express can create a separate account for each user, called an **identity**. You can add, modify, delete, and switch identities.

Add a New E-Mail Account

1. Click the Tools menu, and then click Accounts.

2. Click the Mail tab.

3. Click Add, and then click Mail.

4. Accept the default display name, or type a new name, and then click Next.

5. If your e-mail address appears correctly, click Next to continue; otherwise, type the correct address.

6. Enter the correct information for your e-mail server, and then click Next.

7. Enter your account name and a password, and then click Next.

8. Click Finish.

9. Click Close to save your new account settings.

See Also

See "Setting Up an Account" on page 144 for information about e-mail accounts.

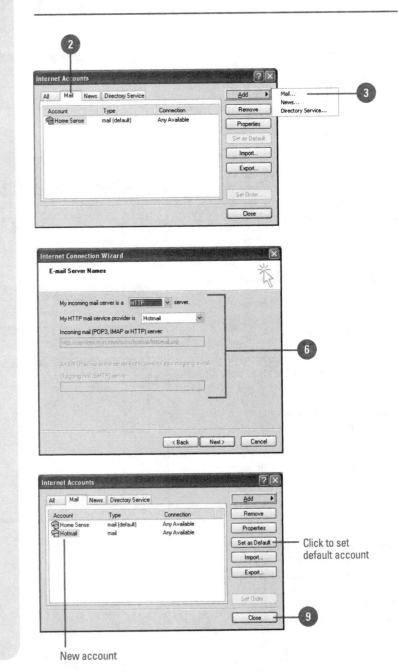

Click to set default account

New account

Add a New Identity

1. Click the File menu, point to Identities, and then click Add New Identity.

2. Type an identity name.

3. If you want, select the Require A Password check box, type a new password, confirm the new password, and then click OK.

4. Click OK.

5. Click No to switch now.

6. Click Close.

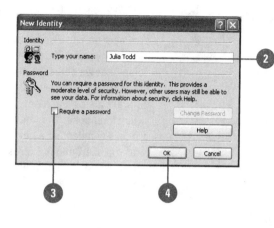

Switch Identities

1. Click the File menu, and then click Switch Identity.

2. Click the name you want to switch to.

3. To add or modify an identity, click Manage Identities.

4. Click OK.

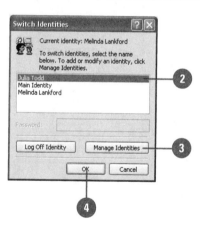

Did You Know?

You can modify an identity. Click the File menu, point to Identities, and then click Manage Identities. Select the identity name you want to change, click Properties or Remove, and then click Close.

You can change the startup identity. Click the File menu, point to Identities, and then click Manage Identities. Click the Use This Identity When Starting A Program list arrow, select the identity you want to start up with, and then click Close.

6

Selecting a News Server

A newsgroup is an electronic forum where people from around the world with a common interest can share ideas, ask and answer questions, and comment on and discuss any subject. You can find newsgroups on almost any topic. Before you can participate in a newsgroup, you must select a **news server**. A news server is a computer located on the Internet, which stores newsgroup messages, also called **articles**, on different topics. Each news server contains several newsgroups from which to choose. The Internet Connection Wizard walks you through the process of selecting a news server. This wizard also appears the first time you use Outlook Express News. To complete the wizard process, you might need an account name and password, and you need to choose a news server that you want to use.

Set up a News Server Using the Internet Connection Wizard

1 On the Outlook Express start page, click the Set up A Newsgroups Account link.

2 Type your name, and then click Next.

3 Read the information in each wizard dialog box, type the required information, and then click Next.

4 In the final wizard dialog box, click Finish.

5 Click Yes to download a list of newsgroups available on the news server.

6 Click OK.

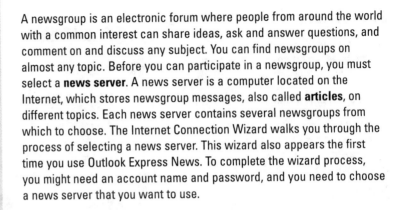

News server address

News server

Newsgroup

> ### Did You Know?
>
> *You can change the news server.*
> Right-click the news server in the Folders list, click Properties, type a name in the News Account text box, and then click OK.

Subscribing to a Newsgroup

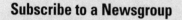

When you add a news server account, Outlook Express retrieves a list of newsgroups available on that server. Once you select a newsgroup, you can merely view its contents, or, if you expect to return to the newsgroup often, you can subscribe to it. Subscribing to a newsgroup places a link to the group in the Folders list, providing easy access to the newsgroup. If you find that you are no longer interested in a newsgroup, you can unsubscribe from it. You can also view a newsgroup without subscribing to see if you might want to add it to your Folders list.

Subscribe to a Newsgroup

1. Click the Tools menu, and then click Newsgroups.

2. Type the word or phrase for which you want to search. As you type, the results appear in the Newsgroup list.

3. Scroll through the list of available newsgroups.

4. Click the newsgroup you want to subscribe to.

5. Click Subscribe.

6. Click Go To to see the posted messages.

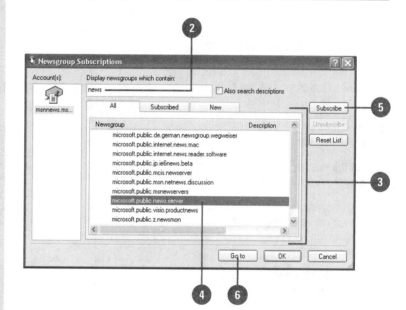

Did You Know?

You can unsubscribe from a newsgroup. If you no longer want to see a newsgroup in your Folders list, right-click the newsgroup name, click Unsubscribe on the shortcut menu, and then click OK.

Reading the News

Once you have subscribed to a newsgroup, you will want to view its messages. Click the newsgroup to display messages, and then click the message you want to read. Newsgroup messages appear in the Preview pane, just as e-mail messages do. If a plus sign (+) appears to the left of a newsgroup message, then the message contains a conversation thread. A **conversation thread** consists of the original message on a particular topic along with any responses that include the original message. Icons appear next to the news messages to indicate whether a conversation thread is expanded or collapsed, and whether or not it has been read.

Open and Read News Messages

1. Click the newsgroup in the Folders list whose message you want to read.

2. Scroll through the list to see the posted messages.

3. Find the message you want to read using the following methods:

   ◆ To display all the responses to a conversation thread, click the plus sign (+) to the left of a message.

   ◆ To hide all the responses to a conversation thread, click the minus sign (-) to the left of a message.

   ◆ To view only unread messages, click the View menu, point to Current View, and then click Hide Read Or Ignored Messages.

   ◆ To sort the messages based on type, click the column button you want to sort by. The column button toggles between sorting the column in ascending and descending order.

4. To read a message, click its header in the message list.

5. Read the message in the Preview pane.

News server

Filtering the News

After you become familiar with a newsgroup, you might decide that you don't want to retrieve messages from a particular person, about a specific subject, of a certain length, or older than a certain number of days. This is called **filtering** newsgroup messages.

Filter Unwanted Messages

1. Click the Tools menu, point to Message Rules, and then click News.

2. If necessary, click New.

3. Select the conditions for your rule.

4. Select the actions for your rule.

5. Click any undefined value, such as the e-mail address you want to divert and the folder where you want to store the unwanted messages, and then provide information.

6. Type a name.

7. Click OK.

8. Click OK.

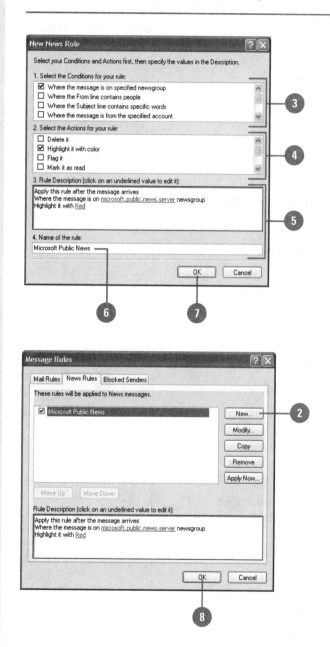

Did You Know?

You can ignore or watch a conversation. Select the conversation you want to ignore or watch, click the Message menu, and then click Ignore Conversation or Watch Conversation.

6

Posting a News Message

Part of the fun of newsgroups is that you can participate in an ongoing discussion, respond privately to a message's author, or start a new thread yourself by posting your own message on a topic of interest to you. If you post a message to a newsgroup and then change your mind, you can cancel the message. Keep in mind that if someone has already downloaded the message, canceling the message will not remove it from that person's computer.

Post a News Message

1 Click the newsgroup in the folder list to which you want to post a message.

2 Click the New Post button on the toolbar.

3 Type a subject for your message.

4 Type your message.

5 Click the Send button on the toolbar.

6 Click OK to confirm your message is being sent to the news server.

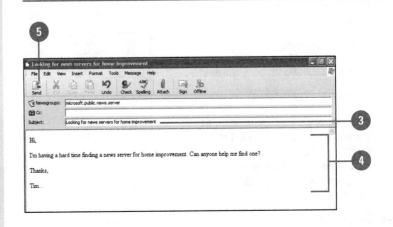

Cancel a Message

1 Select the newsgroup to which you posted the message in the Folders list.

2 Select the message you want to cancel. You will need to wait until the newsgroup posts the message.

3 Click the Message menu, click Cancel Message, and then click OK.

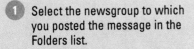

Did You Know?

You need to think before you post. Respond to personal questions posted to a newsgroup directly to the author, not to the entire newsgroup. Remember to click the Reply button.

Reply to a Message

① Click the message to which you want to reply.

② Select the appropriate command.

◆ Click the Reply Group button on the toolbar to post your response to the newsgroup.

◆ Click the Reply button on the toolbar to send the message's author a private e-mail message.

◆ Click the Forward button to send an e-mail message to some other recipient.

③ Type your message, and if you want, delete parts of the original message that are unrelated to your reply.

④ Click the Send button on the toolbar.

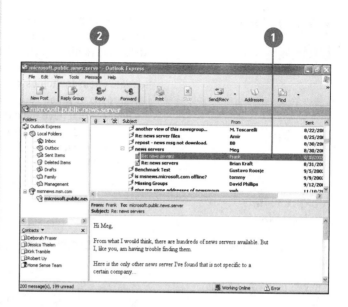

Did You Know?

You should name your messages carefully. When you compose a message, choose a subject that accurately reflects the content of your message so that people can decide whether they want to read it. When you reply to a message, don't change the subject line so that the conversation will remain threaded.

For Your Information

Deleting Old News Messages

Newsgroup messages are stored on your hard drive, so you should delete unneeded messages to free disk space. Outlook Express gives several clean-up options to help you optimize your hard drive space. You can delete entire messages (titles and bodies), compress messages, remove just the message bodies (leaving the title headers), or reset the information stored for selected messages, which allows you to refresh messages (download again). To clean up files on your local hard drive, select a news server in the Folders list, click the Tools menu, click Options, and then click the Maintenance tab. You can select any of the clean-up options to delete or compress news messages at a specified time, or you can click Clean Up Now, and then click the button for the clean-up option you want to perform.

6

Reading News and E-Mail Offline

To keep your phone line free and possibly reduce your Internet connection charges, you can read your newsgroup messages offline, while you are disconnected from the Internet. First, when you are online, set Outlook Express to **download** (transfer to your computer) only the **headers** (message topics, authors, and dates) for the various newsgroups to which you subscribe. Then you can go offline and read the headers that have been downloaded. Mark the messages that look interesting, and then go back online to download the messages you marked. Before disconnecting from your ISP, make sure you set Outlook Express to Work Offline.

Set Outlook Express to Retrieve Only Headers

1. Click the news server in the Folders list.

2. Click the newsgroup you want to view offline.

3. Click the Settings list arrow, and then click Headers Only.

4. If you want, select the New Messages Only check box to download new messages along with the headers.

   Repeat steps 2 through 4 for each newsgroup you want to read offline.

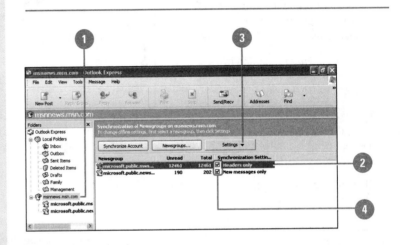

Download Newsgroup Headers

1. Click the news server in the Folders list.

2. Click the newsgroup with synchronization set to Headers Only.

3. Click Synchronize Account.

   Outlook Express will synchronize with news server and download the headers to your computer.

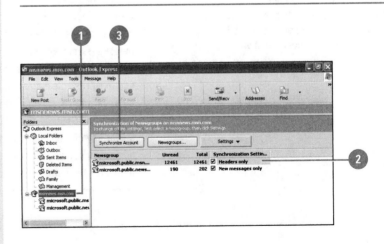

Mark Messages Offline for Downloading

1. While offline, right-click the header of a message you want to read.

2. Click Download Message Later.

3. Repeat for each message you want to retrieve.

4. Click the news server in the Folders list.

5. Click Synchronize Account to download the messages you marked. Click Yes to go online.

Compose Messages and Replies Offline

1. While offline, compose a message, or reply as usual.

2. Click the Send button on the toolbar, and then click OK to confirm your message will go into the Outbox.

3. Click the news server in the Folders list.

4. Click Synchronize Account to post the messages. Click Yes to go online.

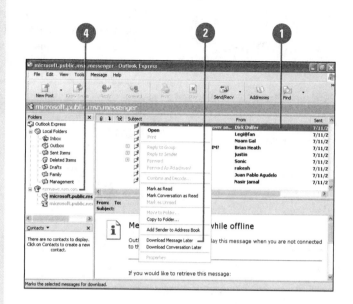

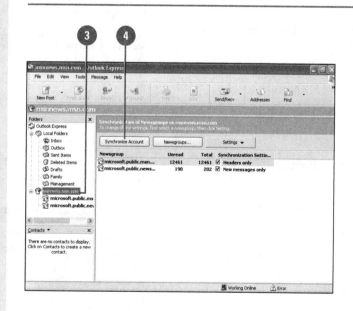

Did You Know?

You can subscribe to a newsgroup offline. While working offline, you can still subscribe to a newsgroup. Click the Newsgroups button on the toolbar, select a newsgroup you are interested in, click the Subscribe button, and then click OK. You won't see any messages until you go back online.

6

Importing and Exporting Information

Outlook Express can import the address book, mail messages, and account settings from many of the most popular e-mail programs. You can also export your messages or Address Book information from Outlook Express to work with other programs.

Import an Address Book

1 Click the File menu, point to Import, and then click Other Address Book.

2 Click an import file type.

3 Click Import.

4 Follow the additional instructions, and then click OK.

5 Click Close.

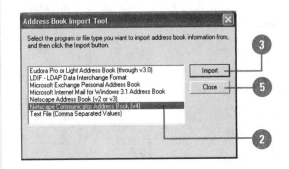

Export Your Address Book to a Text File

1 Click the File menu, point to Export, and then click Address Book.

2 Click an export file type.

3 Click Export.

4 Type a file name, and then click Next.

5 Select the fields for exporting.

6 Click Finish.

7 Click OK, and then click Close.

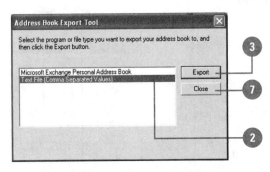

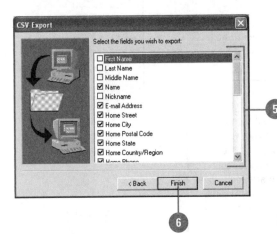

Did You Know?

You can import mail messages from another e-mail program. Click the File menu, point to Import, and then click Messages. Select the e-mail program, and then follow the wizard instructions to import the e-mail messages.

Holding Web Discussions and Video Conferences

Introduction

Windows XP makes communicating with other computers over the Internet easier than ever with Windows Messenger (version 4.7). You can talk to others over the Internet (like you do on a telephone), use video to see and be seen by others while you converse, share programs and files, collaborate on documents, share graphical content on a whiteboard (a drawing canvas), and ask for or get remote online assistance from a contact.

You can use Windows Messenger to exchange instant messages with a designated list of contacts over the Internet. An **instant message** is an online typewritten conversation in real-time between two or more contacts. Unlike an e-mail message, instant messages require both parties to be online, and the communication is instantaneous.

Windows Messenger uses different services to exchange messages, files, and other information. The default service is .NET Messenger Service, which individuals mostly use. For those working in a corporate environment, Windows Messenger supports Communications Service for networks that use SIP-server technology and Exchange Instant Messaging for networks that use Microsoft Exchange Server. You can set up Windows Messenger to access more than one type of messaging service.

Creating .NET Passport

Microsoft .NET Passport (**New!**) is an online service that makes it possible for you to use your e-mail address and a single password to securely sign in to any participating .NET Passport web site or service around the world. Each user on a computer must have a .NET Password to access all MSN Internet Access web sites and use MSN related software, such as MSN Explorer and Windows Messenger. You use the .NET Passport Wizard to help you quickly associate a .NET Password to any existing e-mail address or to create while you sign up for a free MSN or Hotmail e-mail account. Once you create a .NET Passport, you can quickly sign in at any participating web site by clicking the .NET Passport button or you can sign in when you start MSN related software, such MSN Explorer and Windows Messenger. When you finish working with a participating web site, you can click to sign out.

Create a New .NET Passport Association

1. Click the Start button, and then click Control Panel.

2. Double-click the User Accounts icon in Classic view.

3. Click Set Up My Account To Use A .NET Passport and click an account, or click the Advanced tab.

4. Click .NET Passport Wizard, and then click Next.

5. Click the Yes option if you have an e-mail address, and then click Next. If you don't have an e-mail address, follow the alternate instructions.

6. Click the No option to register for a new .NET Password, click Next twice to open the .NET registration web site, and then follow the instructions.

7. After you complete the .NET registration, click Finish.

8. Click the Close button or click OK.

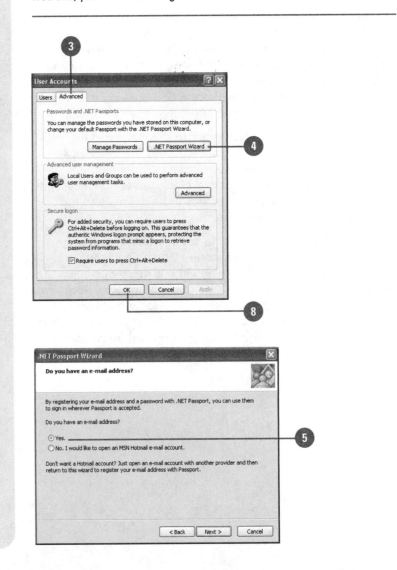

176

Delete a .NET Passport Association

① Click the Start button, and then click Control Panel.

② Double-click the User Accounts icon in Classic view.

③ Click Manage My Network Passwords and click an account, or click the Advanced tab, and then click Manage Passwords.

④ Select your e-mail address or Passport.Net.

⑤ Click Remove.

⑥ Click OK to confirm the removal.

⑦ Click Close.

This procedure doesn't delete the .NET Passport, just the association with the user account.

⑧ Click the Close button or click OK.

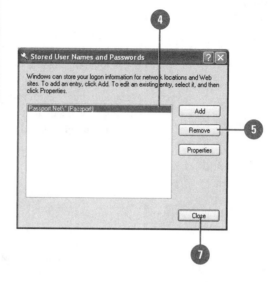

Did You Know?

You can delete a .NET Passport. *To delete a .NET Passport, you need to close your MSN Hotmail or MSN e-mail account or contact .NET Passport member services.*

For Your Information

Making Changes to a .NET Passport

You can find out more about .NET Passport and a directory of partici-pating web sites by visiting the Microsoft .NET Passport web site at www.passport.com. At the web site, you can click the Member Services link to change your .NET Passport information, reset your password, and find out answers to frequently asked questions. You can also access the web site from your account in the User Accounts window. For those who make online purchases, you can also find out how to store financial information in .NET Passport wallet, which helps you make faster, safer online purchases at any .NET Passport express purchase Web site. The .NET Passport wallet uses certificates issued by a trusted certification authority to keep transactions secure.

Starting Windows Messenger

Windows Messenger is an instant messaging program that allows you to exchange instant messages with a designated list of contacts over the Internet. An **instant message** is an online typewritten conversation in real time between two or more contacts. Instant messages require both parties to be online, and the communication is instantaneous. You and your contacts don't have to be MSN members to use Windows Messenger, but you both need a .NET Passport. After you start Windows Messenger, you sign in to let others online know you are connected. When you're done, you sign out.

Start Windows Messenger and Sign In and Out

1 Click the Start button, point to All Programs, and then click Windows Messenger.

   TIMESAVER *Double-click the Windows Messenger icon in the notification area of the taskbar.*

2 If you're not automatically signed in, click the Click Here To Sign In link or click the To Sign In With A Different Account, Click Here link, and then enter your user name and password.

3 If you want to stay signed in, yet still close Windows Messenger, click the Close button.

   When a message arrives, an alert appears. Click the alert to open Windows Messenger.

4 To sign out, click the File menu, and then click Sign Out.

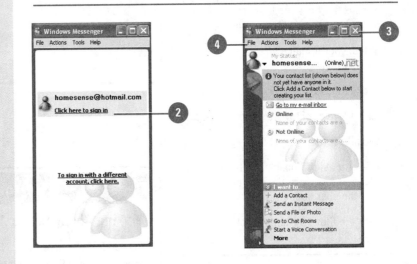

Did You Know?

You can stop signing in automatically. Click the File menu, click Sign Out, click To Sign In With A Different Account, Click Here, and then clear the Sign Me In Automatically On This Computer check box.

For Your Information

Starting Windows Messenger From Outlook Express

While you're working in Outlook Express, you can log on or off to Windows Messenger, send an instant message, change options, and add an online contact. In Outlook Express, click the Tools menu, point to Windows Messenger, and then click the available command you want to access Windows Messenger.

Viewing Windows Messenger

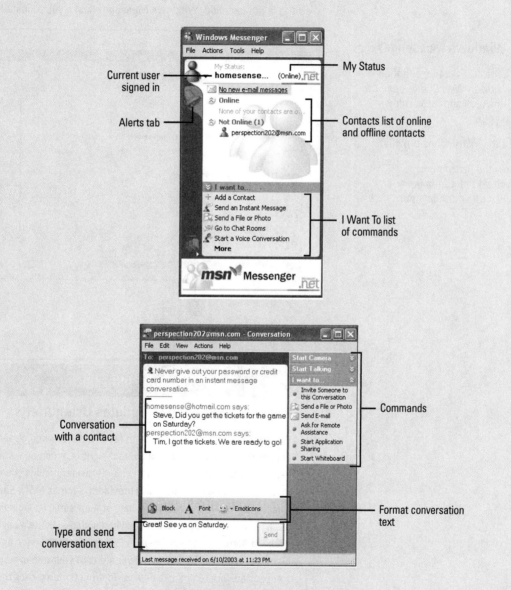

Current user signed in

Alerts tab

My Status

Contacts list of online and offline contacts

I Want To list of commands

Conversation with a contact

Commands

Format conversation text

Type and send conversation text

Updating Windows Messenger

Microsoft is continually updating Windows Messenger with new functionality. You can add functionality to the program using the Add-In web site, which you can access from Windows Messenger. From the web site you can download the latest add-ins and install them on your computer. Sometimes a command or option needs to use an add-in. If the add-in is not installed, Windows Messenger asks you to install it.

Update Windows Messenger

1 Click the Tools menu, and then click Add-In Web Site to open the Add-Ins web site for Windows Messenger.

2 Read the instructions provided.

3 Follow the instructions to download the add-in file and install it on your computer.

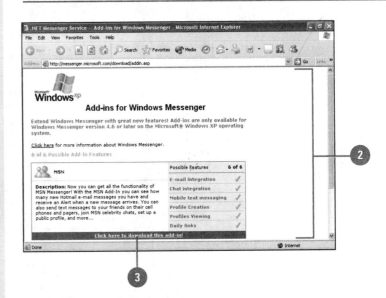

For Your Information

Receiving Information Updates Using Alerts

Windows Messenger allows you to receive alerts when certain actions occur, such as when a contact signs in, when an instant message arrives, or when a third-party alert provider notifies you of a requested action. The third-party providers, such as MSN, Ebay, Nasdaq, or McAfee, provide a variety of Alert services including breaking news, stock updates, and virus updates. In the main window, click the Alerts tab (the bell logo) to sign up for the service and view alerts. You can also decide to deliver alerts to your e-mail inbox, or to a supported wireless mobile device. To turn off alerts, click the Tools menu, select Options, and then click the Preferences tab. In the Alerts section, clear the check box for the alerts you want to turn off. To turn off the third-party alerts, go to the Microsoft Alerts site (at *www.microsoft.com*) where you can turn off the alerts you signed up for.

Changing My Status

When you sign in with Windows Messenger, the program notifies contacts currently online from your Contacts list that you are available to chat. While you're signed in, you might need to leave your computer for a meeting or lunch. Instead of signing out, you can change your online status to let your contacts know that you'll be right back, or that you're busy, away from your desk, on the phone, out to lunch, or offline. You can also change status and program preferences to customize the way Windows Messenger runs, shows status, and displays alerts.

Change My Status

1. Click the File menu, and then point to My Status.

2. Click a status type.

Did You Know?

You can change the name that people see. Click the Tools menu, click Options, click the Personal tab, type a name, and then click OK.

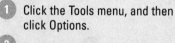

Change Status Preferences

1. Click the Tools menu, and then click Options.

2. Click the Preferences tab.

3. Select or clear the check boxes with the options you want to

   ◆ Run this program when Windows starts

   ◆ Allow this program to run in the background

   ◆ Show me as "Away" when I'm inactive

   ◆ Display alerts or sounds

4. Click OK.

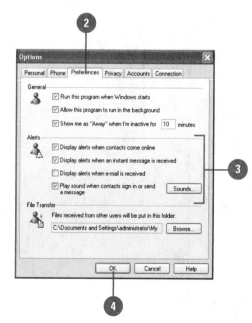

Adding Online Contacts

Before you can send instant messages to other people, they need to be in your Contacts list. You can add a person who has a .NET Passport to your Contacts list by using the Add A Contact wizard. If the person that you want to contact doesn't have a Passport, you can send the person an e-mail with information about getting and installing Windows Messenger and obtaining a Passport. If you don't know a person's e-mail address, the wizard will help you find it. You can have as many as 150 contacts.

Add an Outline Contact

1. Double-click the Windows Messenger icon in the notification area of the taskbar, and then sign in, if necessary.

2. Click Add A Contact.

3. Click the By E-mail Address Or Sign-In Name option, and then click Next.

   TROUBLE? *If the person that you want to contact doesn't have a Passport, follow the instructions to send that person an e-mail explaining how to get a Passport.*

4. Type your contact's complete e-mail address, and then click Next.

5. Click Finish.

Did You Know?

You can quickly delete a contact from your Contacts list. Click a contact in the Contacts list, press Delete, and then click Yes. Users who are removed from your list can still contact you unless you block them.

You can allow others to add you to their Contacts list without seeking your approval. Click the Tools menu, click Options, click the Privacy tab, clear the Alert Me When Other Users Add Me To Their Contact Lists check box, and then click OK.

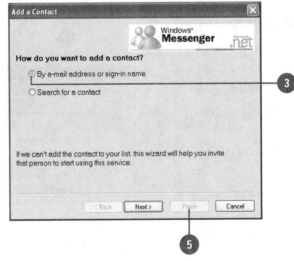

Managing Contacts and Groups ▶

As your Contacts list grows, you may want to organize your contacts into groups. Windows Messenger makes it easy to organize them into predefined groups and groups that you create. Windows Messenger comes with four predefined groups by default: Coworkers, Family, Friends, and Other Contacts. Once you have organized your groups, you can simply drag contacts from one group to another. You can use the Up and Down buttons next to the group name to hide and display contacts in a group.

7

Create a Contacts Group

1 Click the Tools menu, point to Sort Contacts By, and then click Groups.

2 Click the Tools menu, point to Manage Groups, and then click Add A Group.

3 Type a name, and then press Enter.

Move or Copy Contacts to Different Groups

◆ To move a contact, drag the contact to the new group.

◆ To copy a contact, press and hold down the Ctrl key while you drag the contact to the new group.

Did You Know?

You can quickly rename or delete a contacts group. Right-click the contacts group, and then click Delete A Group or click Rename A Group.

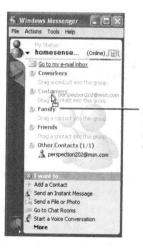

Drag to move contact. Press and hold Ctrl to copy contact.

Sending and Receiving Instant Messages

An instant message is an online typewritten conversation in real-time between two or more contacts. As you type an instant message, you can format your messages by using fonts and color and by inserting graphical symbols called **emoticons**, such as a happy face, which help convey your emotions (New!). Each message can contain up to 400 characters. You cannot send an instant message to more than one person, but you can invite other people using the same messaging service to participate in an existing conversation; you can include up to five people in a conversation.

Send and Receive Instant Messages

1. Double-click the Windows Messenger icon in the notification area of the taskbar, and then sign in, if necessary.

2. Double-click the contact to whom you want to send an instant message.

3. Type your message in the box at the bottom of the window.

   To start a new line while typing, press Shift+Enter.

4. Click Send or press Enter, and then wait for a reply.

5. If you want to add another person to the conversation, click Invite Someone To This Conversation, and then double-click the person you want to add.

6. When you're done, click the Close button to end the session.

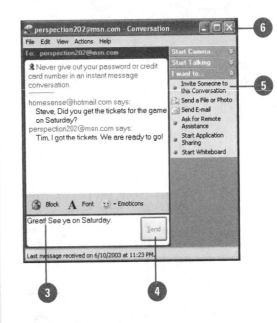

Did You Know?

You can send a message to someone not on your Contacts list. In the main window, click Send An Instant Message, click the Other tab, type the e-mail address, and then click OK.

For Your Information

Stopping Instant Message Pop-up Ads

If you're receiving instant message pop-up ads, known as messenger spam, in Windows Messenger, you can stop them by making sure Windows Firewall is turned on and Messenger Service is turned off in Windows XP; both default settings in SP2 (NewSP2). For instructions to turn them on, see *"Setting Up Windows Firewall"* on page 115. To turn off Message Service, open the Control Panel, double-click the Administrative Tools icon, double-click the Services icon, double-click Messenger in the Services list, click the Startup Type list arrow, click Disabled, click Stop, then click OK. Although Messenger Service is similar to Windows Messenger, the two perform different tasks.

Format Message Text

1. In the Conversation window, click the Font button.

2. Specify the font, font style, size, color, and effect you want, and preview the result in the sample box.

3. Click OK.

4. Type and send the formatted message.

Insert Emoticons

1. In the Conversation window, click the Emoticons button.

2. Click the icon you want to insert into the conversation.

TIMESAVER *You can also type a sequence of characters to quickly insert emoticons as you type your message. To find out the characters, point to an icon on the Emoticons menu.*

Did You Know?

You can save an instant message. In the Conversation window, click the File menu, click Save As, select a folder location, type a file name, and then click Save.

You can keep emoticons from displaying in a message. In the Conversation window, click the View menu, and then click Enable Emoticons to clear the check mark.

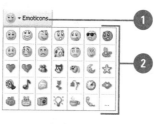

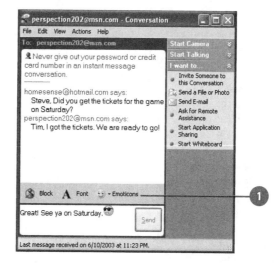

Blocking a Contact

If you no longer want to receive instant messages from a specific contact, you can block the contact from directly sending you instant messages. When you block a contact, you appear to be offline to the person, who doesn't know blocking is turned on. If another contact invites you and someone you blocked into a conversation, the blocked person can send you messages indirectly. Blocking a contact moves them from your Allow list to your Block list. Deleting a blocked contact from your Contacts list does not remove the block.

Block or Unblock a Contact

1 Click the Tools menu, and then click Options.

2 Click the Privacy tab.

3 Select the contacts you want to block, and then click Block.

4 Select the contacts you don't want to block, and then click Allow.

5 To find out which users have added you to their Contacts list, click View, and then click Close.

6 Click OK.

Did You Know?

You can quickly block or unblock a contact. Right-click the contact, and then click Unblock or Block. You can also click the Block button during a conversation.

You can block a person not in your Contacts list. Click Send An Instant Message, click Other, type the person's e-mail address, click OK, and then click the Block button.

You can access the Privacy tab from Outlook Express. In Outlook Express, click the Tools menu, point to Windows Messenger, and then click Options.

Sending a File During an Instant Message

While you are conversing in Windows Messenger, you can send a contact a file (**New!**). You can send many different types of files, including documents, photos, and music. When you send a file, a request to transfer the file is sent to your contact. You are notified when your contact accepts or declines your request. Before you receive files over the Internet, make sure you have up-to-date virus protection software on your computer. When you receive a file, the Attachment Manager (**NewSP2**) provides security information to help you understand more about the file. If your computer is located on a network behind a firewall, you might not be able to send files to those outside the firewall. If you want to send files to those behind the firewall, you need to manually open the connection; check with your network administrator for details.

Send and Receive a File

1. Start a conversation with the contact to whom you want to send the file.

2. Click Send A File Or Photo.

3. Select the drive and folder with the file you want to send.

4. Type a name for the file, or use the suggested name.

5. Click Open, and then wait for the recipient to accept or decline the file.

6. To open a file, click the link in the Conversation window, and follow the security instructions.

Did You Know?

You can follow up on a conversation with an e-mail. Right-click the contact, and then click Send E-Mail (E-Mail Address).

See Also

See "Sending and Retrieving a File" on page 156 for information on security using the Attachment Manager.

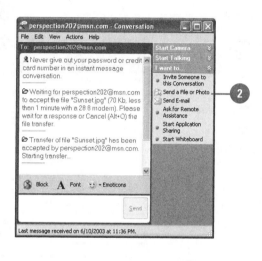

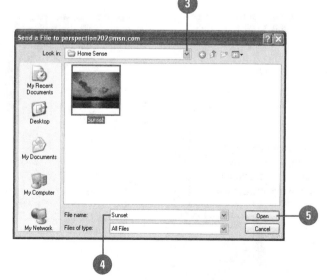

Having a Voice and Video Chat

When used with Windows XP, Windows Messenger provides state-of-the-art computer communications features. With Windows Messenger, you can talk to others over the Internet as you do on a regular phone, and you can use video to see others and let others see you as you converse (New!). Once you set up your computer hardware and software, you're ready to communicate over the Internet. You have two communication choices: audio only, and audio and video. With audio only, you speak into a microphone and hear the other person's response over your computer's speakers. With audio and video, you send video to others so they receive live images as well as sound. If the contacts you call don't have a video camera, they will see you, but you won't see them.

Have a Voice or Video Conversation

1. Double-click the Windows Messenger icon in the notification area of the taskbar, and then sign in, if necessary.

2. Double-click the contact you want to send an instant message.

3. Click Start Talking or Start Camera, and then wait for the other person to accept the invitation.

4. Use the controls to adjust the volume of the speakers or microphone.

5. Start talking.

6. To end the voice or video conversation, click Stop Talking or Stop Camera.

7. Click the Close button.

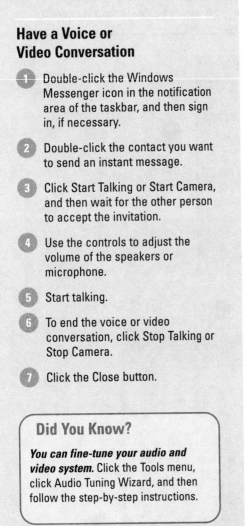

Did You Know?

You can fine-tune your audio and video system. Click the Tools menu, click Audio Tuning Wizard, and then follow the step-by-step instructions.

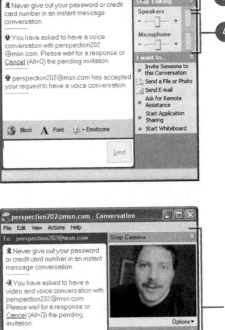

Video and voice conversation

Sharing Graphical Content During a Chat

Windows Messenger includes **whiteboard**, a program that you can use to display and share graphical content. All participants in the Windows Messenger can access a shared whiteboard and make changes interactively to the graphics it displays. A whiteboard can have multiple pages, which users can easily add and delete. You can copy and paste items between the whiteboard and other programs. You can emphasize key points using a highlighter tool or a pointer. Changes to one whiteboard are automatically synchronized with all other whiteboards, unless the user chooses to remove synchronization.

Use the Whiteboard

① Double-click the Windows Messenger icon in the notification area of the taskbar, and then sign in, if necessary.

② Double-click the contact you want to send an instant message.

③ Click Start Whiteboard, and then wait for the other person to accept the invitation.

④ Use the Whiteboard tools to create the graphical content you want to share.

⑤ When you're done, click the Close button.

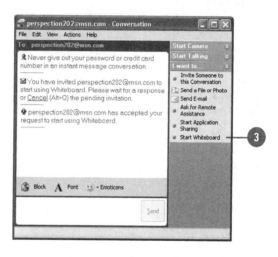

Did You Know?

You can save the content of the Whiteboard. Click the File menu, click Save As, specify a location, and then click Save.

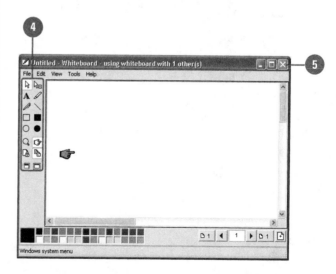

Sharing Programs and Documents

If you need to share information in a specific program or document with others in a conference, you can use Windows Messenger to share your documents and programs. Others can see your document and the program on their computer screens. They cannot work with the document until you give them access to it. The user who clicks the program window "takes control" of the program and can then run any menu commands or make changes to the document. If you have a multi-player game, such as Age of Empires II, installed on both computers, you can play the game using Windows Messenger. Any game installed on your computer that uses the DirectPlayLobby interface appears as an option on the menu.

Share a Program or Document

1. From the desktop, open the program or document you want to share.

2. Double-click the Windows Messenger icon in the notification area of the taskbar, and then sign in, if necessary.

3. Double-click the contact you want to send an instant message.

4. Click Start Application Sharing, and then wait for the other person to accept the invitation.

5. Click App Sharing.

6. Select the item you want to share.

7. Click Share. If you want, share other items.

8. To allow others to control the shared item, click Allow Control.

9. Select the check boxes to specify the type of control you want to allow.

10. When you're done, click the Close button.

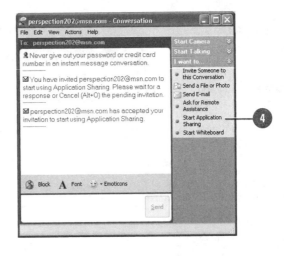

Use the Shared Program or Document

1. Click the shared program or document.

2. Wait for others to ask for control of the program or document. Only one person at a time can have control.

   If you want control of the program or document, click the Control menu, and then click Request Control.

3. Accept or decline the request. If you accept, wait for the person to make changes.

4. To regain control of the program or document, click your mouse.

5. To change sharing setting, click App Sharing, click the program or document you want to change, click Unshare, and then click Close.

6. When you're done, click Close to end the sharing session.

Did You Know?

You can also share your desktop or a folder. Instead of selecting a program or document, you can select the desktop or a folder window.

Getting Remote Assistance

Sometimes the best way to fix a computer problem is to get help from a friend or colleague who knows how to solve it. If your friend or colleague lives too far away to help you in person, you can use Remote Assistance (**New!**) and an Internet connection to help you get the support and answers you need. With Remote Assistance in Windows Messenger, you can ask a trusted contact in another location to connect to your computer over the Internet and provide support in real time. After connecting to your computer, you can invite a contact to view your desktop, chat online using instant messages, talk online using a microphone and speakers, and send files. Instead of simply talking about a solution, sometimes you need someone to show you how to perform the steps before you fully understand the procedure. With Remote Assistance, you can give a contact control of your computer whereby he or she can demonstrate how to perform the procedure using his or her mouse and keyboard while you watch in real time. If your computer is located on a network behind a firewall, you might not be able to use remote assistance; check with your network administrator for details.

Ask for Remote Assistance

1. Double-click the Windows Messenger icon in the notification area of the taskbar, and then sign in, if necessary.

2. Double-click the contact you want to send an instant message.

3. Click Ask For Remote Assistance, and then wait for the other person to accept the invitation.

4. Click Yes to let this person connect to your computer.

5. Type a message to explain your problem, and then press Enter.

6. If you want to talk through your problem, click Start Talking.

7. If the person asks to take control of your computer, click Yes or No.

8. To take back control of your computer, click Stop Control (ESC), or press ESC.

9. When you're done, click Disconnect.

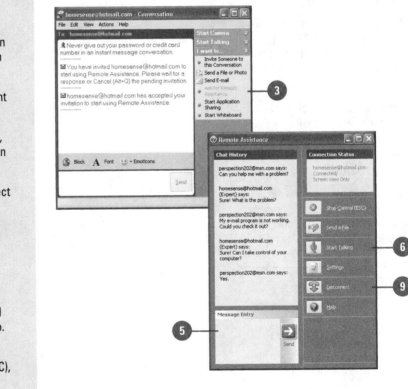

Provide Remote Assistance

1. Sign-in to Windows Messenger, and then wait for an invitation to provide remote assistance.

2. When you receive the invitation, click Accept, and then wait for the Remote Assistance window to open.

3. Type a message to discuss the problem, and then press Enter.

4. If you want to talk through the problem, click Start Talking.

5. Watch the screen of the person you want to help during the conversation.

6. To take control of the person's computer, click the Take Control button on the toolbar, and then wait for the other person's response.

7. Click OK to confirm that you have control.

8. To give back control of the other person's computer, click the Release Control button on the toolbar.

9. When you're done, click Disconnect.

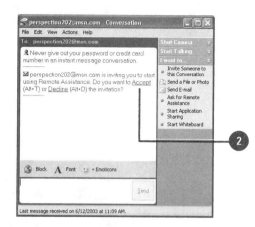

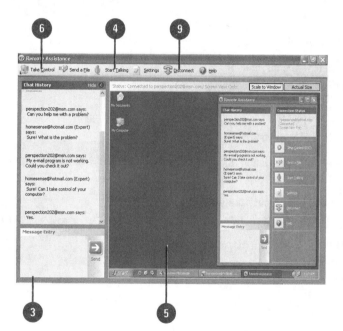

Going to a Chat Room

A **chat room** is a place on the Internet where you can have an online conversation with whom ever is in the room. There are chat rooms for advice, games, business, personal, and a variety of other areas. Unlike an instant message conversation where the people you communicate with are invited to participate, a chat room conversation is open to the public. Anyone can participate in the conversation and read your messages. Windows Messenger makes it easy to access MSN chat rooms (**New!**).

Go to a Chat Room

1. Click the Actions menu, and then click Go To Chat Rooms to open the MSN Chat window.

2. The first time, type an MSN nickname, and then click Save or select one provided.

3. Click a link to a chat room. If necessary, click Yes to download chat software.

4. Type your message in the box at the bottom of the window.

5. Click Send or press Enter, and then wait for a reply.

6. When you're done, click the Close button.

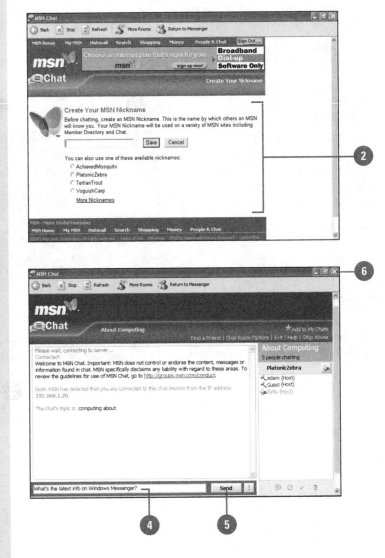

Making a Phone Call with the Internet

Windows Messenger allows you to dial regular phones through a voice service provider using a modem on your computer. Once the modem connects to the number you are dialing, called the **remote party**, you can pick up your phone and talk. This feature is useful for people who spend long periods of time near their computers because it allows them to place calls without first dialing numbers on a phone. When you use Windows Messenger, having your modem's speakers on is helpful so you can hear what is actually happening with the connection. If your computer is located on a network behind a firewall, you might not be able to make phone calls; check with your network administrator for details.

Make a Phone Call

1. Click the Actions menu, and then click Make A Phone Call.

2. If you need a voice service provider, click Get Started Here, and follow the instructions to sign up.

3. Type a phone number, including the area code (even for local calls), and then type a name after it for easy identification on your list.

4. Click Dial.

5. Use the controls to adjust the volume of the speakers or microphone.

6. When you're done, click Hang Up to end the call.

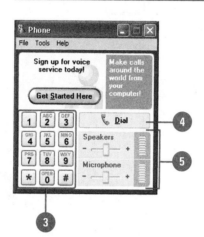

Sending a Message to a Mobile Device

If you have a wireless device, such as a web-enabled cellular phone, a pager, a Microsoft windows CE or Palm OS device, you can set it up to receive instant messages using Windows Messenger (New!). When you send a message to a contact's mobile device, the message includes your e-mail address and phone number unless the mobile device doesn't support the feature. If your contact's mobile device is not turned on, the message might be delayed or not arrive at all.

Set Up an Account for a Mobile Device

1. Click the Tools menu, and then click Edit My Mobile Settings.

2. Click Mobile Settings to open your browser with the MSN Mobile web site.

3. Follow the step-by-step web site instructions.

4. When you're done setting up a mobile account, close your browser, if necessary.

5. Select the Allow People On My Contact List To Send Messages To My Mobile Device check box.

6. Click OK.

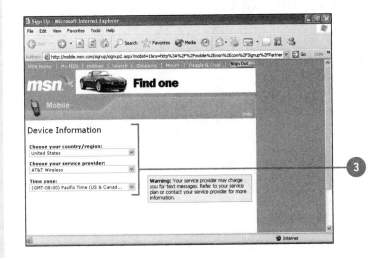

Make Phone Numbers Available to Contacts

1. Click the Tools menu, and then click Publish My Phone Numbers.

2. Click the country you are in, and then type the area code and phone numbers that you want to publish.

3. Click OK.

Send a Message to a Mobile Device

1. Double-click the Windows Messenger icon in the notification area of the taskbar, and then sign in, if necessary.

2. Right-click the contact you want to send a message, and then click Send A Message To A Mobile Device.

   Make sure you have made your phone numbers available to your contacts.

3. Click the phone number at which you can be reached.

4. Type your message.

5. Click Send.

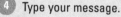

Selecting a Messaging Service

Windows Messenger uses different services to exchange messages, files, and other information. The default service is .NET Messenger Service, which individuals mostly use. For those working in a corporation, Windows Messenger also supports Communications Service for networks that use SIP-server technology, and Exchange Instant Messaging for networks that use Microsoft Exchange Server. You can set up Windows Messenger to access more than one type of messaging service. However, you need to specify which service starts first when you start Windows Messenger.

Select a Messaging Service

1. Click the Tools menu, and then click Options.

2. Click the Accounts tab.

3. Select the option with the primary account in which you want to sign in.

4. If you want, select the check box of another messaging service, and then include sign-in information.

5. Click OK.

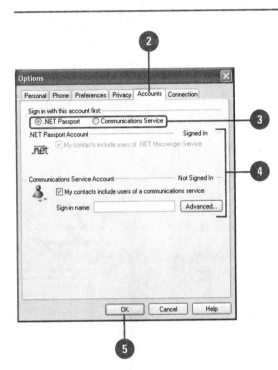

Working with Pictures

Introduction

Windows XP makes it easy to store and work with your pictures using the My Pictures folder. You can quickly access the folder from the Start menu. From the My Pictures folder you can view, organize, and share pictures with others on the Internet. When you download and save pictures from your digital camera or scanner to your computer, Windows stores the digital images in the My Pictures folder by default. (You can specify an alternative location.) You can view your picture files as a slide show or in the Filmstrip view, which displays a larger image above thumbnail images of the pictures. The My Pictures folder also contains links to specialized picture tasks that help you share pictures with others, such as sending pictures in an e-mail, publishing pictures and documents on the Web, printing photographs, and ordering prints from the Internet. You can also create your own pictures or edit existing ones in Paint, a Windows accessory program designed for drawing and painting. Paint is useful for making simple changes to a picture, adding a text caption, or saving a picture in another file format.

Drawing a Picture

Paint is a Windows accessory you can use to create and work with graphics or pictures. Paint is designed to create and edit bitmap (.bmp) files, but you can also open and save pictures created in or for other graphics programs and the Internet using several common file formats, such as .tiff, .gif, or .jpeg. A **bitmap** file is a map of a picture created from small black, white, or colored dots, or bits. Paint comes with a set of tools in the Toolbox located along the left edge of the window you can use for drawing and manipulating pictures. A tool remains turned on until you select another tool in the Toolbox. In addition to the drawing tools, you can also add text to a picture. When you create a text box and type the text, you can edit and format it, but once you deselect the text box, the text becomes part of the picture, which you can't edit.

Draw a Picture

1. Click the Start button, point to All Programs, point to Accessories, and then click Paint.

2. If you want, drag a resize handle on the canvas to resize it.

3. Click a drawing tool.

4. If available, click a fill option for the selected tool.

5. Click the color you want to use with the left mouse button to select the foreground color and the right mouse button to select the background color.

6. Drag the shapes you want by holding down one of the following:

   ◆ The left mouse button to draw with the foreground color

   ◆ The right mouse button to draw with the background color

   ◆ The Shift key to constrain the drawing to a proportional size, such as a circle, square, or horizontal line

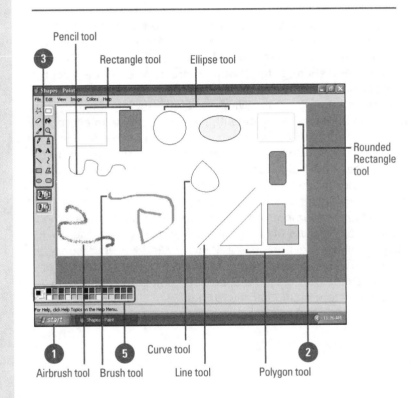

Pencil tool

Rectangle tool

Ellipse tool

Rounded Rectangle tool

Curve tool

Airbrush tool   Brush tool   Line tool   Polygon tool

Add Text to a Picture

1. In Paint, create or open the picture you want to modify.

2. Click the Text tool.

3. Drag a text box.

4. Select the font, font size, and any formatting you want to apply to the text.

5. Click in the text box, if necessary, and then type the text.

6. Drag a text box resize handle to enlarge or reduce the text box.

7. Edit and format the text.

8. Click outside the text box to deselect it and change the text to a bitmap.

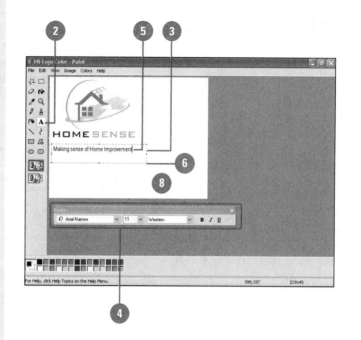

Save a Picture in Different Formats

1. In Paint, create or open the picture you want to save in a different format.

2. Click the File menu, and then click Save As.

3. Select the drive and folder in which you want to save the file.

4. Type a name for the file, or use the suggested name.

5. Click the Save As Type list arrow, and then click a file format.

6. Click Save.

Editing a Picture

After you create or open a picture, you can select all or part of the picture and use commands on the Image menu, such as rotate, stretch, and invert colors, to further modify it in Paint. In addition to the drawing tools, you can also use painting tools, such as Fill With Color, Airbrush, Brush, Pencil, and Pick Color, to transform the picture. The Fill With Color tool is useful if you want to color an entire item or recolor text letter by letter. If you need to remove part of a picture, you can use the Eraser tool, which comes in four different sizes.

Modify a Picture

1. In Paint, create or open the picture you want to edit.

2. Click the Free-Form Select tool to select irregular shapes, or click the Select tool to select rectangle shapes.

3. Drag the selection area you want.

4. Click the Opaque Background option or the Transparent Background option.

5. Click the Image menu, and then click one of the following:

   ◆ Flip/Rotate

   ◆ Stretch/Skew

   ◆ Invert Colors

   ◆ Attributes to change the canvas size.

Change picture stretch and skew

Did You Know?

You can save part of a picture to a file. Select the part of the picture you want to save, click the Edit menu, click Copy To, select a folder, type a name, and then click Save.

You can quickly copy a selection. Hold down the Ctrl key, and then drag the selection.

Fill Part of a Picture

① In Paint, create or open the picture you want to edit.

② Click the color you want to fill, or click the Pick Color tool and click a color from the picture.

③ Click the Fill With Color tool.

④ Point the tip of the paint bucket to the area you want to fill, and then click.

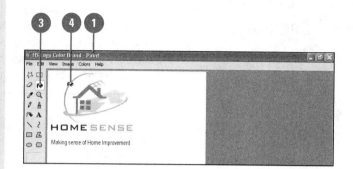

Erase Part of a Picture

① In Paint, create or open the picture you want to edit.

② To magnify an area of the screen, click the Magnifier tool, and then click the area you want to magnify.

③ Click the Eraser tool.

④ Click the Eraser size.

⑤ Drag the Eraser over the area you want to erase.

⑥ If you make a mistake, click the Edit menu, and then click Undo to restore your last action.

⑦ To restore the magnification, click the Magnifier tool, and then click the area again.

Did You Know?

You can replace any color with the background color. Set the foreground color to the color to be replaced and the background color to the replacement color, and then hold down the right mouse button and drag the Eraser over the area you want to replace.

Installing a Scanner or Digital Camera

Windows XP makes it easy to install a scanner or digital camera on your computer using plug-and-play. In most cases, all you need to do is turn off your computer, plug in the hardware device, and restart your computer. Windows recognizes the new hardware and installs it. If for some reason Windows doesn't recognize the hardware, you can start a wizard (**New!**), which walks you through the installation process.

Install a Scanner or Digital Camera

1. Plug your scanner or camera into your computer to start the Scanner And Camera wizard.

   If the wizard doesn't open, click the Start button, click Control Panel, double-click the Scanners And Cameras icon, and then click Add An Imaging Device.

2. Click Next.

3. Click the manufacturer of the scanner or camera you want to install, click the device name, and then click Next.

   TROUBLE? *If your scanner or camera is not listed, try to install it using the Device Manager.*

4. Connect your device to your computer, select a port, and then click Next.

5. Type a name for the device, or use the suggested one, and then click Next.

6. Click Finish.

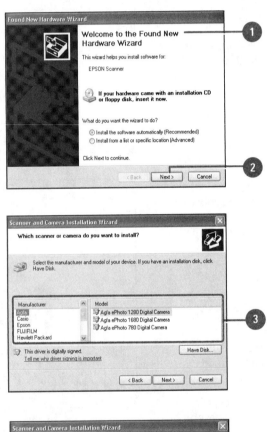

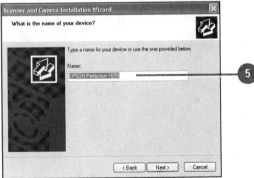

Testing a Scanner or Digital Camera

After you install a scanner or digital camera on your computer, it's a good idea to test the hardware device to make sure it's working properly. When you test a scanner or digital camera, Windows XP checks to see if the hardware device is communicating with the operating system (**New!**).

Install a Scanner or Digital Camera

1 Click the Start button, click Control Panel, and then double-click the Scanners And Cameras icon in Classic view.

2 Right-click the scanner or camera you want to test, and then click Properties.

3 Click the General tab.

4 Click Test Scanner or Test Camera.

A message appears with the results of the test.

5 Click OK.

6 Click OK.

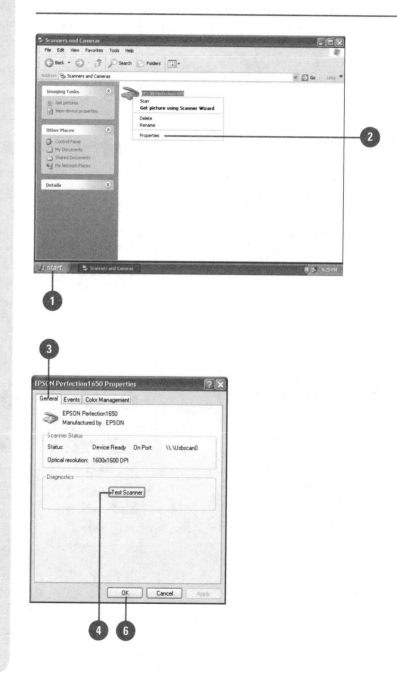

Scanning a Picture

Windows XP makes it easy to scan pictures with the Scanner And Camera Wizard (**New!**). A **scanner** is like a photocopy machine on which you can lay photographs, books, and other documents that you want to save in digital form on your computer. In addition to scanning photographs, many high resolution scanners also allow you to scan a negative from a film strip and enlarge it. With the Scanner And Camera Wizard, you can choose scanning preferences, such as picture type, preview the scanned picture, adjust the scan area, and select a graphic format. As you complete the Scanner And Camera Wizard, you can also choose to publish the scanned pictures to a web site or order prints from a Web site service. In order to use the scanner features of Windows XP, you need to have a scanner attached and installed on your computer.

Scan a Picture

1 Click the Start button, click Control Panel, and then double-click the Scanners And Cameras icon in Classic view.

2 Place the picture on the scanner, and then double-click the Scanner icon.

3 Click a picture type option.

4 To change the resolution and color options, click Custom Settings.

5 Click Preview.

6 If you want, drag the resize handles to change the selected area.

TROUBLE? *If you accidentally click the Preview pane instead of a red resize handle, the selection rectangle changes to a dot. Use the cross-hairs cursor to reselect the picture with green resize handles at the corners.*

7 Click Next.

8 Type a name.

9 Click the File Format list arrow, and then click a file format.

10 If you want, click Browse, select a folder location where you want to save the pictures, and then click OK.

11 Click Next to scan the picture.

12 When it's done, click the Nothing. I'm Finished Working With These Pictures option or a publishing option, and then click Next.

13 Click Finish.

Windows saves the pictures in consecutive order as Family Pictures, Family Pictures 001, Family Pictures 002, and so on.

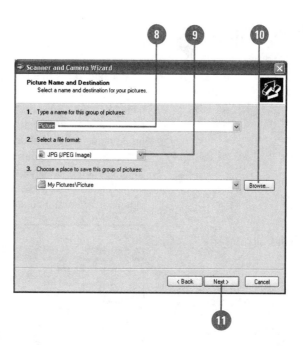

See Also

See "Installing a Scanner or Digital Camera" on page 204 for information on installing a scanner.

See "Installing a Scanner or Digital Camera" on page 204 for information on installing a scanner.

For Your Information

Selecting the Appropriate File Format

Each file type has a different format and recommended use. JPG (Joint Photographic Experts Group; also known as JPEG) and PNG (Portable Network Graphics) are graphic file formats commonly used on web pages, while BMP (Bit-mapped) and TIF (Tagged Image File Format, also known as Tiff) are file formats used in documents. The format specifies how the information in the file is organized internally. JPG and PNG formats are compressible, which means that the file size is smaller and transfers over the Internet faster. Each file format uses a different compression method, which produces different results when you display the graphic files. JPG is designed for photographs and supports millions of colors, but loses some image quality by discarding image data to reduce the file size. PNG is designed for web graphics and supports millions of color without losing image quality, but not all web browsers fully support its capabilities without using a plug-in, which is a software add-on installed on your computer. TIF is designed for all graphics and colors and one of the most widely used graphic formats, but the file size is large. BMP is the standard Windows graphic format and is similar to TIF.

Downloading Digital Camera Pictures

The Scanner And Camera Wizard guides you through the process of downloading pictures from a digital still camera. A **digital still camera** stores pictures digitally rather than on film. The major advantage of digital still cameras is that making photos is fast and inexpensive. With the Scanner And Camera Wizard (**New!**), you can view pictures that you have already taken with the camera and save them in a folder on your computer, view device properties, delete pictures from your camera, or print photos. Instead of using the Scanner And Camera Wizard to work with digital camera pictures, you can also open the Camera window from My Computer and manage pictures from the window. In order to use the digital camera features of Windows XP, you need to have a digital still or video camera attached and installed on your computer.

Download Pictures from a Camera

1. Connect the digital camera to your computer, select an option to start the Scanner And Camera Wizard or open the digital camera in the Scanners And Cameras window.

2. Click Next to download thumbnail images from your camera.

3. Select or clear the check boxes for the pictures you want or don't want, and then click Next.

4. Type a name, or select an existing name for the pictures.

5. If you want, click Browse, and then select a folder location where you want to save the pictures.

6. If you want, select the Delete Pictures From My Device After Copying Them check box.

7. Click Next, and then wait for the pictures to download.

8. Click the Nothing. I'm Finished Working With These Pictures option or a publishing option, and then click Next.

9. Click Finish.

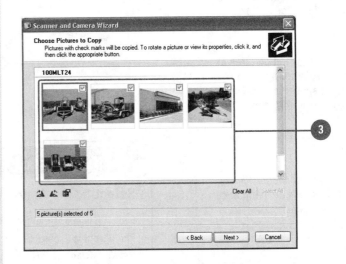

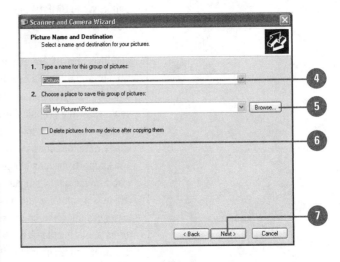

Manage Pictures on the Camera

1. Click the Start button, and then click My Computer.

2. Double-click the digital camera icon, and then wait for the thumbnail images from your camera to appear.

3. Click a picture, and then perform any of the following commands:

    ◆ Right-click a picture, and then click Save In My Pictures.

    ◆ Double-click a picture to display the picture using the Windows Picture And Fax Viewer.

    ◆ Click Delete This File or Delete All Pictures On Camera.

4. When you're done, click the Close button.

Show Camera Properties

1. Click the Start button, and then click My Computer.

2. Double-click the digital camera icon, and then wait for the thumbnail images from your camera to appear.

3. Click Show Camera Properties.

4. Change the properties you want; each camera displays different properties.

5. Click OK.

6. When you're done, click the Close button.

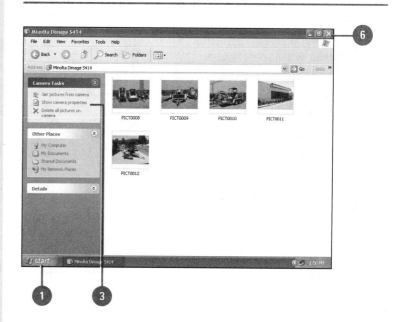

Taking Pictures from a Digital Camera

The Scanner And Camera Wizard guides you through the process of taking pictures from a video camera or digital still camera. A digital video camera displays live or recorded digital video, which is higher in quality than nondigital. With the Scanner And Camera Wizard (New!), you can capture digital snap shots or view those that you have taken already and save them in a folder on your computer, view device properties, delete pictures from your camera, or print photos. In order to use the digital camera features of Windows XP, you need to have a digital still or video camera attached and installed on your computer.

Take a Picture from a Digital Video Camera

1. Connect the video camera to your computer, select an option to start the Scanner And Camera Wizard or open the video camera in the Scanners And Cameras window.

2. Click Next, and then display the image you want.

3. Click the Take Picture button.

4. Select or clear the check boxes for the pictures you want or don't want to download, and then click Next.

5. Type a name, or click the list arrow to select an existing picture name.

6. If you want, click Browse, and then select a folder location where you want to save the pictures.

7. If you want, select the Delete Pictures From My Device After Copying Them check box.

8. Click Next, and then wait for the pictures to download.

9. Click the Nothing. I'm Finished Working With These Pictures option or a publishing option, and then click Next.

10. Click Finish.

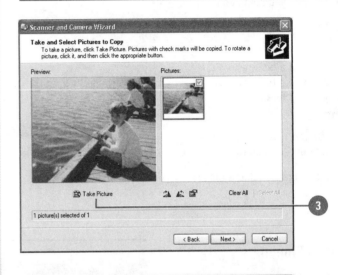

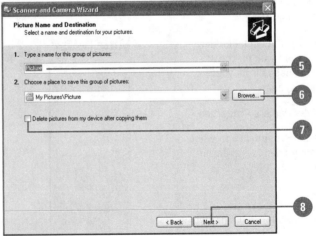

Take a Picture from a Digital Camera

1 Connect the digital camera to your computer, select an option to start the Scanner And Camera Wizard or open the digital camera in the Scanners And Cameras window.

2 Click Next.

3 Focus the camera on the subject of the picture.

> **TROUBLE?** *This functionality is not available for all digital cameras. Check your camera documentation for details.*

4 Click Take Picture.

5 Click Next.

6 Follow the rest of the Scanner And Camera Wizard instructions.

See Also

See "Downloading Digital Camera Pictures" on page 208 for information on using the Scanner And Camera Wizard.

Did You Know?

You can work directly on the camera. When the Scanner And Camera Wizard opens, click the Advanced Users Only link to view the contents of the camera in a folder window.

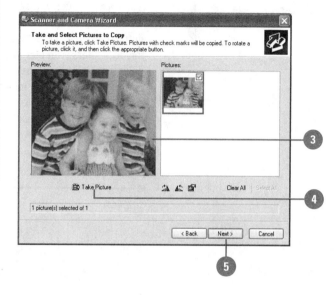

For Your Information

Taking Pictures from the Camera Window

You can also open the Camera window from My Computer and take snap shots in the window. As you take pictures, you can delete individual pictures or all the pictures and save them to your My Pictures folder. To view pictures from the Camera window, click the Start button on the taskbar, click My Computer, and then double-click the Camera icon to open the Camera window. Windows initializes the camera and displays a real-time image. To take a picture, click Take A New Picture in the task pane. The picture appears as a thumbnail at the bottom of the window. You can continue to take pictures, save them to the My Pictures folder, or delete them. To delete or save an individual picture, right-click it, and then click Delete or Save in My Pictures. To delete all the pictures, click Delete All Pictures On Camera in the task pane.

Viewing Pictures

Windows XP gives you several ways to view pictures in a folder. In a picture folder, you can use Filmstrip view (**New!**) to see a larger view of the pictures in a full screen slide show. Filmstrip is a special view available only for folders with pictures. Filmstrip view also includes buttons to make it easy to switch between pictures. If you have a mixture of documents and pictures in a folder or if you receive faxes sent directly to your computer, the best way to view the pictures is to open them in the Windows Picture and Fax Viewer, which is a simple graphics program that comes with Windows XP that allows you to quickly view and annotate select pictures. You can also open the picture in Paint or another editing program to make changes.

View a Picture

1 Open the folder window containing the picture you want to view.

2 Double-click the picture.

> **TROUBLE?** *In Filmstrip view, double-clicking the preview picture doesn't open it. Double-click a thumbnail image.*

3 Use the controls at the bottom of the window to change the picture view or modify it.

4 When you're done, click the Close button.

Did You Know?

You can annotate a picture in the TIF format. When a TIF picture is displayed in the viewer, annotation buttons appear for annotating faxes.

See Also

See "Viewing and Annotating a Fax" on page 368 for information on working with faxes.

View Pictures as a Filmstrip

1. Click the Start button, click My Pictures, and then open the picture folder you want to view.

2. Click the Views button, and then click Filmstrip.

3. Click the Next Image or Previous Image button to view the images in sequence.

   TIMESAVER *Press the Right arrow or Left arrow key to display the images.*

4. To rotate a picture, click the picture, and then click the Rotate buttons.

View Pictures as a Slide Show

1. Click the Start button, click My Pictures, and then open the picture folder you want to view.

2. Select the pictures you want in the show, or click one picture to see all the pictures.

3. Click View As A Slide Show in the task pane, and then watch the show.

4. To manually advance to the next slide, click anywhere in the picture.

5. To control the slide show, move the mouse to display the controls, and then use the toolbar to play, pause, move back or forward, or end the slide show.

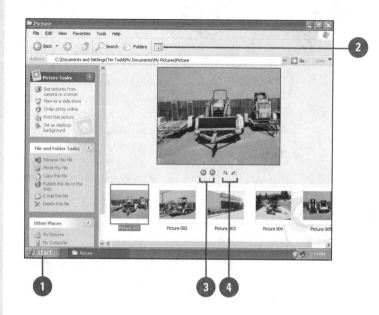

Making a Photo Album

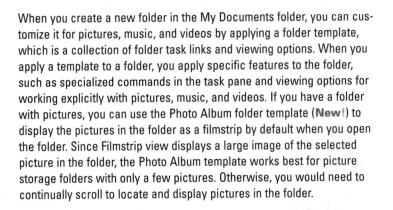

When you create a new folder in the My Documents folder, you can customize it for pictures, music, and videos by applying a folder template, which is a collection of folder task links and viewing options. When you apply a template to a folder, you apply specific features to the folder, such as specialized commands in the task pane and viewing options for working explicitly with pictures, music, and videos. If you have a folder with pictures, you can use the Photo Album folder template (**New!**) to display the pictures in the folder as a filmstrip by default when you open the folder. Since Filmstrip view displays a large image of the selected picture in the folder, the Photo Album template works best for picture storage folders with only a few pictures. Otherwise, you would need to continually scroll to locate and display pictures in the folder.

Make a Photo Album

1. Right-click the folder you want to make a photo album, and then click Properties.

2. Click the Customize tab.

3. Click the Use This Folder Type As A Template list arrow, and then click Photo Album (Best For Fewer Files).

4. If you want, select the Apply This Template To All Subfolders check box.

5. Click OK.

6. Double-click the folder to display the pictures in Flimstrip view.

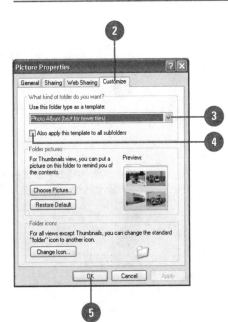

Did You Know?

You can display Thumbnail view by default. Right-click the folder, click Properties, click the Customize tab, select the Pictures template, and then click OK.

E-Mailing a Picture

If you have one or more photos, pictures, or documents that you want to share with others, you can send them in an e-mail as attachments. Before you send photos or pictures in an e-mail as an attachment, you typically need to resize them in a separate graphics program so your recipient can view them with minimal scrolling, open your e-mail program, and then attach the files. With Windows XP you can send a photo or picture in an e-mail message without having to resize it in a separate graphics program, or even open your e-mail program. Using the E-Mail command (**New!**) in the task pane of any folder window, Windows XP simply asks how you want to size the photos and pictures, and then opens an e-mail message window with the attached files from your default e-mail program. All you need to do is address the message, add any message text, and then send it.

E-Mail a Picture

1. Open the folder containing the picture you want to send in e-mail.

2. Select the picture.

3. Click E-Mail This File.

4. Click the Make All My Pictures Smaller or Keep The Original Sizes option.

5. To select a specific picture size, click Show More Options.

6. Click OK to open your e-mail program, displaying an e-mail message with a file attachment.

7. Type an e-mail address.

8. Click Send.

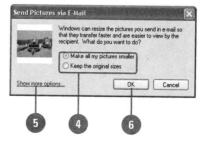

See Also

See "Sending and Retrieving a File" on page 156 for information on sending a file in an e-mail message.

Publishing Pictures to the Web

If you have many pictures to share with others, you can publish them to the web. With the Web Publishing Wizard (**New!**), you can copy an individual file or a folder of files from your computer to a web site or network location, such as a shared folder. When you publish your files to a web site, you can let others view your pictures and documents using their web browser. If you don't have a web site on which to publish your files, you can create a personal web site in MSN Groups. After you publish a file or folder to the web, Windows places a shortcut link to that web site in My Network Places on your computer. When you are connected to the Internet, you can access your published files from My Network Places and add or delete the files in the same way you would on any network.

Publish Files or a Folder to the Web

1. Open the folder containing the picture or folder you want to publish.

2. Select the picture(s) or folder.

3. Click Publish The Selected Items To The Web or Publish This Folder To The Web.

4. Click Next.

5. If you want, select or clear the check boxes next to files to include or exclude them, and then click Next.

6. Select MSN Groups, and then click Next.

   TROUBLE? *If a connection dialog box opens, type your .Net Passport user name and password, and then click OK or click Get A .NET Password to create an account.*

7. Select where you want your files to be stored (create a new group or select an existing one), and then click Next.

8. Follow the specific instructions for your selection.

9. Click Finish.

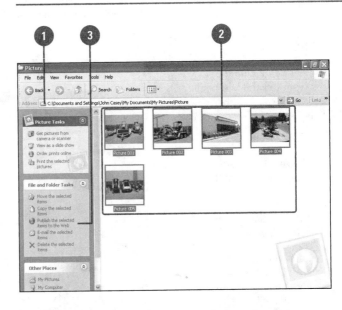

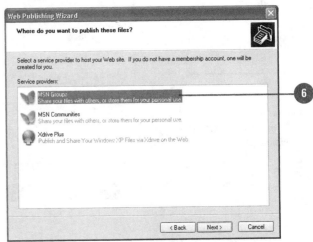

View the Published Files

① Open your web browser.

② Type the web address given when you published the files, and then press Enter.

③ Click Pictures.

④ Use links on the page to add, reposition, or delete pictures, and then change permissions to the web site.

⑤ When you're done, click the Close button.

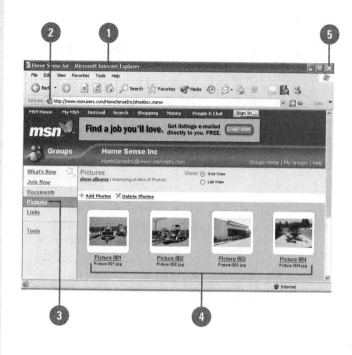

Frequently Asked Questions

What are MSN Groups?

MSN Groups is a service that allows you to create a personal web site to display pictures and documents, and to create an online community to share messages, create a photo album, hold chat sessions, manage a calendar (available for a fee), and add web pages to your site. You don't have to be an MSN member to use MSN Groups, but you do need to have a Microsoft .NET Passport. You can obtain a .NET Passport when you associate an existing e-mail address with a User Account using the .NET Passport Wizard, or you can sign up for a free Hotmail or MSN e-mail account during the setup process.

Formatting and Printing Photos

Windows XP makes it easy to format and print photographs with the Photo Printing Wizard (New!), which allows you to print photographs from a digital camera, scanner, or your computer. With the wizard, you can select the photo(s) to print, the paper type, and a page layout, such as full-page prints, contact-sheet prints, 8 x 10-inch prints, 5 x 7-inch prints, 4 x 6-inch prints, and wallet size prints. To print a photo from your computer, you need a color printer and special photo paper. In order to get the best results when you print photographs, set your printer resolution to the highest setting for the best quality output, and use high-quality glossy paper designed specifically for printing photographs. Check your printer documentation for the best resolution setting suited to print your photographs. When you print photographs with a high resolution setting, the printing process might take longer. Many printer manufacturers also make paper designed to work best with their printers; check your printer manufacturer's web site for more information.

Format and Print a Photo

1 Open the folder containing the picture or folder you want to print.

2 Select the picture(s).

3 Click Print This Picture or Print The Selected Pictures.

4 Click Next.

5 If you want, select or clear the check boxes next to files to include or exclude them, and then click Next.

6 Click the Printer list arrow, and then select a printer.

7 If you want, click Printing Preferences to change printer settings, and then click OK.

8 Click Next.

9 Select the printer layout you want to use; scroll, if necessary.

10 Click Next.

11 Click Finish.

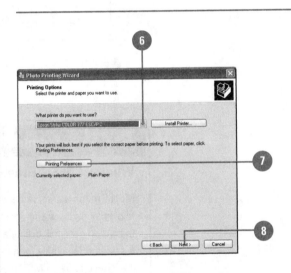

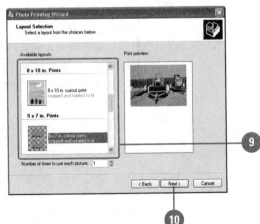

Ordering Photo Prints from the Web

If you have digital photographs taken from a digital camera or scanned into your computer, you can send your digital photographs to an online printing company where they create photo prints and send them to your mailing address. Windows XP makes the process easy with the Online Print Ordering Wizard (**New!**), which walks you through the ordering process. You'll need to provide print sizes, quantities, and billing and shipping information to complete the order.

Order Photo Prints from the Web

1. Open the folder containing the picture or folder you want to print.

2. Select the picture(s).

3. Click Order Prints Online, and then click Next.

4. If you want, select or clear the check boxes next to files to include or exclude them, and then click Next.

5. Select a printing company, and then click Next.

6. Follow the remaining steps to place an order with the specific printing company.

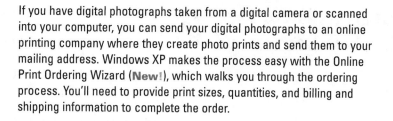

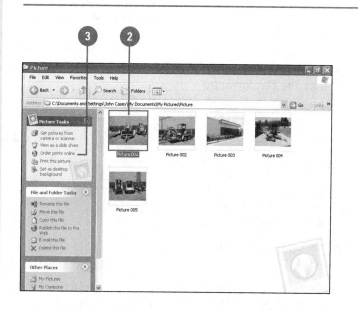

Using a Picture as a Desktop Background

Instead of using one of the pictures provided by Windows XP, you can select a picture on your hard disk or from a web page as the desktop background. You can use Paint or any graphics program to create new background designs or change existing ones. Acceptable formats for background files are Bitmap (the format of a Paint file), JPEG (the format of an Internet graphic file), or HTM (the format of a web page). After you set a picture as the desktop background, Windows adds the picture to the Background list on the Desktop tab in the Display Properties dialog box. When you use a picture from a web page, Windows saves it in the Background list as Internet Explorer Background. Each new picture from a web page you set as a background replaces the previous one.

Set a Picture as the Background

1. Open the folder or the web page with the picture you want to set as the background.

2. Right-click the picture.

3. Click Set As Desktop Background for a picture file, or click Set As Background for a web picture.

   If the picture doesn't appear on your desktop, continue.

4. Right-click a blank area of the desktop, and then click Properties.

5. Click the Desktop tab.

6. Click the picture you set as the background.

7. Click OK.

Did You Know?

You can access the files in the Background list. Open the Windows folder, then the Web folder, then the Wallpaper folder, from which you can remove, rename, or modify them.

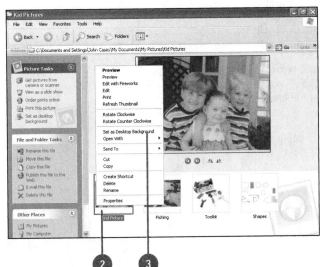

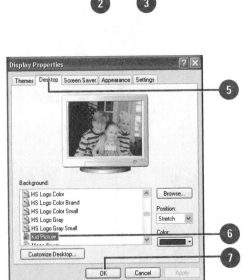

Using Pictures as a Screen Saver

Instead of using screen savers provided by Windows XP, you can use your own pictures to create a slide show screen saver. Windows displays all the pictures in a folder that you create as a full screen slide show. You can add or remove pictures from the folder to modify the slide show.

Use Pictures as a Screen Saver

1 Click the Start button, and then click My Documents.

2 Create a folder, and then place the pictures you want to use in the slide show in the folder.

3 Right-click a blank area of the desktop, and then click Properties.

4 Click the Screen Saver tab.

5 Click the Screen Saver list arrow, and then click My Pictures Slideshow.

6 Click Settings.

7 Click Browse, select the folder with your pictures, and then click OK.

8 Specify the size and for how long you want the pictures to appear in the slide show, and then click OK.

9 Click OK.

10 Click Preview, and then click the mouse to stop it.

11 Click OK.

See Also

See "Using a Screen Saver" on page 87 for more information on screen savers.

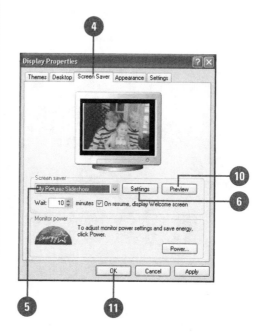

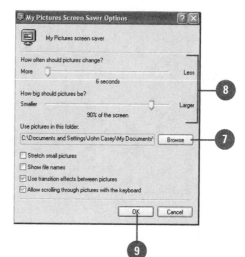

8

Working with Windows Media Player and Sound

Introduction

You can use Windows Media Player (WMP version 10, designed for Windows XP Service Pack 2, NewSP2) to play sounds, music, and digital movies on your computer and on the Internet, or listen to radio stations from all over the world. In addition, you can play and copy CDs, rip music from CDs, create your own CDs, play DVDs or VCDs, and copy music and videos to portable devices, such as portable media players, portable media centers, and Pocket PCs. Using Windows Media Player requires a sound card, speakers, and an Internet connection to view the Guide and other online stores, look for music licenses, and listen to radio stations on the Internet.

When you play music from the Internet, Windows Media Player uses streaming, which is a method of delivering audio and video files across a network or the Internet without downloading an entire file before it plays. All streaming media files buffer before playing. Buffering is the process of sending a certain amount of information to the computer before the content actually plays. Windows Media Player monitors network conditions and makes adjustments to ensure the best reception and playback. If the information in the buffer runs out, you will notice a break in the playback. When a file finishes playing, it is not stored on your computer.

Windows also comes with Sound Recorder, a sound recording utility program you can use to create and modify a sound. You can use the sound to indicate a Windows event, such as starting Windows or an error, has occurred. Using Sound Recorder requires a sound card, speakers, and a microphone.

Starting and Updating Windows Media Player

Before you can use Windows Media Player 10, you need to check to make sure you have version 10 installed on your computer using the About Windows Media Player command on the Help menu for the current player. If it's not, you can download and install it from the web at *www.microsoft.com/window/windowsmedia/mp10/*. You start Windows Media Player like any other Windows program. You can use the Start menu or a button on the Quick Launch toolbar. After you start Windows Media Player, you should check for software updates on the Internet. Microsoft is continually adding features and fixing problems. You can use the Help menu in Windows Media Player to access the updates.

Start and Update Windows Media Player

1 Click the Start button, point to All Programs, and then click Windows Media Player.

2 Click the Help menu, and then click Check For Player Updates.

3 Follow the wizard instructions to complete the upgrade.

Did You Know?

You can show and hide the menu bar. (New10) To show the menu bar, click the down arrow in the upper-right corner, and then click Show Menu Bar. To hide the menu bar, click the View menu, point to Menu Bar Options, and then click Hide Menu Bar.

You can automatically check for software updates. Click the Tools menu, click Options, click the Player tab, and then click the Once A Day, Once A Week, or Once A Month option.

You can display Media Player as a button on the taskbar. Right-click a blank area of the taskbar, point to Toolbars, and then click Windows Media Player.

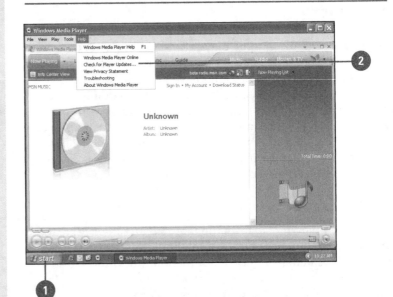

For Your Information

What's New in Windows Media Player 10

Windows Media Player 10 (New10) comes with a new streamline design that makes it easier to access top activities and common tasks, such as ripping from CDs, burning to CDs, syncing to portable devices, and choosing an online store from the Digital Media Mall. The menu bar is hidden by default, which you can show or AutoHide. You can resize the Player to mini Player mode to it available while you work. The WMP supports more than 70 portable music devices and the new Auto Sync feature makes it easy to take your music with you. The improved Library takes the hassle of managing large media collections. WMP is designed to take advantage of the security features in SP2 (NewSP2).

Viewing the Media Player Window (New10)

Mini Player

Show Video and Visual-
ization window button

Quick Access
Panel button

Playback
controls

Restore button;
change to
full player

Full Player

Tabs

Media Information
pane; music files

Display
menus

Minimize button;
change to the
mini-player

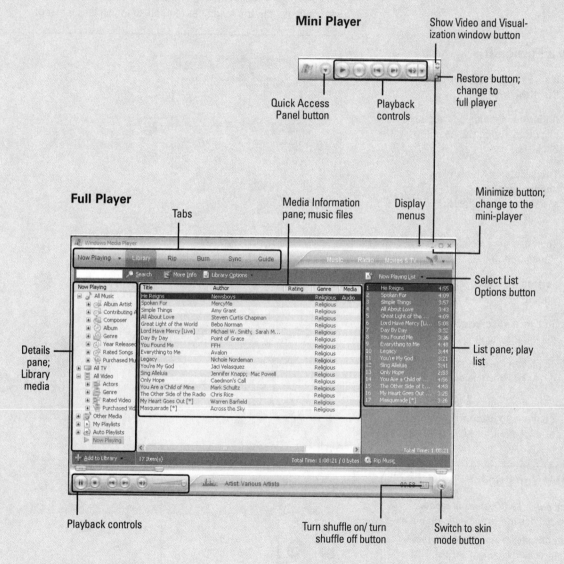

Details
pane;
Library
media

Select List
Options button

List pane; play
list

Playback controls

Turn shuffle on/ turn
shuffle off button

Switch to skin
mode button

Playing Music from CDs

Windows allows you to play music on your computer in the background while you work. After you insert a music CD into your CD-ROM drive and the music starts to play, you can minimize Windows Media Player and continue to work with other programs on your computer. If you are connected to the Internet when you play a music CD, Windows Media Player tries to locate information about the CD from the Internet, such as the name of the artist and the songs on the album. If the information is not available, the track number of each song displays instead.

Play a Music CD

1 Insert a music CD into your CD-ROM drive.

2 If the Audio dialog box appears, click Play Audio CD, and then click OK.

The Windows Media Player window appears, and the CD starts to play on the Now Playing tab.

3 To pause the music, click the Pause button.

4 To stop the music, click the Stop button.

5 To play a specific song, double-click the song in the list.

6 To play the previous or next song, click the Previous or Next button.

7 Click the Minimize button to continue to listen while you work, or click the Close button to exit.

Did You Know?

You can play CD songs in random order. Click the Turn Shuffle On button.

You can stop a song from playing. Right-click the song in the list, and then click Disable Selected Tracks.

You can play a CD continuously. Click the Play menu, and then click Repeat.

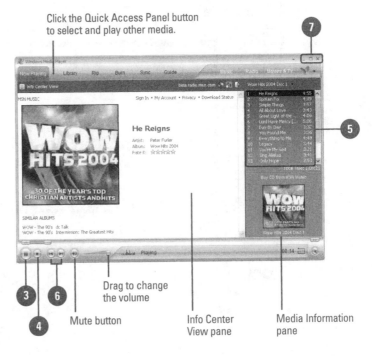

Click the Quick Access Panel button to select and play other media.

Drag to change the volume

Mute button

Info Center View pane

Media Information pane

Playing a DVD or VCD Movie

If you have a DVD drive and decoder hardware or software on your computer, you can play DVD movies with Windows Media Player. If you don't have a decoder, you can purchase one from a third party manufacturer. If you only have a CD player, you can play VCD movies (New 10). A VCD is similar to a DVD, yet the video quality is not as high. When you play a DVD or VCD movie, a list of titles appear with a section of content from the movie. You can use the titles to browse through the contents of the DVD or VCD.

Play a DVD or VCD Movie

1. Insert a DVD into your DVD drive or a VCD into your CD drive.

2. If the Audio dialog box appears, click the option to play the DVD or VCD, and then click OK.

   The Windows Media Player window appears, and the DVD or VCD starts to play.

3. To expand the contents list of the DVD or VCD click the plus sign (+).

4. To pause the movie, click the Pause button.

5. To stop the movie, click the Stop button.

6. To play a specific title, double-click it in the list.

   TIMESAVER *Press Alt+Enter to switch to Full Screen mode.*

7. To play the previous or next section of the movie, click the Previous or Next button.

8. Click the Close button to exit.

Did You Know?

You can display captions and subtitles for a DVD. Click the Play menu, point to Captions And Subtitles, and then click On If Available or the language you want to use.

Click the Quick Access Panel button to select and play other media.

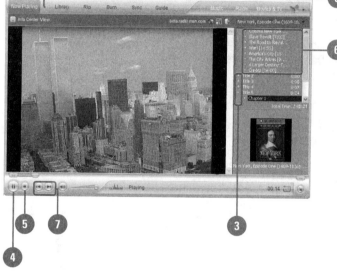

For Your Information

Using the Mini Player

The mini player is a small Windows Media Player that fits on the taskbar. The mini player makes is easy to use Windows Media Player while you work with other programs. You have access to the playback controls and view visualizations and information about the currently playing item. To use the mini player, right-click an open area of the taskbar, point to Toolbars, and then click Windows Media Player. In WMP, click the Minimize button to display the mini player. Click the Restore button to display WMP in full screen mode.

9

Controlling the Volume

Windows comes with master volume controls that allow you to change the volume of all devices on the computer at once. You can increase or decrease the volume, or you can mute (turn off) the sound on your computer. If you frequently change the volume on your computer, you can display the volume control on the notification area on the taskbar. The Speaker icon makes it easy to increase or decrease the volume or mute the sound on your computer. In addition to changing the master volume on your computer, you can also adjust the volume of specific devices, such as a CD or DVD player, without affecting the volume of other devices.

Change the Computer Volume

1. Click the Start button, and then click Control Panel.

2. Double-click the Sounds And Audio Devices icon in Classic view.

3. Click the Volume tab.

4. Drag the slider to increase or decrease the volume.

5. To turn off the sound, select the Mute check box.

6. To display a Volume icon on the taskbar, select the Place Volume Icon In The Taskbar check box.

7. Click OK.

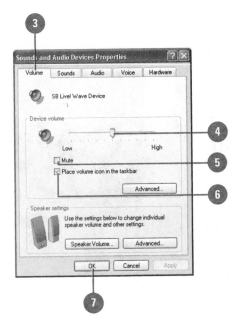

Did You Know?

The volume control is always available. Click the volume icon in the notification area on the taskbar, and then drag the volume slider, or select or clear the Mute check box.

You can change the volume for each speaker separately. On the Volume tab, click Speaker Volume, and then drag the slider for each speaker.

Troubleshooting

Testing Your Sound Hardware

If your are having trouble hearing the sound from Windows Media Player, the best place to start is to test your sound hardware. Click the Start button, click Control Panel, double-click the Sounds And Audio Devices icon in Classic view, click the Voice tab, click Text Hardware, click Next, follow the instructions to test the hardware, click Finish, and then click OK.

Set Volume Levels for Specific Devices

1. Double-click the Volume icon on the taskbar.

2. Click the Options menu, and then click Properties.

3. Click the Playback option.

4. Select the check boxes for the devices you want to display or clear the ones you don't want.

5. Click OK.

6. Drag the sliders to adjust the settings for the devices you want.

7. When you're done, click the Close button.

Did You Know?

You can set the recording volume.
Double-click the Volume icon, click the Options menu, click Properties, click the Recording option, click OK, and then adjust the recording volumes.

You can control the bass and treble.
Double-click the Volume icon, click the Options menu, click Advanced Controls, click Advanced, drag the sliders, and then click Close.

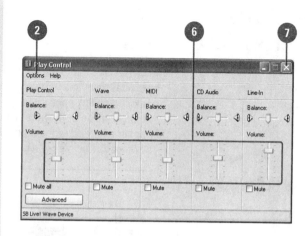

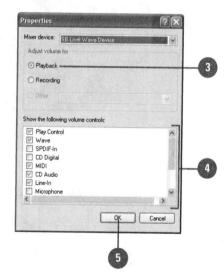

9

Browsing the Guide and Online Stores

The Windows Media Player comes with a built-in Guide that is updated daily with the latest music, movies, and entertainment news from the Internet as well as access to your favorite online media stores (New10), such as napster, CinemaNow, MusicNow, Musicmatch, and Wal-Mart, where you can download music and more. The Guide is a web page that provides links to a variety of media topics ranging from music to sports. Selecting a link opens a web page with more information about the topic, or plays music or movies. Links to media files, such as music or movies, appear with different speeds, which indicate the speed at which the file downloads and plays on your Internet connection.

Use the Guide and Online Stores

1 Start Windows Media Player and connect to the Internet, if necessary.

2 To use the Guide, click the Guide tab.

3 To use an online store, click the Choose An Online Store button, click the store you want, and then click the store tab you want (Music, Radio, Movies, etc.).

4 Click the links you want on the web page.

5 When you're done, click the Close button.

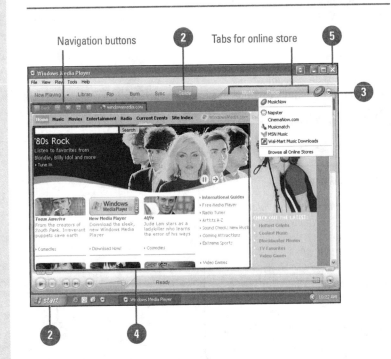

Navigation buttons   **2** Tabs for online store   **5**

Did You Know?

You can automatically hide menus. (New10) To turn on/off Autohide menus, click the View menu, point to Menu Bar Options, and then click Autohide Menu Bar. Point to the menu bar location to show the menu and point away to hide it.

Security Alert

Staying Secure in Windows Media Player

WMP 10 is designed to take advantage of the security features in SP2, yet still offer enhanced security of it's own (New10). The Security tab in the Options dialog box provides options to help you prevent scripts and other web page content on the Internet from running and infecting your computer. Scripts might add functionality, but they also can carry harmful threats. WMP uses the security zone options you set in the Internet Options dialog box, which you can access by using the Zone Settings button. For more information, see "Creating Security Zones" on page 300.

Listening to Radio Stations

You can use Windows Media Player to listen to radio stations around the world that broadcast on the Internet. When you listen to a radio station on the Internet, the audio continuously streams to your computer. The audio is partially downloaded and stored in a buffer, a temporary storage area, before it begins to play. As more audio streams, Windows Media Player continues to buffer it, which minimizes the interruptions to the radio broadcast. When you play a radio station, a web page for the radio station is displayed in your web browser behind Windows Media Player. While you listen to a radio station, you can browse the web or work in other programs.

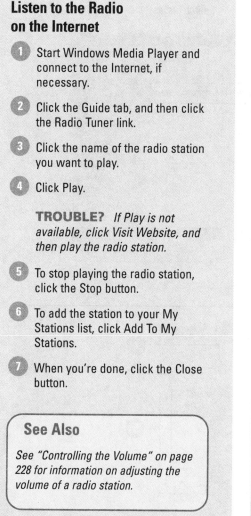

Listen to the Radio on the Internet

1. Start Windows Media Player and connect to the Internet, if necessary.

2. Click the Guide tab, and then click the Radio Tuner link.

3. Click the name of the radio station you want to play.

4. Click Play.

   TROUBLE? *If Play is not available, click Visit Website, and then play the radio station.*

5. To stop playing the radio station, click the Stop button.

6. To add the station to your My Stations list, click Add To My Stations.

7. When you're done, click the Close button.

> **See Also**
>
> *See "Controlling the Volume" on page 228 for information on adjusting the volume of a radio station.*

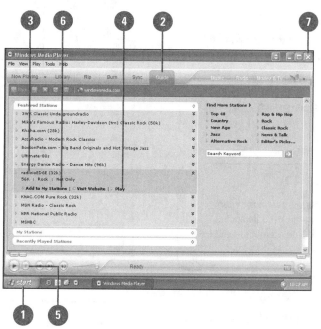

> ## Security Alert
>
> ### Protecting Privacy in Windows Media Player
>
> Windows Media Player uses the privacy settings you set in the Internet Options dialog box to block cookies (New 10). You can access the privacy settings from Windows Media Player by using the Cookies button on the Privacy tab in the Options dialog box. For more information, see "Protecting Internet Privacy" on page 304.

Playing Media Files

With Windows Media Player, you can play sound and video files on your computer. You can find and download sound and video files from the Internet or copy media files from a CD or DVD. The Library makes it easy to manage and organize your media. You can quickly search for media by name or you can have the Library in Windows Media Player search your computer or monitor a specific folder for media files and organize them by category, such as Album, Genre, Rated Songs, Year Released, or Purchased Music. You can browse the Library and select the media file that you want to play.

Perform a Quick Search

① Click the Library tab.

② Type the text that you want to search by.

③ Click the Search button.

TIMESAVER *Click Search Results in the Library list to display it at any time.*

Did You Know?

You can delete an item from the Library. Right-click the item, click Delete, click a delete option, and then click OK.

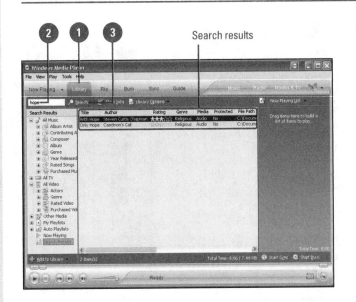

Search results

Search for and Add Media Files

① Click the Tools menu, and then click Search For Media Files.

② Click the Search On list arrow, and then select a drive.

③ If you want, click Browse to select a specific location.

④ Click Advanced Options.

⑤ Specify options for adding new media files.

⑥ Click Search, and then click Close.

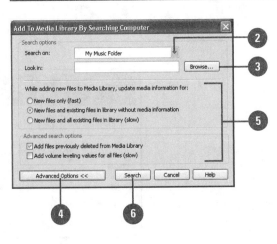

Add Media Files to the Library

1 Click the Library tab.

2 To add a currently playing track or playlist to the Library, play it now.

3 Click the Add To Library button, and then click the option you want:

- ◆ Add Currently Playing Item
- ◆ Add Currently Playing Playlist
- ◆ Add Folder
- ◆ Add File or Playlist
- ◆ Add URL

Play Media Files from the Library

1 Click the Library tab.

2 Click a plus sign (+) next to the category you want to view.

3 Click a category.

4 Double-click the media file to play it.

Did You Know?

You can monitor folders to automatically add media files to the Library. Click the File menu, point to Add To Library, click By Monitoring Folders, click Add, select a folder, and then click OK twice.

You can automatically add media files to the Library. Click the Tools menu, click Options, click the Player tab, select the Add Music Files To Library When Played check box, and then click OK.

9

Playing Media Using a Playlist

Instead of playing digital media files, such as music tracks, video clips, and DVD segments, one at a time or in sequential order from a CD or DVD, you can use Windows Media Player to create a playlist. A **playlist** is a customized list or sequence of digital media that you want to listen to or watch. A playlist allows you to group together media files and specify the order in which you want to play back the media. You can mix and match the media files on your computer, a network, a CD, or the Internet, creating a personal juke box. You can create an easy access general playlist called Now Playing List (New10), create one with a specify name, or specify criteria to create an Auto Playlist.

Create a Now Playing List

1. Click the Library tab.

2. Click the Select List Options button, and then click Now Playing List.

3. To clear the Now Playing List, click the Select List Options button, and then click Clear List.

   TIMESAVER Click the File menu, and then click New Now Playing List.

4. Display the media files you want to add to the playlist, and then drag them to the playlist.

Create a Playlist

1. Click the Library tab.

2. Click the Select List Options button, point to New List, and then click New Playlist.

3. Display the media files you want to add to the playlist, and then drag them to the playlist.

4. Click the Select List Options button, and then click Save Playlist As.

5. Type a name for the playlist.

6. Click Save.

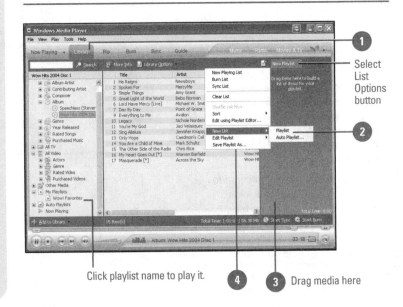

Drag media here

Select List Options button

Click playlist name to play it.

Drag media here

Create an Auto Playlist

① Click the Library tab.

② Click the Select List Options button, point to New List, and then click Auto Playlist.

③ Type a name for the Auto Playlist.

④ Select the criteria options you want.

⑤ Click OK.

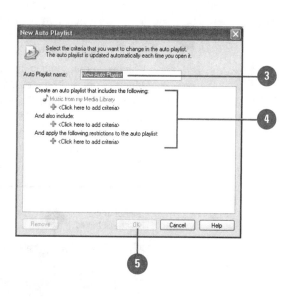

Add Media Files from Your Hard Disk to a Playlist

① Open the folder window that contains the files or folders you want to add to a playlist.

② Select the file(s) or folder(s) you want to include in the playlist.

③ Right-click the selection, and then click Add To Playlist.

④ Click a playlist.

⑤ Click OK.

Click to add to Now Playing List.

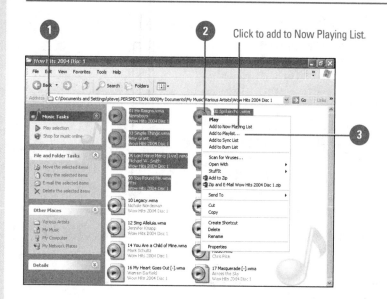

Did You Know?

You can quickly play a playlist. Click the Quick Access Panel button, point to My Playlists, and then click a playlist.

You can edit playlist. Click the Library tab, click the Select List Options button, click Edit Using Playlist Editor, delete and add items, and then click OK.

9

Ripping CD Music

Windows Media Player allows you to **rip** (New 10), or copy, one music track or an entire album from a music CD to your computer. When you rip music from a CD or download music from the Web to your computer, Windows copies music by the same artist into one folder in the My Music folder and creates subfolders for each album, unless you change the location using the Rip Music tab in the Options dialog box. You can also use the Rip Music tab to specify the file format and sound quality, and to protect tracks from illegal distribution, copying and sharing. Remember audio recordings take up a lot of hard disk space. To reduce the amount, rip your music at a lower audio-quality level.

Rip Tracks from a Music CD

1 Insert your music CD into the CD-ROM drive.

2 Click the Rip tab.

3 Clear the check boxes next to the tracks you don't want to copy.

4 Click Rip Music.

5 Click the Change My Current Format Settings or Keep My Current Format Settings option.

6 Click OK.

7 If you're changing current format setting, select the settings you want, and then click OK.

The music is copied to the My Music folder by default unless you specify a different location.

8 To stop the copy at any time, click Stop Rip.

Did You Know?

You can rip files from the Library. Select the files you want to rip on the Rip tab, click the Library tab, and then click Rip Music (bottom of List pane).

Select or clear all check boxes **2**

Button toggles between Rip Music and Stop Rip **8**

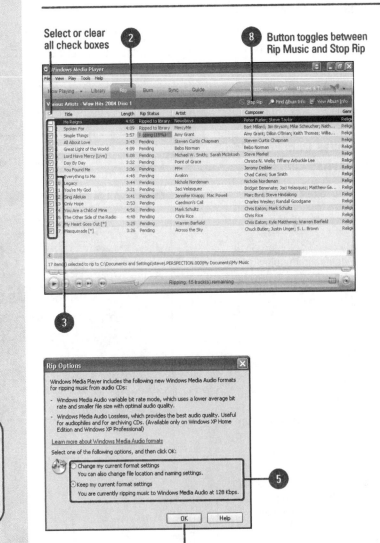

Select Rip Music Settings

1. Click the Tools menu, and then click Options.

2. Click the Rip Music tab.

3. To change the location where Windows Media Player stores ripped music, click Change, select a new folder location, and then click OK.

4. Select the format and copy setting you want.

   - **Windows Media Audio.** Most common WMA format with widest range of quality and file size

   - **Windows Media Audio (variable bit rate).** High quality with variable file size

   - **Windows Media Audio Lossless.** Quality closest to the original with high file size

   - **MP3.** Common and flexible format (New10)

5. Drag the slider to adjust audio quality.

6. Click OK.

Did You Know?

You can use error correction during a copy. Click the Tools menu, click Options, click the Device tab, select the CD-ROM drive, click Properties, click Digital, select the Use Error Correction check box, and then click OK.

For Your Information

Getting a License to Copy Music

Most CD music is secured with a license to prevent illegal distribution. A license is a legal agreement that specifies whether the license expires or how you can use the file. The terms of the license are entirely dependent upon the person or company that provided the file. Windows Media Player cannot play licensed files without a license. When you copy music from a CD with the Acquire Licenses Automatically For Protected Content option selected on the Privacy tab in the Options dialog box, WMP searches the Internet for the license and copies it to your computer. If the license is not available, you can still acquire a license by copying the music and selecting the Copy Protect Music check box on the Rip Music tab in the Options dialog box. As you copy the music, the licenses are issued. The license allows you to copy the music to your hard disk, a portable device, or a CD. If you want to view the license for a file, right-click the file, click Properties, and then click the License tab. If you copy music without a license, you could be violating the music's copyright. You can avoid license problems by backing them up. Click the Tools menu, click Manage Licenses, click Browse, select a folder, click OK, and then click Backup Now. Click Restore Now to get back lost or corrupted ones.

Copying Media Files to a CD or Portable Device

Windows Media Player makes it easy to burn (copy) music to a CD using a CD burner or copy the music and video you want to a portable device and keep it in sync . Portable handheld devices, such as Personal Digital Assistants (PDAs), provide a convenient way to keep computer files up-to-date while you're on the road. If you have a Portable Music Player, you can download music from an online store and play it on the go. With a new Portable Media Center (PMC), you can synchronize music, video, and picture files to the device so you can bring your whole library with you (New 10). You can choose to automatically or manually sync your digital media between WMP and your device, known as a **partnership**. Set up Auto Sync once, and every time you connect your device to your computer, WMP updates the digital media between them, so devices that allow you to rate your music can automatically send them back to WMP.

Burn Music to a CD

 Click the Library tab.

 Click the Select List Options button, and then click Burn List.

> **TROUBLE?** To clear the burn list, click the Select List Options button, and then click Clear List.

 Display and drag the media files you want to the burn list.

 Click the Start Burn list arrow, and then click Audio CD.

 Insert a blank CD in your CD recorder.

> **TIMESAVER** If you don't need to change any properties, click the Start Burn button to start it now.

 Click the Burn tab.

 If you need to erase a CD-RW disc, click the Erase Disk button, and then click Yes.

 To change recording speed and music quality, click the Display Properties And Settings button, select the options you want, and then click OK.

 Click the Start Burn button.

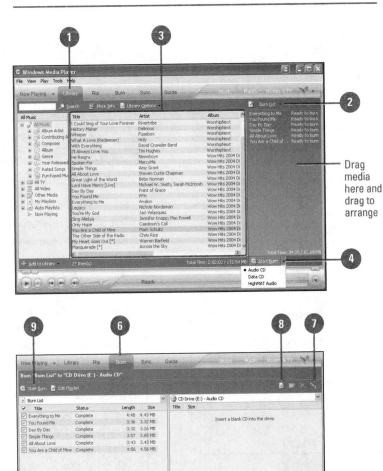

Drag media here and drag to arrange

Copy Music to a Portable Device

1. Start Windows Media Player, and then connect the portable device to your computer.

2. If sync setup needed for the device, click the Automatic or Manual option, and then click Finish.

3. If you setup Auto Sync, synchronization begins, click Stop Sync.

4. Click the Library tab.

5. Click the Select List Options button, and then click Sync List.

   TROUBLE? *To clear the sync list, click the Select List Options button, and then click Clear List.*

6. Display and drag the media files you want to the sync list.

   TIMESAVER *If you don't need to change any properties, click the Start Sync button to start it now.*

7. Click the Sync tab.

8. To change sync priority order, sync method, and other settings, click the Set Up Sync button, specify options, and then click OK.

9. To delete items from the device, select the content, and then click the Delete button.

10. Click the Start Sync button.

    Upon completion, status information appears next to files indicating success or failure.

See Also

See "Managing Files Using a CD" on page 78 for information on working with different types of CDs.

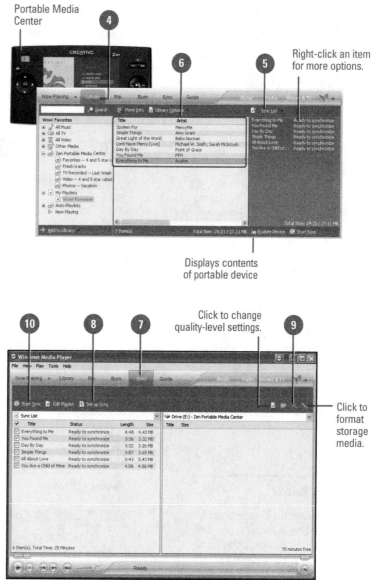

Portable Media Center

Right-click an item for more options.

Displays contents of portable device

Click to change quality-level settings.

Click to format storage media.

9

Adding Functionality to Media Player

Windows Media Player allows you to add functionality to the player using plug-ins. Plug-ins add or enhance the media experience with audio and video effects, new rendering types, and visualizations. Before you can use a plug-in, you need to download it from the Web and add it to the Media Player. You can find lots of Media Player plug-ins at *www.wmplugins.com*. Before you download a plug-in, read the online information about the plug-in for additional instructions.

Work with Plug-Ins

1. Click the View menu, point to Plug-Ins, and then click Options.

2. To download a plug-in, click Look For Plug-ins On The Internet link, and then follow the instructions on the Web page.

3. To add a plug-in, click Add, select the plug-in, and then click Open.

4. Select a plug-in category.

5. Select a plug-in option, if available.

6. To modify a plug-in, click Properties.

7. To remove a plug-in, click Remove.

8. Click OK.

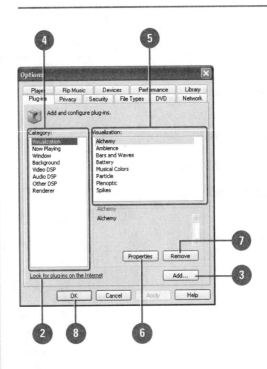

Did You Know?

You can download a creativity fun pack for the Media Player. Open your browser, go to *www.wmplugins.com*, and then search for the Creativity Fun Pack for Windows Media Player download link.

Plug-ins web site

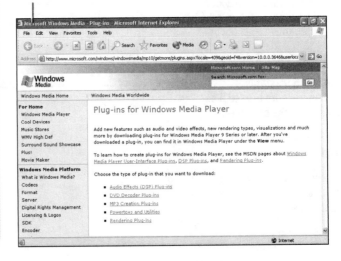

Enhancing the Media Player Display

Visualizations are plug-ins that display geometric shapes and color on the Now Playing tab when you play music. Visualizations are grouped together into collections. You can add and remove visualizations or download additional collections from the Microsoft web site. You can also display special enhancement controls to change video settings, play speed, or audio levels with a graphics equalizer, choose color effects, and send a media link in an e-mail.

Select Visualizations

1. Click the Now Playing tab.

2. Click the Info Center View button, and then point to Visualizations.

   TIMESAVER *Right-click the Info Center View pane to quickly access visualizations.*

3. Point to a category, and then click the visualization you want to display.

4. To display other visualizations in the collection, click the Previous Visualization button or Next Visualization button.

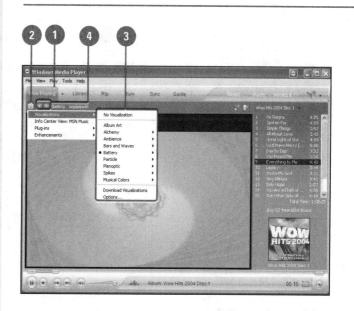

Select Enhancements

1. Click the Now Playing tab.

2. Click the Info Center View button, and then point to Enhancements.

3. Click the enhancement you want to display.

4. Adjust the enhancement controls.

5. To display other visualizations in the collection, click the Previous Visualization button or Next Visualization button.

6. When you're done, click the Close button.

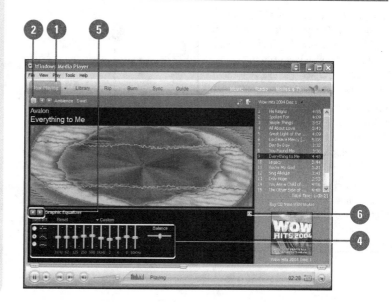

Changing the Media Player Look

Windows Media Player gives you the freedom of expression to change the look, known as the **skin**, of the Media Player. Windows Media Player includes several skins from which you can select the one you like the best. When you select a skin, Windows Media Player changes from full mode to skin mode. You can use skins only when Media Player is in skin mode. Skin mode displays a smaller player, which provides more room on the screen for other programs.

Apply a Skin

1. Click the View menu, and then click Skin Chooser.

2. Click a design.

3. Click Apply Skin.

4. Use the controls to play a media file.

5. To return to the full window, click the Return To Full Mode button.

   TIMESAVER *Press Ctrl+1 to return to full mode.*

6. To switch back to skin mode, click the Switch To Skin Mode button.

Did You Know?

You can download more skins from the Internet. Click the View menu, click Skin Chooser, click More Skins, click the link to the skin you want to download, follow the instructions, and then click View Now.

You can delete a skin. Click the View menu, click Skin Chooser, select the skin you want to delete, click the Delete Selected Skin button, and then click Yes.

You can access a shortcut menu of commands in skin mode. Press Shift+F10 to display a shortcut menu of convenient commands.

Delete Selected Skin button

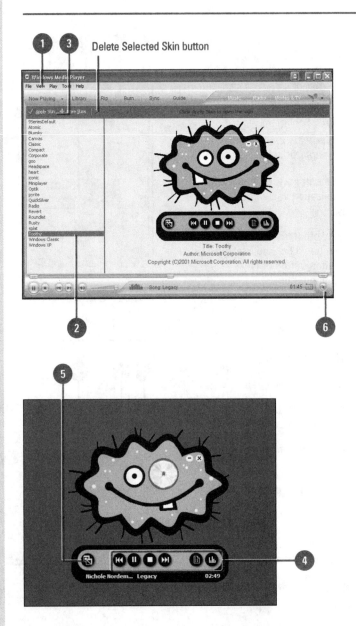

Viewing and Playing Music Files

You can view and play music files with relative easy in the My Music folder. The My Music folder (New!), which is located in the My Documents folder, is a folder specifically designated to play and manage music files. When you copy music files from a CD or download them from the Internet, the files are copied to the My Music folder by default unless you specify a different location. The My Music folder contains links to specialized music tasks that can help you play the music you store on your computer. In the My Music folder, you can click Play All or Play Selection in the task pane or double-click an individual music file to open and play the music in Windows Media Player. If you click Play All in the My Music folder, Windows Media Player opens and plays all the music in your My Music folder and subfolder in random order. If you click Play All in a subfolder within your My Music folder, Windows Media Player opens and plays all the music in the folder in consecutive order.

View and Play Music Files

1. Click the Start button, and then click My Music.

2. Select the music files or folder you want to play.

3. Click Play All or Play Selection.

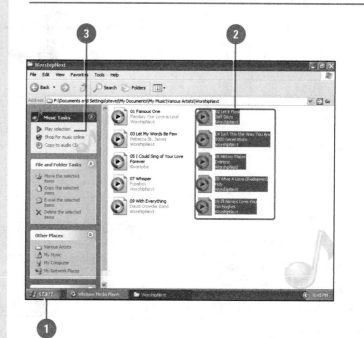

Did You Know?

You can shop for music online. From an album folder in the My Music folder, click Shop For Music Online, which opens the *WindowsMedia.com* web page where you can buy other albums by the same artist.

See Also

See *"Customizing Personal Folders"* on page 74 for information on creating a music folder, such as the My Music folder.

Creating a Sound File

Using Sound Recorder and a microphone, you can record and play your own sound files. Sound Recorder creates Wave files with the .wav file extension, a typical sound file Windows uses, but you can also change the sound format to MPEG or Windows Media Audio. Using Sound Recorder, you can record, mix, play, and edit sounds. You can also copy or link sounds into another document.

Record a Sound

1. Click the Start button, point to All Programs, point to Accessories, point to Entertainment, and then click Sound Recorder.

2. Click the Record button, and then record the sounds you want.

3. When you're done, click the Stop button.

4. Click the File menu, and then click Save.

5. Select a folder, type a name for the file, and then click Save.

6. Click the Close button.

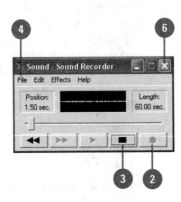

Playback a Sound

1. Open the file you want to modify.

2. If you want, drag the slider to where you want to play the sound.

3. Click the Play button.

    The slider indicates the current position in the recording.

4. When you're done, click the Stop button.

5. Click the Rewind button or Forward button to move to the beginning or end of the sound.

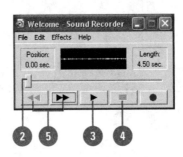

Change a Sound Format

1. Open the file you want to modify.

2. Click the File menu, and then click Save As.

3. Click Change.

4. Click the Name list arrow, and then select a preset format, or specify a sampling frequency sound attribute and a specific format, such as MPEG or Windows Media Audio.

5. Click OK.

6. Select a folder, and then type a name for the file, and then click Save.

7. Click Save.

8. Click the Close button.

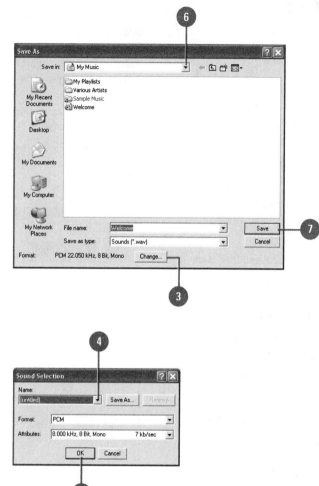

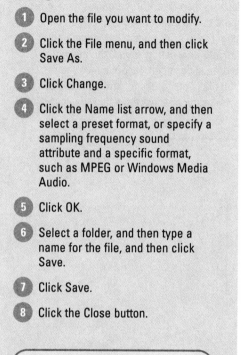

Did You Know?

You can link a sound to a document. Copy the sound in Sound Recorder, switch to the document, click the Edit menu, click Paste Special, click Paste Link, and then click OK.

You can copy a sound into a document. Record or open the sound you want to copy, click the Edit menu, click Copy, open the document where you want to copy the sound, place the insertion point, if necessary, click the Edit menu, and then click Paste.

Modifying a Sound File

After you create a sound, you can make simple changes to the file, such as delete parts of the sound. You can also insert or merge a sound to an existing sound or add some simple sound effects, such as add an echo, play the sound backwards, and increase or decrease the volume and speed. When you insert a sound into an existing sound, the new sound replaces the original sound after the slider point. If you do not see a green line in Sound Recorder, the file is compressed, and you cannot modify it using Sound Recorder unless you adjust the sound quality to an uncompressed format.

Open and Insert a Sound

1. Click the Start button, point to All Programs, point to Accessories, point to Entertainment, and then click Sound Recorder.

2. Click the File menu, and then click Open.

3. Select the file you want to open, and then click Open.

4. Move the slider to where you want to insert the sound.

5. Click the Edit menu, and then click Insert File.

6. Select the file you want to insert.

7. Click Open.

8. Click the File menu, and then click Save.

Did You Know?

You can revert back to the last saved version. Click the File menu, click Revert, and then click Yes.

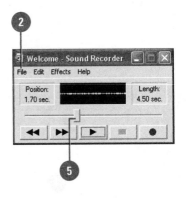

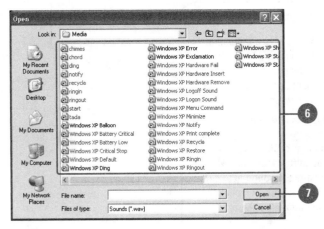

Convert a Sound Format

1. Open the file you want to modify.

2. Click the File menu, and then click Properties.

3. Click the Format Conversion list arrow, and then select the type of format you want.

4. Click Convert Now.

5. Select the format and attributes you want.

   TROUBLE? *If you're not sure which format to choose, click the Help menu, click Help Topics, click the Search Tab, and then search for Compressing Sound Files.*

6. Click OK.

7. Click OK.

8. Click the File menu, and then click Save As.

9. Select a folder, type a name for the file, and then click Save.

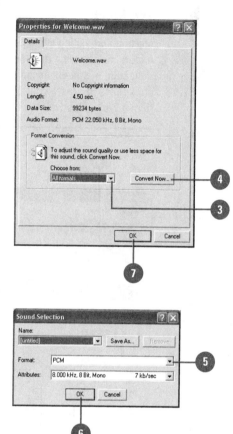

Add Sound Effects

1. Open the file you want to modify.

2. Click the Effects menu, and then click one of the following effects:

   ◆ Increase Volume or Decrease Volume

   ◆ Increase Speed or Decrease Speed

   ◆ Add Echo

   ◆ Reverse

3. Click the File menu, and then click Save.

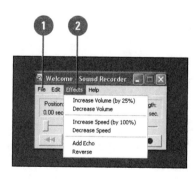

9

Associating a Sound with an Event

Besides customizing the desktop appearance of Windows XP, you can also add sound effects to common Windows commands and functions, such as starting and exiting Windows, printing complete, opening and closing folders, or emptying the Recycle Bin. You can select a sound scheme (a collection of sounds associated with events), or you can mix and match sound files to create your own sound scheme for your computer. You need to use Wave files with the .wav file extension.

Create and Select a Sound Scheme

1. Click the Start button, click Control Panel, and then double-click the Sounds And Audio Devices icon in Classic view.

2. Click the Sounds tab.

3. Click an event to which you want to associate a sound.

4. Click the Sounds list arrow, and then select a sound, or click Browse and locate the sound file you want to use.

5. Click the Play button to preview the sound.

6. Click Save As, type a name for the sound scheme, and then click OK.

7. To select a sound scheme, click the Sound Scheme list arrow, and then select a scheme.

8. Click OK.

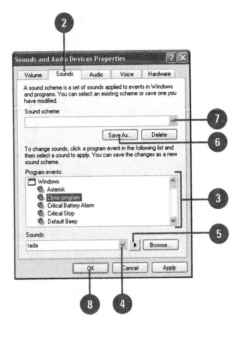

Did You Know?

You can add sounds to the list. If you put WAV files in the Media folder, located in the Windows folder, the sound files appear in the Sounds list.

You can remove a sound associated with an event. On the Sounds tab, click an event, click the Sounds list arrow, and then click (None).

Creating Movies Using Movie Maker

Introduction

Windows XP comes with an accessory called Windows Movie Maker (version 2.1) that lets you combine video, audio, and image files with special effects to create movies you can show on your computer or CD, e-mail to others, record on a digital camera, or place on a web page.

In Movie Maker, you create a project that contains the arrangement and timing information of audio and video clips, video transitions, video effects, and titles in a storyboard or timeline. You drag video and audio clips from a collection to the storyboard or timeline. After you arrange the video and audio clips in the sequence you want, you can add video transitions, video effects, and titles and credits. After you preview your project using the monitor, you save it as a movie file to your computer or to a recordable CD, send it as an attachment in an e-mail message, save and send it to the web, or record your movie to a digital video tape. The movie you create can be watched in a media player, such as Microsoft Windows Media Player, or in a web browser.

Before using Movie Maker, you need to connect and install the equipment needed to transfer video content to your computer, such as a digital video or web camera. Movie Maker must detect the video device on your computer, and you must properly connect the device to a USB port, a video capture card, or an IEEE 1394 port. (Check your computer documentation for details.)

Planning a Movie Maker Project

Movie Maker lets you combine video, audio, and image files to create movies you can show on your computer, e-mail to others, or place on a web page. You save the movie you create as a file, just as you would save a word processing or spreadsheet file, and you can play and view it at any time. However, movies and their accompanying files are larger than most other documents you create—usually exceeding 5 MB. Before you begin, it's a good idea to plan your content.

Decide the purpose of the movie

Your movie might be a promotional piece or catalog for business use, or a vacation movie to share with family and friends. Your purpose determines the subject, type, and quality of the **source material**, which is the video and audio material you will use.

Determine how to share the movie with others

You might want to show your movie on a computer projection screen at a meeting, send it as an attachment in an e-mail message, or place it on a web site. When you place a movie on a web site, viewers might download it, which means to transfer it to their computers and store it for future viewing. If your movie is very long or has many high-quality images, the movie file will be large and will take a long time to download.

Choose source material

If you have a digital video or digital web camera, you can record or capture digital images directly into Movie Maker on your computer. To use existing video or audio segments, called **clips**, you must import them, or bring them into, Movie Maker. You can also import clips from videotape, but your computer must have a video capture card to convert clips from analog to digital format. You can start the System Information accessory on the System Tools submenu to determine whether you have a video capture card installed on your computer.

Sketch the movie

Before putting your movie together in Movie Maker, it's important to make a sketch of your movie that shows the order of the audio and video components. What audio clips do you want to play with what video clips?

Review the process used to create a movie

First, you bring clips of source material into a Movie Maker project file. A **project file**, which is the working copy of your movie, is a Movie Maker document with the file name extension .mswmm. You then use the project file to do the following: set the order of your movie segments; **trim** (delete) portions of clips you don't want to use; specify how clips display from one to the next, called **transitions**; add a video special effect to clips; add titles and credits to the beginning and end of the movie or individual clips; and, lastly, preview your work. Finally, you save your project file as a movie with the file name extension .wmv and display the completed movie using the Windows Media Player program.

Starting Movie Maker ▶

Before you start Movie Maker, use Display Properties in the Control Panel to make sure the screen resolution is set correctly. Movie Maker is a Windows accessory program that you can start from the Start menu. You can achieve the best results in Movie Maker when the screen resolution is set to 1024 by 768 or higher. When you start Movie Maker, a new untitled movie project is displayed. You can either create a new movie project or open an existing one.

Start Movie Maker

1. Click the Start button.
2. Point to All Programs.
3. Click Windows Movie Maker.

Did You Know?

You can check online for the latest version of Movie Maker. Click the Start button, point to All Programs, click Windows Update, connect to the Internet, scan for updates, check for a new version of Movie Maker, and then download it.

See Also

See "Changing the Display" on page 88 for information on changing the screen resolution.

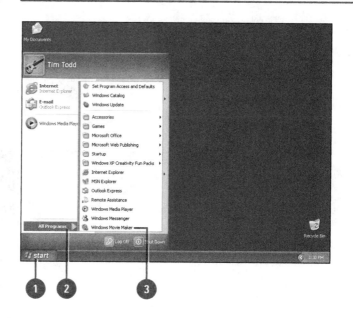

Viewing the Movie Maker Window (New!)

Collections pane
The collections pane displays your
collections, which contains clips.

Movie Tasks button
The button displays the Movie Tasks pane. The Movie Tasks pane lists the
common tasks that you may need to perform when making a movie.

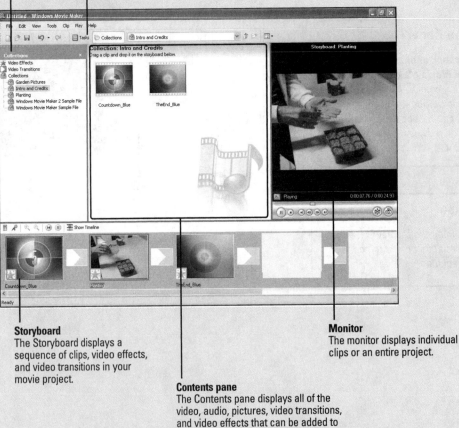

Storyboard
The Storyboard displays a
sequence of clips, video effects,
and video transitions in your
movie project.

Contents pane
The Contents pane displays all of the
video, audio, pictures, video transitions,
and video effects that can be added to
the storyboard/timeline to include in
your movie project.

Monitor
The monitor displays individual
clips or an entire project.

Opening an Existing Project

After you save a project in Movie Maker, you can open it and continue to work on the project. A Movie Maker project file is saved with a .mswmm file name extension, which you can open using the Open Project button on the toolbar.

Open an Existing Project

1. Click the Start button, point to All Programs, and then click Windows Movie Maker.

2. Click the Open Project button on the toolbar.

3. Select the drive and folder that contains the project you want to open.

4. Select the project file.

5. Click Open.

Did You Know?

You can automatically open a project. Click the Tools menu, click Options, click the General tab, select the Open Last Project On Startup check box, and then click OK.

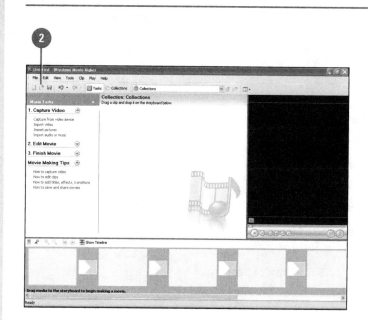

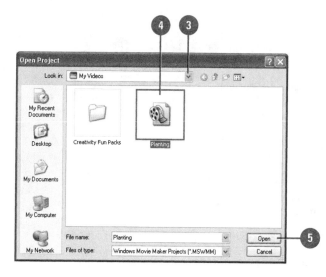

Capturing Video and Audio

You can capture video and audio to your computer from a digital video (DV) or analog camera, web camera, videotape (VCR), or television tuner card directly in Movie Maker (**New!**). Similarly, you can record audio source material from a microphone, radio, audio or video tape, or a CD. Before you can capture video and audio, a video capture device must be connected properly and detected on your computer by Windows Movie Maker. If you record clips from any commercial source, however, be aware of copyright restrictions that regulate how you may or may not use the content. In the capturing process, Movie Maker converts the material to Windows Media format.

Capture Video from a Video Camera

1. Make sure the digital video camera is connected properly, and then set the camera to play recorded video.

2. Click Capture From Video Device in the Movie Tasks pane.

3. Click the digital video camera, and then click Next.

4. Type a file name for your captured video file.

5. Select the location where you want to save the video, and then click Next.

6. Specify the video settings you want for capturing video and audio, and then click Next.

7. Click Capture Parts Of The Tape Manually.

8. To separate the video into smaller clips, select the Create Clips When Wizard Finishes check box.

9. Click Start Capture.

10. To stop capturing video, click Stop Capture.

11. Click Finish.

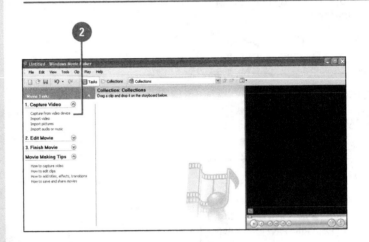

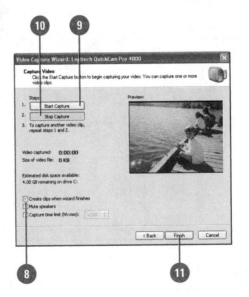

Capture Live Video

1. Make sure the digital video camera is connected properly, and then set the camera to play recorded video.

2. Click Capture From Video Device in the Movie Tasks pane.

3. Click the digital video camera, and then click Next.

4. Type a file name for your captured video file.

5. Select the location where you want to save the video, and then click Next.

6. Specify the video settings you want, and then click Next.

7. To separate the video into smaller clips, select the Create Clips When Wizard Finishes check box.

8. To automatically stop the capture, select the Capture Time Limit check box, and then type or select a time limit.

9. Click Start Capture.

10. To stop capturing video, click Stop Capture.

11. Click Finish.

Did You Know?

Twenty hours of video take a gigabyte of hard disk space. You can store more than 20 hours of video for each gigabyte of hard disk space on your computer.

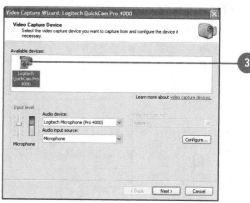

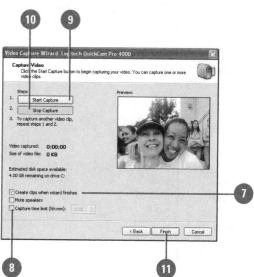

10

Importing Video and Audio

If you want to use existing video and audio clips in your movie instead of recording them yourself, you can obtain them from various companies that specialize in video processing, or you can download them from the Web. Commercial CDs are excellent sources for audio clips. You can import the video and audio clips into Movie Maker from files on your computer, from your CD drive, or from the Web. If you already imported a video clip and need a still picture of a frame from a video, you can take a picture of the video frame and save it as a file, which you can import back into Movie Maker.

Import Video or Audio

1. Click the File menu, and then click Import Into Collections.

2. Select the folder that contains the video or audio files you want to import.

3. To select a specific media type, click the Files Of Type list arrow, and then select a file type.

4. Select the files you want to import.

   TIMESAVER *To import several files at one time, press and hold down the Ctrl key, and then click each file that you want to import.*

5. To import clips as separate smaller clips, select the Create Clips For Video Files check box.

6. Click Import.

   Movie Maker creates a new collection for the imported video or audio clips.

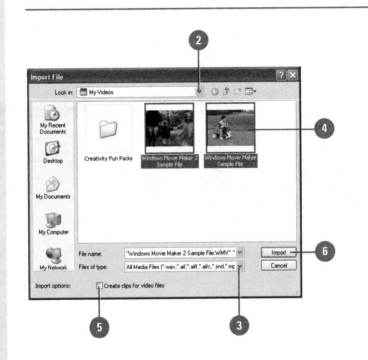

Did You Know?

You can use the Movie Tasks pane to import files. Click the Tasks button on the toolbar to open the Movie Task pane, if necessary, click the Details button for Capture Video, if necessary, and then click an import link.

Display Clip Properties

1. Right-click the clip you want, and then click Properties.

2. Scroll the list of properties.

3. Click OK.

Did You Know?

You can rename a media clip. Click the Collection folder that contains the clip you want to rename, right-click the clip in the Collection area, click Rename, type a name, and then press Enter.

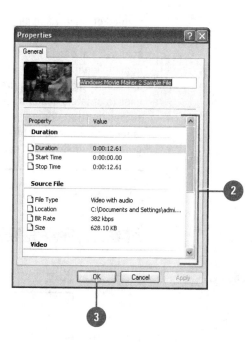

Movie Maker Import File Types	
File Type	**File Extensions**
Video	.asf, .avi, .m1v, .mp2, .mp2v, .mpe, .mpeg, .mpg, .mpv2, .wm, and .wmv
Audio	.aif, .aifc, .aiff, .asf, .au, .mp2, .mp3, .mpa, .snd, .wav, and .wma
Pictures	.bmp, .dib, .emf, .gif, .jfif, .jpe, .jpeg, .jpg, .png, .tif, .tiff, and .wmf

10

Adding Slides to a Movie

Instead of using video clips, you can create slide shows in Movie Maker with still images that you create using a digital camera, web camera, or scanner. You can import the clips into Movie Maker and create transitions between them, just as you would in a movie. You can change the duration of individual pictures in Timeline view. You can also add sound clips to create a sound track that plays as your pictures appear on the screen. Portrait-oriented pictures in Movie Maker are the same height as landscape-oriented pictures, and Movie Maker inserts a black background on either side of each one.

Set Picture Duration

1. Click the Tools menu, and then click Options.

2. Click the Advanced tab.

3. Specify the picture duration in seconds.

4. Click OK.

Import Pictures

① Click the Collections button, and then click the collection where you want to place the imported pictures.

② Click the Tasks button on the toolbar, if necessary, and then click Import Pictures.

③ Select the folder that contains the picture files you want to import.

④ Select the files you want to import.

TIMESAVER *To import several files at one time, press and hold down the Ctrl key, and then click each file that you want to import.*

⑤ Click Import.

Movie Maker adds the imported pictures into the selected collection.

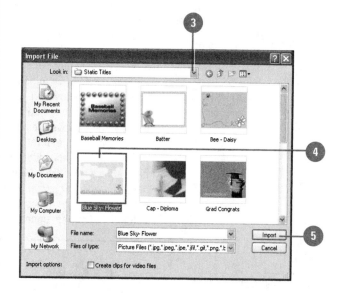

Take a Picture from Video

① Click the video clip from which you want to take a picture.

② Drag the Playback indicator on the Seek bar to the frame that you want to capture as a picture.

③ Click the Take Picture button.

④ Select a folder, type a name, and then click Save.

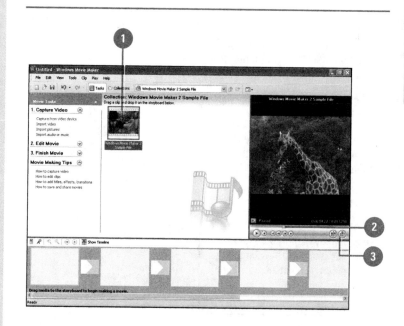

10

Organizing Clips and Collections

When you bring video clips, audio clips, or pictures into Movie Maker, the program stores them in a collection folder in the **Collections pane**. The contents of the selected collection folder appear in the **Collections area**. As you continue to collect media clips for use in different movie projects, the number of clips in a collection and in Movie Maker can grow rapidly and become hard to manage. You can use the same management techniques you use in Windows Explorer to help you organize and remove clips and collections. Once you have clips in your collections, you can move them around and rename the clips and collections as you would a file or folder and use them to create a movie. When you no longer need individual video and audio clips or entire collections, you can remove them from Movie Maker. When you remove video and sound clips and collections, they are deleted only from Movie Maker; the original video and sound files, which you imported into Movie Maker, are not deleted and remain unchanged on your hard drive.

View a Collection

1. Click the Collections button on the toolbar.

2. Click the Collection folder you want to view.

3. Click the Views button on the toolbar, and then click Thumbnails or Details.

4. Click the Views button on the toolbar, point to Arrange Icons By, and then click an arrangement type.

5. To close the Collection pane, click the Close button.

6. To open the Movie Tasks pane, click the Tasks button on the toolbar.

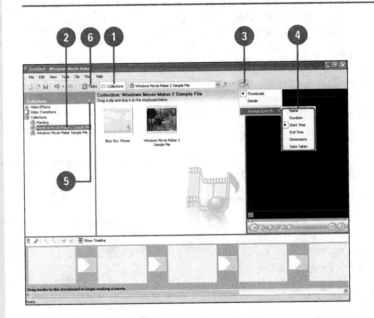

> ### Did You Know?
>
> **You can quickly display a collection.** Click the Location list arrow on the toolbar, and then select the collection you want to display.

Move a Clip to a Collection

1. Click the Collections button on the toolbar.

2. Click the Collection folder that contains the clip you want to move.

3. Drag the clip to another Collection folder.

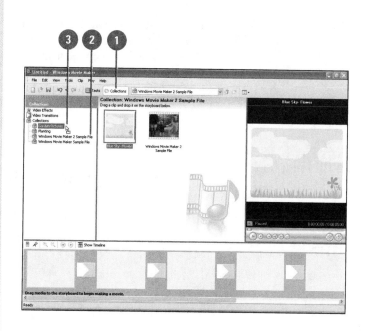

Rename a Collection

1. Click the Collections button on the toolbar.

2. Right-click the Collection folder you want to rename, and then click Rename.

3. Type a name, and then press Enter.

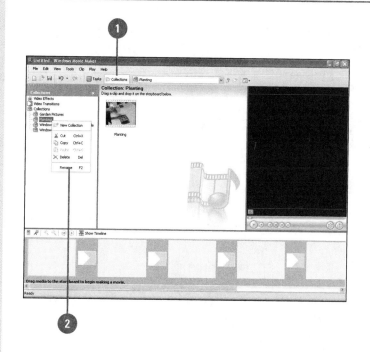

Did You Know?

You can delete a media clip. Click the Collection folder that contains the clip you want to delete, click the clip in the Collections area, and then press Delete.

You can create a collection folder. Click the Collections button on the toolbar, click the folder where you want the new folder, click the New Collection Folder button on the toolbar, type a name, and then press Enter.

10

Working with Clips

After you capture or import a video clip or audio clip, you can preview the individual clips within a collection in the monitor. The monitor works similarly to a VCR. If you have a long clip that you want to divide into smaller clips, you can split the clip on your own or let Movie Maker try to do it. Movie Maker creates clips automatically based on time stamps insert by the digital video camera or significant frame change in the video.

Preview a Clip in a Collection

1 Click the Collections button on the toolbar.

2 Click the Collection folder you want to preview.

3 Click the clip you want to preview.

4 Click the Play button.

TIMESAVER *Press Spacebar to play or pause a clip quickly.*

5 To pause the clip, click the Pause button. Click the Play button again to continue.

6 To stop the clip, click the Stop button.

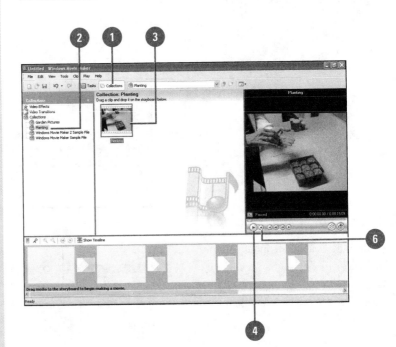

Did You Know?

You can drag a clip to play it. You can drag any clip from the Collections area to the monitor to begin playing that clip.

Split a Clip

 Click the clip from which you want to split.

② Drag the Playback indicator on the Seek bar to the frame where you want to split the clip.

③ Click the Split the Clip button.

TIMESAVER *Press Ctrl+L to split a clip.*

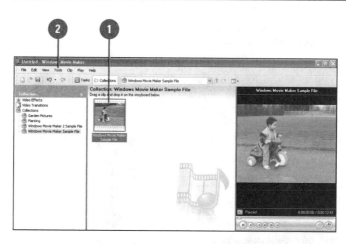

Create Clips Automatically

① Click the video clip for which you want to detect and create clips.

② Click the Tools menu, and then click Create Clips.

Did You Know?

You can combine clips. Hold down Ctrl, click the consecutive clips you want to combine, click the Clip menu, and then click Combine.

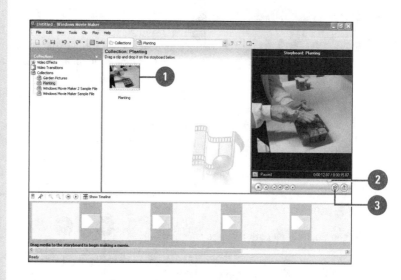

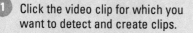
Creates individual clips from one clip

10

Creating a Movie Maker Project File

When you start Movie Maker, a new, untitled project opens. A project contains the arrangement and timing information of audio and video clips, video transitions, video effects, and titles you have added to the storyboard/timeline. You can view a project in one of two views: **Storyboard view**, which shows the order of your clips, and **Timeline view**, which shows the duration of each clip and the types of transitions between them as well as the sound track. To create a movie, you drag video and audio clips from your Collections area to the project file's storyboard or timeline and rearrange the clips in any order you want. After you preview your project using the monitor and are satisfied with the results, you save it as a movie file.

Create a Project

1. Click the Collections button on the toolbar.

2. Click the Collection folder that contains the clips you want to use in your project.

3. Click the Show Timeline button or Show Storyboard button.

4. Drag clips from the Collections area to the place in the storyboard or timeline where you want them.

5. To rearrange the order of clips, drag clips on the storyboard or timeline.

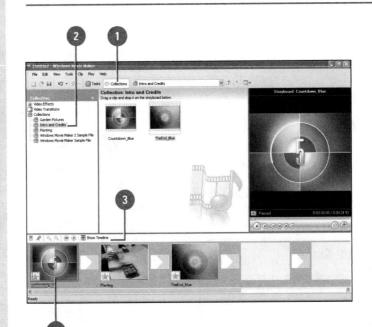

Did You Know?

You can delete a clip from the storyboard. If you drag the wrong clip to the storyboard, select it, and then press Delete. The clip remains in the Collections area and on your hard drive.

Preview a Project

① Click the Rewind Storyboard button or click Rewind Timeline button.

The buttons change depending on the view.

② Click the Play Storyboard button or click the Play Timeline button.

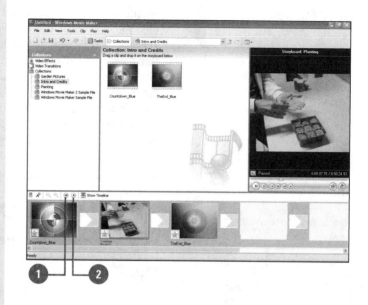

Change the Preview Monitor Size

① Click the video you want to preview.

② Click the View menu, and then point to Preview Monitor Size.

③ Click Small (320x240) or Large (640x480).

TROUBLE? *This option is available when there is enough room to resize the monitor without resizing the storyboard/timeline.*

Did You Know?

You can play the video using the entire screen. Click the View menu, and then click Full Screen.

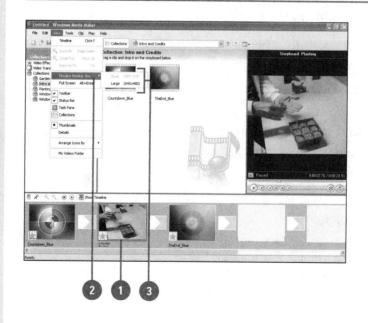

Trimming Clips

Frequently, the clips you record or import into Movie Maker run longer than you want them to in your final movie. You can easily trim clips in Timeline view by playing the clip and setting the **start trim point** and **end trim point**. The portion between the trim points remains in your movie. The frames before and after the trim points are deleted from your movie, but the original clip in your collection is not affected and retains its original length. You can trim a clip as it plays, or you can pause and set the trim points. You can use the Start Trim Point and End Trim Point commands on the Clip menu or drag the timeline **trim handles** (small triangles at the beginning and end of a selected clip).

Crop a Clip

1. Click the Show Timeline button, if necessary.

2. Select the clip you want to crop.

3. Drag the Seek bar to the point where you want to start the clip.

4. Click the Clip menu, and then click Set Start Trim Point.

   TIMESAVER *Position the pointer on the left edge or right edge of the clip, and then drag the trim handles to crop the clip.*

5. Drag the Seek bar to the point where you want to end the clip.

6. Click the Clip menu, and then click Set End Trim Point.

> ### Did You Know?
>
> **You can restore a clip to its original length.** Click Clip on the menu bar, and then click Clear Trim Points.

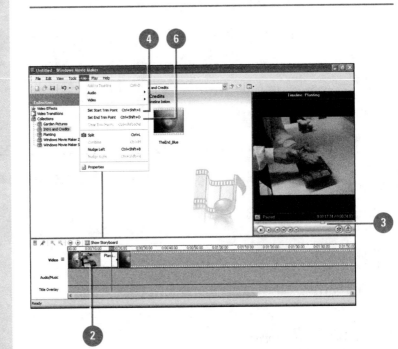

Adding Transitions Between Clips

A **transition** is an effect that provides a smoother, more gradual change between clips in a movie. A transition plays before one clip ends while another starts to play. You can add a transition between two video clips, pictures, or titles on the storyboard or timeline. Movie Maker provides a variety of video transitions (**New!**) that you can quickly add to a movie project, such as Bow Tie, Eye, Diamond, Fan Up, and Shatter In.

Adding a Transition

1. Click the Locations list arrow on the toolbar, and then click Video Transitions.

2. Click the Show Storyboard button or Show Timeline button.

3. To view the Transition track in the timeline, click the plus sign (+) next to the Video track in the timeline.

4. Drag a transition to the video transition cell in the storyboard or between the two clips in the timeline.

5. To increase the transition duration in the timeline, drag the beginning of the transition towards the beginning of the timeline.

6. To decrease the transition duration in the timeline, drag the beginning of the transition towards the end of the timeline.

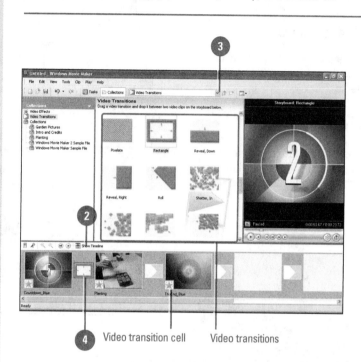

Video transition cell   Video transitions

Did You Know?

You can change the default transition duration. Click the Tools menu, click Options, click the Advanced tab, type a value for the transition duration, and then click OK.

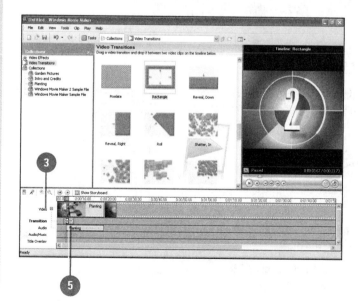

10

Adding Video Effects

Movie Maker offers a variety of video effects (**New!**) that you can add to a movie project, such as Ease In, Blur, Film Age Old, Mirror Vertical, Speed Up Double, and Watercolor. A video effect is applied for the entire duration of a clip, picture, or title in a movie project. You can add multiple video effects to the same clip, as well as customize the order. If you no longer want to use a video effect, you can remove it.

Add a Video Effects

1. Click the Locations list arrow on the toolbar, and then click Video Effects.

2. Click the Show Storyboard button or Show Timeline button.

3. Drag the effect to the video effect cell of the clip in the storyboard or on the clip on the Video track in the timeline.

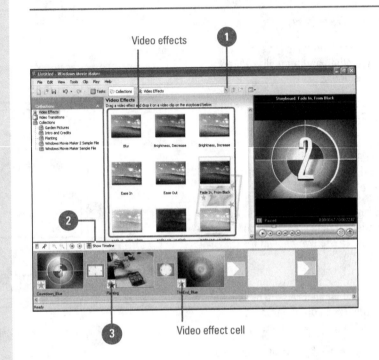

Video effects

Video effect cell

Change Order or Remove Video Effects

1. Right-click the clip with the effects you want to change, and then click Video Effects.

2. Click the displayed effect you want to move or remove.

3. To remove the effect, click Remove.

4. To move the effect, click Move Up or Move Down.

5. When you're done, click OK.

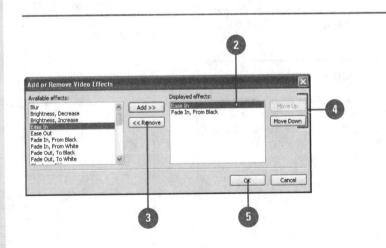

Adding Titles and Credits

You can add titles and credits to your movies just like the professionals (**New!**). You can add any text you want, such as the title of your movie, your name, captions, and credits at the end. You can add a title at the beginning of a movie, before or after a clip, or overlapping a clip or credits at the end of a movie. You can also change the appearance of the title or credits, and you can add special animation effects, which play for the time you specify in the Title Overlay track in the timeline.

Add Titles and Credits

1. Select the clip you want to add a title.

2. Click the Tasks button on the toolbar, if necessary, and then click Make Titles Or Credits under Edit Movie.

3. Click the link to where you want to add a title or credit.

4. Type the text you want to appear as the title.

5. Click Change The Text Font And Color, and then click a font, font color, font size, formatting, background color, transparency, and position.

6. Click Change The Title Animation, and then select a title animation.

7. Click Done, Add Title To Movie.

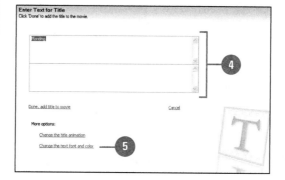

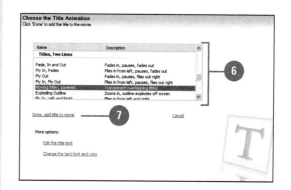

Did You Know?

You can change the title or credit duration. In the timeline, select the title or credit in the Title Overlay track, and then drag the edge to change the duration.

You can remove a title. Select the title in the storyboard or timeline, and then press Delete.

Adding a Soundtrack

With Movie Maker, you can play a video clip sound and soundtrack simultaneously and have one play louder than the other. You can put two types of sounds in your movies: sounds that are part of a video clip, and separate sounds, such as music or narration, that appear on the Audio bar of the timeline. You can import and edit sound clips in the soundtrack the same way you edit video clips using the Audio bar. Remember that if you use a clip from a CD, you must obtain permission from the publisher.

Add a Soundtrack

1. Click the Tasks button on the toolbar, if necessary, and then click Import Audio Or Music.

2. Select the folder that contains the files you want to import.

3. Select the files you want to import, and then click Import.

4. Click the Show Timeline button, if necessary.

5. Drag the sound clip onto the Audio/Music bar at the location where you want the clip to play.

6. Click the Set Audio Levels button.

7. Click the Rewind Timeline button, and then click the Play Timeline button.

8. Drag the Audio Levels slider to adjust the balance between the video click and the soundtrack.

9. When you're done adjusting the volume, click the Close button.

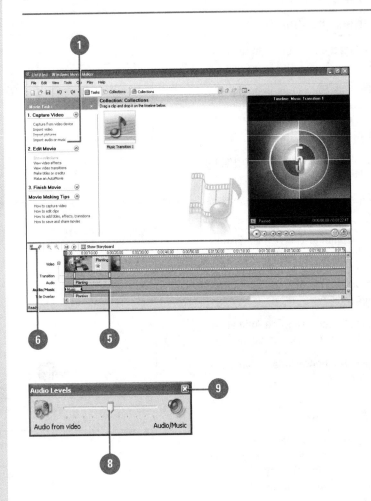

Adding a Narration

If you have a microphone attached to your computer, you can record a narration to accompany your movie. Your narration is saved as a .wav sound file directly in your Collections area so that you can place it in the Audio bar like any other audio clip.

Add a Narration

1. Click the Show Timeline button, if necessary, and then drag the playback indicator to the place where you want to start the narration.

2. Click the Tools menu, and then click Narrate Timeline.

3. To select an audio device, input source, and other settings, click Show More Options.

4. Drag the slide to adjust the input levels.

5. Click Start Narration.

6. When you're done speaking, click Stop Narration.

7. Save the audio file.

8. Click Done.

See Also

See "Adding a Soundtrack" on page 270 for information on changing the audio levels.

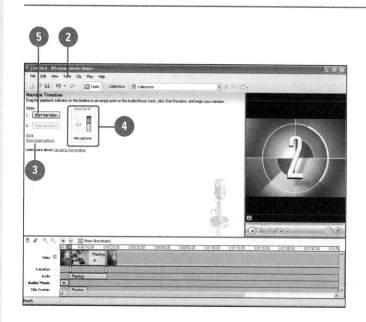

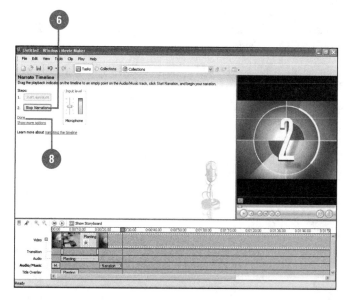

10

Using AutoMovie

You can use AutoMovie (**New!**) to help you automatically create a movie based on the selected clips or collection. AutoMovie analyzes the selected video clips, pictures, and music and combines them into a movie based on your AutoMovie editing style. To use AutoMovie, the total length of the clips you use need to last for at least 30 seconds; each picture needs to play at least 6 seconds, and an audio clip needs to play at least 30 seconds.

Use AutoMovie

1. Select the clips, pictures, and audio you want in the Collections area.

2. Click the Tools menu, and then click AutoMovie.

3. Click an AutoMovie editing style.

4. Click Enter A Title For The Movie.

5. Type the text you want to appear as the title.

6. Click Select Audio Or Background Music.

7. To select an audio or music file, click Browse, locate and select the audio or music file you want to use, and then click Open.

8. Drag the slider to adjust the audio balance level.

9. Click Done, Edit Movie.

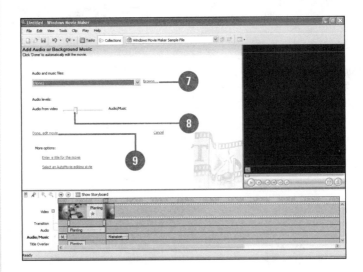

Saving a Project

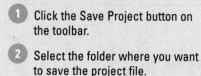

If you're still working on a project, you can save the project file and open it later to continue working with your movie. A saved project file in Movie Maker has an .mswmm file name extension. Before you save your project, you can include general information about the movie, such as the title, author, copyright, a rating, and a description, that is often displayed during playback by many media players.

Save a Movie Project

1 Click the Save Project button on the toolbar.

2 Select the folder where you want to save the project file.

3 Type a project name.

4 Click Save.

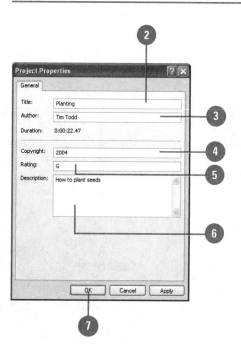

Add Project Properties

1 Click the File menu, and then click Properties.

2 Type the movie title.

3 Type the author name.

4 Type any copyright information.

5 Type a rating for the movie.

6 Type a description.

7 Click OK.

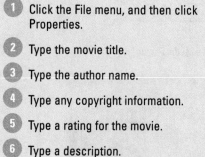

See Also

See "Saving a Movie" on page 274 for information on creating a movie from a project file.

10

Saving a Movie

After you preview the final project using the monitor, you can save the project file as a movie file. Using the Save Movie Wizard, you can save the movie file to your computer or a recordable CD, send it as an attachment in an e-mail message, or save and send it to the web. If you have a digital video camera connected to your computer, you can also record your movie to a tape. After you save the movie in the .wmv format, you can play it in a media player, such as Windows Media Player, or in a web browser.

Save a Movie to Your Computer

1. Click the Tasks button on the toolbar, if necessary, and then click Save To My Computer.

2. Type a file name for your captured video file.

3. Select the location where you want to save the video, and then click Next.

4. Click Show More Choices, click a movie quality option, and then click Next.

5. To play the movie, select the Play Movie When I Click Finish check box.

6. Click Finish.

Did You Know?

You can send a movie in e-mail. Click the Tasks button on the toolbar, if necessary, click Send In E-mail under Finish Movie, click Next to open a new e-mail message with the attached movie file, type an address and message, and then click Send.

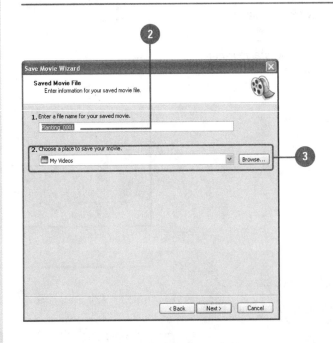

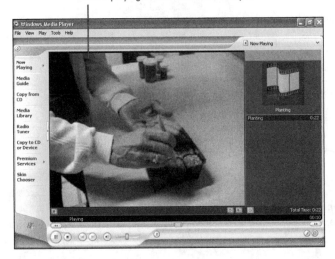

Movie playing in Windows Media Player

Save a Movie to a CD

1. Insert a blank CD into your CD-R or CD-RW drive.

2. Click the Tasks button on the toolbar if necessary, and then click Save To CD.

3. Type a file name for your saved movie.

4. Type a name for the CD, and then click Next.

5. Click Show More Choices, click a movie quality option, and then click Next.

6. Wait while Movie Maker saves the file to the CD.

7. To save the movie to another recordable CD, select the Save This Movie To Another Recordable CD check box.

8. Click Finish.

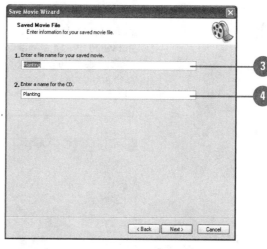

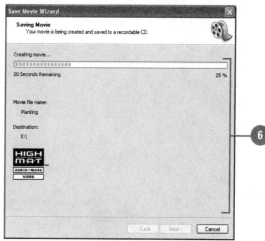

Did You Know?

You can save a movie to a digital video camera. Turn on your digital camera, and connect it to your computer. In Movie Maker, click the Tasks button, click Send To DV Camera in the Movie Tasks pane (under Finish Movie), select your digital camera, click Next, use your video camera controls to cue the tape, click Next, click Yes, and then click Finish.

10

Having More Fun with Movie Maker

Microsoft Windows XP provides additional Power Toys in Creativity Fun Packs (**New!**) you can download from the Web. The Creativity Fun pack for Movie Maker 2 includes sound effects, music tracks and transitions, and video titles and end credits that make it fun to create movies. Before you can use the Movie Maker fun pack, you need to download it from the Web and install it. The fun pack movie files are stored in your My Videos folder.

Download and Install the Fun Pack

1. Click the Help menu, and then click Windows Movie Maker On The Web.

   The Movie Maker Web site opens in your web browser.

2. Locate and click the link to the Movie Maker 2 Creativity Fun Pack.

   TROUBLE? *Web pages change, so you may need to use Search to find the link.*

3. Download the file, save it to your hard disk, and then double-click it to install it.

4. Follow the wizard instructions to complete the installation.

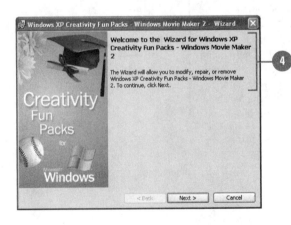

Setting Up Accounts and Maintaining Security

Introduction

With user accounts, you can customize and personalize Windows for each user on your computer. Each user can have their own My Documents folder and list of Web favorites, customize computer preferences, and protect private files. When you set up a new user account, the account appears on the Welcome screen, where the new user can log on.

You can use User Accounts in the Control Panel to add or delete user accounts, create a guest account, change a user's group or account type, change the way Windows starts, change the account picture, and set, change, and reset an account password.

Keeping your computer safe and secure is a continuing battle. With the Windows Security Center, you can manage computer security from one place. The Security Center makes it easy to find information about the latest virus or security threat, check the status of essential security settings, and quickly get support from Microsoft for a security-related issue.

While you're browsing the Internet or working in your e-mail program, you need to be aware of viruses and other harmful attacks so you can protect your computer from being infected by one. Internet Explorer and Outlook Express include security enhancements to help you make your computer more secure. In Internet Explorer, you can create security zones to designate trusted web sites, set web site ratings to restrict user access, use the Profile Assistant to protect personal information on the Internet, and manage cookies to protect your personal identity from unauthorized access. If you're tired to closing unwanted pop-up ads, you can use Pop-up Blocker in Internet Explorer to prevent most pop-up windows from appearing. In Outlook Express, you can select a security zone, set options to prevent viruses in attachments and spam, and send secure e-mail using digital IDs and encryption.

Securing a Computer

Windows XP provides several ways to secure your computer.

Create User Accounts

For a shared or workgroup computer, there are two main types of user accounts: computer administrator and limited. For a domain network computer, different account types (administrator, standard user, restricted user) provide similar permissions as the ones on a shared or workgroup computer.

The **computer administrator** account is for the person who needs to make changes to anything on the computer as well as manage user accounts. A computer administrator account can install programs and hardware, make system-wide changes, access and read all non private files, create and delete user accounts, change other people's accounts, change your own account name and type, change your own picture, and create, change, or remove your own password.

The **limited** account is for the person who needs to manage personal files and run programs. The limited account cannot install software or hardware or change most computer settings.

The **guest** account doesn't have a password for easy access and contains more restrictions than the limited account. The guest account is disabled by default and needs to be turned on.

Use Security Center

Use the Security Center to check your security settings— Window Firewall, Automatic Updates, and antivirus software—and learn how to improve the security of your computer.

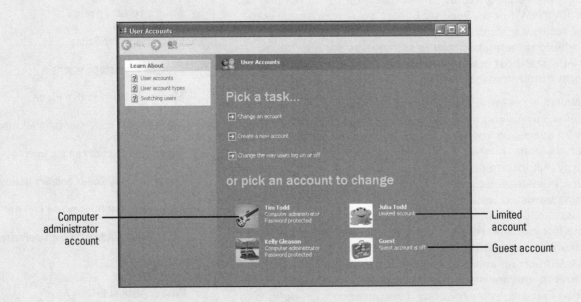

Computer administrator account

Limited account

Guest account

Enable Windows Firewall

Windows Firewall is a security system that creates a protective barrier between your computer or network and others on the Internet. Windows Firewall (NewSP2) monitors all communication between your computer and the Internet and prevents unsolicited inbound traffic from the Internet from entering your computer. For more information on Windows Firewall, see "Connecting to the Internet" on page 113 and "Setting Up Windows Firewall" on page 115.

Enable Automatic Updates

Windows Automatic Updates (NewSP2) allows you to keep your computer up-to-date with the latest system software and security updates over the Internet. For more information, see "Updating Windows" on page 390.

Enable Internet Security Options

Internet Explorer provides security zones to browse secure web sites and a rating system to screen content, protects personal information and your privacy on the Internet, blocks pop-up ads, and displays information to help you make security decisions. For more information, see "Understanding Security on the Internet" on page 298.

Enable E-Mail Security Options

Outlook Express provides security zones to help you to determine whether or not to run potentially harmful content from inside an e-mail, prevents program from sending mail with your e-mail address to contacts in your address book (which is a common way propagate a virus), and stops pictures and other content from automatically downloading inside and e-mail to your computer (which is a com-

mon way spammers confirm your e-mail address to send more spam). For more information, see "Sending and Retrieving a File" on page 156, "Reading and Replying to E-Mail" on page 154, and "Protecting Against E-Mail Attacks" on page 309.

Protect Files and Folders

Another way to protect the files on your computer is to use the built-in security provided by the NTFS file system. The NTFS file system is available for Windows NT-based computers, which doesn't include Windows 95, Windows 98, or Windows Me. You can select your hard disk in My Computer and display Details on the task pane to determine whether your computer uses the NTFS file system.

The NTFS file system provides additional security for your files and folders. You can make a folder private, use the advanced Encrypting File System (EFS) to protect sensitive data files on your computer. If someone tries to gain access to encrypted files or a folder on your computer, a unique file encryption key prevents that person from viewing it. While these security options are more advanced, they could be helpful for securing very sensitive information. For more information, see "Making a Folder Private" on page 291 and "Encrypting Files for Safety" on page 292.

Understand the Enemy

Knowing your enemy (harmful intruders) can help you make safe computing decisions that lead to a secure computer rather than unsafe ones that lead to potential disaster. For information, see "Avoiding Viruses and Other Harmful Attacks" on page 296.

11

Adding and Deleting User Accounts

If you have a computer administrator account or are a member of the Administrators group, you can create a new user account or delete an existing one. When you add a new user to your computer, Windows creates a separate identity, allowing the user to keep files completely private and customize the operating system with personal preferences. The name you assign to the user appears on the Log On screen and the Start menu. The steps to add and delete user accounts differ, depending on whether your computer is part of a domain network or shared/workgroup computer.

Add an Account

1. Click the Start button, and then click Control Panel.

2. Double-click the User Accounts icon in Classic view.

3. Click Create A New Account.

4. Type an account name, and then click Next.

5. Click the Computer Administrator option, or click the Limited option.

6. Click Create Account.

7. Click the Close button.

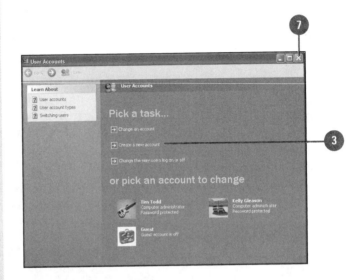

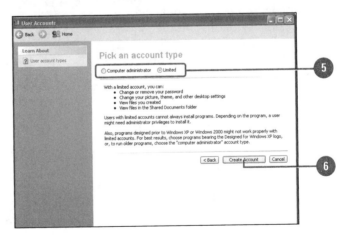

Did You Know?

You can delete an account. In User Accounts, click the account you want to remove, click Delete The Account, click Keep Files to save account file to the desktop or click Delete Files, and then click the Close button.

See Also

See "Securing a Computer" on page 278 for information on computer accounts.

Add an Account on a Domain Network

① Click the Start button, and then click Control Panel.

② Double-click the User Accounts icon in Classic view.

③ Click the Users tab.

④ Click Add to start the Add New User Wizard.

⑤ Type a user name and domain, and then click Next.

⑥ Click a user access level option: Standard, Restricted, or Other.

⑦ Click Finish.

⑧ Click OK.

Did You Know?

You can delete an account on a domain network. In the User Accounts dialog box, click the Users tab, select the user you want to delete, click Remove, click Yes to confirm, and then click OK.

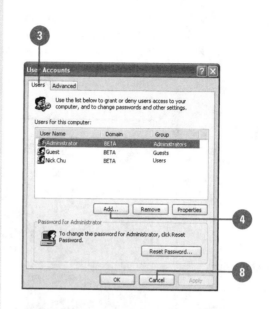

11

Creating a Guest Account

If you have a computer administrator account or are a member of the Administrators group, you can create a guest account. A guest account provides access to a computer for anyone who doesn't have a user account. The steps to create a guest account differ, depending on whether your computer is part of a domain network or shared/workgroup computer.

Create a Guest Account

1 Click the Start button, and then click Control Panel.

2 Double-click the User Accounts icon in Classic view.

3 Click the Guest Account.

4 Click Turn On The Guest Account.

5 Click the Close button.

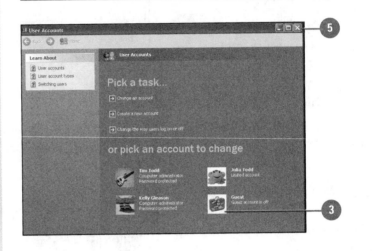

Create a Guest Account on a Domain Network

1 Click the Start button, and then click Control Panel.

2 Double-click the Administrative Tools icon in Classic view, and then double-click the Computer Management icon.

3 Click Local Users and Groups, and then double-click Users.

4 Double-click the Guest icon.

5 Clear the Account Is Disabled check box.

6 Click OK, click the Close button twice.

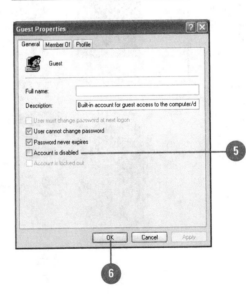

Changing a User's Group or Account Type

If you have a computer administrator account or are a member of the Administrators group, you can change a user's account type or user group on a domain network. A user account or group grants permissions to a user to perform certain types of tasks based on the account type or user group (domain network). The steps to create a guest account differ, depending on whether your computer is part of a network domain or shared/workgroup computer.

Change a User's Account Type

1. Click the Start button, and then click Control Panel.

2. Double-click the User Accounts icon in Classic view.

3. Click the user's account name.

4. Click Change The Account Type.

5. Click the type of account you want.

6. Click Change Account Type.

7. Click the Close button.

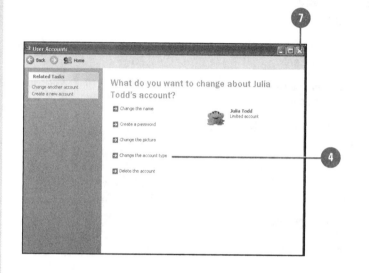

Change a User's Group on a Domain Network

1. Click the Start button, and then click Control Panel.

2. Double-click the User Accounts icon in Classic view.

3. Click the Users tab.

4. Select the user account name you want to change.

5. Click Properties, and then click the Group Membership tab.

6. Click the group you want.

7. Click OK, and then click OK again.

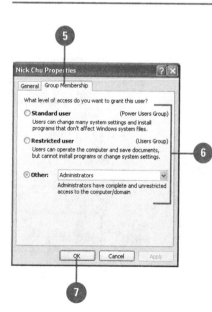

11

Changing the Start Up Screen

For added security, you can turn off the Welcome screen and Fast User Switching (New!). This requires users to use the classic logon prompt and to type a user account name. If you are using a domain network, you can require users to use Ctrl+Alt+Delete, which protects your computer from automatic logins. The steps to change the way Windows starts differ, depending on whether your computer is part of a network domain or shared/workgroup computer.

Change the Way Users Logon and Logoff

1. Click the Start button, and then click Control Panel.

2. Double-click the User Accounts icon in Classic view.

3. Click Change The Way Users Log On Or Off.

4. Clear the Use The Welcome Screen check box. This turns off Fast User Switching too.

5. Click Apply Options.

6. Click the Close button.

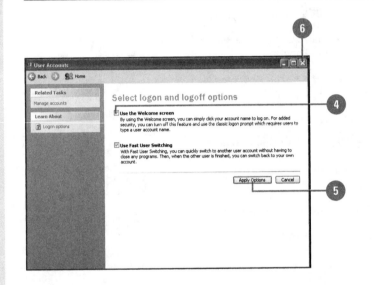

Increase Logon Security on a Domain Network

1. Click the Start button, and then click Control Panel.

2. Double-click the User Accounts icon in Classic view.

3. Click the Advanced tab.

4. Select the Require Users To Press Ctrl+Alt+Delete check box.

5. Click OK.

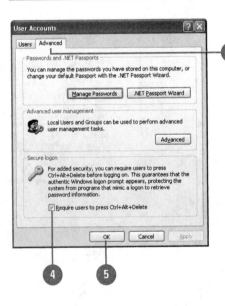

Changing an Account Picture

When you log on to Windows, the Welcome screen appears, displaying a list of user accounts with a picture next to each one. When you complete the logon process, the picture associated with your account appears at the top of the Start menu along with your user name. This identifies you as the current user of the computer. You can change the picture to suit your own personality. Changing your account picture is not available for computers on a domain network.

Change an Account Picture

1. Click the Start button, and then click Control Panel.

2. Double-click the User Accounts icon in Classic view.

3. Click the user's account name.

4. Click Change The Picture or click Change My Picture.

5. Click the picture you want.

6. Click Change Picture, or click Browse For More Pictures and double-click the picture you want.

7. Click the Close button.

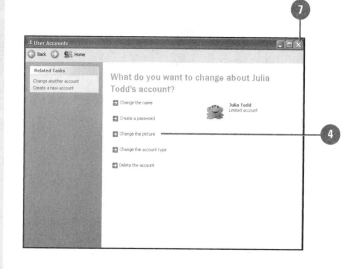

See Also

See Chapter 8,"Working with Pictures" on page 199 for information on creating, scanning, and using pictures.

11

Setting and Changing a Password

If you don't have a password associated with your user account, anyone can access your files. A password controls who has access to your files. When you create a password, enter one that is easy for you to remember, yet difficult for others to guess. Good passwords are typically at least seven characters and include letters (uppercase and lowercase), numbers, and symbols. Once you create a password, you can always change it (**New!**).

Create a Password

1. Click the Start button, and then click Control Panel.

2. Double-click the User Accounts icon in Classic view.

3. Click the user's account name.

4. Click Create A Password.

5. Type a password, and then type it again.

6. Type a hint that reminds you of the password.

7. Click Create Password.

8. If your computer uses NTFS, click Yes, Make Private to make your files private, or click No.

9. Click the Close button.

Did You Know?

You can change a password. In User Accounts, click the account you want to change, click Change My Password, type your current password, if necessary, type a new password, type it again, type a hint, and then click Change Password.

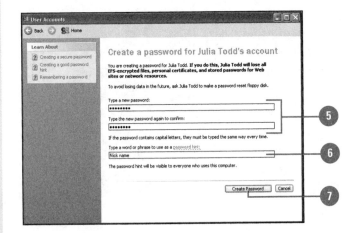

Change an Administrator Password on a Domain Network

1️⃣ Click the Start button, and then click Control Panel.

2️⃣ Double-click the User Accounts icon in Classic view.

3️⃣ Click the Users tab.

4️⃣ Click the administrator account.

5️⃣ Click Reset Password.

6️⃣ Type the new password, and then type it again.

7️⃣ Click OK.

8️⃣ Click OK.

See Also

See "Making a Folder Private" on page 291 for information on NTFS and private folders.

11

Security Alert

Working Smarter as the Administrator

If you are an administrator, it's recommended that you log out and use another account for general work to avoid harmful damage to your computer by a virus or malicious user. For example, if a hacker received access to your computer with administrator privileges, the attacker could reformat your hard drive, delete files, or create a new administrator account.

Resetting a Password

If you have ever forgotten your password, you understand how important it is to write it down. However, writing down a password is not very secure. You can create a Password Reset disk (**New!**) to help you log on and reset your password. If you have any security credentials and certificates on your computer, the Password Reset disk restores them. If you have forgotten your password and don't have a Password Reset disk, you can ask your administrator to reset it for you. Resetting your password also erases any security credentials and certificates on your computer.

Create a Password Reset Disk

1. Click the Start button, and then click Control Panel.

2. Double-click the User Accounts icon in Classic view.

3. Click the user's account name.

4. Click Prevent A Forgotten Password.

5. Insert a blank disk in the Floppy drive, and then follow the instructions in the Forgotten Password Wizard to create a password reset disk.

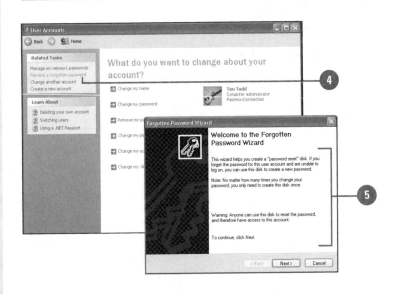

Reset Your Password

1. At the Welcome screen, click the Help button to see your password hint, and then type the password if you remember it.

2. Click the green arrow.

3. Click User Your Password Reset Disk, follow the instructions in the Password Reset Wizard to create a new password.

4. Type your new password, and then press Enter.

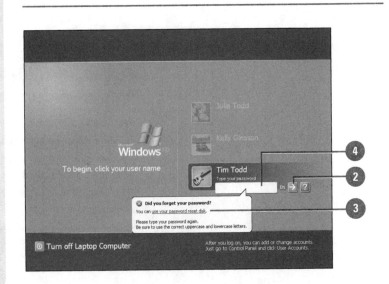

Locking the Computer ▶

If you are working on sensitive material and need to leave your computer unattended for a while, you can lock it so that no one can use it without your permission. While your computer is locked, all your programs continue to run. When you return to your computer, you can access your computer in the same way you started Windows. If you have Fast User Switching turned on, the Welcome screen appears (**New!**). If it is turned off or you work on a network domain, the Locked Computer dialog box appears.

Lock and Unlock the Computer

1 Press ⊞+L to lock the computer.

> **TIMESAVER** *The Windows key* ⊞ *is located in the lower-left corner of the keyboard.*

2 If the Welcome screen appears, click your name, type your password, and then press Enter.

3 If the Computer Locked dialog box appears, press Ctrl+Alt+Del, type your password, and then click OK.

See Also

See "Starting Windows XP" on page 6 and "Switching Users" on page 20 for information on logging on to Windows XP.

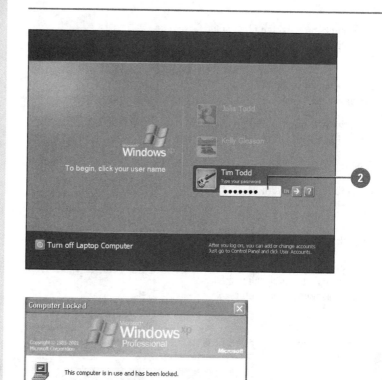

Protecting Files with a Password

If you have files that contain sensitive information on a shared computer, network, or removable disk, or if you want to send confidential files in an e-mail message, you can compress the files in a folder and assign a password. You need the password to open the files, so don't forget it.

Compress and Protect Files

1 Select the files you want to protect.

2 Right-click the selected files, point to Send To, and then click Compressed (Zipped) Folder.

3 Double-click the compressed folder.

4 Click the File menu, and then click Add A Password.

5 Type a case-sensitive password.

6 Re-enter the password.

7 Click OK.

8 Click the Close button.

9 To access the compressed folder, double-click it, double-click a file, type a password, and then click OK.

See Also

See "Compressing Files and Folders" on page 76 for information on working with compressed files.

Making a Folder Private

If you share your computer with other people, you may want to keep some files private. If your computer uses NTFS and you have a user account, you can make a folder private. Any files or folder in the private folder become protected, too. When you log on to Windows, you can access the files in the private folder.

Make a Folder Private

1. Click the Start button, and then click My Computer.

2. Display the folder you want to make private.

3. Right-click the folder, and then click Sharing And Security.

4. Click the Sharing tab.

5. Select the Make This Folder Private check box.

6. Click OK.

7. If you don't have a password, click Yes to create one.

See Also

See "Understanding Disk File Systems" on page 374 for information on the NTFS file system.

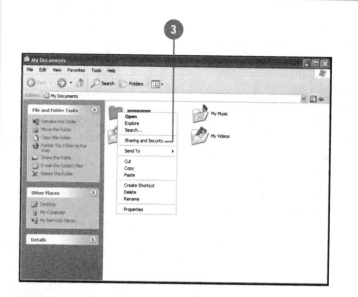

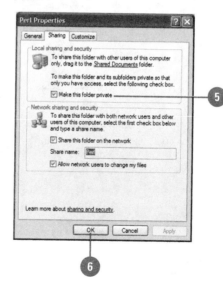

11

Encrypting Files for Safety

If your computer uses NTFS, you can use the advanced Encrypting File System (EFS) to protect sensitive data files on your computer. If someone tries to gain access to encrypted files or a folder on your computer, a unique file encryption key prevents that person from viewing it. When you encrypt a file, you also need to decide whether you want to encrypt the folder, too. When you encrypt a folder, you need to decide whether you want to encrypt all files and subfolders within it.

Encrypt or Decrypt a File or Folder

1. Right-click the file or folder you want to encrypt, and then click Properties.

2. Click the General tab.

3. Click Advanced.

4. Select the Encrypt Contents To Secure Data check box to encrypt the file or folder or clear the check box to decrypt it.

5. Click OK.

6. Click OK.

7. Click an option to apply changes to this folder only or to this folder, subfolders, and files.

8. Click OK.

Did You Know?

You can compress files and folders with NTFS. Right-click the file or folder, click Properties, click the General tab, click Advanced, select the Compress Contents To Save Disk Space check box, and then click OK twice.

Analyzing Computer Security

Microsoft Baseline Security Analyzer (MBSA) (**New!**) is a tool available for download from the Internet that allows you to scan your computer for common security misconfigurations and potential security vulnerabilities. It can also check whether your computer is up-to-date with respect to critical security updates. Descriptions of each check are detailed in a security report that includes instructions for fixing any issues that were found. You must have administrator privileges for each computer you want to scan. You can download MBSA from the Microsoft TechNet Web site at *www.microsoft.com/technet*. Perform a search for MBSA, and then follow the instructions to download and install the product.

Analyze a Computer Security

1. Click the Start button, point to All Programs, and then click Microsoft Baseline Security Analyzer.

2. Click Scan A Computer.

3. Select the computer you want to scan.

4. Select the check boxes with the option you want, and clear the other ones.

5. Click Start Scan.

6. View the report.

7. Click the Close button.

See Also

See "Updating Windows" on page 390 for information on installing the latest security updates.

Did You Know?

You can view existing reports. Start MBSA, click Pick A Security Report To View, and then click a report.

You can print an existing report. Start MBSA, click Pick A Security Report To View, click a report, and then click Print.

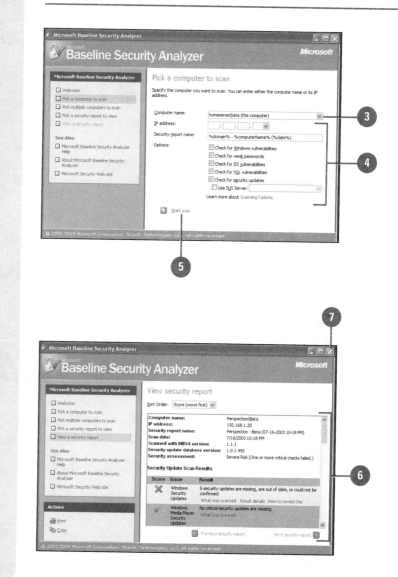

Managing Security in One Place

The Windows Security Center (NewSP2) provides a single place to manage your three security essentials, Windows Firewall, Automatic Updates, and Virus Protection using your antivirus software. The Security Center recommends security settings that you can use to help protect your computer. It also provides links to important information about the latest virus or other security threat, or to get customer support from Microsoft for a security related issue. As you work, Windows XP uses security alerts and icons (NewSP2) in the notification area on the taskbar to help you recognize potential security risks, such as a new virus, out of date antivirus software or an important security option is turned off, and choose appropriate settings.

View Essential Security Settings Using the Security Center

1. Click the Start button, and then click Control Panel.

2. Double-click the Security Center icon in Classic view.

   IMPORTANT *If you're part of a network, options might be grayed out; your security settings are managed by your network administrator.*

3. To manage security settings, click the link (Internet Options, Automatic Updates, or Windows Firewall) for the one you want.

4. To find out information about security options and issues, click the link you want.

5. When you're done, click the Close button.

Did You Know?

Windows Firewall could be on when it says off. If you use the Advanced tab to turn off Windows Firewall for one or more individual connections, the Security Center indicates the firewall is turned off, even though it is still on for other connections.

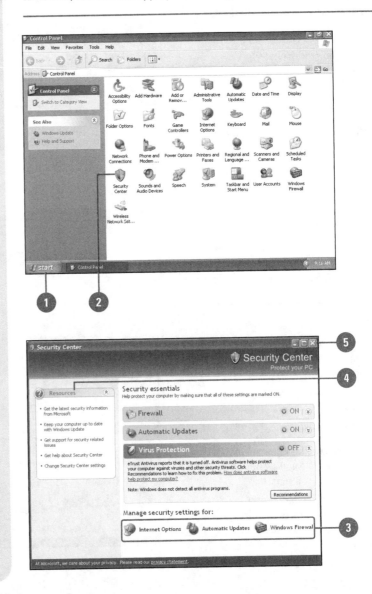

Act Upon Security Alerts

1. If the Security Center detects that your computer needs enhanced security, it displays an alert in the notification area.

2. Read the security alert, and then click it.

3. To find out information on a security option, click the down arrow next to it.

4. To find out how to address the problem, click Recommendations, and then follow the instructions.

5. When you're done, click the Close button.

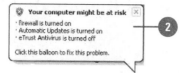

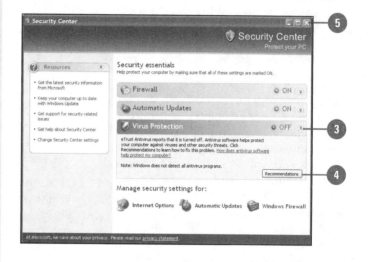

Did You Know?

You can disable virus alerts when Security Center doesn't recognize an installed antivirus software. Double-click the Security Center icon in the Control Panel, click Recommendations (under Virus Protection), select the I Have Antivirus Software That I'll Monitor Myself check box, and then click OK.

You can disable firewall alerts when Security Center doesn't recognize an installed third-party firewall. Double-click the Security Center icon in the Control Panel, click Recommendations (under Firewall), select the I Have A Firewall Solution That I'll Monitor Myself check box, and then click OK.

You can disable Security Center alerts. Not recommended; only for an expert. Double-click the Security Center icon in the Control Panel, click Change The Way Security Center Alerts Me (under Resources), clear the Firewall, Automatic Updates, Or Virus Protection check box, and then click OK.

Security Icons

Icon	Description
	Security Settings: Indicates important security information and settings are available, such as the Windows Security Center.
	Potential Risk: Indicates your computer encountered a potential security risk; act upon the security alert.
	No Risk: Indicates your computer is more secure and using recommended security settings; no action needed.
	Security Warning: Indicates your computer encountered a warning alert, which is potentially harmful; consider adjusting security settings.
	Security Problem: Indicates your computer is not using recommended security settings; consider adjusting them.

11

Avoiding Viruses and Other Harmful Attacks

Understanding Harmful Attacks

Using the Internet can expose your computer to a wide variety of harmful attacks, such as viruses, worms, and Trojan Horses. These attacks can come through e-mail, file transferring, and even possibly through Java and ActiveX, which are both programming languages used to enhance web pages.

A **virus** is an executable program whose functions range from just being annoying to causing havoc to your computer. A virus may display an innocuous warning on a particular day, such as Friday the 13th, or it may cause a more serious problem, such as wiping out your entire hard disk. Viruses are found in executable (.exe and .com) files, along with Microsoft Word and Microsoft Excel macro files. A **worm** is like a virus, but it can spread without human action across networks. For example, a worm might send e-mail copies of itself to everyone in your e-mail Address Book. A worm can consume memory causing your computer to stop responding or even take it over. A **Trojan Horse**, like it's mythological counterpart, is a program that appears to be useful and comes from a legitimate source, but actually causes problems.

Spreading Harmful Infections

Many viruses and other harmful attacks spread through file downloads and attachments in e-mail messages. Virus writers capitalize on people's curiosity and willingness to accept files from people they know or work with, in order to transmit malicious files disguised as or attached to benign files. When you start downloading files to your computer, you must be aware of the potential for catching a computer virus, worm, or Trojan Horse. Typically, you can't catch a one from just reading a mail message or downloading a file, but you can catch a one from opening or running an infected program, such as a file attached to an e-mail message, or one you download for free. And even though most viruses and other harmful attacks take the form of executable programs, data files that have macros or Visual Basic code attached to them, such as Word or Excel files, can also be infected with viruses.

Avoiding Harmful Attacks

There are a few things you can do to keep your system safe from the infiltration of viruses and other harmful attacks.

1) Make sure Windows Firewall is turned on. Windows Firewall (NewSP2) helps block viruses and worms from reaching your computer, but it doesn't detect or disable them if they are already on your computer or come through e-mail. Windows Firewall doesn't block unsolicited e-mail or stop you from opening e-mail with harmful attachments. For more information on Windows Firewall, see "Connecting to the Internet" on page 113 and "Setting Up Windows Firewall" on page 115.

2) Make sure Automatic Updates is turned on. Windows Automatic Updates (NewSP2) regularly checks the Windows Update web site for important updates that your computer needs, such as security updates, critical updates, and service packs. Each file that you download using Automatic Update has a digital signature from Microsoft to ensure it's authenticity and security. For more information, see "Updating Windows" on page 390.

3) Make sure you are using the most up-to-date antivirus software. New viruses and more virulent strains of existing viruses are discovered every day. Unless you update your virus checking software, new viruses can easily bypass outdated virus checking software.

Companies such as McAfee and Symantec offer shareware virus checking programs available for download directly from their web sites. These programs monitor your system, checking each time a file is added to your computer to make sure it's not in some way trying to change or damage valuable system files.

4) Be very careful of the sites from which you download files. Major file repository sites, such as FileZ, Download.com, or TuCows, regularly check the files they receive for viruses before posting them to their web sites. Don't download files from web sites unless you are certain that the sites check their files for viruses. Internet Explorer monitors downloads and warns you about potentially harmful files and gives you the option to block them (NewSP2). For more information, see "Downloading Files from the Web" on page 136.

5) Be very careful of file attachments in e-mail you open. As you receive e-mail, don't open or run an attached file unless you know who sent it and what it contains. If you're not sure, you should delete it. The Attachment Manager (NewSP2) provides security information to help you understand more about the file you're opening. To protect your computer from harmful attacks, see "Sending and Retrieving a File" on page 156, "Reading and Replying to E-Mail" on page 154, and "Protecting Against E-Mail Attacks" on page 309.

6) Make sure you activate macro virus checking protection in both Word and Excel. To do so, click the Tools menu, point to Macro on the expanded menu, click Security, and then make sure that the High Security Level option is selected. (In Office 2000, XP, or later, click the Tools menu, click Options, click the General tab, and then make sure the Macro Virus Protection option is selected.) And always elect not to run macros when opening a Word or Excel file that you received from someone who might not be using proper virus protection.

Avoiding Other Intruders

Spyware is software that collects personal information without your knowledge or permission. Typically, spyware is downloaded and installed on your computer along with free software, such as freeware, games, or music file-sharing programs. Spyware is often associated with **Adware** software that displays advertisements, such as a pop-up ad. Examples of spyware and unauthorized adware include programs that change your home page or search page without your permission. To avoid spyware and adware, read the fine print in license agreements when you install software, scan your computer for spyware and adware with detection and removal software (such as Ad-aware from Lavasoft), and turn on Pop-up Blocker. For details, see "Blocking Pop-Up Ads" on page 306.

Spam is unsolicited e-mail, which is often annoying and time-consuming to get rid of. Spammers harvest e-mail addresses from Web pages and unsolicited e-mail. To avoid spam, use multiple e-mail addresses (one for web forms and another for private e-mail), opt-out and remove yourself from e-mail lists, and turn on the Block Images And Other External Content In HTML E-mail option. For details, see "Protecting Against E-Mail Attacks" on page 309.

Phishing is an e-mail scam that tries to steal your identity by sending deceptive e-mail asking you for bank and credit card information online. Don't be fooled by spoofed web site that look like the official site. Never respond to requests for personal information via e-mail; call the institution to investigate and report it.

11

Understanding Security on the Internet

No other web browser offers as many customizable features as Internet Explorer does, particularly advanced security features that are built into the program. To understand all the Internet Explorer security features, you first have to learn about security on the Internet in general.

When you send information from your computer to another computer, the two computers are not linked directly together. Your data may travel through multiple networks as it works its way across the Internet. Since your data is broadcast to the Internet, any computer on any of these networks could be listening in and capturing your data. (They typically aren't, but they could be.)

In addition, on the Internet it's possible to masquerade as someone else. E-mail addresses can be forged, domain names of sites can easily be misleading, and so on. You need some way to protect not only the data you send, but also yourself from sending data to the wrong place.

Furthermore, there is always the potential that someone (referred to as a "hacker") or something, such as a virus or worm, could infiltrate your computer systems. Once infiltrated, a hacker or virus can delete, rename, or even copy valuable information from your computer without your knowledge.

Security Zones

Through the use of **security zones**, you can easily tell Internet Explorer which sites you trust to not damage your computer and which sites you simply don't trust. In your company's intranet you would most likely trust all the information supplied on web pages through your company's network, but on the Internet you may want to be warned first of potential dangers a site could cause your system. You can set up different levels of security based on different zones.

Certificates

When shopping on the Internet, you want to do business with only those companies that offer a certain level of security and promise to protect your buying information. In turn, those companies want to do business with legitimate customers only. A **certificate** or **digital ID** provides both the browser and the company with a kind of guarantee confirming that you are who you say you are and that the site is secure and genuine, not a fraud or scam. When you send an e-mail message, it also verifies your identity to your recipients.

A digital ID is made up of a public key, a private key, and a digital signature. When you digitally sign an e-mail, Outlook Express adds your public key and digital signature (the two together is the certificate) to the message. When your recipients receive the e-mail, your digital signature verifies your identity and your public key is stored in their Address Book so they can send you encrypted messages, which only you can open with your private key.

An independent company, called a **credentials agency**, issues three types of certificates: personal, authority, and publisher. A **personal certificate** identifies you so that you can access web sites that require positive identification, such as banks that allow online transactions. You can obtain a personal certificate from a credentials agency called VeriSign using the Security tab of the Options dialog box in Outlook Express. An **authority certificate** ensures that the web site you are visiting is not a fraud. Internet Explorer automatically checks site certificates to make sure that they're valid. A **publisher certificate** enables you to trust software that you download, such as ActiveX controls. Internet Explorer maintains a list of software companies whose certificates are valid and trustworthy. You can view your certificate settings on the Content tab of the Internet Options dialog box.

Content Advisor

Just about everyone can find objectionable material on the Internet. Parents might not want to subject their children to some of this material, such as strong language, violence, and other adult themes. However, most parents cannot spend every online minute with their children, censoring objectionable sites. In such cases, you can employ Internet Explorer's **Content Advisor** to screen out inappropriate sites, preventing youngsters from seeing things they shouldn't.

The Content Advisor works with different rating bureaus, such as the Recreational Software Advisory Council (RSAC), to rate sites within certain ranges. The RSAC's rating system is based on research that compiled a rating system to reflect different levels of violence, strong language, and so on. You decide exactly what kind of sites that your children can access, what ratings systems are used, which ranges are available to users within those sites, and whether users of your computer can see unrated sites.

You can also assign a supervisor password to allow a user to view such sites. As long as the user supplies the password you specified when you initially set up the content rating systems, the user can view sites where the material rates above the level chosen. You can turn off the Content Advisor at any time, opening up all sites on the Internet for viewing by any user without having to enter a password.

In order for the rating system to work, sites must subscribe to the system so that their ratings are passed to your computer when you access the sites. Most sites that want to offer quality information for children and those adult sites interested in making sure only individuals 18 years old or older are accessing their sites subscribe to rating systems like the RSAC. A site that voluntarily rates itself usually displays the RSAC logo on its home page. This logo is your indication that the site has properly rated itself and offers only materials that are appropriate to its rating.

Cookies

When you browse the Internet, you can access and gather information from web sites, but web sites can also gather information about you without your knowledge unless you set up Internet security on your computer. You can set Internet privacy options to protect your personal identity from unauthorized access. When you visit a web site, the site creates a **cookie** file, known as a **first-party cookie**, which stores information on your computer, such as your web site preferences or personal identifiable information, including your name and e-mail address. Not all cookies are harmful; many first-party-cookies save you time re-entering information on a return visit to a web site. However, there are also **third-party cookies**, such as advertising banners, which are created by web sites you are not currently viewing. Once a cookie is saved on your computer, only the web site that created it can read it. The privacy options allow you to block or permit cookies for web sites in the Internet zone; however, when you block cookies, you might not be able to access all the features of a web site. When a web site violates your cookie policy, a red icon appears on the status bar.

11

Creating Security Zones

Internet Explorer lets you create security zones based on where information comes from. For example, you might want to restrict access to web pages that can be viewed from the Internet, but not to those sites within your company's intranet. You can specify the level of security for each of the four available security zones: Local Intranet, Trusted Sites, Restricted Sites, and Internet. When you access a web page or download content from the site, Internet Explorer checks its security settings and determines the web site's zone. Internet Explorer displays a padlock icon in the status bar to indicate the web site is secure. All Internet web sites are assigned to the Internet zone until you assign individual web sites to other zones.

Select a Security Zone and Its Security Level

1. Click the Start button, and then click Control Panel, double-click the Internet Options in Classic view.

2. Click the Security tab.

3. Click the zone to which you want to assign security options.

4. If you want, click Default Level to reset the settings to Microsoft's suggested level.

5. Move the slider to the level of security you want to apply.

   TROUBLE? *If the slider is not available, click Default Level to change the security level to Medium and display the slider.*

6. If you want to specify individual security options, click Custom Level.

7. Scroll to a settings area, and then click the Enable, Prompt, or Disable option button.

8. Click OK.

9. Click OK.

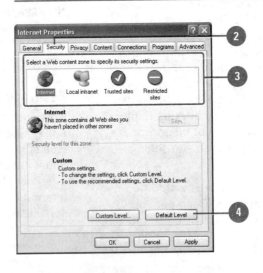

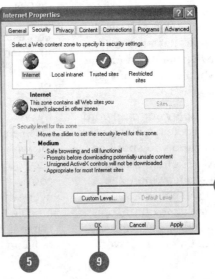

Add Sites to Your Restricted Sites Zone

1 Click the Start button, and then click Control Panel, double-click the Internet Options in Classic view.

2 Click the Security tab.

3 Click Restricted Sites.

4 Click Sites.

5 Type the full URL for the site.

6 Click Add.

7 Click OK, and then click OK again.

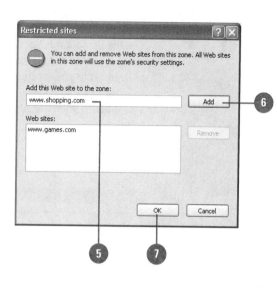

Did You Know?

You can reset default settings for security options. To return each option to its default settings for a specified security level, click the Reset Custom Settings list arrow, select a security level, and then click Reset.

You can remove a site from your Restricted Sites zone. Click the Tools menu, click Internet Options, click the Security tab, click Restricted Sites, and then click the Sites button. In the Web Sites box, click the site you want to remove, click Remove, and then click OK. Click OK to close the Internet Options dialog box.

Security Zones	
Zone	**Description**
Internet	Contains all web sites that are not assigned to any other zone; default is Medium
Local intranet	Contains all web sites that are on your organization's intranet and don't require a proxy server; default is Medium
Trusted sites	Contains web sites that you trust not to threaten the security of your computer; default is Low (allows all cookies)
Restricted sites	Contains web sites that you believe threaten the security of your computer; default is High (blocks all cookies)

For Your Information

Setting a Stronger Zone Defense

Internet Explorer also uses another zone called Local Machine, which provides security for your hard disk, but doesn't appear on the Security tab. In earlier versions of Internet Explorer, hackers were using low security levels to attack your computer. This is now stopped (NewSP2).

11

Setting Ratings Using the Content Advisor

If you have children who surf the Internet and you don't want to subject them to strong language, violence, or sexually explicit material, you can use the Content Advisor to restrict their access to inappropriate web sites. If a rated site matches your ratings specifications, the site can be viewed. If the site is rated above the level you've set, or if the site is not rated and you've restricted access to unrated sites, the site can be viewed only when the supervisor password is supplied.

Enable the Content Advisor Ratings

1. Click the Start button, and then click Control Panel, double-click the Internet Options in Classic view.

2. Click the Content tab.

3. Click Enable. This button toggles between Enable and Disable.

    The first time you use Content Advisor, set your initial settings.

4. Click OK, type a supervisor password twice, and then click OK.

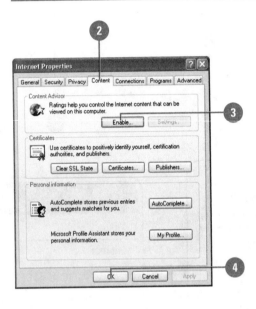

Set the Content Advisor Ratings

1. Click the Start button, and then click Control Panel, double-click the Internet Options in Classic view.

2. Click the Content tab.

3. Click Settings. If necessary, type the supervisor password, and then click OK.

4. Click the category for which you want to set the rating.

5. Move the Rating slider to the rating level you want.

6. Click OK, and then click OK again.

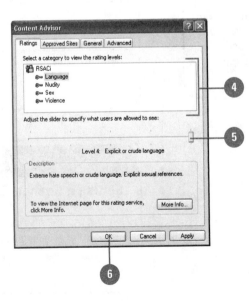

Protecting Personal Information on the Internet

Using Internet Explorer, you can store personal, home, business, and other information in a single location to make communicating and shopping on the Internet quick and easy. The **Profile Assistant (New!)** stores your name, address, and other important information. The Profile Assistant can save you from having to enter the same information every time you visit a new web site that requests such information. The information is stored on your computer and cannot be viewed without your permission. If a web site requests information, the Profile Assistant lets you know.

Enter Information About You Using the Profile Assistant

1. Click the Start button, and then click Control Panel, double-click the Internet Options in Classic view.

2. Click the Content tab.

3. Click My Profile.

4. If necessary, click the option you want to create a new profile or select an existing one, and then click OK.

5. Click each tab to enter the information.

6. Enter or modify the necessary information in the boxes.

7. Click OK.

8. Click OK.

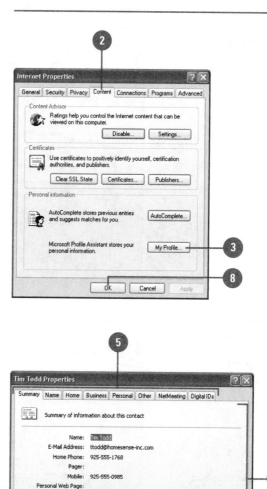

Protecting Internet Privacy

You can set Internet privacy options to protect your personal identity from unauthorized access (**New!**). The privacy options allow you to block or permit cookies for web sites in the Internet zone; however, when you block cookies, you might not be able to access all the features of a web site. When a web site violates your cookie policy, a red icon appears on the status bar. To find out if the web site you are viewing in Internet Explorer contains third-party cookies or whether any cookies have been restricted, you can get a privacy report. The privacy report lists all the web sites with content on the current Web page and shows how all the web sites handle cookies.

Control the Use of Cookies

1. Click the Start button, and then click Control Panel, double-click the Internet Options in Classic view.

2. Click the Privacy tab.

3. Drag the slider to select the level of privacy you want.

4. Click OK.

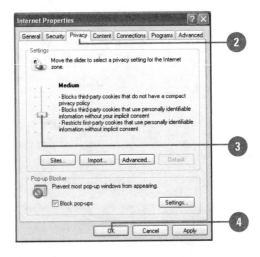

Delete All Cookies

1. Click the Tools menu, and then click Internet Options.

2. Click the General tab.

3. Click Delete Cookies.

4. Click OK, and then click OK again.

Did You Know?

You can view a web site's privacy policy summary. Click the Start button, click Internet, click the View menu, click Privacy Report, select a web site, and then click Summary.

Protecting an Internet Identity

To further protect your privacy, you can use certificates to verify your identity and protect important information, such as your credit card number, on the Internet (New!). A certificate is a statement verifying the identity of a person or the security of a web site. You can obtain your personal security certification from an independent Certification Authority (CA). A personal certificate verifies your identity to a secure web site that requires a certificate, while a web site certificate verifies its security to you before you send it information. When you visit a secure web site (one whose address may start with "https" instead of "http"), the site automatically sends you its certificate, and Internet Explorer displays a lock icon on the status bar. A certificate is also known as a Digital ID in other programs, such as Outlook Express, or the Address Book.

Import a Certificate

1. Click the Start button, and then click Control Panel, double-click the Internet Options in Classic view.

2. Click the Content tab.

3. Click Certificates.

4. Click the tab with the type of certificate you want.

5. Click Import.

6. Follow the instructions in the Certificate Import Wizard to import a certificate.

7. Click Close.

8. Click OK.

Did You Know?

You can let e-mail recipients know a message is from you with a certificate. Click the Start button, click Outlook Express, click the Tools menu, click Options, click the Security tab, select the Digitally Sign All Outgoing Messages check box, then click OK.

Blocking Pop-Up Ads

The Pop-up Blocker (NewSP2) prevents most unwanted pop-up windows from appearing. When Internet Explorer blocks an ad, a new window appears with an alert message in the Information Bar at the top. Blocked items are replaced in the window with a red "x". The Information Bar in Internet Explorer lets you temporarily or permanently open pop-ups, change Pop-up Blocker settings, and get Information Bar help. With the Pop-up Blocker Settings dialog box, you can allow or disallow pop-ups from specific sites, play a sound or show the Information Bar when a pop-up is blocked, and set a filter level to block pop-ups.

Set Options to Block Pop-Up Ads

1. Click the Start button, and then click Control Panel, double-click the Internet Options in Classic view.

2. Click the Privacy tab.

3. Select the Block Pop-ups check box.

   TIMESAVER *In Internet Explorer, click the Tools menu, point to Pop-up Blocker, and then click Turn On Pop-up Blocker.*

4. Click Settings.

   TIMESAVER *In Internet Explorer, click the Tools menu, point to Pop-up Blocker, and then click Pop-up Blocker Settings.*

5. To add an pop-up exception, enter a web site address, then click Add.

6. Select or clear check boxes to play sound or show an Information Bar when an ad is blocked.

7. Click the Filter Level list arrow, then click a pop-up filter: High, Medium, Low.

8. Click Close.

9. Click OK.

Default filter is set to Medium

Using the Information Bar

Security Information Bar for Browsing

The Information Bar (NewSP2) in Internet Explorer makes it easier for you to make informed decisions about potentially harmful content entering your computer. Internet Explorer displays the Information Bar below the address bar where you can view important security information about blocked pop-ups, downloads, security risks, and other harmful threats. When Internet Explorer blocks a pop-up ad or program from running on your computer, the Information Bar appears at the top of the window with information and options. If the default settings in Internet Explorer are turned on, the Information Bar appears when a web site tries to install an add-on, such as an ActiveX control, open a pop-up window, or download a file to your computer. A pop-up window typically display annoying ads. ActiveX controls provide added functionality to Internet Explorer, which makes using the Internet more enjoyable. However, it also opens the door for Spyware and Adware to invade your computer and privacy. When an outsider tries to enter your computer, the Information Bar appears, where you can click the message to take an action, such as block or unblock the content, or get more information. See "Blocking Pop-Up Ads" on page 306 for information on turning on the Information Bar.

Security Information Bar for E-Mail

Outlook Express adds a security option to stop pictures and other content from automatically downloading to your computer from contacts who are not in your address book (NewSP2). Spammers commonly use automatic picture download to confirm your e-mail address and send you more spam. Blocking the picture download provides a faster display, reduces spam e-mail. When Outlook Express blocks images and other potential harm content in an e-mail message from downloading to your computer, the Information Bar appears at the top of the e-mail message with status information. Blocked items in e-mail are replaced with a red "x". You can follow the instructions on the Information Bar to view the blocked content. However, when you edit, print, forward, or reply to an e-mail message with blocked items, the blocked content is downloaded. See "Protecting Against E-Mail Attacks" on page 309 for information on setting e-mail security options.

Information Bar for a pop-up window   Information Bar menu

Information Bar for an e-mail

Information Bar for an ActiveX control

Blocked image

11

Managing Add-Ons

Add-on are programs that extend the functionality of Internet Explorer to perform a unique task, such as provide search toolbars or display Flash content. In most cases, add-ons are useful, but sometimes poorly built or old ones can slow down your computer, cause system crashes, or invade your privacy (such as Spyware or Adware that are sometimes deceptively installed). To help you work with add-ons, Internet Explorer includes the Add-on Manager (NewSP2), which provides a list of add-ons currently loaded or used by Internet Explorer. You can use the Add-on Manager to individually enable, disable, or update add-ons. The Add-on Manager can also detect add-ons related crashes in Internet Explorer and displays an option to disable it.

Manage Browser Add-Ons

1. Click the Start button, and then click Control Panel, double-click the Internet Options in Classic view.

2. Click the Programs tab.

3. Click Manage Add-Ons.

    TIMESAVER *In Internet Explorer, click the Tools menu, and then click Manage Add-ons.*

4. Click Show list arrow, and then click the option with the type of add-ons you want to display.

5. Click the add-on you want to manage.

6. Click the Enable or Disable option.

7. If needed, click the Update button to get the latest version of the software, which could fix a problem.

    NOTE *The Update button changes to Update ActiveX or Update Extension depending on the type add-on you select.*

8. Click OK.

9. Click OK.

Protecting Against E-Mail Attacks

In Outlook Express, security zones allow you to determine whether or not to run active content, such as ActiveX controls, from inside HTML e-mail messages, which potentially can carry viruses and other harmful threats. You can adjust the security zone levels using Internet Options in the Control Panel. To provide further protection, you can set options to let you know when an program tries to send mail with your e-mail address to contacts in your address book (which is a common way propagate a virus), to not allow attachments to be saved or opened that might contain a virus, and to stop pictures and other content from automatically downloading to your computer (which is a common way spammers confirm your e-mail address to send more spam) from contacts who are not in your Address Book until you have a chance to read the message (New**SP2**).

Protect Against E-Mail Attacks in Outlook Express

1. Click the Start button, then click Outlook Express.

2. Click the Tools menu, then click Options.

3. Click the Security tab.

4. Click the security zone option you want: Internet zone (Less secure) or Restricted sites zone (More secure).

5. Select the Warn Me When Other Applications Try To Send Mail As Me check box.

6. Select the Do Not Allow Attachments To Be Saved Or Opened That Could Potentially Be A Virus check box.

7. Select the Block Images And Other External Content In HTML E-mail check box.

8. Click OK.

See Also

See "Avoiding Viruses and Other Harmful Attacks" on page 296 for information on security threats in e-mail.

11

Sending Secure E-Mail

In Outlook Express, you can set security options to send e-mail messages with a digital ID or encryption (**New!**). A digital ID verifies your identity to your recipients in the same way a picture ID verifies your identify when you write a check. Before you can send a digitally signed e-mail, you need to get a digital ID from an independent certification authority, which you can access from Outlook Express. Encryption prevents others on the Internet from intercepting and reading your e-mail. Before you can send an encrypted e-mail, your Address Book needs to contain a digital ID for each recipient, which allows them to decrypt the message for reading.

Set Options to Send Secure E-Mail in Outlook Express

1. Click the Start button, then click Outlook Express.

2. Click the Tools menu, then click Options.

3. Click the Security tab.

4. To get a digital ID, click Get Digital ID, and then follow the instructions.

5. To encrypt e-mail, select the Encrypt Contents And Attachments For All Outgoing Messages check box.

6. To digitally sign e-mail, select the Digitally Sign All Outgoing Messages check box.

7. Click Advanced.

8. Select the check boxes to include my digital ID and add sender's certificates to my address book.

9. To check for a revoked digital ID, click the Only When Online option.

10. Click OK.

11. Click OK again.

See Also

See "Understanding Security on the Internet" on page 298 for information on how digital IDs work in e-mail.

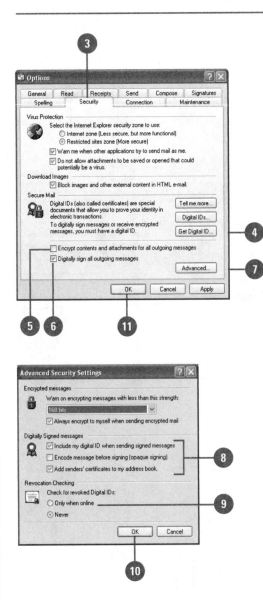

Managing Files Using a Network

Introduction

Windows XP comes with many tools for managing files and folders across multiple computers. One of the more powerful tools is My Network Places. A network is a system of two or more computers connected together to share resources. It consists of at least one host and one client. My Network Places is integrated with Windows Explorer and My Computer, allowing you to view the entire network (hosts and clients) and to share files and folders with people from other parts of the network. Using My Network Places (accessed from the Start menu), you create and manage your network connections to these other computers. This chapter helps you set up you host and client computers so they can easily share files across your network.

In addition, Windows provides tools for sharing files and folders with computers that are not located in your home or in the same office (commonly referred to as remote computers). You can connect your computer to a network in a different location via modem, or via the internet using the Communications accessory provided. With wireless technology, such as laptop computers or Bluetooth-enabled devices (keyboards, cell phones and PDAs), you can seamlessly setup, discover and connect to wireless networks. You can also share and synchronize files between your laptop and your desktop computers using the Briefcase.

Understanding Network Services

Windows is a secure, reliable network operating system that allows people using many different computers to share resources, such as programs, files, folders, printers, and an Internet connection. A single computer on the network, called a **server**, can be designated to store these resources. Other computers on the network, called **clients** or **workstations**, can access the resources on the server instead of having to store them. You can share resources using two or more client computers, or you can designate one computer to serve specifically as the server. If the workstation computers are close together in a single building or group of buildings, the network is called a **local area network (LAN)**. If the workstation computers are spread out in multiple buildings or throughout the entire country using dial-up or wireless connections, the network is called a **wide area network (WAN)**. To set up a network with multiple computers, you need to install a network adapter for each computer on your network and connect each computer to a network hub using network cable or wireless technology, known as Wi-Fi. Network adapters are usually hardware cards, called **network interface cards**, or **NICs**, inserted in a slot, or **USB (Universal Serial Bus)**, port in the back of your computer that connects it to the network. A **network hub** is a hardware device that connects multiple computers at a central location. When data arrives at one port of the network hub, it is copied to the other ports so that all connected network devices see the data. If you have two LANs or two sections of the same LAN on different floors of the same building with different network adapter types, you can connect them together with a hardware device called a **bridge**. If you have any number of LANs, you can connect them together with a

hardware device called a **router**. If you want to share a printer or Internet connection with the computers on a network, you simply connect the printer or modem to the server, a computer on the network, or directly to a network hub, router, or bridge.

Share central resources through client/server networking

Windows offers a network configuration called **client/server networking**. Under this arrangement, a single computer is designated as a server, allowing access to resources for any qualified user. Client/server networking provides all users on a network a central location for accessing shared files. In a client/server network, individual computers are often grouped into domains. A **domain** is a collection of computers that the person managing the network creates to group together computers used for the same tasks and to simplify the set up and maintenance of the network. The network administrator defines the domains that exist on the network and controls access to computers within those domains. Domains are available only with the Professional edition.

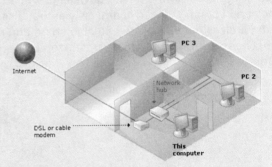

Share resources through peer-to-peer networking

Windows also offers a network configuration called **peer-to-peer networking**. Peer-to-peer networking enables two or more computers to link together without designating a central server. In a peer-to-peer network, individual computers are often organized into workgroups. A **workgroup** is a group of computers that perform common tasks or belong to users who share common duties and interests. In this configuration, any computer user can access resources stored on any other computer, as long as those resources are available for sharing. Peer-to-peer networking allows individual computer users to share files and other resources, such as a printer, with other users on the network without having to access a server. Workgroups are available on all Windows XP computers.

Share resources through network connections

Windows provides connectivity between your computer and a network, another computer, or the Internet using **Network Connections**. Whether you are physically connected using a direct cable or connected remotely using a dial-up or cable modem, you can connect securely to a network over the Internet using a **Virtual Private Network (VPN)** connection or set up your computer to let other computers connect to yours using an **incoming network connection**. VPN and incoming network connection are examples of WANs.

Share designated files and folders on your computer with other network users

Windows provides support for security, so even though your computer is connected to a network, you can designate which resources on your computer you want to share with others. Before network users can use any resources on your computer, they must be granted the required permission.

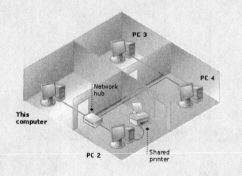

12

Viewing Network Connection Properties

A computer that uses a network must be configured so that other machines on the network recognize it. On a small network, you might be responsible for configuring your computer, or that responsibility might fall to the network administrator. You can view the status of the network connection and modify some of the network settings for your computer using the Network Connections window. A network connection consists of a network adapter and three types of components: client, service, and protocol. The **client** type allows you to access computers and files on the network. The **service** type allows you to share your computer resources, such as files and printers, with other networked computers. **Protocol** is the language that the computer uses to communicate with other computers on the network, such as TCP/IP. Knowing which components are installed on your computer helps you understand the capabilities and limitations of your computer on the network.

View Network Connection Properties

1. Click the Start button, and then click Control Panel.

2. Double-click the Network Connections icon in Classic view.

3. Click a network connection icon.

4. Click View Status Of This Connection.

5. Click Close.

6. Click Change Settings Of This Connection.

7. To display a network connection icon on the taskbar, select the Show Icon In Notification Area When Connected check box.

8. Click OK.

Did You Know?

You can troubleshoot network adapter problems. In the Network Connections window, right-click the Network Connection icon, click Properties, click Configure, click Troubleshoot, and then follow the instructions.

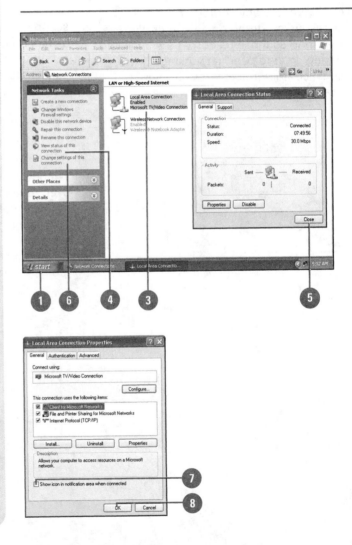

Viewing Network Computer Properties

Names and locations are used to identify computers on a network. The computer's name refers to the individual machine, and the computer's location refers to how the machine is grouped together with other computers. Computers anywhere on the network can be located easily through the naming hierarchy and can be addressed individually by name. You can find the name and workgroup or domain of a computer on the network by examining the system properties. Workgroups are available on all Windows XP computers, but domains are available only with the Professional edition.

View Network Computer Properties

1. Click the Start button, and then click Control Panel.

2. Double-click the System icon in Classic view.

3. Click the Computer Name tab.

4. To change a workgroup or domain, click Change, specify a new name, and then click OK.

5. Click OK.

Security Alert

Networking with Windows Firewall

For security purposes, Windows Firewall is turned on (the default setting) to protect your computer against security threats, such as viruses, worms, and Trojan Horses, spread over the Internet or a network (NewSP2). When Windows Firewall is enabled, you might have to adjust Windows Firewall settings for some programs, such as Internet games, to allow them to work properly. See "Setting Up Windows Firewall" on page 115.

Viewing a Network

The key to managing files and folders in a network environment is understanding the structure of your particular network. Most networks consist of multiple types of computers and operating systems. My Network Places lets you view the entire network or just your part of the network to give you access to the servers, domains, and workgroups on the network. My Network Places also displays shared folders available on your immediate network. The Entire Network window allows you to view a list of servers not in your workgroup and to view other network domains. The Entire Network window displays various segments and computers connected to your network, such as Microsoft Windows Network. If you are on a large network, you might have other choices that display more segments of the network.

View a Workgroup Network

1. Click the Start button, and then click My Network Places.

2. Click View Workgroup Computers.

3. Double-click a network computer icon to display the shared files, folders, and devices on the computer.

4. When you're done, click the Close button.

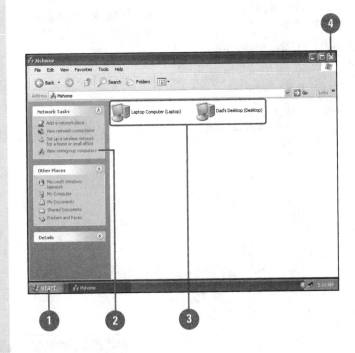

View a Domain Network

1. Click the Start button, and then click My Network Places.

2. Click Entire Network in the task pane.

3. Double-click a network icon.

4. Double-click a domain icon.

5. Double-click a network computer or server icon to display the shared files, folders, and devices on the computer.

6. When you're done, click the Close button.

View a Shared Folder

1. Click the Start button, and then click My Network Places.

2. Double-click a shared folder to display the shared files and folders in the folder.

3. When you're done, click the Close button.

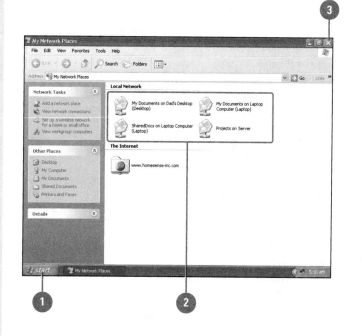

12

Setting Up a Home Network ▶

Before you can set up and configure a network at home or small office, you need to physically attach the hardware so the computers can communicate. This includes installing the network cards in all the computers, connecting the computers together using cables or wireless technology, installing a modem on the host computer, turning on all computers, printers, and external modems, and establishing a connection to the Internet. A home or small office network is typically a peer-to-peer network where individual computers are organized into workgroups with a host and several clients. The host is a computer on the network who shares an Internet connection with the other client computers on the network. The host computer must be turned on whenever a client computer needs to access the Internet. Depending on your hardware setup, your Network Setup Wizard options might differ.

Set Up the Host Computer

1 Install network cards, connect all the computers together, and then turn them on.

2 Click the Start button, point to All Programs, point to Accessories, point to Communications, and then click Network Setup Wizard (**New!**).

3 Click Next, and then click Next again.

4 Click the This Computer Connects Directly To The Internet option, and then click Next.

5 If necessary, select an Internet connection, and then click Next.

6 Type a computer description and a computer name, and then click Next.

7 Type a workgroup name, and then click Next.

8 Click Next to continue.

9 Click an option to create a Network Setup Disk or Use My Windows XP CD, and then click Next and follow the instructions.

10 Click Finish.

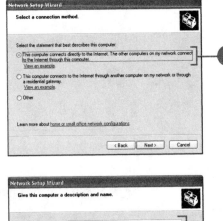

Set Up a Client Computer

1. Click the Start button, point to All Programs, point to Accessories, point to Communications, and then click Network Setup Wizard.

   If the computer isn't running Windows XP, insert the Windows XP CD, click Perform Additional Tasks from the menu, and then click Set Up A Home Or Small Office Network.

   If you created a Network Setup Disk, click the Start button, click Run, type **a:netsetup**, and then click OK.

2. Click Next, and then click Next again.

3. Click the This Computer Connects To The Internet Through Another Computer option, and then click Next.

4. Type a computer description and a computer name, and then click Next.

5. Type the same workgroup name as the host computer, and then click Next.

6. Click Next to continue.

7. Click the Just Finish The Wizard option, and then click Next.

8. Click Finish.

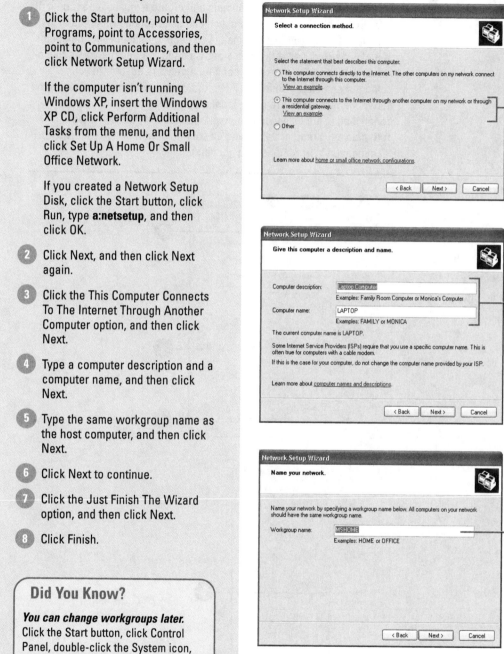

Did You Know?

You can change workgroups later. Click the Start button, click Control Panel, double-click the System icon, click the Computer Name tab, click Change, type a new workgroup name, and then click OK twice.

12

Joining a Domain Network

If you are not connected to a domain network, you can use the Network Identification Wizard to join a domain and create a local user account. If you already have a user account, you can use System Properties to join a domain. Before you join a domain, you need to connect your computer to a client/server network using a network adapter and network cable or wireless technology. After you connect a network adapter to your computer and start Windows XP Professional, your computer detects the network adapter and creates a local area connection. A local area connection is the only type of network connection that Windows automatically creates. Depending on your hardware setup, your Network Identification Wizard options might differ.

Join a Domain Network

1. Click the Start button, and then click Control Panel.

2. Double-click the System icon in Classic view.

3. Click the Computer Name tab.

4. Click Change.

5. Click the Domain option.

6. Type the domain name.

7. Click OK.

8. Click OK.

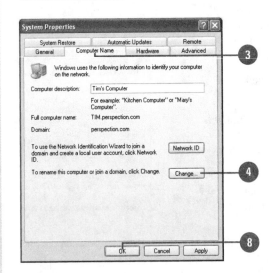

Join a Domain Network and Create a User Account

1. Click the Start button, and then click Control Panel.

2. Double-click the System icon in Classic view.

3. Click the Computer Name tab.

4. Click Network ID, and then click Next.

5. Click a business network option, and then click Next.

6. Click the My Company Uses A Network With A Domain option, and then click Next.

7. Read the page, and then click Next.

8. Type a user name and password.

9. Type a domain name, and then click Next.

10. Type a computer name, and then click Next.

11. Click the Add The Following User option, and then click Next.

12. Click an access user level, and then click Next.

13. Click Finish, and then restart your computer.

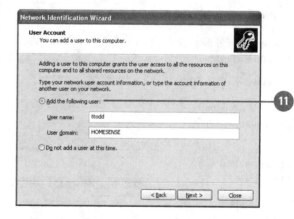

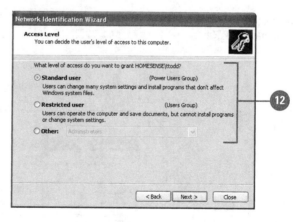

12

Connecting to a Network Using a Modem

If you have a modem installed on your computer, you can use the New Connection Wizard to set up a dial-up connection to another computer or a network. Connecting to another computer or a network is useful when you need access to information stored on another computer or a network. You only need to set up a dial-up connection to a computer or a network once. After you set up the connection using the New Connection Wizard, you can use the connection icon in the Connection window or the Connect To submenu on the Start menu to establish a dial-up connection. When you are connected, Windows displays a connection icon in the notification area on the taskbar. You can point to the icon to display information about the connection or right-click the icon to perform tasks.

Create a Dial-Up Connection

1. Click the Start button, point to All Programs, point to Accessories, point to Communications, and then click New Connection Wizard.

2. Click Next to continue.

3. Click the Connect To The Network At My Workplace option, and then click Next.

4. Click the Dial-Up Connection option, and then click Next.

5. Type a name for the connection, and then click Next.

6. Type the phone number for calling the network, and then click Next.

7. Click Finish.

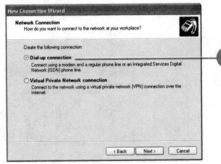

Establish a Dial-Up Connection

1. Click the Start button, point to Connect To, and then click the dial-up connection name.

2. Type your assigned user name and password.

3. To save your user name and password information, select the Save This User Name And Password For The Following Users check box, and then click an option to specify who can use the information.

4. Click Dial, and then wait for the connection.

5. When you're done, right-click the Connection icon in the notification area of the taskbar, and then click Disconnect.

See Also

See "Changing Phone Dialing Options" on page 407 for information on changing the settings for a dial-up connection.

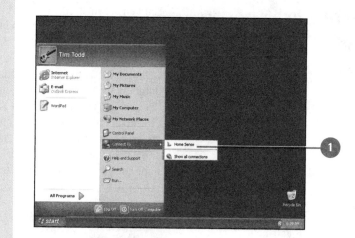

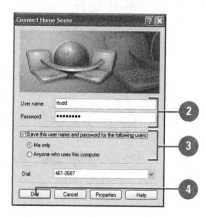

Connecting to a Network over the Internet

You can create a VPN (Virtual Private Network) (New!) connection to connect to a network over the Internet. A VPN provides a secure connection between your computer and the network. The computer to which you want to connect must support a VPN and Internet connection. Before you create a connection, you need to have the name or IP (Internet Protocol) address of the VPN computer. You can use the New Connection Wizard to set up a VPN connection. You only need to set up a VPN connection to a network once. When you are connected, Windows displays a connection icon in the notification area on the taskbar. You can point to the icon to display information about the connection or right-click the icon to perform tasks.

Create a VPN Connection

① Click the Start button, point to All Programs, point to Accessories, point to Communications, and then click New Connection Wizard.

② Click Next to continue.

③ Click the Connect To The Network At My Workplace option, and then click Next.

④ Click the Virtual Private Network Connection option, and then click Next.

⑤ Type a name for the connection, and then click Next.

⑥ Click an option to use a dial-up connection or other connection (such as a DSL line), and then click Next.

⑦ Type the host name or IP address to the computer to which you want to connect, and then click Next.

⑧ Click the Anyone's Use option or click the My Use Only option, and then click Next.

⑨ Click Finish.

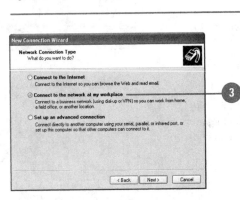

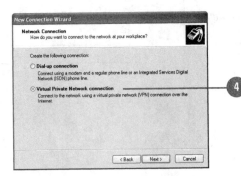

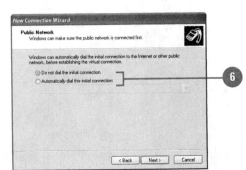

Establish a VPN Connection

1. Click the Start button, point to Connect To, and then click the dial-up connection name.

2. Type your assigned user name and password.

3. To save your user name and password information, select the Save This User Name And Password For The Following Users check box, and then click an option to specify who can use the information.

4. Click Connect, and then wait for the connection.

5. When you're done, right-click the Connection icon in the notification area of the taskbar, and then click Disconnect.

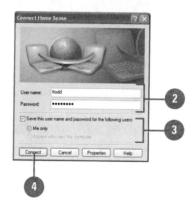

Connecting to a Computer from Another Location

You can set up an incoming connection on a computer so you can connect to the computer from another location. An incoming connection allows you to connect to the computer to access files and to print documents on attached printers and network drives. Before you can set up an incoming connection, you need to log on as the administrator. During the setup process, you can specify whether you want to allow a Virtual Private Network (VPN) connection, and which users you want to connect to your computer. When you are connected, Windows displays a connection icon in the notification area on the taskbar. You can point to the icon to display information about the connection or right-click the icon to disconnect, change properties, and perform other tasks.

Create an Incoming Connection

1. Click the Start button, point to All Programs, point to Accessories, point to Communications, and then click New Connection Wizard.

2. Click Next to continue.

3. Click the Set Up An Advanced Connection option, and then click Next.

4. Click the Accept Incoming Connections option, and then click Next.

5. Select the connection device, and then click Next.

6. Click the Do Not Allow Virtual Private Connections option, and then click Next.

7. Select the check boxes for the users who are allowed to access the computer, and then click Next.

8. Select the check boxes for the type of networking software you want enabled, and then click Next.

9. Click Next, and then click Finish.

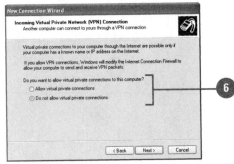

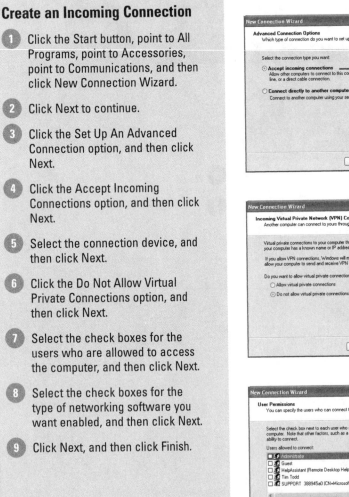

Connecting to a Computer Directly

You can set up a direct connection to another computer using your serial, parallel, or infrared port. An incoming direct connection allows you to connect to another computer to access files and to print documents on attached printers and network drives. Before you can set up a direct connection, you need to either connect the two computer together using a cable or line up the infrared ports. During the setup process, you specify the role of each computer, either host or guest, and select a connection method and which users you want to connect to your computer. When you are connected, Windows displays a connection icon in the notification area on the taskbar. You can point to the icon to display information about the connection or right-click the icon to disconnect, change properties, and perform other tasks.

Create a Direct Connection

1. Click the Start button, point to All Programs, point to Accessories, point to Communications, and then click New Connection Wizard.

2. Click Next to continue.

3. Click the Set Up An Advanced Connection option, and then click Next.

4. Click the Connect Directly To Another Computer option, and then click Next.

5. Click the Host or Guest option, and then click Next.

6. Specify a connection device, and then click Next.

7. Select the check boxes for the users who are allowed to access the computer, and then click Next.

8. Click Finish.

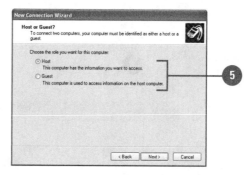

12

Connecting to a Wireless Network

Windows XP provides updated wireless networking (NewSP2), enabling you to setup and manage wireless connections with a broad range of wireless hot spots. discover and connect to wireless networks (known as Wi-Fi). The Wireless Network Setup Wizard makes it easy to setup a Wi-Fi network. As you walk through the process, you'll specify a network name, called the SSID (Service Set Identifier) and use a USB Flash drive (UFD)—recommended—to transfer and configure your network settings to your other wireless computers or devices. The SSID is broadcasted from your access point (AP)—typically a wireless router—to your other wireless devices. Windows XP also provides updated support for Bluetooth-enabled hardware devices (NewSP2), allowing you to take advantage of the latest wireless devices, including wireless keyboards and mice, wireless printers, and connections with cell phones and PDAs.

Connect to a Wireless Network

1. Click the Start button, click Control Panel, and then double-click the Wireless Network Setup Wizard icon in Classic view.

2. Click Next to continue.

3. Click the Setup A New Wireless Network option, and then click Next (if screen appears).

4. Enter the name of your wireless network (SSID).

5. Click the Automatically Assign A Network Key (recommended) option. For more advanced users, you can use the manually assign option.

6. If you want to use WPA encryption, select the Use WPA Encryption check box, and then click Next.

7. Click the Use A USB Flash Drive (recommended) or the Set Up A Network Manually option.

8. Click Next to save your network settings to the flash drive and continue, or print out the network settings for each wireless device and complete the manual installation.

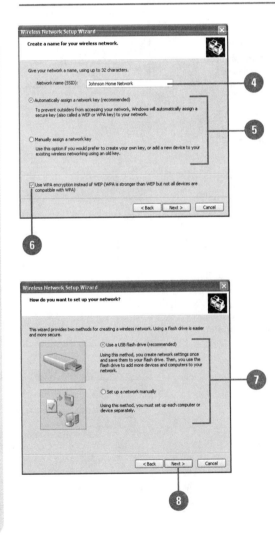

9 Click the Flash Drive list arrow, select your flash drive, and then click Next.

10 Follow the instructions carefully to transfer your network settings to your other computers or devices.

IMPORTANT *If you plug into a computer running Windows XP SP2, the Wireless Setup Wizard runs and asks you to join the wireless network, and then creates a wireless profile and connection.*

11 When you're done following the transfer instructions, click Next to complete the setup.

The wizard lists the configured wireless computers and devices.

12 If you want to use the UFD to configure additional wireless computers or devices at a later time, clear the For Security Reasons, Remove Network Settings From My Flash Drive check box.

13 Click Finish.

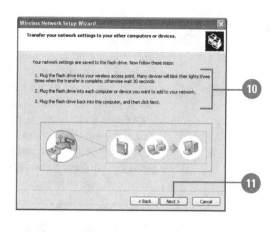

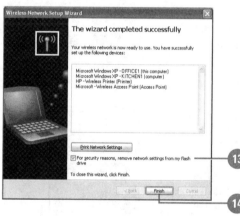

Did You Know?

You can perform a security check on your wireless network. After implementing lock down security measures, you can perform a security check. Install the free program NetStumbler available at *www.netstumber.com* onto a laptop or PDA.

Security Alert

Locking Down Your Wireless Network

Wireless networks (Wi-Fi) are a popular way to network home and small office computers. Unless you lock it down, hackers can take advantage of unsecure Wi-Fi networks. The following security techniques can keep you safe: (1) disable the SSID (Service Set Identifier) broadcast, so you no longer tell computers near by that you have a wireless network, (2) change the password on your access point, (3) use encryption, either WEP (Wired Equivalent Privacy), which is older and less secure (uses 64- or 128-bit non-changing encryption), or WPA (Wi-Fi Protected Access), which is much more secure (uses 256-bit constantly changes encryption), and (4) enable Media Access Control (MAC) filtering, which tells your access point to grant access to only MAC addresses you enter. MAC is a unique address assigned to each wireless card.

12

Working with a Wireless Connection

After you setup and connect to a wireless network, you can use the Wireless Network Connection dialog box (NewSP2) to view a list of the type—indicated by an icon—and name, or SSID, of detected wireless networks, and to connect a wireless network connection by name. Each connection also displays status information, including a signal strength level, and whether the network is preferred (the star icon), connected (the Connected" label), and security-enabled (the lock icon and the "Security-enabled wireless network" label). From the Wireless Network Connection dialog box, you perform a refresh scan of wireless networks, start the Wireless Network Setup Wizard, change the order of preferred networks, and change other advanced settings.

View Wireless Connections

1. Click the Start button, click Control Panel, and then double-click the Network Connections icon in Classic view.

2. Click a wireless network connection icon.

3. Click Change Settings Of This Connection.

4. Click Refresh Network List.

5. To connect to a network, click a non connected network, and then click Connect.

6. To disconnect from a network, click a connected network, then click Disconnect.

7. Click the Close button.

Did You Know?

You can quickly identify a wireless network type by the icon. The antenna icon indicates an infrastructure mode wireless network. The icon with two wireless computers indicates an ad hoc mode wireless network. An icon for the log of a wireless Internet Service Provider (ISP) indicates that the wireless network uses WPS to automate and secure registration.

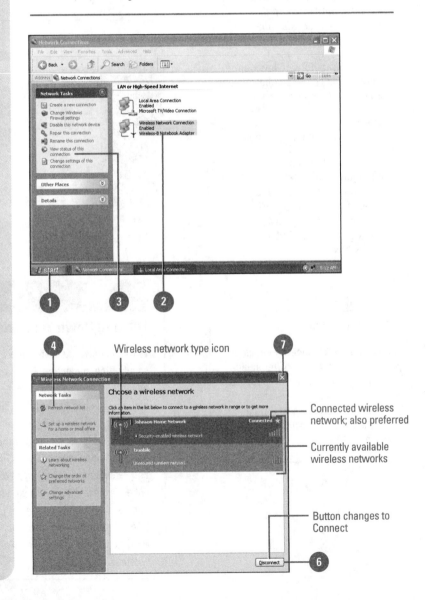

Wireless network type icon

Connected wireless network; also preferred

Currently available wireless networks

Button changes to Connect

Change the Order of Preferred Wireless Networks

1. Click the Start button, click Control Panel, and then double-click the Network Connections icon in Classic view.

2. Click a wireless network connection icon, and then click Change Settings Of This Connection.

3. Click Change The Order Of Preferred Networks.

4. Click the Wireless Networks tab.

5. Use the Add, Remove, Move Up, and Move Down buttons to change the network order.

6. Click OK, and then click the Close button.

Change Wireless Connection and Security Properties

1. Click the Start button, click Control Panel, and then double-click the Network Connections icon in Classic view.

2. Click a wireless network connection icon, and then click Change Settings Of This Connection.

3. Click Change Advanced Settings.

4. Click a tab.

   ◆ **Association.** Changes SSID and data encryption key type.

   ◆ **Authentication.** Changes security authentication settings.

   ◆ **Connection.** Allows for automatic connection.

5. Click OK, and then click the Close button.

Wireless Network Connection Properties

General | Wireless Networks | Advanced

☑ Use Windows to configure my wireless network settings

Available networks:
To connect to, disconnect from, or find out more information about wireless networks in range, click the button below.

[View Wireless Networks]

Preferred networks:
Automatically connect to available networks in the order listed below.

- tmobile (Automatic)
- Johnson Home Network (Automatic)

[Move up]
[Move down]

[Add...] [Remove] [Properties]

Learn about setting up wireless network configuration. [Advanced]

[OK] [Cancel]

Wireless network name

Johnson Home Network properties

Association | Authentication | Connection

Network name (SSID): [Johnson Home Network]

Wireless network key

This network requires a key for the following:

Network Authentication: [Open]

Data encryption: [WEP]

Network key:

Confirm network key:

Key index (advanced): [1]

☑ The key is provided for me automatically

☐ This is a computer-to-computer (ad hoc) network; wireless access points are not used

[OK] [Cancel]

Click to have Windows provide a network key for you.

Open: Uses the open system authentication method
Shared: Uses the shared key entered in Network key and Confirm network key
WPA: Uses WPA; select EAP type configured on Authentication tab
WPA-PSK: Uses WPA and a pre-shared key entered in Network key and Confirm network key

Disabled: Disables encryption
WEP: Uses Wired Equivalent Privacy (WEP) encryption
TKIP: Uses WPA Temporal Key Integrity Protocol (TKIP) encryption
AES: Uses Advanced Encryption Standard (AES) encryption

Select to create a computer-to-computer (ad hoc) network

12

Mapping and Disconnecting a Network Drive

Windows networking enables you to connect your computer to other computers on the network quite easily. If you connect to a network location frequently, you might want to designate a drive letter on your computer as a direct connection to a shared drive or folder on another computer. Instead of spending unnecessary time opening My Network Places and the shared drive or folder each time you want to access it, you can create a direct connection, called **mapping** a drive, to the network location for quick and easy access. If you no longer use a mapped drive, you can right-click the mapped drive in My Computer and then click Disconnect.

Map a Network Drive

1. Click the Start button, and then click My Network Places.

2. Click the Tools menu, and then click Map Network Drive.

3. Click the Drive list arrow, and then select a drive letter.

4. Click Browse.

5. Select the folder you want to connect to.

6. Click OK.

7. To reconnect each time you log on to your computer, select the Reconnect At Login check box.

8. Click Finish.

9. To disconnect from a mapped drive, right-click the drive in My Computer, and then click Disconnect.

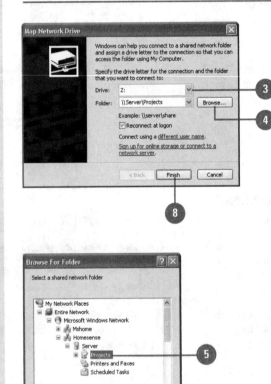

> ## Did You Know?
>
> **You can add a Map Drive button to the toolbar.** Click the Start button, click My Computer, right-click the toolbar, click Customize, click Map Drive, click Add, and then click Close.

Creating a Shortcut to a Network

Instead of clicking numerous icons in My Network Places to access a network location, by using the Add Network Place Wizard you can create a shortcut to the network location in the My Network Places window for easy access. The wizard provides step-by-step instructions to select the network location and create a shortcut. The wizard also allows you to create a shortcut to a web or FTP (File Transfer Protocol) site. If you need storage space on the Internet to manage, organize, and share documents, you can also use the Add Network Place Wizard to help you sign up for a service that offers online storage space.

Add a Network Place

1. Click the Start button, and then click My Network Places.

2. Click Add A Network Place, and then click Next.

3. Click Choose Another Network Location, and then click Next.

4. Type the Internet or network address, or click Browse, select a network location, and then click OK. Click Next to continue.

   TROUBLE? *If the addresses are not working, click View Some Examples for help.*

5. Type a name for the network place or use the suggested one, and then click Next.

6. To open the network, select the Open This Network Place When I Click Finish check box.

7. Click Finish.

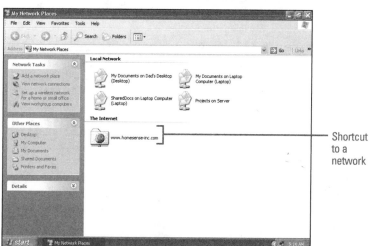

Shortcut to a network

12

Sharing a Folder over a Network

You can share a folder and its contents on a network and specify whether you want to give network users permission to change the contents of the shared folder. You can create a new folder to share, or you can use an existing one anywhere on your computer. For example, you can create a shared folder in a subfolder within your My Documents folder. When you create a shared folder, you have the option to use the name of the folder or another name as the **share name**, which is the name network users see on the network in My Network Places. Once you create shared folders, copying and moving shared files and folders in Windows is as easy as managing files on your own computer. The only difference is that data transfer can take longer over a network than it does on your local computer.

Share a Folder on a Workgroup Network

1. Click the Start button, and then click My Computer.

2. Locate the folder you want to share.

3. Right-click the folder, and then click Sharing And Security.

4. Click the Sharing tab.

5. Select the Share This Folder On The Network check box.

6. Type a share name or use the suggested one.

7. To give the user full control of the folder, select the Allow Network Users To Change My Files check box. Clear the check box to give read-only access.

8. Click OK.

See Also

See "Sharing Files or Folders with Others" on page 75 for information on using the Shared Documents folder.

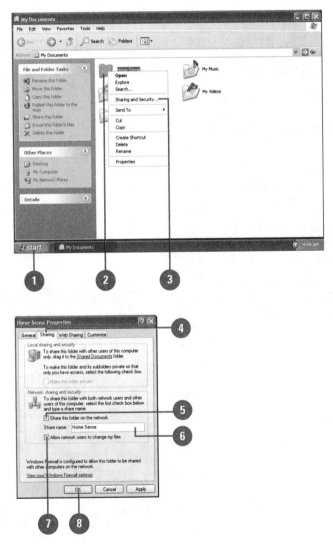

Share a Folder on a Domain Network

1. Click the Start button, and then click My Computer.

2. Locate the folder you want to share.

3. Right-click the folder, and then click Sharing And Security.

4. Click the Sharing tab.

5. Click the Share This Folder option.

6. Type a share name or use the suggested one.

7. Click Permissions.

8. Select the user you want to change permissions.

9. Select the check boxes for the permissions you want.

10. Click OK.

11. Click OK.

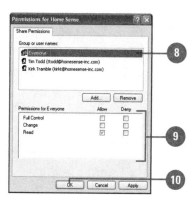

For Your Information

Understanding File Permission Properties

Every file in the Windows file system includes **permissions** for each user, or settings that designate what each user can and cannot do to each file. Three basic types of file permissions are available for users: read and full. **Read permission** allows the user to open and view the file but not to make changes that can be saved in the file. When you open a read-only file, the words "Read Only" appear in the title bar. You can save the file with a new name in a different location and have full access to it. **Change permission** allows the user to open and edit the file and save changes. **Full Control permission** allows the user to edit and save changes to the file (or "write") and execute programs on server or client computers. Qualified users or system administrators use file permissions and passwords to control who can access any specific area of the network.

12

Using Briefcase to Update Files

If you want to work with files that are copied onto two different computers, such as your work computer and your home computer, you can synchronize the files and keep the various copies updated between computers using Briefcase. Before you can use Briefcase, you need to create one. To use Briefcase, drag the files you want to copy to your other computer from a folder window to the Briefcase icon. Then, drag the Briefcase icon to the removable disk drive, and remove the disk. You can now insert the removable disk in a different computer. After you modify the files in the Briefcase, you need to synchronize them when you return to your main computer. Do not rename or move the original files and do not rename the files in the Briefcase. Otherwise, Briefcase will not be able to update them.

Create a Briefcase

1. Right-click a blank area on the desktop, point to New, and then click Briefcase.

2. Click the Start button, click My Documents, and then click the Folders button on the toolbar.

3. Locate and drag the files you want to work with while away from your computer to the Briefcase icon.

4. Insert a floppy disk or other removable disk into a drive on your computer.

5. Drag the Briefcase to the drive that contains the disk.

   You can open and edit the files in the Briefcase on another computer.

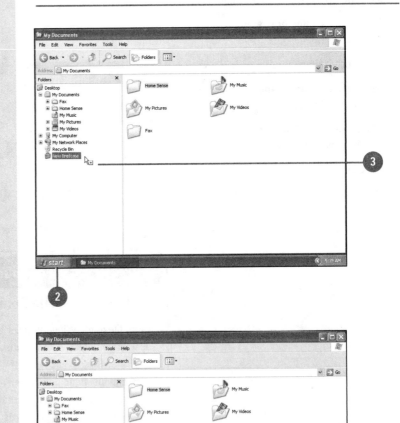

Did You Know?

You can create a new file in Briefcase. If you create a new file in an existing folder in the Briefcase, the file is updated on your computer. If you create a file any other place, Windows doesn't know where to store it.

Update Briefcase Files

1. Insert the disk into a drive on your computer.

2. Click the Start button, click My Computer, and then double-click the drive that contains the disk.

   If the Welcome To The Windows Briefcase dialog box opens, read it, and then click Finish.

3. Double-click the Briefcase icon.

4. Select the updated file in Briefcase.

5. Click the Update Selection button on the toolbar, or click the Update All button on the toolbar.

6. To change the way a file updates, right-click the file, and then click an option.

7. Click Update.

Did You Know?

You can prevent Briefcase from updating a file. Select the file you don't want to update in the Briefcase window, click the Briefcase menu, and then click Split From Original. The file in Briefcase is labeled an orphan file.

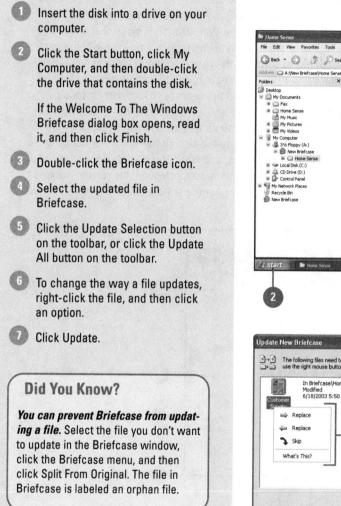

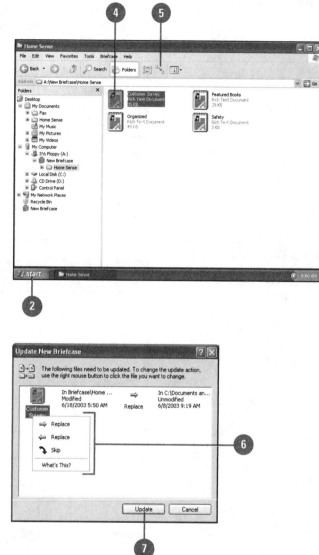

12

Controlling a Remote Computer

You can use Remote Desktop Connection (**New!**) to connect to a remote computer on your network or the Internet and use the remote computer as if you were working on it. Before you can connect to a remote computer, you need to turn on the Windows XP Professional computer and set the option to allow users to connect remotely to the computer. Doing this provides security for the remote computer. You can allow anyone to connect to the remote computer, or you can specify users with a password. You also need to have the name or IP (Internet Protocol) address of the remote computer and the user name and password you use to log on to the computer. You can also customize settings for the remote connection, which include the display size and color depth, when to use local or remote resources, and what programs to use and options to allow. Once you connect to the remote computer, the remote desktop appears on your screen. You can use the remote desktop as if you were working at the computer.

Set Up a Remote Computer

1. Click the Start button, and then click Control Panel.

2. Double-click the System icon in Classic view.

3. Click the Remote tab.

4. Select the Allow Users To Connect Remotely To This Computer check box.

5. Click Select Remote Users.

6. Click Add, type user names, and then click OK.

   TROUBLE? *If the user names are not working, click Examples for help.*

7. Click OK.

8. Click OK.

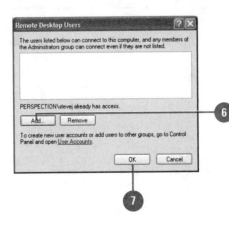

338

Connect to a Remote Computer

1. Establish a connection to your network.

2. Click the Start button, point to All Programs, point to Accessories, point to Communications, and then click Remote Desktop Connection.

3. Type the name or IP address of the remote computer.

4. Click Options.

5. Type the user name, password, and domain name.

6. Click Connect.

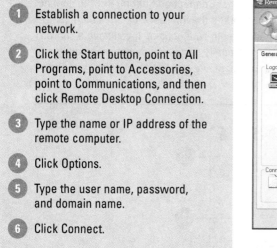

Control a Remote Computer

1. Connect to the remote computer.

2. Use the remote desktop as if you were sitting in front of the remote computer.

3. Click the Minimize or Restore Down button to resize the remote desktop and to display the local desktop.

4. Use the local desktop.

5. When you're done, click the Close button, and then click Yes to disconnect.

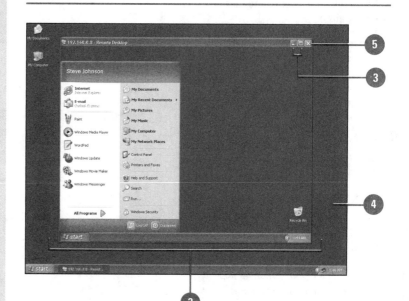

12

Sharing an Internet Connection ▶

If you have a home or small office network using Windows XP Professional, you can use Internet Connection Sharing (ICS) to connect all the computers on the network to the Internet with one connection, which saves you money on multiple connections. If you have a shared dial-up Internet connection no one is using, you can change settings to have the connection end automatically, or you can manually end the connection from your computer.

Share an Internet Connection

1. Click the Start button, point to All Programs, point to Accessories, point to Communications, and then click Network Connections.

2. Right-click the Internet Connection icon, and then click Properties.

3. Click the Advanced tab.

4. Select the Allow Other Network Users To Connect Through This Computer's Internet Connection check box.

5. If you want this connection to dial automatically, select the Establish A Dial-up Connection Whenever A Computer On My Network Attempts To Access The Internet check box.

6. For a home network, select the adapter that connects you to the other networked computers.

7. Click OK.

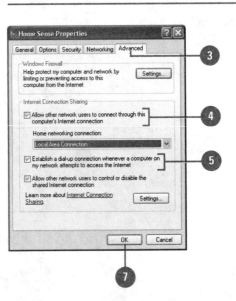

See Also

See "Creating an Internet Connection" on page 114 for information on creating a new shared Internet connection using the New Connection Wizard.

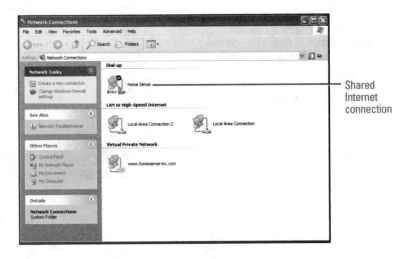

Shared Internet connection

End an Internet Connection

1. Double-click the Connection icon in the notification area on the taskbar.

2. Click Disconnect.

   TIMESAVER *Right-click the Connection icon in the notification area on the taskbar, and then click Disconnect.*

3. Click Close.

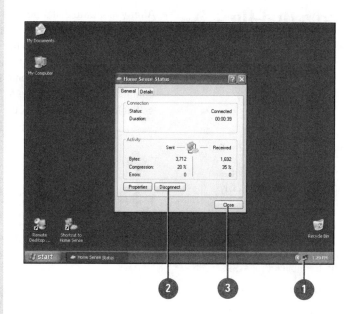

12

Changing a Dial-Up Connection

After you create a dial-up connection, you can change the settings to specify how the computer creates a dial-up connection to another computer. You can change the phone number, add dialing rules, and modify redial and hang up settings. You need to log on as an administrator to change some settings for a dial-up connection. When a computer is set up to share a dial-up connection to the Internet, these settings control the connection for the network users.

Change a Dial-Up Connection

1 On the host computer, click the Start button, and then click My Network Places.

2 Click View Network Connections.

3 Right-click the Dial-Up connection icon, and then click Properties.

4 Click the General tab.

5 To change the number, double-click the text box, and then type a new number.

6 To use dialing rules, select the Use Dialog Rules check box, and then specify the area and country codes.

7 Click the Options tab.

8 Select the check boxes for the dialog options you want, and clear the others.

9 Set the idle time you want before the dial-up connection hangs up, and any redial options.

10 Click OK.

> ### See Also
>
> *See "Connecting to a Network Using a Modem" on page 322 for information on creating a dial-up connection.*

4

Home Sense Properties

General | Options | Security | Networking | Advanced

Connect using:
Modem - Actiontec MD560RD V92 MDC Modem (COM3)

[Configure...]

Phone number

Area code | Phone number:
461-0687 | [Alternates]   **5**

Country/region code:

☐ Use dialing rules   [Dialing Rules]   **6**

☑ Show icon in notification area when connected

[OK] [Cancel]

7

Home Sense Properties

General | Options | Security | Networking | Advanced

Dialing options
☑ Display progress while connecting
☑ Prompt for name and password, certificate, etc.
☐ Include Windows logon domain
☑ Prompt for phone number   **8**

Redialing options
Redial attempts: 3
Time between redial attempts: 1 minute   **9**
Idle time before hanging up: never
☐ Redial if line is dropped

[X.25]

[OK] [Cancel]

10

Printing and Faxing

13

Introduction

After you create a document or picture, or open a web page or an e-mail, you can use Windows printing options to create a hard copy. You can print files from a folder window or within a program. The Add A Printer Wizard makes it easy to install a printer directly attached to your computer or connected to a network. After you send a print job to the printer, you can check the status, pause and resume the print job, or cancel it. If a printer is not working the way you want, you can change printer properties, such as a printer's computer connection or network location, sharing options, related software drivers, color management options, graphics settings, installed fonts, and other advanced settings. To customize your print jobs, you can also change printer preferences, such as orientation, page order, pages per sheet, paper size, paper tray selection, copy count, and print quality and color.

Windows also provides you with complete fax facilities from your computer. After the fax is installed, you can configure fax settings, send and receive faxes, track and monitor fax activity, and view faxes. Using Fax, you can choose to send and receive faxes with a local fax device attached to your computer, or with a remote fax device connected to fax resources located on a network. You can also change the send and receive properties for the fax to work with your phone line.

Understanding Printers

Although there are many different kinds of printers, there are two main categories: ink-jet and laser. An **ink-jet printer** works by spraying ionized ink on a sheet of paper. Ink-jet printers are less expensive and considerably slower than laser printers, but they still produce a good quality output. A **laser printer** utilizes a laser beam to produce an image on a drum, which is rolled through a reservoir of toner and transferred to the paper through a combination of heat and pressure. Laser printers are faster and produce a higher quality output than ink-jets, but they are also more expensive. Ink-jet and laser printers are combined with other hardware devices, such as a copier and scanner, into a multi-function device. A **multi-function device** provides common device functionality at a lower cost than purchasing each device separately. Printers are classified by two main characteristics: resolution and speed. Printer resolution refers to the sharpness and clarity of a printed page. For printers, the resolution indicates the number of dots per inch (dpi). For example, a 300-dpi printer is one that is capable of printing 300 distinct dots in a line one-inch long, or 90,000 dots per square inch. The higher the dpi, the sharper the print quality. Printer speed is measured in pages per minute (ppm). The speed of printers varies widely. In general, ink-jet printers range from about 4 to 10 ppm, while laser printers range from about 10 to 30 ppm. The speed depends on the amount of printer memory (the more the better) and the page's contents: if there is just text or the page has only one color, the ppm is in the high range, but when a page contains graphics and/or has multiple colors, the ppm rate falls to the low range.

Ink-jet printer

Laser printer

Multi-function device

Viewing Printers

After you install a printer, the printer appears in the Printers and Faxes window and in a program's Print dialog box, where you can view and change printer properties and personal preferences. Every installed printer on your computer is represented by an icon in the Printers and Faxes window. When you select a printer icon, status information for that printer appears in the Details section of the task pane, such as number of documents to be printed, and whether the printer is ready to print. A printer icon appears in the window without a cable indicates a **local printer**, while a printer icon with a cable indicates a **network printer**. A local printer is a printer connected directly to your computer, and a network printer is one connected to a network to which you have access. A printer icon that appears with a hand indicates that other network users share the printer directly connected to your computer, known as a **shared printer**.

View Printer Properties

1 Click the Start button, and then click Printers And Other Hardware (Home) or Printers And Faxes (Pro).

   TROUBLE? *If the Printers And Others Hardware (Home) or Printers And Faxes (Pro) are not available on the Start menu, click Control Panel, and then double-click the Printers And Faxes icon in Classic view.*

2 Click a printer icon.

3 Click the Details button to display printer properties.

4 Click the Close button.

> **See Also**
>
> *See "Sharing a Printer" on page 350 for information on creating a shared printer.*

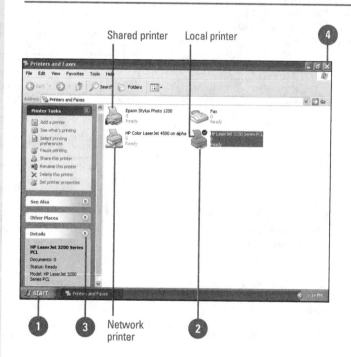

Installing a Printer

To install a printer, you do not need to shut down your computer. Simply attach the printer cable to the appropriate connector on your computer, according to the manufacturer's instructions, and plug in the power cord. If you connect your printer to your computer through a USB port, Windows detects the new hardware device and installs the printer, and you are ready to print. Otherwise, you can use the Add Printer Wizard in conjunction with the Found New Hardware Wizard to detect and install the printer. The Add Printer Wizard asks you a series of questions to help you install either a local or network printer, establish a connection, and print a test page.

Set Up a Local Printer Using the Add Printer Wizard

1. Click the Start button, and then click Printers And Other Hardware (Home) or Printers And Faxes (Pro).

2. Click Add A Printer, and then click Next.

3. Click the Local Printer Attached To This Computer option.

4. Select the Automatically Detect And Install My Plug And Play Printer check box, and then click Next.

5. Click the Port list arrow, select the port to which the printer is connected, and then click Next.

6. Select the printer manufacturer and model, and then click Next.

7. Type a printer name.

8. Click the Yes or No option to use the printer as the default printer, and then click Next.

9. Click the Do Not Share This Printer option, or click the Share Name Option and type a share printer name, and then click Next.

10. Click the Yes or No option to print a test page, and then click Next.

11. Click Finish.

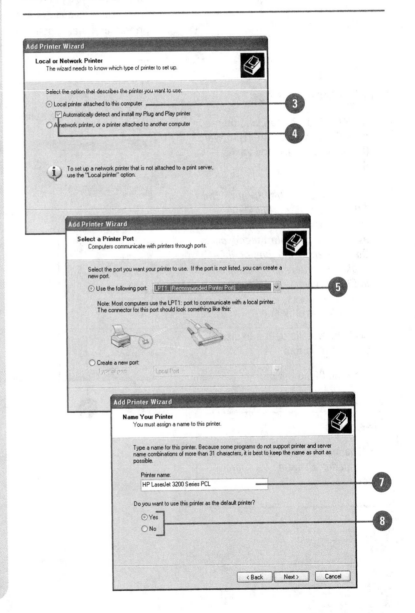

Set Up a Network Printer Using the Add Printer Wizard

1. Click the Start button, and then click Printers And Other Hardware (Home) or Printers And Faxes (Pro).

2. Click Add A Printer, and then click Next.

3. Click the A Network Printer, Or A Printer Attached To Another Computer option, and then click Next.

4. Click an option to specify a printer or find one, and then click Next.

5. Click the Yes or No option to use the printer as the default printer, and then click Next.

6. Click Finish.

For Your Information

Understanding USB Ports

A **port** is the location on the back of your computer where you connect the printer cable. You can connect the cable to either a printer port, which is labeled LPT1 or LPT2, to a communications port, which is labeled COM1 or COM2, or to a Universal Serial Bus port, which is labeled USB. A printer port is called a **parallel port**, which sends more than one byte simultaneously. A communications port is called a **serial port**, which sends information one byte at a time. The USB port is a new technology that is expected to replace parallel and serial ports. A **USB (Universal Serial Bus) port** is an external hardware interface on the computer that allows you to connect a USB device. A single USB port can be used to connect up to 127 peripheral devices, such as mice, modems, and keyboards, and supports data transfer rates of 480 Mbs (480 million bits per second). USB also supports plug and play installation and **hot plugging**, which is the ability to add and remove devices to a computer while the computer is running and have the operating system automatically recognize the change.

Specifying a Default Printer

If your computer is connected to more than one printer, you can choose the default printer you want Windows to use to print your files unless you specify another one. The default printer is typically the printer that you use most often. When you start a print job without specifying a particular printer, the job is sent to the default printer. You can select a default printer in the Printers and Faxes window or when you set up a new printer. The default printer displays a black dot with a check mark in the printer icon.

Select a Default Printer

1. Click the Start button, and then click Printers And Other Hardware (Home) or Printers And Faxes (Pro).

2. Right-click the printer icon you want to set as the default, and then click Set As Default Printer.

3. Click the Close button.

Current default printer

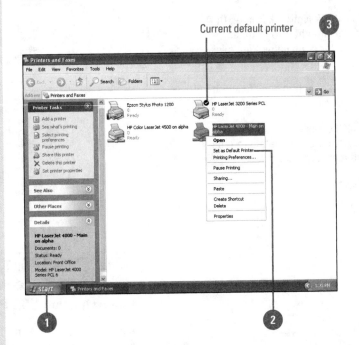

Renaming or Deleting a Printer

If you have trouble identifying a printer, or if you just want a change, you can rename it. You rename it the same way you rename a file or folder. When you rename a printer, the new name appears in the Print dialog box for all your programs. If you no longer use a printer, you can delete it. When you delete the default printer, Windows displays a warning message and changes the default printer to another available printer.

Rename a Printer

1. Click the Start button, and then click Printers And Other Hardware (Home) or Printers And Faxes (Pro).

2. Right-click the printer icon you want to rename, and then click Rename.

3. Type a new name for the printer, and then press Enter.

4. Click the Close button.

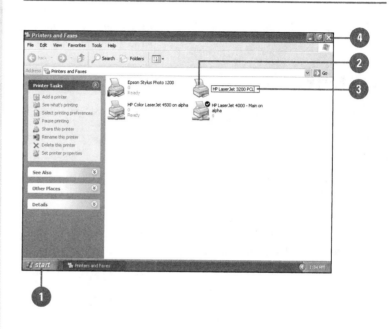

Delete a Printer

1. Click the Start button, and then click Printers And Other Hardware (Home) or Printers And Faxes (Pro).

2. Right-click the printer icon you want to delete, and then click Delete.

3. Click OK to confirm the deletion.

4. If the printer is the default, click OK.

5. Click the Close button.

Printing and Faxing   **349**

Sharing a Printer

If you have a printer connected to your computer and your computer is connected to a network, you can share your printer with other network users. Before you can share a printer, you need to turn on printer sharing using the Network Setup Wizard, which you can accomplish by using the Sharing tab in the Printer Properties dialog box. After you share a printer, the printer icon appears with a hand in the Printers and Faxes window. For security purposes, if Windows Firewall is enabled (the default setting) on the computer with the shared computer, then you need to select File and Printer Sharing on the Exceptions tab in Windows Firewall for others to use the shared printer (NewSP2).

Share a Printer

1. Click the Start button, and then click Printers And Other Hardware (Home) or Printers And Faxes (Pro).

2. Right-click the printer you want to share, and then click Sharing.

    TROUBLE? *If sharing options are not available, click the link, and then follow the instructions to turn on print sharing.*

3. Click the Share This Printer option.

4. Type a name for the printer (eight characters recommended), or use the suggested one.

5. If other computers on the network don't use Windows XP or Windows 2000, click Additional Drivers to install other drivers for them.

6. Select the check boxes for the operating systems you want.

7. Click OK.

8. If prompted, insert the Windows XP CD into your CD-ROM drive or provide a driver location, and then click OK.

9. Click OK.

10. Click OK.

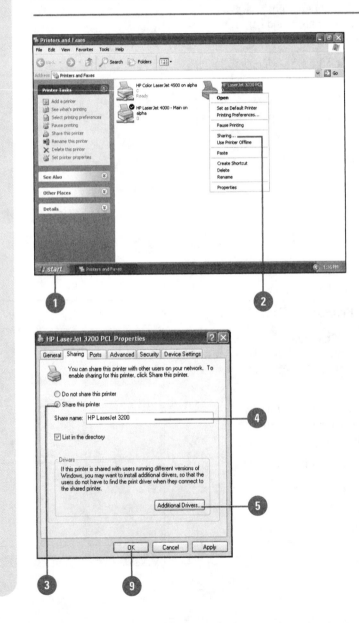

Printing Documents

If you have a group of documents that you want to print, you can print them all directly from a folder window without having to open each one in its program. The program needs to be installed on your computer to complete the job.

Print Documents Using the Default Printer

1. Open the folder that contains the documents you want to print.

2. Select the documents.

3. Right-click a selected document, and then click Print.

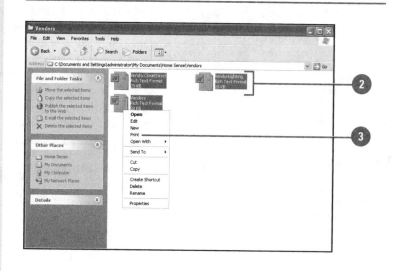

Print Documents Using a Specific Printer

1. Click the Start button, and then click Printers And Other Hardware (Home) or Printers And Faxes (Pro).

2. Open the folder (in a separate window) that contains the documents you want to print.

3. Select the documents.

4. Drag the selected documents onto the printer you want to use.

   TROUBLE? *If a program requires the use of the default printer, you need to change the printer to the default.*

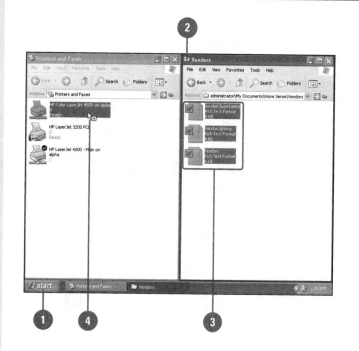

Managing Printers and Print Jobs

After you send a print job to the printer from the Print dialog box in a program, or drag files to the Printer icon in the Printers and Faxes window, you can check the status. To check the status of a printer or manage multiple print jobs, you can double-click the appropriate printer icon in the Printers and Faxes window or on the taskbar in the notification area. A window opens showing the **print queue**, which is the list of files to be printed. You can use this window to cancel print jobs, temporarily pause print jobs, view printer properties, and so on. If you are having problems with a printer or print job, you can **defer**, or halt, the printing process to avoid getting error messages. With deferred printing, you can send a job to be printed even if your computer is not connected to a printer. To do this, you pause printing, and the file waits in the print queue until you turn off pause printing.

Pause Printing

1. Click the Start button, and then click Printers And Other Hardware (Home) or Printers And Faxes (Pro).

2. Double-click the printer icon.

3. Click the Printer menu, and then click Pause Printing.

4. To resume printing, click the Printer menu, and then click Pause Printing again.

5. Click the Close button.

Did You Know?

You can troubleshoot print problems. Open the Printers and Faxes window, click Troubleshoot Printing in the task pane, and then follow the trouble-shooting instructions.

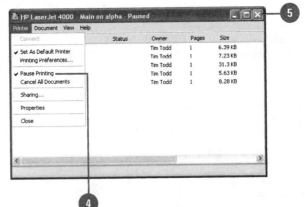

Pause a Print Job

1 Click the Start button, and then click Printers And Other Hardware (Home) or Printers And Faxes (Pro).

2 Double-click the printer icon.

3 Right-click the document you want to pause, and then click Pause.

4 To resume the document printing, right-click the document you want to resume, and then click Restart.

5 Click the Close button.

Cancel a Print Job

1 Click the Start button, and then click Printers And Other Hardware (Home) or Printers And Faxes (Pro).

2 Double-click the printer icon.

3 Right-click the document you want to stop, and then click Cancel.

4 To cancel all documents, click the Printer menu, click Cancel All Documents, and then click Yes to confirm the cancelation.

5 Click the Close button.

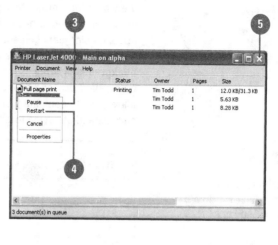

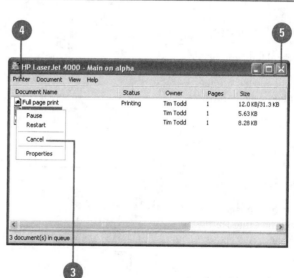

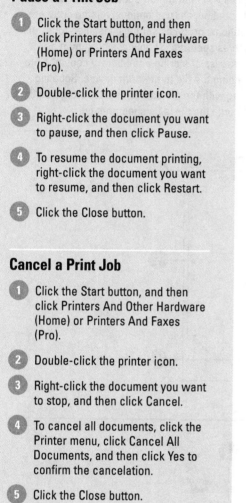

Security Alert

Displaying Printer Notification

For security purposes, if Windows Firewall is turned on (the default setting), printer notification information, such as "Ready" or "Paused," in the Printers and Faxes folder is slightly delayed and your computer no longer receives other printer notifications, such as "Print job completed" or "Printer out of paper" (NewSP2).

Changing Printer Properties

Viewing printer properties gives you information about a printer's computer connection or network location, sharing options, related software drivers, color management options, graphics settings, installed fonts, and other advanced settings, such as **spooling**. Spooling, also known as **background printing**, is the process of storing a temporary copy of a file on the hard disk and then sending the file to the print device. Spooling allows you to continue working with the file as soon as it is stored on the disk instead of having to wait until the file is finished printing.

Change General Properties

1. Click the Start button, and then click Printers And Other Hardware (Home) or Printers And Faxes (Pro).

2. Select the printer icon you want to change.

3. Click Set Printer Properties.

4. Click the General tab.

5. If you want, change the printer name or location, and then type a comment.

6. Click OK.

Change Device Properties

1. Click the Start button, and then click Printers And Other Hardware (Home) or Printers And Faxes (Pro).

2. Right-click the the printer icon you want to change, and then click Properties.

3. Click the Device Settings tab.

4. Click the plus sign (+) to expand the options you want to change.

5. Click an option link.

6. Click an option list arrow, and then select a setting.

7. Click OK.

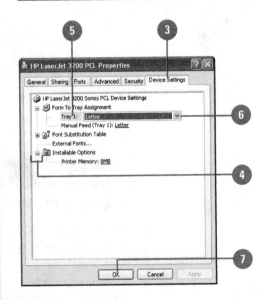

Change Spooling Settings

1. Click the Start button, and then click Printers And Other Hardware (Home) or Printers And Faxes (Pro).

2. Right-click the the the printer icon you want to change, and then click Properties.

3. Click the Advanced tab.

4. Click the Spool Print Documents So Program Finishes Printing Faster option.

5. Click a spooling option to specify when you want the printer to start printing your documents.

6. To keep documents in the spooler after they are printed, select the Keep Printed Documents check box.

7. To print documents that have completed spooling before other documents, select Print Spooled Documents First check box.

8. Click OK.

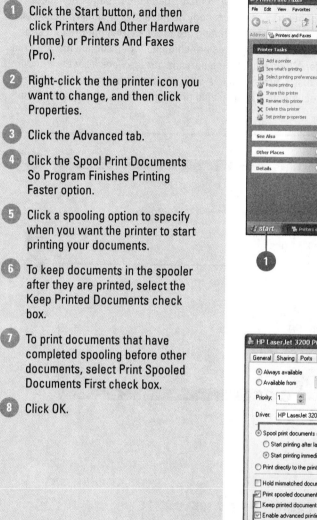

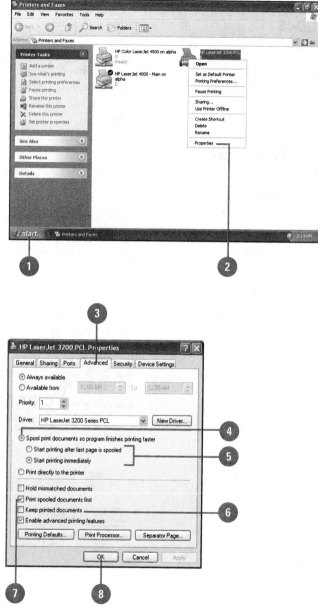

13

Changing Printer Preferences

In addition to printer properties, you can also view and change personal printer preferences, such as orientation, page order, pages per sheet, paper size, paper tray selection, copy count, and print quality and color. When you change personal printing preferences from the Printers and Faxes folder, the default settings are changed for all documents you print to that printer. When you change personal preferences from the Print or Page Setup dialog boxes within a program, the settings are changed for individual documents. The available printing preferences depend on the printer.

Change Printer Preferences

① Click the Start button, and then click Printers And Other Hardware (Home) or Printers And Faxes (Pro).

② Select the printer icon you want to change.

③ Click Select Printing Preferences.

④ Click the tab with the option you want to change.

⑤ Change the printer preferences you want to modify.

⑥ Click OK.

⑦ Click the Close button.

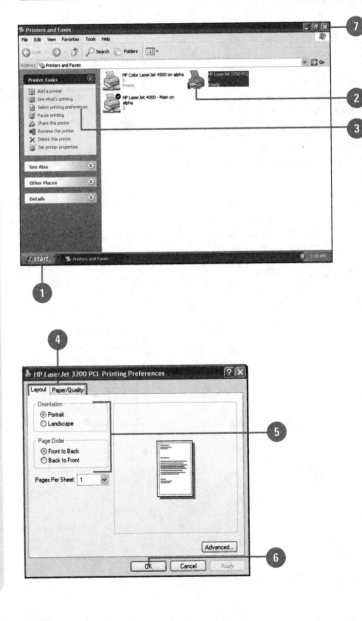

Understanding Faxes

Windows XP comes with several fax components that you can use to configure fax devices, send and receive faxes, and monitor fax activity. These components include the Fax Configuration Wizard, Send Fax Wizard, Fax Cover Page Editor, and Fax Console.

Before you can use a fax component, you need a fax device for sending and receiving faxes. The fax device can be directly attached to your computer, known as a **local fax**, or located on a network, known as a **remote fax**. Once Fax is installed, you can use the fax components to configure the fax device, send and receive faxes, manage incoming and outgoing faxes, and change fax device properties.

The **Fax Configuration Wizard** walks you through the process to configure a fax device. After you configure a local fax or connect to a remote fax, you can use the **Send Fax Wizard**

to send faxes from a folder window or the Print dialog box in a program. The Send Fax Wizard starts when you print using a fax printer.

With the **Fax Cover Page Editor**, you can create and edit cover pages to use when you send a fax. The Fax Cover Page Editor is a full page editor that makes it easy to insert common fax page items, such as recipient, subject, number of pages, and message, and to format the page to create a professional look. You can also customize a few samples that come with the program.

You can use the **Fax Console** to monitor incoming and outgoing fax activity. From Fax Console, you can also access Fax Monitor, a tool used to track the progress of faxes being sent and received. You can also send faxes directly from the Fax Console.

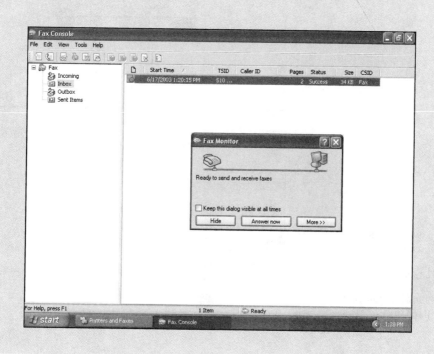

Setting Up a Fax

If your computer has a fax modem installed, you can send and receive faxes through your computer. The Fax Configuration Wizard helps you set up the Fax Service. You need to enter some personal information for the fax cover page, a phone number, and some option for the way you want to send and receive faxes. As part of the setup, you also need to specify the use of a Transmitting Station Identifier (TSID), which is an identification sent along with a fax to identify the source, and a Called Subscriber Identifier (CSID), which is an identification sent back to the sending fax device to confirm the identity of the source. Fax is not installed by default during Windows Setup, so you need to install it. If it is not installed, the Fax Configuration Wizard asks you to install it.

Install a Modem

1. Click the Start button, and then click Control Panel.

2. Double-click the Phone And Modem Options icon.

3. Click the Modems Tab.

4. Click Add, and then click Next.

5. Select a country/region, and then type the area code, carrier code, and access number as necessary.

6. Click the Tone Dialing or Pulse Dialing option.

7. Click OK.

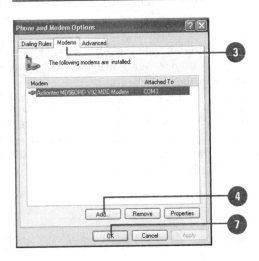

Set Up a Fax

1. Click the Start button, and then click Printers And Faxes.

2. Insert the Windows XP installation CD into your CD-ROM drive.

3. Click Set Up Faxing, and then wait for the installation to complete.

4. Click Install A Local Fax Printer.

5. Follow any Windows installation instruction as necessary.

Configure a Fax

1 In the Printers And Faxes window, double-click the Fax icon.

   TROUBLE? *If a modem is not available, follow the instructions to install one, or if the Fax Console opens, click the Tools menu, and then click Configure Fax.*

2 Click Next.

3 Enter sender information, and then click Next.

4 Select the Enable Send check box.

5 Select the Enable Receive check box.

6 Select the Manual Answer or Automatically Answer After (number) Rings option.

7 Click Next.

8 Type the fax number, your name for the TSID, and then click Next.

9 Type the fax number, your name for the CSID, and then click Next.

10 If you want, select routing options, and then click Next.

11 Click Finish.

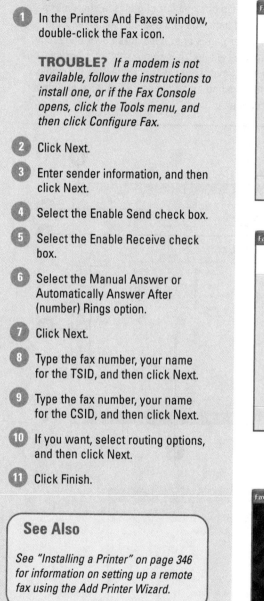

See Also

See "Installing a Printer" on page 346 for information on setting up a remote fax using the Add Printer Wizard.

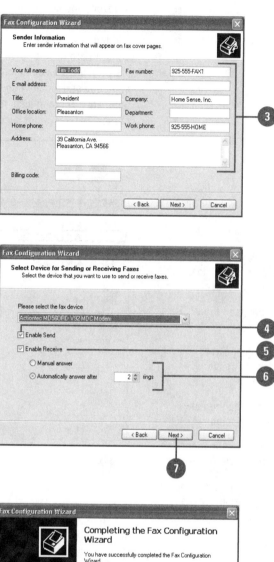

Creating a Fax Cover Page

A cover page is typically a one page cover memo sent along with a fax containing the fax sender, a recipient, number of pages, a short message, and the transmission date and time. You can use the Fax Cover Page Editor to create your own cover pages or to customize cover page templates, known as common cover pages, that come with the program. You can copy and modify common cover pages without affecting the original templates. You can also edit existing cover pages and rename or delete personal cover pages as needed.

Create a Cover Page from Scratch

1. Click the Start button, point to All Programs, point to Accessories, and then point to Communications.

2. Point to Fax, click Fax Cover Page Editor, and then click OK to close the Tip dialog box, if necessary.

3. Click the View menu, and then click Grid Lines.

4. Click the Insert menu, point to Recipient, Sender, or Message, and then click an item.

5. Press and hold Ctrl, and then click the items you want to select.

6. Drag the items to a new location, or use the alignment buttons on the toolbar.

7. Use the formatting buttons on the toolbar to format the text.

8. Use the drawing tools on the toolbar to add shapes and lines.

9. Click the File menu, and then click Save As.

10. Type a name for the cover page.

11. Click Save.

12. Click the Close button.

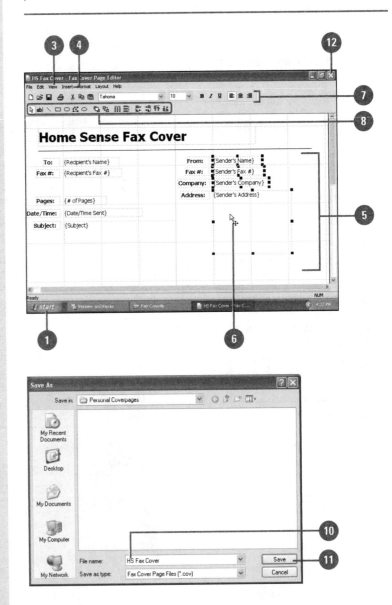

360

Copy a Cover Page Template

1. Click the Start button, and then click Printers And Other Hardware (Home) or Printers And Faxes (Pro).

2. Double-click the Fax icon.

3. Click the Tools menu, and then click Personal Cover Pages.

4. Click Copy.

5. Select a common fax cover page.

6. Click Open.

7. Click Close.

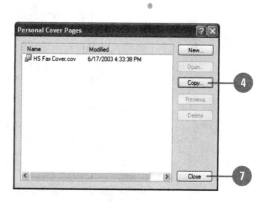

Rename or Delete a Cover Page

1. Click the Start button, and then click Printers And Other Hardware (Home) or Printers And Faxes (Pro).

2. Double-click the Fax icon.

3. Click the Tools menu, and then click Personal Cover Pages.

4. Click a cover page.

5. To rename the cover page, click Rename, type a new name (include the extension .cov), and then press Enter.

6. To delete the cover page, click Delete, and then click Yes to confirm it.

7. Click Close.

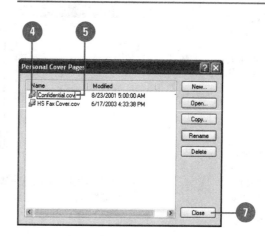

13

Sending a Fax

After you install and configure your fax, you can send a fax using the Send Fax Wizard. The Send Fax Wizard walks you through the process of sending a fax. You can send a cover page fax from the Printer and Faxes window or from within Fax Console, or a document fax from a program. When you send a cover page fax, the Send Fax Wizard opens to help you create and send a cover page fax. When you send a document fax, the program in which you open or create the document prints it to the fax device. When you print to a fax device, the Send Fax Wizard opens to help you send the fax.

Send a Cover Page Fax

1. Click the Start button, and then click Printers And Other Hardware (Home) or Printers And Faxes (Pro).

2. Double-click the Fax icon.

3. Click the File menu, click Send A Fax, and then click Next.

4. Type the recipient name and fax number, or click Address Book and select one.

5. If you typed a recipient's name, click Add to add the person to your list of fax recipients. Repeat the process to add other recipients.

6. To include an area or country code, click the Use Dialing Rules check box.

7. Click Next.

8. Select the Select A Cover Page Template With The Following Information check box, click the Cover Page Template list arrow, and then select a cover page.

9. Type the subject and notes for the fax, and then click Next.

10. Click the option to specify when you want to send the fax.

11. Click Next, preview the fax if you want, and then click Finish.

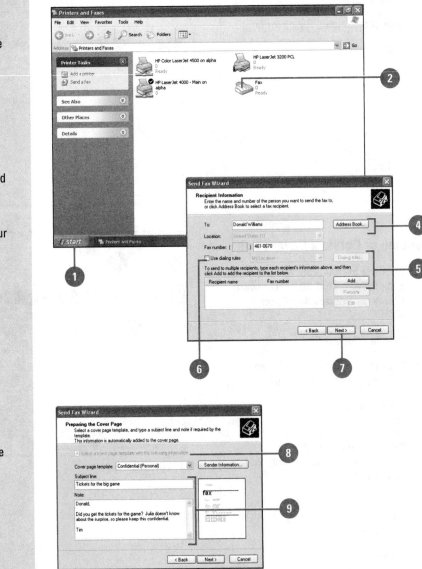

Send a Fax from a Document

1. Start the program and open or create the document you want to send as a fax.

2. Click the File menu, and then click Print.

3. Click the Fax printer as your printer.

4. Click Print.

5. Follow the Send A Fax Wizard instructions, specifying the following:

   ◆ The recipient(s)

   ◆ Cover page

   ◆ Subject and notes

   ◆ When to send the fax

6. Preview the fax, and then click Finish.

Did You Know?

You can scan and fax a document. Scan the document using a scanner, open the scanned document in a program, and then print it to the fax directly from the program.

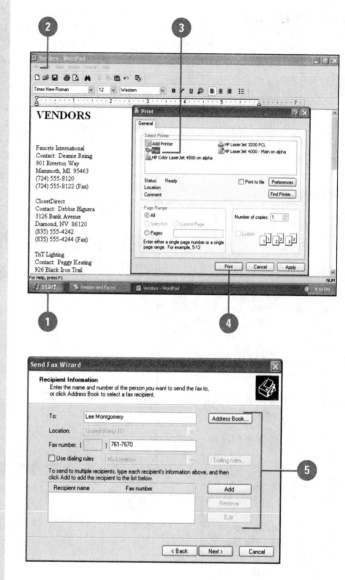

Managing Outgoing Faxes

After you send a fax, its sent to the Outbox folder of the Fax Console. The Outbox is a storage area for all faxes waiting to be sent, or in the process of being sent. From the Outbox, you can pause and resume faxes, restart failed faxes, and remove individual faxes as necessary. If a fax is being sent to multiple recipients, the fax for each recipient appears separately, so you can pause or delete a fax to one of the multiple recipients without affecting the others. When you change the status of a fax in the Outbox, the Status column changes to indicate the new state of the fax. Once a fax is sent successfully, it is moved to the Sent Items folder.

Cancel or Restart an Outgoing Fax

1. Click the Start button, and then click Printers And Other Hardware (Home) or Printers And Faxes (Pro).

2. Double-click the Fax icon.

3. Click the Outbox icon.

4. To cancel a fax, click the fax, and then click the Delete button.

5. To restart a failed fax, click the fax, and then click the Restart button.

6. When you're done, click the Close button.

Did You Know?

You can't remove a fax from a remote fax printer without deleting the fax printer. Click the remote fax printer from the Printer and Faxes window, and then click Delete This Printer.

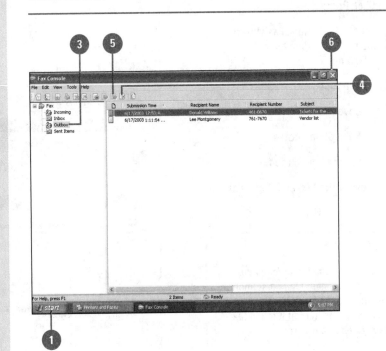

Pause or Resume an Outgoing Fax

1. Click the Start button, and then click Printers And Other Hardware (Home) or Printers And Faxes (Pro).

2. Double-click the Fax icon.

3. Click the Outbox icon.

4. To pause a fax, click the fax, and then click the Pause button.

5. To resume a fax, click the paused fax, and then click the Resume button.

6. When you're done, click the Close button.

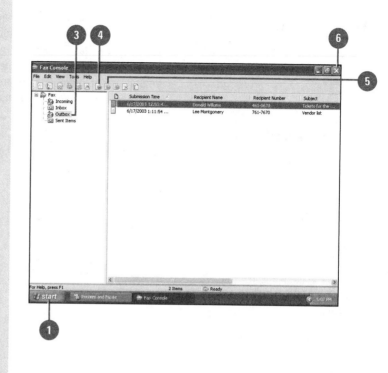

View a Sent Fax

1. Click the Start button, and then click Printers And Other Hardware (Home) or Printers And Faxes (Pro).

2. Double-click the Fax icon.

3. Click the Sent Items icon.

4. Review the fax information.

5. When you're done, click the Close button.

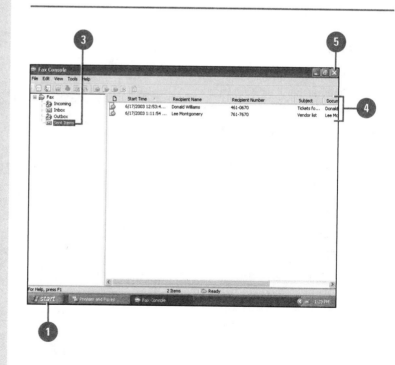

Receiving a Fax

If you have a phone line attached to your computer, you can set up the Fax Console to receive faxes automatically or manually. If the phone line is a dedicated fax line and set to receive faxes automatically, the Fax Console automatically stores the fax in your Inbox, just like an e-mail in your e-mail program. If the phone line is used for voice and fax calls, the Fax Console waits for you to answer the call before it receives the fax.

Receive a Fax Manually

1 When you receive a call for a fax, click to receive the call to open the Fax Monitor dialog box.

2 Click Answer Now, if necessary.

3 Click More to see details about the call.

4 If there are problems with the fax or if you don't want to receive it, click Disconnect.

5 To hide the Fax Monitor dialog box while you receive the fax, click Hide.

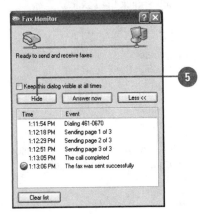

Change Receive Answer Mode

1 Click the Start button, and then click Printers and Other Hardware (Home) or Printers and Faxes (Pro).

2 Right-click the Fax icon, and then click Properties.

3 Click the Devices tab, and then click Properties.

4 Click the Receive tab.

5 Click the Manual or Automatic After Number Of Rings option.

6 Click OK, and then click OK again.

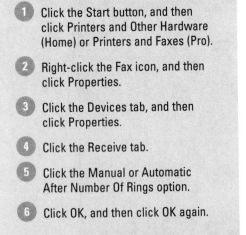

Reviewing a Fax

Review a Received Fax

1 Click the Start button, and then click Printers And Other Hardware (Home) or Printers And Faxes (Pro).

2 Double-click the Fax icon.

3 To review the status of a fax being received, click the Incoming icon.

4 Click the Inbox icon.

5 Click the fax you want to view.

6 Use the buttons on the toolbar to do the following:

   ◆ Print the fax to your printer

   ◆ View the fax on the screen

   ◆ Save the fax to a folder as a TIF document

   ◆ E-mail the fax as an attachment to a message

7 When you're done, click the Close button.

After you receive a fax, you can use Fax Console to view, print, save, or e-mail the fax. The Fax Console informs you when a fax arrived, who sent it, how many pages were received, and the status of the job.

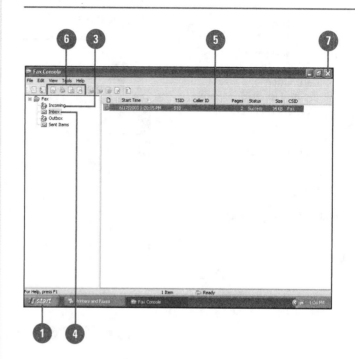

Viewing and Annotating a Fax

When you view a fax, the file opens in Windows Picture and Fax Viewer. The Windows Picture and Fax Viewer (**New!**) opens fax files in the TIF format, which allows you to mark up the fax file using additional annotation tools. With the annotation tools, you can draw straight lines, rectangles, and freehand shapes, highlight text and graphics, and attach notes.

View a Fax

1. Click the Start button, and then click Printers And Other Hardware (Home) or Printers And Faxes (Pro).

2. Double-click the Fax icon.

3. Click the icon that contains the fax you want to view.

4. Double-click the fax you want to view.

5. Use the buttons in the Windows Picture And Fax Viewer to view the fax.

6. When you're done, click the Close button.

7. Click the Close button again.

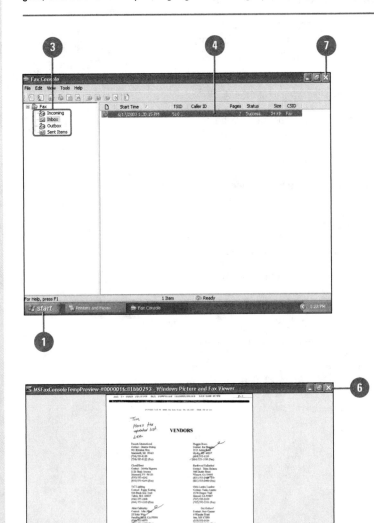

Annotate a Fax

1. Open and view the fax in the Windows Picture And Fax Viewer.

2. Use the annotation tools to mark up the fax.

3. To select, move, or resize an annotation, click the Select Annotation tool.

4. To delete an annotation, select it, and then press Delete.

5. To change annotation properties, select the annotation, click the Edit Info button, change the properties, such as line width, font, color, and transparency, you want, and then click OK.

6. Click the Copy To, and then save the fax.

7. Select the folder where you want to save the fax.

8. Click Save.

9. When you're done, click the Close button.

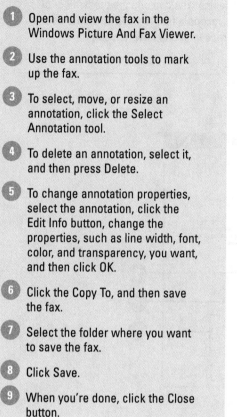

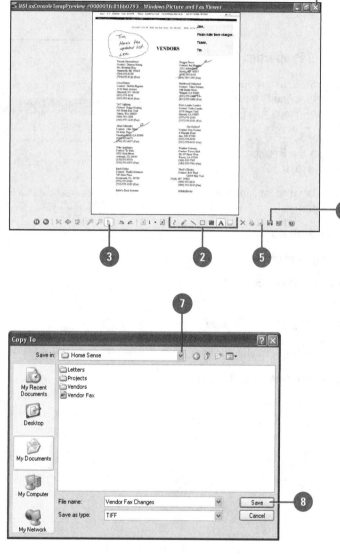

13

Changing Fax Properties

You can change the send and receive properties for a fax device to effectively work with your phone line. You can change the number of times the the fax device tries to resend a fax. You can also change where to store a fax when you receive it and how to clean up a failed fax.

Change Send Properties

1. Click the Start button, and then click Printers And Other Hardware (Home) or Printers And Faxes (Pro).

2. Right-click the Fax icon, and then click Properties.

3. Click the Devices tab, and then click Properties.

4. Click the Send tab.

5. Type number of retries.

6. Type retries after number of minutes.

7. To send faxes at a specific time when discount phone charges apply, specify a start and end time.

8. Click OK, and then click OK again.

Change Receive Properties

1. Click the Start button, and then click Printers And Other Hardware (Home) or Printers And Faxes (Pro).

2. Right-click the Fax icon, and then click Properties.

3. Click the Devices tab, and then click Properties.

4. Click the Receive tab.

5. Click the Manual or Automatic After Number Of Rings option.

6. If you want, select the Print It On check box, and then select a printer.

7. If you want, select the Save A Copy In Folder check box, and then select a folder.

8. Click OK, and then click OK again.

Automatically Clean Up Faxes

1. Click the Start button, and then click Printers And Other Hardware (Home) or Printers And Faxes (Pro).

2. Right-click the Fax icon, and then click Properties.

3. Click the Devices tab, and then click Properties.

4. Click the Cleanup tab.

5. Select the Automatically Delete Failed Faxes After Number Of Days check box.

6. Type in the number of days.

7. Click OK, and then click OK again.

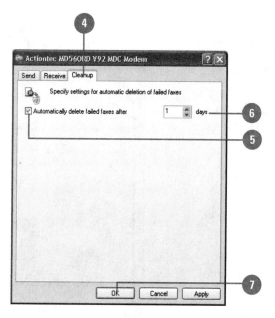

Changing Fax Options

As you send and receive faxes, you can have fax track and notify you when events take place. For example, you can show a progress indicator when faxes are incoming or outgoing and display notifications when faxes arrive. You can also set fax options to automatically open the Fax Monitor when a fax is being sent or received and archive faxes for backup purposes.

Change Tracking Options

1. Click the Start button, and then click Printers And Other Hardware (Home) or Printers And Faxes (Pro).

2. Right-click the Fax icon, and then click Properties.

3. Click the Tracking tab.

4. Select the check boxes in the Notification Area you want.

5. Select the check boxes for the Fax Monitor you want.

6. Click OK.

Change Archive Options

1. Click the Start button, and then click Printers And Other Hardware (Home) or Printers And Faxes (Pro).

2. Right-click the Fax icon, and then click Properties.

3. Click the Archives tab.

4. Select the archive check boxes in which you want to enable.

5. Click Browse, select a folder, and then click OK.

6. Click OK.

Maintaining Your Computer

Introduction

Windows XP offers a number of useful tools for managing such routine tasks as installing and removing programs, and formatting, copying, and repairing disks. Windows XP also provides tools to find and fix disk problems, speed up disk access, and clean up disk space. By periodically finding and repairing disk errors, you can keep your files in good working condition and prevent disk problems that might cause you to lose your work. You can also schedule these tasks to run on a regular basis. If you find Windows performing sluggishly even after performing routine maintenance, you can adjust system processing and memory settings to improve performance.

Keeping your computer up-to-date is another way to keep your computer in good working condition and protect it against new and ongoing attacks over the Internet. Windows Automatic Update scans your computer for any software components or fixes (including security and high priority updates) that need to be installed and automatically or manually downloads them from the Internet. Each file that you download using Automatic Update has a digital signature from Microsoft to ensure it's authenticity and security. If problems do occur, you can undo harmful changes to your computer and restore its settings, or you can use one of several startup options to help you start Windows in a safe environment with basic files and drivers where you can restore settings and fix the problem.

What You'll Do

Understand Disk File Systems

Format a Disk

Display Disk and Folder Information

Transfer Files Using a Disk

Copy a Disk

Detect and Repair Disk Errors

Optimize and Clean Up a Disk

Schedule Maintenance

Add or Remove Windows Components

Install or Uninstall a Program

Set Program Access and Defaults

Improve Computer Performance

Update Windows

Restore Computer Settings

Start Windows When Problems Occur

Set Startup and Recovery Options

Understanding Disk File Systems

A disk must be formatted with a **file system** that allows it to work with the operating system to store, manage, and access data. Two of the most common file systems are FAT (or FAT32, which is an improvement on FAT technology) and NTFS. Disks on DOS, Windows 3.1, or Windows 98/Me computers use the FAT file system, while disks on computers running Windows NT 4.0, Windows 2000, Windows XP and later can use either the NTFS or FAT system. NTFS is a newer file system that improves on some of the shortcomings of FAT disks that make them less desirable on a network. Which file system your disks are most likely to use and why depends on the type of disk, whether your computer is on a network, and your computer's role as a resource on the network.

There are important differences between FAT and NTFS file systems:

FAT

When you format a disk with the FAT file system, a formatting program divides the disk into storage compartments. First it creates a series of rings, called **tracks**, around the circumference of the disk. Then it divides the tracks into equal parts, like pieces of a pie, to form sectors. The number of sectors and tracks depends on the size of the disk.

Although the physical surface of a disk is made of tracks and sectors, a file is stored in clusters. A cluster, also called an **allocation unit**, is one or more sectors of storage space. It represents the minimum amount of space that an operating system reserves when saving the contents of a file to a disk. Thus, a file might be stored in more than one cluster. Each cluster is identified by a unique number. The first two clusters are reserved by the operating system. The operating system maintains a file allocation table (or FAT) on each disk that lists the clusters on the disk and records the status of each cluster, whether it is occupied (and by which file), available, or defective. Each cluster in a file "remembers" its order in the chain of clusters—and each cluster points to the next one until the last cluster, which marks the end of the file. The FAT and FAT32 formats provide compatibility with other operating systems on your computer, which means you can configure your computer for a dual-boot or multiboot setup and you can backup a previous operating system.

NTFS

NTFS features a built-in security system that does not allow users to access the disk unless they have a user account and password with the necessary rights and permissions. NTFS protects disks from damage by automatically redirecting data from a bad sector to a good sector without requiring you to run a diskchecking utility. Given the reliability and the built-in repair mechanisms of NTFS disks, only rarely do they require maintenance. This is an example of **fault tolerance**, the ability of a disk to resist damage, which is a critical issue with disks on a network computer.

Selecting a file system

NTFS does not support floppy disks, so all floppies are formatted with FAT. If you are running Windows XP on a stand-alone computer, you can choose either FAT or NTFS, but in most cases, the file system has already been determined either by the person who originally set up the computer or by the manufacturer from whom you purchased the computer. If your computer is a client on a Windows XP network, it is likely that your hard disk uses

NTFS. Because NTFS is more suited to network demands, such as a high level of security and resistance to system failure, network administrators format network disks with NTFS whenever possible. Sometimes, however, users on a network want or need to use a non-Windows XP operating system. Also, a user might need a computer that is capable of running Windows XP or Windows 98/Me. The disks on that computer would then be formatted with FAT.

User Interface Differences		
Feature	**FAT**	**NTFS**
Security	Vulnerable to "hackers"—unauthorized users who break into other people's files	Includes built-in security measures that allow only people who have permission to access files
Recoverability	Likely to fail if a sector containing system data is lost because it stores critical system files in single sectors	Highly reliable because it uses redundant storage—it stores everything in vital sectors twice, so if a disk error in a vital sector occurs, NTFS can access file system data from the redundant sector
File size	Designed for small disks (originally less than 1 MB in size); can handle a maximum file size of 4 GB	Handles files up to 64 GB in size

Formatting a Disk

Formatting a disk prepares it so that you can store information on it. Formatting removes all information from the disk, so you should never format a disk that has files you want to keep. When you format a disk, you need to specify the disk capacity, file system, and allocation unit size; default settings are recommended. Capacity is how much data the disk or partition can hold, such as the physical size, storage size, and sector size. A file system is the overall structure in which files are named, stored, and organized. NTFS and FAT32 are types of file systems. Disk allocation unit size, or cluster size, is a group of sectors on a disk. The operating system assigns a unique number to each cluster and then keeps track of files according to which clusters they use. The default allocation size is typically selected. If your hard disk uses the FAT or FAT32 file system, you can convert the hard disk to the NTFS format.

Format a Disk

1. With a disk in the drive, click the Start button, and then click My Computer.

2. Right-click the drive, and then click Format.

3. Specify the capacity, file system, and allocation unit size.

4. Select the Quick Format check box to perform a quick format, or clear the Quick Format check box to perform a full format and disk scan for bad sectors.

5. To format an NTFS drive so that folders and files are compressed, select the Enable Compression check box.

6. To use a floppy disk to start up your computer and run MS-DOS, select the Create An MS-DOS Startup Disk check box.

7. Click Start, click OK to format the disk, and then click OK when it's done.

8. Click Close.

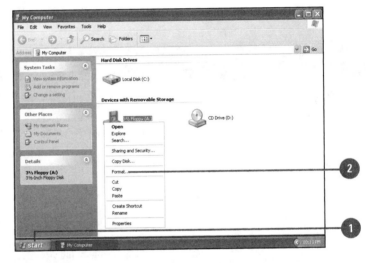

Convert a Disk

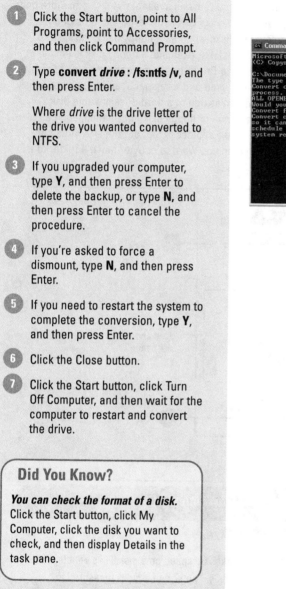

1. Click the Start button, point to All Programs, point to Accessories, and then click Command Prompt.

2. Type **convert** *drive* : **/fs:ntfs /v**, and then press Enter.

   Where *drive* is the drive letter of the drive you wanted converted to NTFS.

3. If you upgraded your computer, type **Y**, and then press Enter to delete the backup, or type **N**, and then press Enter to cancel the procedure.

4. If you're asked to force a dismount, type **N**, and then press Enter.

5. If you need to restart the system to complete the conversion, type **Y**, and then press Enter.

6. Click the Close button.

7. Click the Start button, click Turn Off Computer, and then wait for the computer to restart and convert the drive.

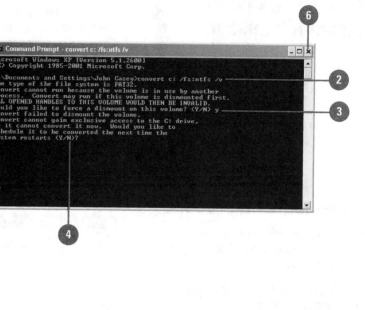

Did You Know?

You can check the format of a disk.
Click the Start button, click My Computer, click the disk you want to check, and then display Details in the task pane.

See Also

See "Detecting and Repairing Disk Errors" on page 381 for information on bad sectors.

14

Displaying Disk and Folder Information

As you work with files, folders, and programs, you should know the size of the disk and how much space remains available. A disk can store only a limited amount of data. Hard disks can store large amounts of data (in gigabytes), while removable disks, such as a floppy or ZIP disk, store smaller amounts (in megabytes). For example, a floppy disk is limited to 1.4 MB of data. You can use the Properties command on a disk to display the disk size or the amount of used and free space, and to change a disk label, which is a name you can assign to a hard or removable disk. Besides checking hard disk drive or floppy disk information, you can also use the Properties command on a folder to find out the size of its contents. This can be helpful when you want to copy or move a folder to a removable disk or CD.

Determine Free Space on a Disk

1. With a disk in the drive, click the Start button, and then click My Computer.

2. Right-click the drive, and then click Properties.

3. On the General tab, identify the amount of free space on the disk.

4. Click OK.

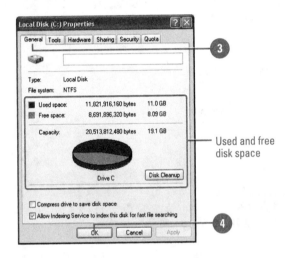

Used and free disk space

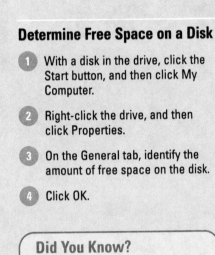

Did You Know?

A 1.44 MB floppy disk holds about 3,000 pages of text. A 1.44 MB floppy disk is capable of storing approximately 1.4 million characters, or about 3,000 pages of information.

For Your Information

Understanding File Sizes

When you create a file, it takes up space on a disk. Files with text are smaller than files with graphics. The size of a file is measured in bytes. A byte is a unit of storage capable of holding a single character or pixel. It's the base measurement for all other incremental units, which are kilobyte, megabyte, and gigabyte. A kilobyte (KB) is 1,024 bytes of information while a megabyte (MB) is 1,048,576 bytes, which is equal to 1,024 kilobytes. A gigabyte (GB) is equal to 1,024 megabytes.

Transferring Files Using a Disk

You can copy files from your computer to a disk if you need to either transfer files from one stand-alone computer to another or save a copy of important files to prevent losing them in the event of a power failure or a computer problem.

Copy Files to a Disk

1. With the disk in the drive, click the Start button, and then click My Computer.

2. Open the folder, and then select the files you want to copy.

3. Right-click the selected files, and then point to Send To.

4. Click a disk from the submenu.

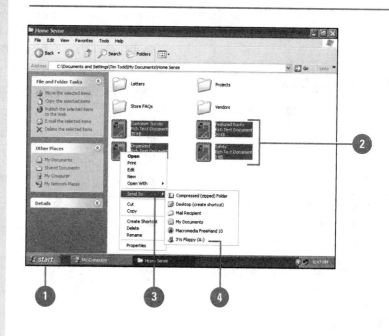

Copy Files from a Disk

1. With the disk in the drive, click the Start button, and then click My Computer.

2. Open the disk window, and then select the files you want to copy.

3. Drag the selected files to copy the selected items.

Copying a Disk

One way to protect the information on a disk from possible problems is to copy the disk, placing copies of all the files on it to another disk. Then, if information goes bad on a disk, you still have the copied information. You can use Windows to copy information from one disk to another using the same disk drive. When you copy disks, the disk must be the same type and not write-protected. A floppy disk is not write-protected when the tab in the upper-left corner on the back of the floppy disk is pushed down so that you cannot see through the square hole.

Copy a Floppy Disk

1. Click the Start button, and then click My Computer.

2. Right-click the floppy disk drive, and then click Copy Disk.

3. Select the source disk (Copy from) and destination disk (Copy to), if necessary.

4. Click Start, and then click OK.

5. When a Copy Disk message opens, remove the source disk, insert the destination disk, and then click OK.

6. When it's done, click Close.

See Also

See "Transferring Files Using a Disk" on page 379 for information on copying files to and from a disk.

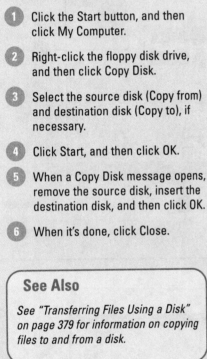

Detecting and Repairing Disk Errors

Sometimes an unexpected power loss or program error can create inaccessible file segments that take up space on a disk. The Check Disk program that comes with Windows helps you find and repair damaged sections of a disk. Check Disk can also be used to find physical disk errors or **bad sectors**. The program doesn't physically repair your media, but it moves data away from any bad sectors it finds. To keep your hard disk drive working properly, you should run Check Disk from time to time. When you run Check Disk, all files must be closed for the process to run. While the Check Disk process is running, your hard disk will not be available to perform any other task.

Check a Disk for Errors

1. Click the Start button, and then click My Computer.

2. Right-click the disk you want to check, and then click Properties.

3. Click the Tools tab.

4. Click Check Now.

5. Select the Automatically Fix File System Errors check box.

6. Select the Scan For And Attempt Recovery Of Bad Sectors check box.

7. Click Start.

8. When it's done, click OK.

9. Click OK.

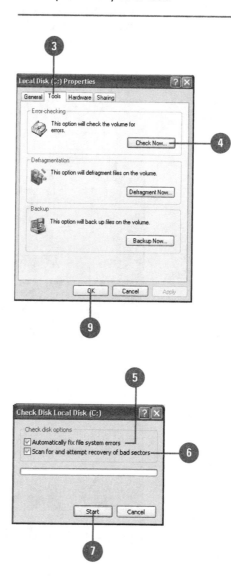

Optimizing a Disk

When you delete files from a disk, you create empty spaces that might be fragmented over different areas of the disk. When you create a new file on a fragmented disk, parts of the file are stored in these empty spaces, resulting in a single file that is broken into many parts, which takes longer to retrieve or store when you open or save the file. A file broken up in this way is called a **fragmented file**, which is undetectable to the user. You can use Disk Defragmenter to place all of the parts of a file in one **contiguous**, or adjacent, location. This procedure, which efficiently arranges all of the files and unused space, is called **optimization**. Optimization makes your programs run faster and your files open more quickly. While the Disk Defragmenter works, you can use your computer to carry out other tasks; however, your computer will operate more slowly. The Analysis display shows you the defragmentation process.

Defragment a Disk

1. Click the Start button, point to All Programs, point to Accessories, point to System Tools, and then click Disk Defragmenter.

2. Click the drive you want to defragment.

3. Click Analyze, and then click Close.

4. Click Defragment.

5. To pause and resume the process, click Pause and Resume.

6. To stop the process, click Stop.

7. When it's done, click Close.

8. Click the Close button.

Did You Know?

You should run Check Disk before the Disk Defragmenter. For best results, run Check Disk to check for errors on your disk before you start the disk defragmentation process.

You can view a defragment report. In Disk Defragmenter, click View Report.

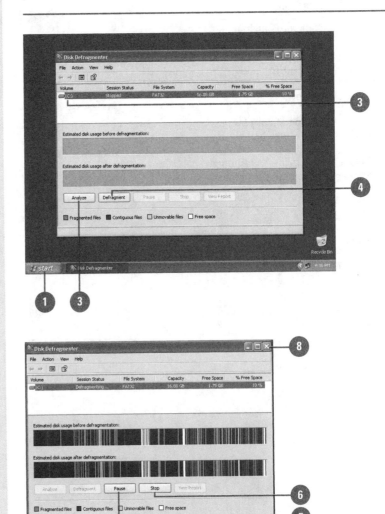

Cleaning Up a Disk

Cleaning up a disk involves removing unneeded files to make room for other files on your computer, which can be difficult if you don't know the significance of each file. You can use a Windows XP program called Disk Cleanup to clean up your hard disk drive safely and effectively. You can also empty the Recycle Bin to clear space on the hard disk. Disk Cleanup searches your drive, then lists temporary files, Internet cache files, and unnecessary program files that you can safely delete. You can select the types of files you want Disk Cleanup to delete. Before you select and delete files, make sure you will not need them in the future. Disk Cleanup also gives you the option to remove Windows components and installed programs that you no longer use.

Clean Up a Disk

1. Click the Start button, point to All Programs, point to Accessories, point to System Tools, and then click Disk Cleanup.

   Wait while Disk Cleanup calculates how much space it can free up.

2. Select the check boxes for the folders and files you want to delete.

3. To view the contents of a folder, click View Files, and then click the Close button.

4. Click OK, and then click Yes.

Did You Know?

You can remove programs from Disk Cleanup. In the Disk Cleanup window, click the More Options tab, click the Clean Up button you want, and then use the program to delete the program.

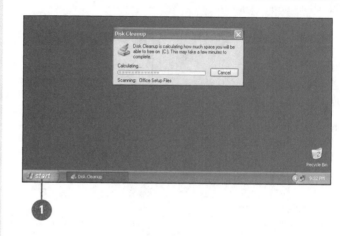

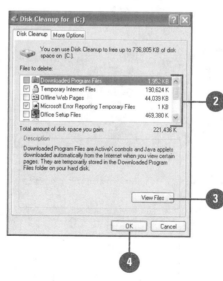

Scheduling Maintenance

Task Scheduler is a program that enables you to schedule tasks, to run regularly such as Disk Cleanup or Disk Defragmenter, at a time convenient for you. Task Scheduler starts each time you start Windows. With Task Scheduler, you can schedule a task to run daily, weekly, monthly, or at certain times (such as when the computer starts or idles), change the schedule for or turn off an existing task, or customize how a task runs at its scheduled time. Before you schedule a task, be sure that the system date and time on your computer are accurate, as Task Scheduler relies on this information to run.

Add a Scheduled Task

1. Click the Start button, and then click Control Panel.

2. Double-click the Scheduled Tasks icon in Classic view.

3. Double-click the Add Scheduled Task icon, and then click Next.

4. Click the program you want to schedule, and then click Next.

5. Type a name for the scheduled task.

6. Click a scheduled task time interval option, and then click Next.

7. Specify a start time.

8. Select the check boxes with the days you want the task to run, and then click Next.

9. If asked, type your password twice, and then click Next.

10. Click Finish.

> ### Did You Know?
>
> **You can stop a scheduled task.** In the Scheduled Tasks window, right-click the task that you want to stop, then click End Task.

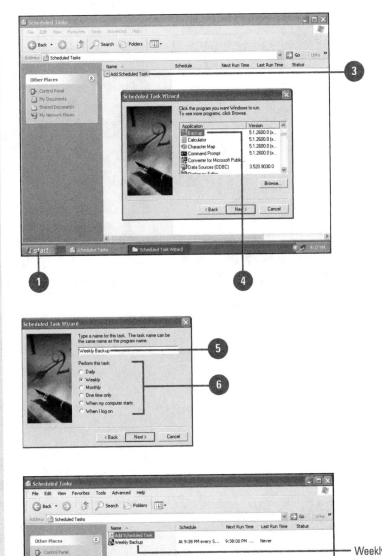

Weekly backup scheduled task

Adding or Removing Windows Components

Windows XP comes with a collection of components, such as Internet Explorer, Outlook Express, Windows Media Player, or Windows Messenger, you can use to get work done and have fun on your computer. When you install Windows XP, not all the components on the installation CD are installed on your computer. You can use the Windows Components Wizard to install additional components. When you install a new program on your computer, the Start menu highlights the menus you need to click to start the program. If you are no longer using a Windows component, you can remove it to save disk space.

Add or Remove a Windows Component

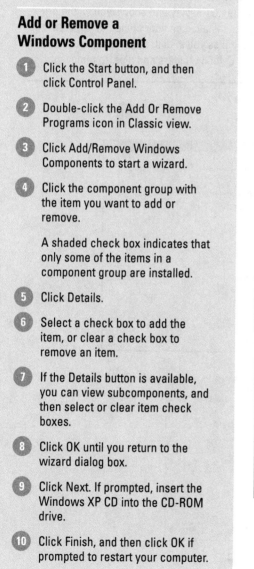

1. Click the Start button, and then click Control Panel.

2. Double-click the Add Or Remove Programs icon in Classic view.

3. Click Add/Remove Windows Components to start a wizard.

4. Click the component group with the item you want to add or remove.

   A shaded check box indicates that only some of the items in a component group are installed.

5. Click Details.

6. Select a check box to add the item, or clear a check box to remove an item.

7. If the Details button is available, you can view subcomponents, and then select or clear item check boxes.

8. Click OK until you return to the wizard dialog box.

9. Click Next. If prompted, insert the Windows XP CD into the CD-ROM drive.

10. Click Finish, and then click OK if prompted to restart your computer.

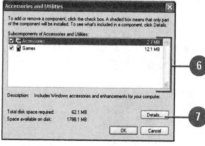

Installing or Uninstalling a Program

Windows comes with a collection of accessory programs with simple functionality. If you need more functionality, software programs are available for purchase. Before you can use a software program, you need to install it first using Add Or Remove Programs in the Control Panel or a separate installer program. Most software programs come with their own installation program, which copies the program files to different places on your computer, some in a program folder and others in the Windows folder. When you install a new program on your computer, the Start menu highlights the menus you need to click to start the program (**New!**). If you no longer use a program or a Windows update, you can remove it from your computer, which saves hard disk space. Add Or Remove Programs provides a faster display and shows you all the programs and/or software updates installed on your computer (**NewSP2**). Windows keeps track of all the files you install, so you should uninstall a program or update, instead of deleting folders and files, to remove it.

Install a Software Program

1. Close all running programs, and then insert the program installation CD into the CD-ROM drive.

   If the CD starts, follow the instructions provided to install the software.

   IMPORTANT *Only users with administrator privileges can add or remove programs.*

2. If the CD doesn't start or you're installing from a network or different drive, click the Start button, and then click Control Panel.

3. Double-click the Add Or Remove Programs icon in Classic view.

4. Click Add New Programs.

5. Click CD Or Floppy, and then click Next.

6. If the setup program doesn't appear, click Browse to locate it on the CD or a network, and then click Next.

7. Click Finish, and then follow the installation instructions.

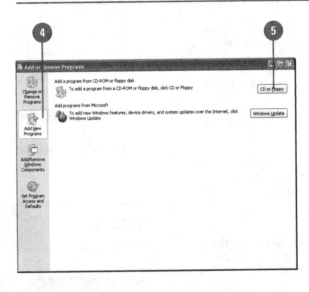

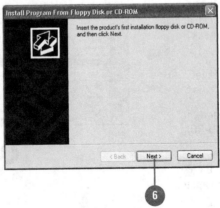

Uninstall a Software Program

1. Click the Start button, and then click Control Panel.

2. Double-click the Add Or Remove Programs icon in Classic view.

3. Click Change Or Remove Programs.

4. Click the program you want to uninstall.

5. Click Change/Remove.

6. Click Yes to confirm the removal. If an uninstall program starts, follow the instructions.

7. When it's done, click OK.

Did You Know?

You can turn the Start menu highlight off. Right-click the Start button, click Properties, click Customize, click the Advanced tab, clear the Highlight Newly Installed Programs check box, and then click OK twice.

You can show or hide software updates. In the Add Or Remove Programs dialog box, select or clear the Show Updates check box (NewSP2). If you no longer need a Windows update, you can remove it like any other program.

See Also

If you encounter a problem after removing a Windows update or component, see "Restoring Computer Settings" on page 392 for information on restoring Windows to a previous state using the System Restore Wizard.

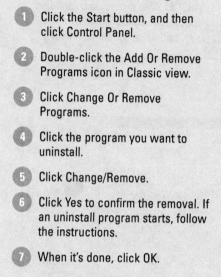

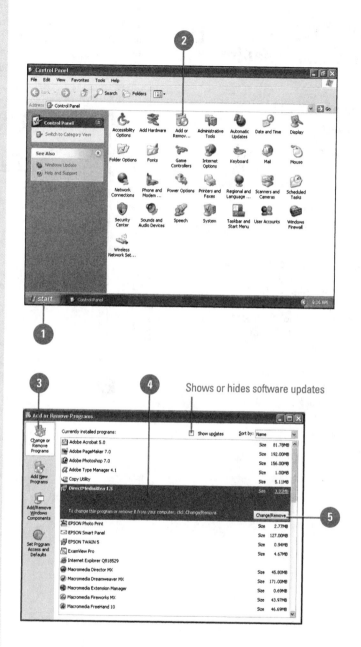

Shows or hides software updates

Setting Program Access and Defaults

You can use Add or Remove Programs in the Control Panel to choose default programs for common tasks, such as Web browsing or sending e-mail and instant messages, and to specify which programs are accessible from the Start menu, desktop, and other locations (**New!**).

Set Program Access and Defaults

1. Click the Start button, point to All Programs, and then click Set Program Access And Defaults.

2. Click the Details button, if necessary, to display option details.

3. To set Microsoft programs as the default, click the Microsoft Windows option.

4. To set non-Microsoft programs as the default, click the non-Microsoft option.

5. To set a mix of Microsoft and Non-Microsoft programs as the defaults, click the Custom option, and then click the specific options you want.

6. When you're done, click OK.

Set individual program options

Improving Computer Performance

You can adjust Windows XP to improve its performance by changing the way Windows XP manages system processing and memory. You can set Windows XP to give a greater proportion of processor time to the program in which you are currently working, known as a foreground process. The greater the processor time, the faster response time you receive from the program in which you are currently working. If you have background processes, such as printing, that you want to run while you work, you might want to have Windows XP share processor time equally between background and foreground programs. When your computer is running low on RAM and more is needed immediately to complete your current task, Windows XP uses hard disk drive space to simulate system RAM. This is known as **virtual memory**. For processes that require a lot of RAM, you can optimize virtual memory use by allocating more available space on your hard disk drive.

14

Optimize Computer Performance

1. Click the Start button, and then click Control Panel.

2. Double-click the System icon in Classic view.

3. Click the Advanced tab, and then click Settings (under Performance).

4. Click the Visual Effects tab.

5. Click the Adjust For Best Performance option.

6. Click the Advanced tab.

7. To optimize program performance, click the Programs option.

8. To optimize system performance, click the Background Services option and the System Cache option.

9. To optimize virtual memory settings, click Change, click the System Managed Size option, and then click OK.

10. Click OK, and then click OK again.

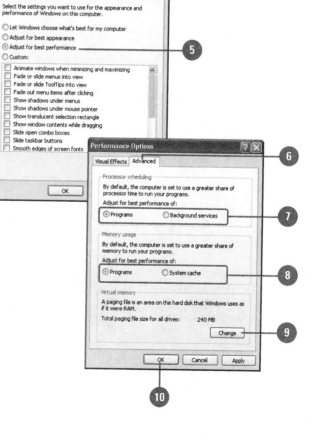

Updating Windows

Microsoft continues to improve Windows XP with new features or security fixes, known as updates. Windows Automatic Updates (New SP2) allows you to keep your computer up-to-date with the latest system software and security updates over the Internet. You can choose to have Windows regularly check for critical updates and download them in the background (which doesn't interfere with other downloads), or you can manually select the ones you want to install using the Windows Update web site. Automatic updates occur at scheduled times or by notification acceptance. If you're busy, you can ignore/hide the update to install it later. The Windows Update web site displays express (only high priority) and custom (high priority, software, and hardware) installation update options. High priority updates are critical for your system to run properly, while software and hardware updates are optional. Windows Update confidentially scans your computer for updates that need to be installed.

Update Windows Automatically

1 Click the Start button, and then click Control Panel.

2 Double-click the Automatic Updates icon in Classic view.

IMPORTANT *If you're part of a network, options are grayed out.*

3 Click the automatic update option you want to use:

♦ Automatic (recommended), then specify a time.

♦ Download updates for me, but let me choose when to install them.

♦ Notify me, but don't automatically download or install them.

♦ Turn off Automatic Updates.

IMPORTANT *Only users with administrator privileges can install updates, unless you use the Automatic (recommended) option.*

4 Click OK.

5 If a Windows Update icon appears in the notification area, click the alert or icon, and then follow any instructions as needed.

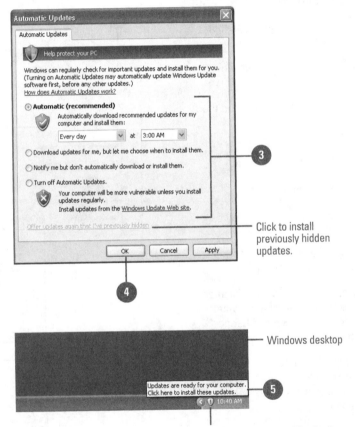

Click to install previously hidden updates.

Windows desktop

Windows Update notification icon

Update Windows Manually

1. Click the Start button, point to All Programs, and then click Windows Update.

   Windows connects to the Internet.

2. If prompted, click Yes to install Windows Update software.

3. Click Express Install or Custom Install, and then wait for the update scan to complete.

   For the Express Install, skip to step 7.

4. Click an update category.

5. Select the check box next to the update you want to install, or clear the check box next to the updates you do not want to install.

6. To review the updates you want to install, click Go To Install Updates.

7. Click Install, and then accept the license agreement, if necessary.

8. Wait for the updates to be downloaded from the Web and installed on your computer.

9. If prompted, click OK to restart your computer.

10. Click the Close button.

Did You Know?

You can install updates when not available or resume after an interruption. If your computer is turned off or in hibernate or standby mode during a scheduled update, updates are installed the next time you start your computer. If you lose an Internet connection during a download, Windows Update resumes where it left off.

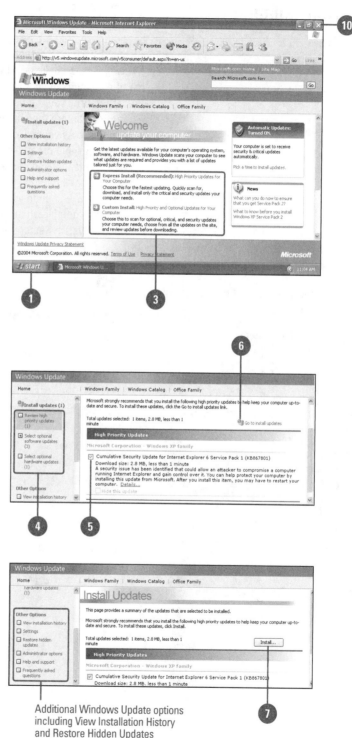

Additional Windows Update options including View Installation History and Restore Hidden Updates

Restoring Computer Settings ▶

Windows XP is a reliable operating system, but any time you make changes to your computer, such as adding or removing software and hardware, you run the risk of causing problems with your operating system. To alleviate potential problems, you can use System Restore (**New!**), a program installed with Windows XP Professional, to undo harmful changes to your computer and restore its settings. System Restore returns your computer system, but not your personal files, to an earlier time, before the changes were made to your computer, called a **restore point**. As you work with your computer, System Restore monitors your changes and creates restore points on a daily basis or at important system events, but you can also create your own restore point at any time. If you have recently performed a system restoration, you can use System Restore to undo your most recent restoration. System Restore is turned on by default when you install Windows XP, but you can turn it off or change System Restore options.

Change Restore System Settings

1. Click the Start button, and then click Control Panel.

2. Double-click the System icon in Classic view.

3. Click the System Restore tab.

4. To turn off System Restore, select the Turn Off System Restore check box.

5. Drag the slide to increase or decrease the amount of disk space for System Restore.

6. Click OK.

Restore the System

1. Close all programs and make sure no one else is logged on to the computer.

2. Click the Start button, point to All Programs, point to Accessories, point to System Tools, and then click System Restore.

3. Click the Restore My Computer To An Earlier Time option.

4. Click Next.

5. Select a date in bold type that contains a restore point.

6. Click the restore point you want to use, and then click Next.

7. Review the restore point information, and then click Next.

8. Wait for the system to be restored, and log on when prompted.

9. When it's done, click OK.

Create a Restore Point

1. Click the Start button, point to All Programs, point to Accessories, point to System Tools, and then click System Restore.

2. Click the Create A Restore Point option, and then click Next.

3. Type a restore point name.

4. Click Create.

5. When it's done, click Close.

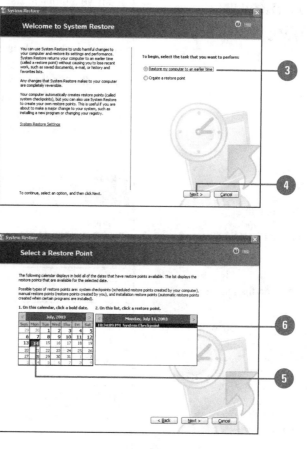

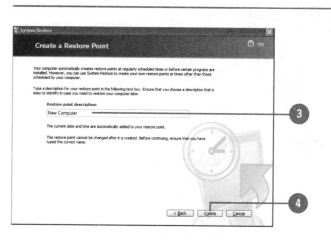

14

Starting Windows When Problems Occur

If you have a problem starting Windows, you can use one of several startup options to help you start Windows in a safe environment where you can restore settings and fix the problem. Safe Mode is a good place to start. If a problem does not occur when you start in Safe Mode, you can eliminate basic Windows files and drivers as possible causes of the problem. If you added a device or changed driver, you can use Safe Mode to remove the device or restore the changed driver, or you can use Choosing Last Known Good Configuration to restore settings saved when your computer was last shut down properly.

Start Windows When Problems Occur

1. Restart your computer.

2. As your computer boots, press and hold F8.

3. Use the arrow keys to select a startup option, and then press Enter.

4. If you have a dual-boot system, select the operating system you want, and then press Enter.

5. Restore any recent system changes, or remove any newly installed software that might be causing the problem.

6. Shutdown your computer.

7. Start your computer to see if it works properly.

8. If problems persist, try a different startup option, or seek assistance from a support technician.

Computer Startup Options

Option	Description
Safe Mode	Starts with basic files and drivers and without a network connection
Safe Mode With Networking	Starts with basic files and drivers and a network connection
Safe Mode With Command Prompt	Starts with basic files and drivers and without a network connection to the command prompt
Enable Boot Logging	Starts and logs startup information in the *ntbtlog.txt* file
Enable VGA Mode	Starts using the basic VGA driver
Last Know Good Configuration	Starts using Registry settings saved at the last properly done shutdown
Directory Services Restore Mode	Restores active directory services for Windows XP Professional only
Debugging Mode	Starts and sends debugging information to another computer using a serial cable
Start Windows Normally	Starts the computer normally
Reboot	Restarts the computer
Return To OS Choices Menu	Displays operating system selection screen

Setting Startup and Recovery Options

If you installed more than one operating system on your computer (known as a **dual-boot**), such as Windows 98 and Windows XP, you can select the default operating system you want to use when you start up your computer. If you have problems starting Windows, you can set options to instruct Windows what to do.

Set Windows Startup and Recovery Options

1. Click the Start button, and then click Control Panel.

2. Double-click the System icon in Classic view.

3. Click the Advanced tab.

4. Click Settings (under Startup And Recovery).

5. Click the Default Operating System list arrow, and then select the operating system you want to start as default.

6. Select the system startup check boxes you want to use and specify the time you want to wait to select the operating system or recovery options.

7. Select the system failure check boxes you want to use.

8. Click OK.

9. Click OK.

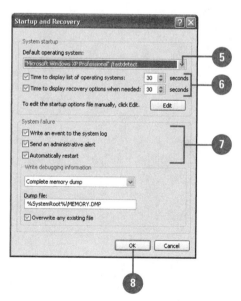

Managing Hardware

15

Introduction

A **hardware device** is any physical device that you plug into and is controlled by your computer. This device can be, for example, a network or modem card that you install inside your computer. It can be a printer or a scanner that you plug into the outside of the computer. When you plug or insert a hardware device into the appropriate port or expansion slot, Windows attempts to recognize the device and configure it for you using plug-and-play technology. Plug-and-play automatically tells the device drivers (software that operates the hardware and comes with Windows XP) where to find the hardware device. After a hardware device is installed, you change settings and options to customize the way the device works. Plug-and-play technology will recognize most any kind of hardware device, such as a mouse, modem, keyboard, game controller, laptop battery, or secondary monitor to name a few.

All hardware devices can be managed or removed from the Control Panel. You can even specify which devices to start when you start your computer by creating a hardware **profile**. Most hardware devices are managed under the Device Manager, but some have their own program for managing them (for example, a Game Controller located in the Control Panel).

Understanding Plug and Play Hardware

Windows XP includes **plug and play** support for hardware, making it easy to install and uninstall devices quickly. With plug and play support, you simply plug the device in, and Windows sets the device to work with your existing hardware and resolves any system conflicts. When you install a hardware device, Windows installs related software, known as a **driver**, that allows the hardware to communicate with Windows and other software applications. Plug and play tells the device drivers where to find the hardware devices. Plug and play matches up physical hardware devices with the software device drivers that operate them and establish channels of communication between each physical device and its driver. With plug and play, you can be confident that any new device will work properly with your computer and that your computer will restart correctly after you install or uninstall hardware. Microsoft recommends that you use only device drivers with the Designed for Microsoft Windows XP logo, which have a digital signature from Microsoft, indicating that the product was tested for compatibility with Windows. You might need to be logged on as an administrator or a member of the Administrators group in order to install a hardware device. In order to install a plug and play device, you need to do the following:

1) Gather your original Windows XP CD-ROMs, the hardware device that you want to install, and the disks that come with the device, if available.

2) Turn off your computer before you physically install a hardware device, such as a network card or a sound card, inside your computer. To install a hardware device that plugs into the outside of your computer, such as a scanner or printer, you can use the Add Hardware utility program in the Control Panel without turning off your computer.

3) Follow the manufacturer's instructions to plug the new device into your computer.

4) Turn on your computer, or start the Add Hardware utility program in the Control Panel. Windows tries to detect the new device and install the device drivers. If Windows doesn't recognize the new hardware device, the device might not be plug and play compatible or installed correctly. Turn off your computer, check the device documentation and installation carefully, and then turn on your computer again. If the device driver is not available on your computer, Windows asks you to insert into the appropriate drive the Windows XP installation CD-ROM or the disk that comes with the device from the manufacturer.

5) Follow the instructions on the screen until a message indicates that you are finished. Windows notifies all other devices of the new device so there are no conflicts and manages the power requirements of your hardware and peripherals by shutting them down or conserving power when you are not using them. If you are working in another program when you install or uninstall a device, plug and play lets you know that it is about to change your computer configuration and warns you to save your work.

6) Use the Safely Remove Hardware icon in the notification area to safely unplug or eject plug and play hardware. The Safely Remove Hardware dialog box helps you stop the device, so it's safe to remove.

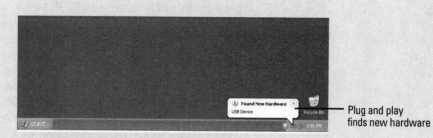
Plug and play
finds new hardware

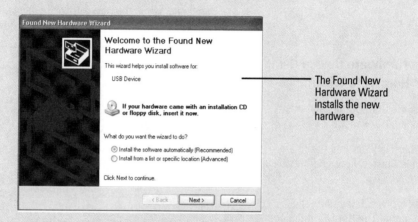
The Found New
Hardware Wizard
installs the new
hardware

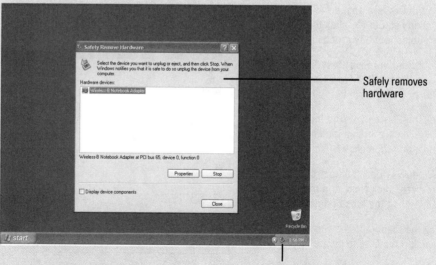
Safely removes
hardware

Safely Remove Hardware icon

Installing Hardware Devices

Before you install a new hardware device, be sure to carefully read the product installation guide provided by the manufacturer. If the hardware device comes with an installation CD-ROM, it is recommended that you use the manufacturer's CD-ROM and related instructions to install the hardware. If the product documentation instructs you to perform a typical plug and play installation, turn off your computer, physically connect your hardware to your computer, and then turn on your computer again. In most cases, Windows detects your new hardware device and installs it or starts the Add Hardware Wizard. The Add Hardware Wizard installs hardware devices by asking you a series of questions to set up the necessary software for the new hardware device. If Windows doesn't detect the new hardware, you can start the Add Hardware Wizard in the Control Panel and select the new hardware device to install it. You might need to be logged on as an administrator in order to install a hardware device.

Install a Hardware Device Using the Add Hardware Wizard

1. Click the Start button, and then click Control Panel.

2. Double-click the Add Hardware icon in Classic view, and then click Next.

3. Click the Yes, I Have Already Connected The Hardware option, and then click Next.

4. If your hardware appears in the installed list, double-click the item to troubleshoot any problems.

5. If your hardware isn't listed, double-click Add A New Hardware Device.

6. Click the Search For And Install The Hardware Automatically option, and then click Next.

7. If Windows doesn't detect the hardware, click Next, and then double-click the type of device.

8. Click the manufacturer and model, or click Have Disk to locate files.

9. Click Next twice, and then click Finish.

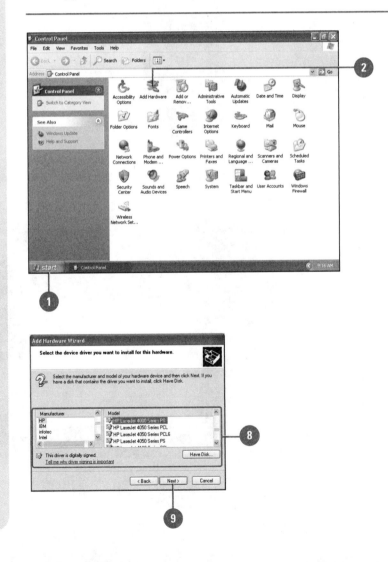

Viewing System Hardware

When you install a new operating system, such as Windows XP, it is important to make sure that you are using the latest software drivers with your system hardware. If you are not using the latest software drivers, your hardware devices might not work to full capacity. You can view your system hardware using a Windows utility called the Device Manager. Device Manager provides you with a list of the hardware types, also known as **hardware classes**, which are attached to your computer. With the Device Manager, you can determine the software driver versions being used with your system hardware, update the software driver with a newer version, roll back to a previous driver version if the device fails with the new one, or uninstall a driver. After viewing your software driver version numbers, you can contact the manufacturer or visit their web site to determine the latest versions. Most manufacturers allow you to download drivers from their web sites for free.

Use the Device Manager

1. Click the Start button, and then click Control Panel.

2. Double-click the System icon in Classic view.

3. Click the Hardware tab.

4. Click Device Manager.

5. Click the plus sign (+) next to the hardware category you want to expand.

6. Click the device you want to view.

7. Click the Properties button on the toolbar.

8. To troubleshoot a problem, click the General tab, and then click Troubleshoot.

9. To work with drivers, click the Driver tab.

10. Click OK.

11. Click the Close button.

12. Click OK.

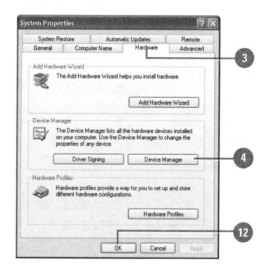

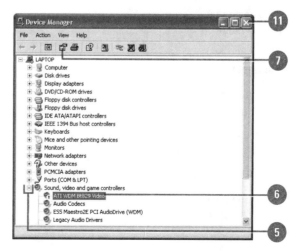

Viewing Hardware Settings

One reason you might want to view hardware settings is if you plan to install any legacy hardware. **Legacy hardware** is any device not designed for Windows XP plug and play support. If you have a hardware device that is not designed for Windows XP plug and play, it is important to find out current hardware resource settings to avoid conflicts during installation, such as having two devices with the same resource settings. Before you actually place a legacy hardware device in your computer, you should browse through the devices currently attached to your computer system and ensure that your computer has the available resources to install the hardware device. With the Device Manager, you can view the device resources that are being used with your system hardware and determine whether your computer has the available resources to install a legacy or plug and play hardware device. Generally, you cannot install non plug and play hardware without performing some manual setup with the Device Manager. Instead of writing down your computer resource information on paper, you can print a system summary report.

View Hardware Settings

1. Click the Start button, and then click Control Panel.

2. Double-click the System icon in Classic view.

3. Click the Hardware tab.

4. Click Device Manager.

5. Click the View menu, and then click Resources By Type or Resources By Connection.

6. Click the plus sign (+) next to the resource category you want to expand.

7. Click the device you want to view.

8. Click the Properties button on the toolbar.

9. Use the tabs to view or modify device settings.

10. Click OK.

11. Click the Close button, and then click OK.

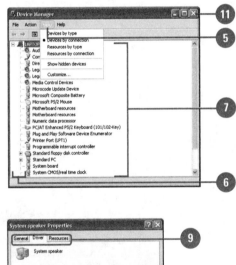

Print a Resource Summary Report

1. Click the Start button, and then click Control Panel.

2. Double-click the System icon in Classic view.

3. Click the Hardware tab, and then click Device Manager.

4. Click the View menu, and then click Resources By Type or Resources By Connection.

5. Click the plus sign (+) next to the resource category you want to expand.

6. Click the device you want to view.

7. Click the Print button on the toolbar.

8. Click the report type option you want.

9. Click Print.

10. Click the Close button, and then click OK.

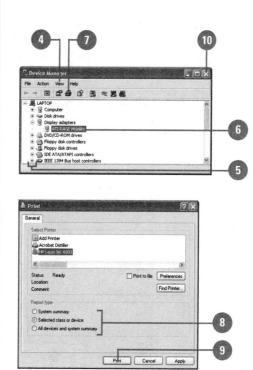

For Your Information

Understanding Resources

When you install a legacy hardware device, the device's instructions might ask you to provide a resource setting. When prompted by the device instructions, provide a resource setting that is not already in use. **Direct Memory Access (DMA)** channel is a communication process in which data is transferred between memory and a hardware device, such as a disk drive. **Input/Output (I/O)** is a channel through which data is transferred between hardware and the computer processor. Each installed device requires a communication line called an **Interrupt Request Line (IRQ)**, which allows the physical hardware device to communicate with your computer's software. Any IRQ number between 0 and 15 that is not listed is available. **Memory** address is a portion of memory that can be used by a hardware device or program. Each resource assigned to your device must be unique, or the device will not function properly. Two devices attempting to share a resource create a conflict, and neither device will work properly.

Changing Mouse Settings

A mouse does not require adjustments after you plug it in and start Windows. It should just work. However, you can use Mouse properties in the Control Panel to change the way your mouse works and the way the pointer looks and behaves. For the mouse, you can switch the role of the buttons, or you can change the double-clicking speed. For the mouse pointer, you can modify its appearance using a pointer scheme, increase or decrease its speed, improve its visibility with a pointer trail, or set it to be hidden when you are typing. If your button has a wheel, roll the wheel with your forefinger to move up or down in a document or on a web page.

Change Button Settings

1 Click the Start button, and then click Control Panel.

2 Double-click the Mouse icon in Classic view.

3 Click the Buttons tab.

4 To reverse the mouse buttons, select the Switch Primary And Secondary Buttons check box.

5 To adjust the double-click speed, drag the slider.

6 Click OK.

Did You Know?

You can change the mouse wheel speed. In the Control Panel, double-click the Mouse icon, click the Wheel tab, click the The Following Number Of Lines At A Time option, type a number or click the One Screen At A Time option, and then click OK.

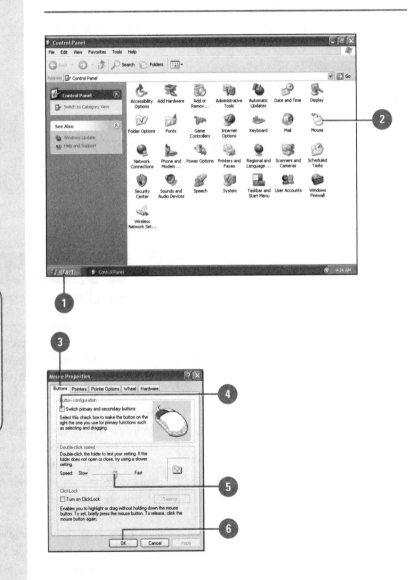

Change Pointer Appearance

1. Click the Start button, and then click Control Panel.

2. Double-click the Mouse icon in Classic view.

3. Click the Pointers tab.

4. Click the Scheme list arrow, and then select a pointer scheme.

5. Click OK.

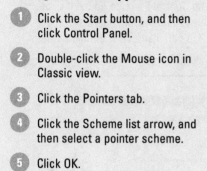

Change Pointer Options

1. Click the Start button, and then click Control Panel.

2. Double-click the Mouse icon in Classic view.

3. Click the Pointer Options tab.

4. To adjust the pointer speed, drag the Motion slider.

5. To snap the pointer to a button, select the Automatically Move Pointer To The Default Button In A Dialog Box check box.

6. To display a trail after the pointer, hide the pointer while you type, or show the pointer location, select the visibility check box you want.

7. Click OK.

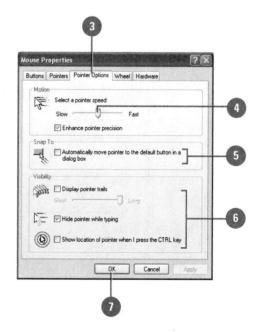

15

Changing Keyboard Settings

While your keyboard should just work when you start up your computer, you can use Keyboard properties in the Control Panel to adjust the rate at which a character is repeated when you hold down a key, and the time delay before it starts repeating. You can also adjust the blink rate of the insertion point.

Change Keyboard Settings

1. Click the Start button, and then click Control Panel.

2. Double-click the Keyboard icon in Classic view.

3. Click the Speed tab.

4. To adjust the character repeat delay, drag the slider.

5. To adjust the character repeat rate, drag the slider.

6. Click OK.

See Also

See "Changing Language Options" on page 94 for information on changing languages and keyboard layouts.

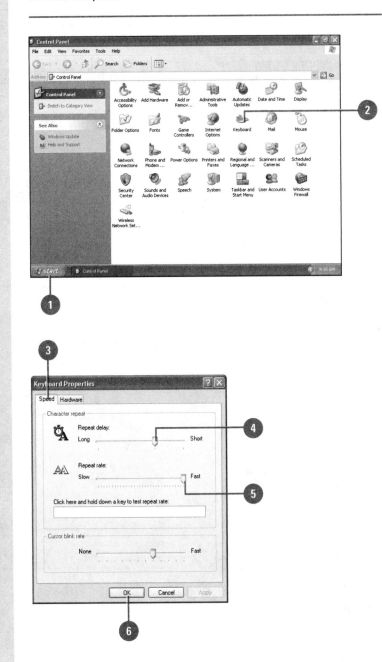

Changing Phone Dialing Options

When phone numbers or dialing settings to an Internet Service Provider or a network change, you need to update the phone dialing options your modem uses to make a dial-up connection. You can use Phone and Modem properties in the Control Panel to add, edit, and customize phone dialing options on your computer for one or more locations. For example, you can change country, region or area codes, disable call waiting, and set up a credit card number to pay for calls. You can also set access rules for dialing local, long distance, and international calls. If you no longer use a dialing location, you can remove it.

Change Phone Dialing Options

1. Click the Start button, and then click Control Panel.

2. Double-click the Phone And Modem Options icon in Classic view.

3. Click the Dialing Rules tab, and then click a dialing location.

4. Click Edit, and then click the General tab.

5. Change the country/region or area code.

6. Specify the dialing rules you want.

7. If you want, select the To Disable Call Waiting check box.

8. To apply area code dialing rules, click the Area Code Rules tab, and then click New to create one.

9. To use a calling card, click the Calling Card tab, select a calling card option, or click New to create your own.

10. Click OK.

11. Click OK.

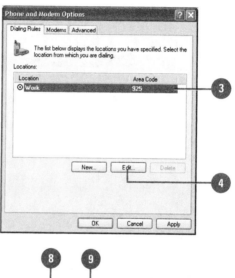

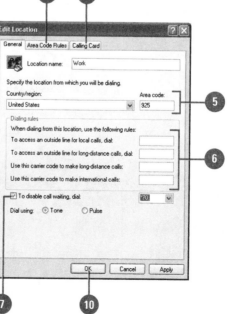

15

Changing Modem Options

A **modem** is a hardware device that allows two computers to transmit information over a phone line. A modem translates the binary information from the computer to an analog signal (known as modulation) that can pass over the phone line. At the receiving end, another modem translates the analog signal back to binary information (known as demodulation) that can be used by the computer. If you are having problems with your modem, you can test it. With the results of the test you can consult the modem documentation or a support technician to help you fix the problem. If requested, you can change data transmission settings, such as data bits, parity, stop bits, or modulation.

Test a Modem

① Click the Start button, and then click Control Panel.

② Double-click the Phone And Modem Options icon in Classic view.

③ Click the Modems tab.

④ Click the modem you want to test.

⑤ Click Properties.

⑥ Click the Diagnostics tab.

⑦ Click Query Modem, and then wait for the results.

⑧ Scroll through the results for any failure indicators.

⑨ Click OK.

⑩ Click OK.

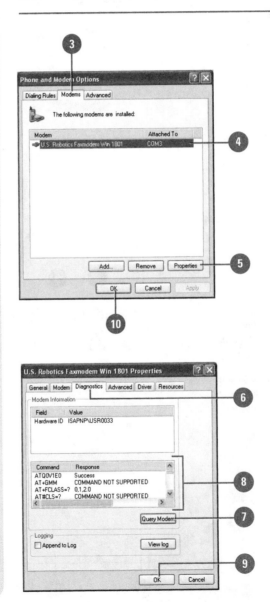

Change Modem Hardware Settings

1 Click the Start button, and then click Control Panel.

2 Double-click the Phone And Modem Options icon in Classic view.

3 Click the Modems tab.

4 Click the modem you want to change, and then click Properties.

5 Click the Modem tab.

6 Change the maximum port speed and speaker volume.

7 Click the Advanced tab, and then click Change Default Preferences.

8 Click the Advanced tab.

9 Change the setting for data bits, parity, stop bits, or modulation.

10 Click OK.

11 Click OK, and then click OK again.

Did You Know?

You can troubleshoot a modem problem. In the Control Panel, double-click the Phone And Modem Options icon, click the Modems tab, click the modem, click Properties, click Troubleshoot, and then answer the troubleshooting questions.

Changing Game Controller Settings

A **game controller** is a hardware device, such as a joystick or game pad, that controls a program, typically a game. You can use Game Controllers properties in the Control Panel to add, configure, and customize game controllers on your computer. For example, you can add older gaming devices so you can play those games on your computer. You can also test, calibrate, and troubleshoot your game controllers. If you no longer use a game controller, you can remove it from your computer.

Test a Game Controller

① Click the Start button, and then click Control Panel.

② Double-click the Game Controllers icon in Classic view.

③ Click the controller you want to test.

④ Click Properties.

⑤ Click the Test tab.

⑥ Test the controller by moving or pressing each control, and then view the results.

⑦ Click OK.

⑧ Click OK.

Did You Know?

You can select a preferred game controller. In the Control Panel, double-click the Game Controller icon, click a controller, click Advanced, click your preferred game controller, and then click OK twice.

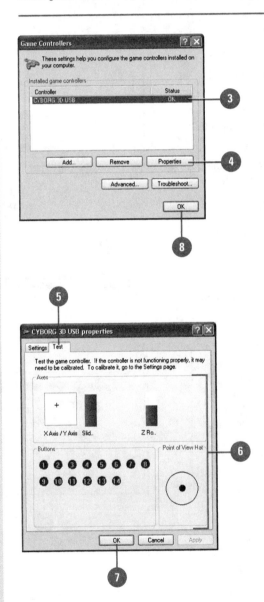

Calibrate a Game Controller

1. Click the Start button, and then click Control Panel.

2. Double-click the Game Controller icon in Classic view.

3. Click the controller you want to calibrate.

4. Click Properties.

5. Click the Settings tab.

6. Click Calibrate.

7. Follow the Game Device Calibration Wizard instructions.

8. Click OK.

9. Click OK.

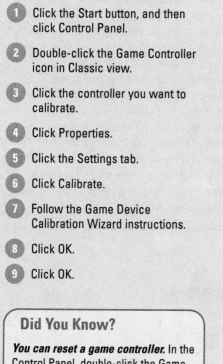

Did You Know?

You can reset a game controller. In the Control Panel, double-click the Game Controller icon, click a controller, click Properties, click the Settings tab, click Reset To Default, and then click OK twice.

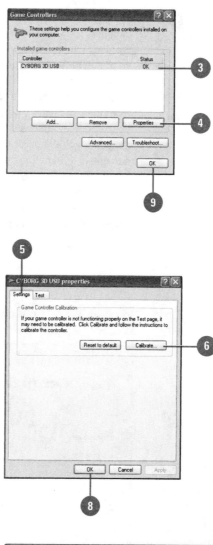

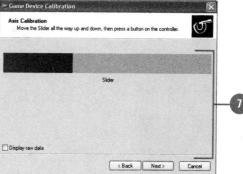

15

Controlling Power Options

You can change power options properties for a portable or laptop computer to reduce power consumption and maximize battery life. For example, if you often leave your computer for a short time while working, you can set your computer to go into **standby**, a state in which your monitor and hard disks turn off after being idle for a set time. If you are often away from your computer for an extended time, you can set it to go into **hibernation**, a state in which your computer first saves everything in memory on your hard disk and then shuts down. To help you set power options, you can choose one of the power schemes included with Windows or modify one to suit your needs. A **power scheme** is a predefined collection of power usage settings. You can also set alarms and passwords and show the power icon on the taskbar. The power options you see vary depending on your computer's hardware configuration. Windows detects what is available on your computer and shows you only the options that you can control.

Select or Create a Power Scheme

1. Click the Start button, and then click Control Panel.

2. Double-click the Power Options icon in Classic view.

3. Click the Power Schemes Tab.

4. Click the Power Schemes list arrow, and then select a power scheme.

5. If you want, modify the power scheme settings.

6. Click Save As, type a name for the new scheme, and then click OK.

7. Click OK.

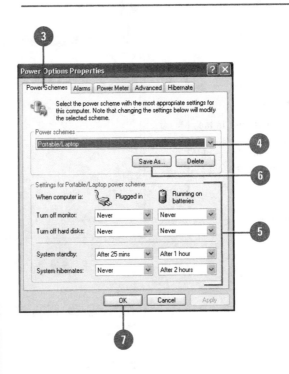

Did You Know?

You can enable hibernation. In the Power Options dialog box, click the Hibernate tab, select the Enable Hibernation check box, and then click OK.

Set Battery Options

1. Click the Start button, and then click Control Panel.

2. Double-click the Power Options icon in Classic view.

3. Click the Alarms tab.

4. Select the check boxes to activate a battery alarm when power reaches a certain level.

5. Drag a Power Level slider to adjust the alarm setting.

6. To set an action when the power level is reached, click Alarm Action, select an action, and then click OK.

7. Click the Power Meter tab, and then check battery power levels.

8. Click OK.

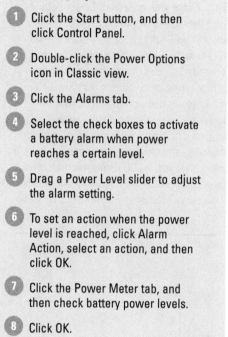

Set Advanced Options

1. Click the Start button, and then click Control Panel.

2. Double-click the Power Options icon in Classic view.

3. Click the Advanced tab.

4. Select the Always Show Icon On The Taskbar check box.

5. Select the Prompt For Password When Computer Resumes From Standby check box.

6. Specify the actions you want to occur when you press a power button.

7. Click OK.

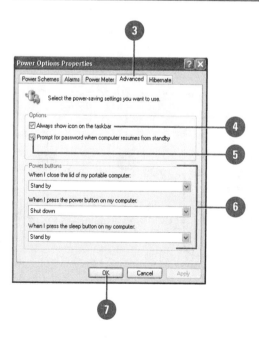

15

Adding a Secondary Monitor

If you need more space on your desktop to work, you can add a secondary monitor to your computer. This allows you to view and work with more than one full size window on the screen at the same time. One monitor serves as the primary display while the other serves as the secondary display. You can set different screen resolutions and different color quality settings for each monitor. You can connect multiple monitors to individual video cards or to a single card that supports multiple video ports. If you have a docked or undocked portable computer or desktop computer with two video ports on one video card, you use DualView to add a secondary monitor and expand the size of your desktop. DualView is similar to the multiple monitor feature, but you cannot select the primary display, which is always the LCD display screen on a portable computer and the monitor attached to the first video out port on a desktop computer. You don't need to purchase and install another video adapter on your computer.

Set Secondary Monitor Options

1. Click the Start button, and then click Control Panel.

2. Double-click the Display icon in Classic view.

3. Click the Settings tab.

4. Click the secondary monitor.

5. Select the Extend My Windows Desktop Onto This Monitor check box.

6. Click OK.

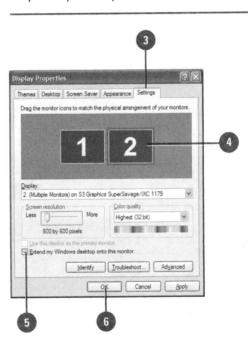

> ### Did You Know?
>
> **You can change resolution and color quality on either monitor.** On the Settings tab, click the monitor icon for the monitor you want to change, adjust the resolution or color quality, and then click OK.

Change the Movement Between Monitors

1. Click the Start button, and then click Control Panel.

2. Double-click the Display icon in Classic view.

3. Click the Settings tab.

4. Click Identify.

5. Click the monitor icons and drag them to positions that represent how you want to move items from one monitor to another.

6. Click OK.

You can drag items across the primary monitor until it appears on the secondary monitor.

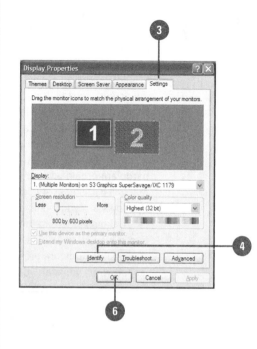

Change the Primary Monitor

1. Click the Start button, and then click Control Panel.

2. Double-click the Display icon in Classic view.

3. Click the Settings tab.

4. Click the monitor icon that represents the monitor you want as the primary one.

5. Select the Use This Device As The Primary Monitor check box.

TROUBLE? *This check box is unavailable if you select the current primary monitor.*

6. Click OK.

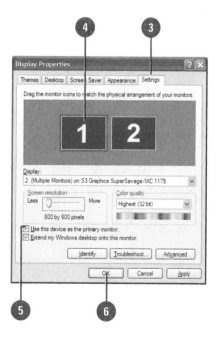

15

Creating Hardware Profiles

A **hardware profile** is a set of instructions that tells Windows which devices to start when you start your computer or which settings to use for each device. When you first install Windows, a hardware profile called Profile 1 (for laptops, the profiles are Docked Profile or Undocked Profile) is created. By default, every device installed on your computer at the time you install Windows is enabled in the Profile 1 hardware profile. Hardware profiles are especially useful if you have a portable computer. Most portable computers are used in a variety of locations, and hardware profiles will let you change which devices your computer uses when you move it from location to location. If there is more than one hardware profile on your computer, you can designate a default profile that will be used every time you start your computer. You can also have Windows ask you which profile to use every time you start your computer. Once you create a hardware profile, you can use Device Manager to disable and enable devices that are in the profile. When you disable a device in a hardware profile, the device drivers for the device are not loaded when you start your computer.

Create a Hardware Profile

1. Click the Start button, and then click Control Panel.

2. Double-click the System icon in Classic view.

3. Click the Hardware tab, and then click Hardware Profiles.

4. Click the current Profile or another profile you want to copy.

5. Click Copy.

6. Type a name for the profile, and then click OK.

7. Click OK, and then click OK again.

8. Open the Device Manager and enable or disable devices to customize the new profiles.

> ### See Also
>
> See "Viewing System Hardware" on page 401 for information on using the Device Manager.

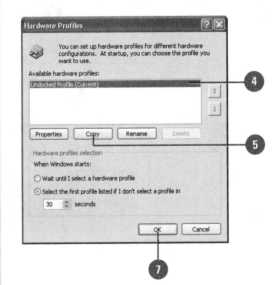

Select a Default Hardware Profile for Startup

1 Click the Start button, and then click Control Panel.

2 Double-click the System icon in Classic view.

3 Click the Hardware tab.

4 Click Hardware Profiles.

5 Click the profile you want to use for startup.

6 Click the Up Arrow button to position the profile at the top of the list, if necessary.

7 Click the Select The First Profile Listed If I Don't Select A Profile In number of Seconds.

8 Click OK.

9 Click OK.

Did You Know?

You can rename a profile. In the Hardware Profiles dialog box, click the profile you want to change, click Rename, type a new name, and then click OK.

You can delete a profile. In the Hardware Profiles dialog box, click the profile you want to remove, click Delete, and then click Yes.

15

Removing Hardware Devices

If you no longer use a hardware device, or if you have an older hardware device that you want to upgrade, you need to remove the hardware device drivers and related software before you remove the physical hardware device from your computer. With the Device Manager, you can quickly and easily remove hardware devices and any related device drivers. Before you remove a legacy device, printing the device settings is a good idea in case you need to reinstall the device later.

Remove a Hardware Device

1 Click the Start button, and then click Control Panel.

2 Double-click the System icon in Classic view.

3 Click the Hardware tab.

4 Click Device Manager.

5 Click the plus sign (+) next to the hardware category you want to expand.

6 Click the device you want to remove.

7 Click the Uninstall button on the toolbar, and then click OK.

8 Click the Close button, and then click OK.

9 Click OK.

Did You Know?

You can quickly delete a printer. Click the Start button, click Printers And Faxes, right-click the printer you want to delete, click Delete, and then click Yes.

You can safely unplug or eject plug and play hardware from the notification area. If the Safely Remove Hardware icon appears in the notification area on the taskbar, double-click it, select a device, click Stop, click Close, and then unplug or eject the device.

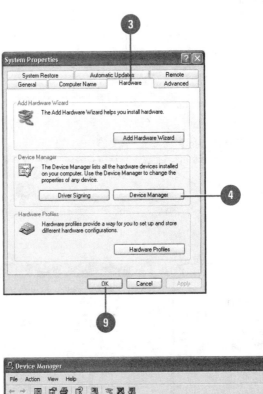

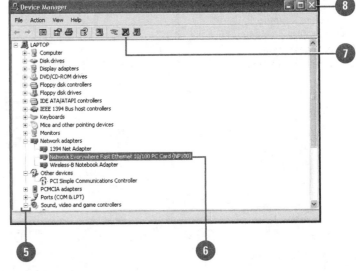

Backing Up Your Computer

Introduction

It is vital that you make backup copies of the files on your computer on a regular basis so you don't lose valuable data if your computer encounters problems. The term **back up** (or **backup**, when referring to the noun or adjective) refers to the process of using a special software program designed to read your data quickly, compress it into a small, efficient space, then store it on an external medium, such as a set of disks or a tape cartridge.

Windows XP Professional includes a program called Backup. Using Backup has several advantages over simply copying files to a removable disk. Your files are compressed as they are copied so that you can fit more onto a removable disk, and it splits a large file across two or more disks (saving disk space), something you cannot do with the Copy command. Also, in an emergency, Backup offers several data-recovery aids to help you locate and restore important files quickly.

If your computer system crashes and Windows XP cannot start, you can't use Backup to restore the files. To avoid the event of a major system failure and prepare for possible problems in the future, you can use the Automated System Recovery Preparation Wizard to help you create an Automated System Recovery (ASR) disk and backup of your system files. The ASR disk and the Windows XP installation CD allow you to start Windows XP and retrieve a backup of your system and personal files to restore your system.

Developing a Backup Strategy

With Backup, you can back up files from a local or network hard drive to a removable disk, a network drive, or a tape drive that is attached to your computer. Before you back up files, it is a good idea to develop a backup strategy. A **backup strategy** is a method for regularly backing up your work that balances tradeoffs between safety, time, and media space. For example, if safety were your only concern, you could back up your entire hard drive every hour. But you would not have any time to work, and you would spend a fortune on backup tapes. If spending minimal time and money on backups were your only concern, you might back up only a few crucial files once a month. The best choice is a balance between the two extremes. The **backup medium** that you use to store backed up files from a hard drive is usually a set of removable disks or a tape cartridge designed to store computer data. Removable disks and tape cartridges are large capacity backup media that require special hardware on your computer, such as a zip or tape drive. This extra expense may be worthwhile if you depend on your computer for business.

Because backups take time each time you perform them, you should back up only the files that change on a regular basis; back up all of the files on your computer at less frequent intervals. For example, because software program files don't change, you can easily reinstall them from their original program CDs or disks, so you do not need to back them up as often as your personal document files, which might change on a daily or weekly basis. Ask yourself how much work you can afford to lose. If you cannot afford to lose the work accomplished in one day, then you should back up once a day. If your work does not change much during the week, back up once a week.

Depending on the number and size of your files and the backup device you are using, the backup can take a few minutes to a few hours to complete. If you are planning to back up large amounts of information, such as your entire hard drive, it is best to start the backup at the end of the day and use a large capacity tape or removable disk, if possible, so you do not have to swap multiple disks. When a file does not fit on a tape or disk, Backup splits the file, fitting what it can on the current disk and then prompting you to insert the next tape or disk. When you perform a backup, Backup creates a **backup set**, also known as a **backup job**, which contains the compressed copies of the files you backed up. The backup job is stored in the backup file with the .bkf extension. You can store more than one backup job in a specified backup file. There are several different methods for backing up files with Backup:

A **normal backup** copies all selected files to the backup medium, regardless of when the files were last changed and clears the archive attribute for each file in order to mark the file as backed up. An **archive attribute** is an internal Windows file marker indicating whether a file needs to be backed up.

An **incremental backup** copies only the files that have changed since your most recent normal or incremental backup. It also clears the archive attribute for each file that is backed up. Therefore, the first incremental backup after a normal backup copies all files that have changed since the normal backup, and the second incremental backup copies only those files that have changed since the first incremental backup, and so on.

A **differential backup** copies only the selected files that have changed since your most recent normal or incremental backup. Unlike incremental backups, however, the archive attribute is not cleared during a differential backup. Therefore, successive differential backups copy all the files that have changed since the last normal or incremental backup, not just the ones that have changed since the last differential backup. The first differential backup after a normal backup copies all files that have changed since the normal backup, and the second differential backup copies all the files that have changed since the normal

backup, including all files that changed from both differential backups. Since differential backups copy more changed files, they take longer than incremental backups and require more disk or tape space.

A **copy backup** copies all selected files, like a normal backup, but it does not clear the archive attribute. Therefore, you can use it to perform a special backup without affecting your normal backup routine.

A **daily backup** copies all selected files that were changed on the day the backup is done. It does not clear the archive attribute. You can use daily backups to save your day's work without affecting your normal backup routine.

Typical Backup Schedule	
Day	**Tasks to do**
Monday, Week 1	Label your medium (removable disk or tape). If your backup requires more than one medium, label and number all the media in advance so you can recognize them easily. Insert your first medium into the backup device, and perform a normal backup with the Back Up Everything On This Computer option.
Tuesday, Week 1	Reinsert the medium you used for the normal backup, and perform an incremental backup. The incremental backup is appended automatically to the normal backup.
Wednesday through Friday, Week 1	Perform incremental backups. Each subsequent incremental backup is appended to the previous backup. If you need more than one medium, you will be prompted to insert another one. After your Thursday backup, you will have a complete rotation set.
Monday through Friday, Week 2	Repeat the cycle with a second set of media. If you need to perform a special backup of selected files, insert a different medium, perform a copy backup, re-insert the previous medium, and then continue the normal cycle.
Monday through Friday, Week 3	Repeat the cycle with the first set of media; continue rotating. If you need to back up only the files that have changed during a day, insert a different medium, perform a daily backup, re-insert the previous medium, and then continue the normal cycle.

16

Starting Backup

When you start the Backup Utility, either the Backup or Restore Wizard dialog box opens (known as Wizard Mode), in which you can back up or restore files, or the Backup Utility window opens (known as Advanced Mode), displaying the Welcome tab, in which you can start the Backup Wizard or Restore Wizard separately, or manually perform your own back up or restore files.

Start Backup and Switch Modes

1. Click the Start button, point to All Programs, point to Accessories, point to System Tools, and then click Backup.

2. To start Backup in Advanced Mode, select the Always Start In Wizard Mode check box.

3. Click Advanced Mode or Wizard Mode.

4. Click the Close button, or click Cancel.

Did You Know?

You can use Backup with Windows XP Home. By default, the NTBackup program is not installed on the home version. You can find it on the CD in the \VALUEADD\MSFT\NTBACKUP folder.

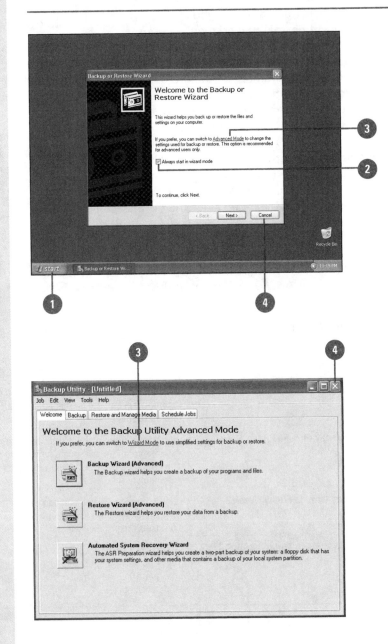

Understanding Backup Permissions

Backup Permissions

You must have certain permissions to back up files and folders. If you are an administrator or a backup operator in a local group using Windows XP Professional, you can back up any file and folder on the computer to which the local group applies. However, if you are not an administrator or a backup operator and you want to back up files, then you must be the owner of the files and folders you want to back up, or you must have one or more of the following permissions for the files and folders you want to back up: Read, Read and Execute, Modify, or Full Control. You can also restrict access to a backup file by selecting the Allow Only The Owner And The Administrator Access To The Backup Data check box in the Backup Job Information dialog box. If you select this option, only an administrator or the person who created the backup file will be able to restore the files and folders. To add a user to the Backup Operators group, double-click the Administrative Tools icon in the Control Panel, double-click the Computer Management icon in the Administrative Tools window to open the Computer Management Window, click the Expand indicator next to Local Users and Groups in the console tree, click Groups in the console tree, double-click Backup Operators in the Details pane, click Add in the Backup Operators Properties dialog box, type the domain and user name of the person you want to make a backup operator in the form \\Domain\user name, and then click OK. For more information about using Computer Management, see Chapter 17, "Administering Your Computer."

File Systems

You can use Backup to back up and restore data on either FAT or NTFS volumes. However, if you have backed up data from an NTFS volume used in Windows XP, it is recommended that you restore the data to an NTFS volume used in Windows XP instead of Windows 2000, or you could lose data as well as some file and folder features. For more information about FAT and NTFS disk file systems, see Chapter 14, "Maintaining Your Computer."

16

Performing a Backup Using a Wizard

In Wizard Mode, the Backup Wizard walks you through the process of backing up files on your computer. You can back up every file on your computer, selected files, drives, or network data, or only the System State data. The **System State data** is a collection of Windows operating system-specific data, such as the registry and boot files, that have been customized during normal usage for your computer. When you back up your System State data and restore it after a system problem, you bring back your customized version of the files instead of the general System State data reinstalled with the Windows XP CD.

Back up Every File Using a Wizard

1. Click the Start button, point to All Programs, point to Accessories, point to System Tools, and then click Backup.

2. Click Wizard Mode if necessary, and then click Next.

3. Click the Back Up Files And Settings option, and then click Next.

4. Click the All Information On This Computer option, and then click Next.

5. Select the location where you want to back up every file on your computer.

6. Type a name for the backup, and then click Next.

7. Insert a disk in the appropriate drive, if necessary.

8. Click Finish to start the backup.

Back up Selected Files Using a Wizard

1. Click the Start button, point to All Programs, point to Accessories, point to System Tools, and then click Backup.

2. Click Wizard Mode if necessary, and then click Next.

3. Click the Back Up Files And Settings option, and then click Next.

4. Click the Let Me Choose What To Back Up option, and then click Next.

5. Click the plus sign (+) or minus sign (-) to expand the file hierarchy.

6. Select the check boxes with the files or folders you want to back up, and then click Next.

7. Select the location where you want to back up the selected files or folders.

8. Type a name for the backup, and then click Next.

9. Insert a disk in the appropriate drive, if necessary.

10. Click Finish to start the backup.

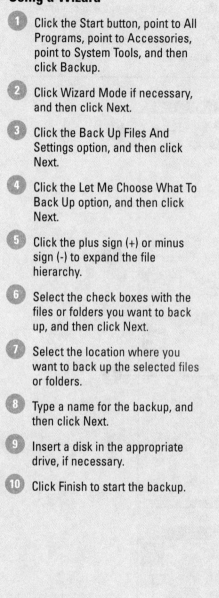

16

Selecting Advanced Options Using a Wizard

Before you click the Finish button in the Backup Wizard, you can set additional options using the Advanced button. The advanced options allow you to select a backup type (normal, copy differential, incremental, or daily), verify data after the backup, use hardware compression, if available, append this backup to an existing one or replace it, and schedule the backup for a specific date and time.

Select Advanced Options Using a Wizard

1. Click the Start button, point to All Programs, point to Accessories, point to System Tools, and then click Backup.

2. Click Wizard Mode if necessary, and then click Next.

3. Follow the instructions until you reach the Finish button.

4. Click Advanced.

5. Click the Select The Type Of Backup list arrow, select a backup type, and then click Next.

6. Select the verification, compression, and shadow copy check boxes you want, and then click Next.

7 Click the Append This Backup To The Existing Backups option or the Replace The Existing Backups option, and then click Next.

8 Click the Now option, and then click Next.

9 Click Finish to start the backup.

See Also

See "Performing a Backup Using a Wizard" on page 424 for information on using the Backup Wizard.

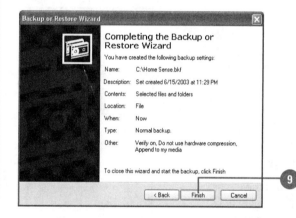

16

Power User Technique

Using Batch Files to Back Up Data

You can perform backup operations from batch files using the ntbackup command followed by various command line parameters. The ntbackup command you can only backup folders and cannot specify individual files. However, you can use a backup selection file (.bks) from the command line, which contains a list of files you want to back up. You can use Backup to create backup selection files. The ntbackup command does not support the use of wildcard characters. For example, typing *.doc will not back up files with a .doc extension. To start a backup using ntbackup, click the Start button, point to All Programs, point to Accessories, click Command Prompt, type **ntbackup** *folder name*, and then press Enter.

Performing a Backup

Instead of using the Backup Wizard to back up files, you can use Advanced Mode to manually perform a backup. When backing up only some of the files on your disk, you need to display and then select the folders and files that you want to back up in the Backup Utility window. Working in this window is similar to working with the Folders list. After using the plus and minus sign to display and hide the appropriate files, you select the check boxes next to the folders and files you want to back up. A blue checked box means all the folders and files it contains are selected for backup, while a gray checked box means only some of the folders and files are selected for backup. When you perform a backup, Backup creates a **backup set**, also known as a **backup job**, which contains the compressed copies of the files you backed up. The backup job is stored in the backup file with the .bkf extension. You can store more than one backup job in a specified backup file.

Perform a Backup

1. Click the Start button, point to All Programs, point to Accessories, point to System Tools, and then click Backup.

2. Click Advanced Mode, if necessary.

3. Click the Backup tab.

4. Select the check boxes with the files or folders you want to back up.

5. Click the Tools menu, and then click Options.

6. Click the Backup Type tab.

7. Click the Default Backup Type list arrow, and then select a backup type.

8. Click OK.

9. Click Browse, select the location where you want to save the backup file.

10. Type a name for the backup file, and then click Save.

11. Click Start Backup.

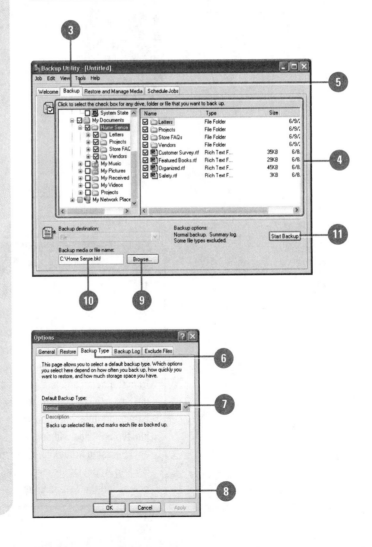

12 Click the Append This Backup To The Media option or the Replace The Data On The Media With This Backup option.

13 Click Start Backup.

The Backup Progress dialog box opens.

14 Click Close.

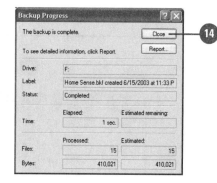

For Your Information

Excluding File Types from a Backup

When you want to back up all but a few files of a specific type on your computer, it is more efficient to back up all the files on your computer and then exclude the ones you don't want to back up instead of selecting each individual file you want to back up. To exclude file types from a backup, click Tools on the Backup Utility menu bar, click Options, click the Exclude Files tab, and then click Add new under the Files excluded for all users list if you want to exclude files that are owned by all users, or click Add New under the Files Excluded for User list if you want to exclude only files that you own. In the Add Excluded Files dialog box, click the file type to exclude in the Registered File Type list, or type a period and then the one, two, or three letter file extension in the Custom File Mask text box to exclude a custom file type. Type a path in the Applies To Path text box if you want to restrict the excluded file type to a specific folder or hard disk drive, and then click OK. If you restrict excluded files to a specific path or folder, the files will be restricted from all subfolders of that path unless you click the Applies To All Subfolders check box to deselect it.

16

Scheduling a Backup ▶

Scheduling backups according to a backup strategy can help you perform backups on a regular basis and protect your data. Typically, late at night or on weekends, when nobody is around, is a good time to perform backups. Backup makes it easy to schedule backups any time you want to perform them. You can schedule a backup to run once, every day, every week, or every month. You can also set additional options that start or stop the backup if the computer is idle, meaning that it is not processing any tasks. After you finish the Backup Wizard, a Backup Schedule icon appears in the Schedule Jobs tab on the backup date. On the scheduled day and time, the Task Scheduler starts Backup and performs the backup operation.

Schedule a Backup Job

1. Click the Start button, point to All Programs, point to Accessories, point to System Tools, and then click Backup.

2. Click Advanced Mode, if necessary.

3. Click the Schedule Jobs tab.

4. Double-click the day you want to schedule a backup to start, and then click Next.

5. Click the backup option you want, and then click Next. Select files, and then click Next, if necessary.

6. Select the location where you want to back up every file on your computer.

7. Type a name for the backup, and then click Next.

8. Click the Select The Type Of Backup list arrow, select a backup type, and then click Next.

9. Select the verification, compression, and shadow copy check boxes you want, and then click Next.

10. Click the Append This Backup To The Existing Backups option or the Replace The Existing Backups option, and then click Next.

11. Type a backup name.

12. Click Set Schedule.

13. Click the Schedule Task list arrow, and then select a backup interval.

14. Click the Start time up or down arrow to specify a backup time.

15. Click OK.

16. Click Next, enter a password twice as indicated, and then click OK.

17. Click Finish.

See Also

See "Scheduling Maintenance" on page 384 for information on scheduling a task.

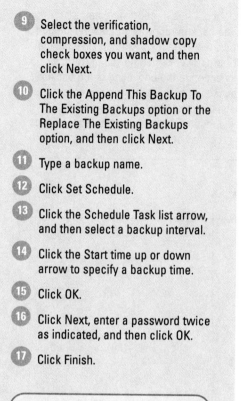

For Your Information

Using a Tape Drive to Back Up Files

Using a tape drive can make backing up large amounts of information, such as an entire hard drive, fast and easy. A tape drive is a hardware device that reads data from and writes onto a tape. Before you use a tape drive with Backup, make sure the tape drive is compatible with Backup. For a complete list of compatible tape drives, click Help Topics on the Help menu in the Backup Utility window. After connecting the tape drive to your computer and loading a tape cartridge into the tape drive, you can click the Restore and Manage Media tab, right-click the tape media to restore the tape tension, and then format or erase a tape cartridge to back up your files. To format a tape cartridge, you need to have a DC-2000-type tape drive, which requires that you format a tape before you use it.

Viewing and Printing a Report

After performing a backup, Backup creates a report with status information about the backup. The backup report is created in Notepad (a text-editing program that comes with Windows XP) and saved in the Backup program folder on your hard drive. Each time you perform a backup, the report information is added to the beginning of the backup report file in order to create a backup history. To make it easier to manage your backup jobs, it is important to view and print a backup report after each backup so you can have a hard copy reference of the backed up files and make sure no errors occurred.

View a Report

1. Click the Start button, point to All Programs, point to Accessories, point to System Tools, and then click Backup.

2. Click Advanced Mode, if necessary.

3. Click the Tools menu, and then click Report.

4. Click the report you want to view.

5. Click View.

6. Read the report in Notepad.

7. When you're done, click the Close button.

8. Click Cancel.

Print a Report

1. Click the Start button, point to All Programs, point to Accessories, point to System Tools, and then click Backup.

2. Click Advanced Mode, if necessary.

3. Click the Tools menu, and then click Report.

4. Click the report you want to print.

5. Click Print.

6. Click Cancel.

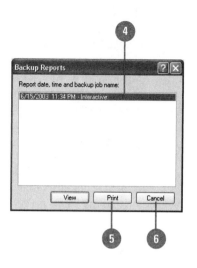

Select Report Options

1. Click the Start button, point to All Programs, point to Accessories, point to System Tools, and then click Backup.

2. Click Advanced Mode, if necessary.

3. Click the Tools menu, and then click Options.

4. Click the Backup Log tab.

5. Click the Detailed, Summary, or None option.

6. Click OK.

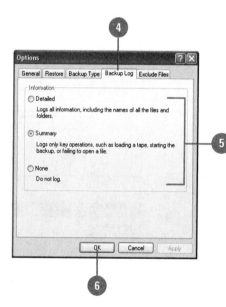

16

Restoring Backed Up Files

The real value in backing up your files becomes apparent if you lose or damage some files or need information from a document that has changed a great deal over time. You can restore a single file, several files, or an entire hard drive. Using the Restore Wizard, you can specify which files you want to restore and where you want them to be placed. When you create a backup set, a **catalog**, or index of the backed up files, is built and stored on the backup medium. When you store the catalog on the backup medium, it speeds up the process when you want to restore files. Instead of re-creating the catalog, the Restore function opens the catalog on the backup medium. However, if you want to restore data from several tapes, and the tape with the catalog is missing, or if you want to restore data from media that are damaged, you should not select the Use The Catalogs On The Media option.

Restore Backed Up Files Using a Wizard

1. Click the Start button, point to All Programs, point to Accessories, point to System Tools, and then click Backup.

2. Click Advanced Mode, if necessary.

3. Click the Welcome tab.

4. Click the Restore Wizard (Advanced) button, and then click Next.

5. Click the plus sign (+) to display the backup file.

6. Click the plus sign (+) to display the backup sets and folders.

7. Select the check boxes with the folders or files you want to restore.

8. Click Next, and then click Advanced.

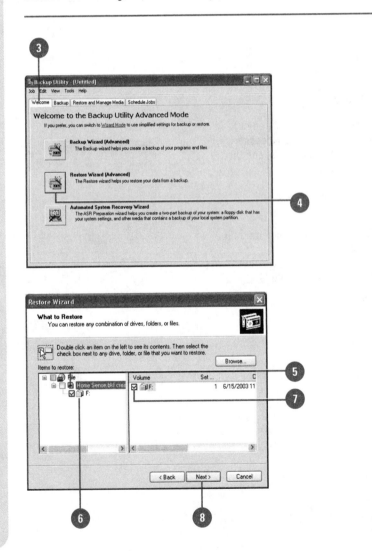

9. Click the Restore Files To list arrow, select a destination, and then click Next.

10. Click a restoring existing files option, and then click Next.

11. Select the restore security check boxes you want, and then click Next.

12. Click Finish.

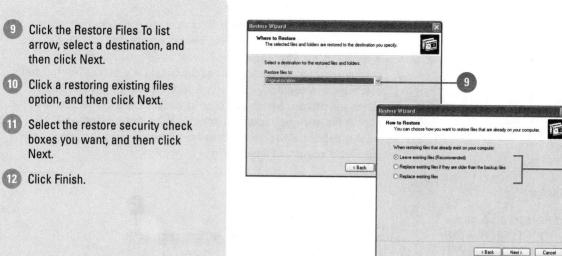

Perform a Restore

1. Click the Start button, point to All Programs, point to Accessories, point to System Tools, and then click Backup.

2. Click Advanced Mode, if necessary.

3. Click the Restore And Manage Media tab.

4. Select the check boxes with the folders or files you want to restore.

5. Click the Restore Files To list arrow, and then select a destination.

6. Click Start Restore.

7. Click OK, and then click Close.

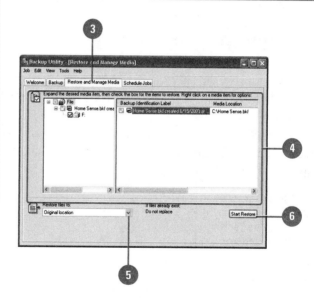

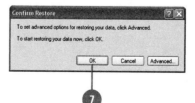

Did You Know?

You can set restore replacement options. Click the Tools menu, click Options, click the Restore tab, click the restore replacement option you want, and then click OK.

16

Deleting a Backup Set

Each time you perform a backup, Backup creates a backup set containing the backed up files. You can store more than one backup set in a backup file. After backing up files for a while, you might find a number of unneeded backup sets accumulating in a backup file. You can delete these sets quickly and easily from the backup file within Backup. When you delete a backup set, only the backup set is deleted, but the backup file, such as Backup.bkf, remains in the backup location. If you want to delete the backup file, drag the file icon into the Recycle Bin as you would any other Windows file.

Delete a Backup Set

1. Click the Start button, point to All Programs, point to Accessories, point to System Tools, and then click Backup.

2. Click Advanced Mode, if necessary.

3. Click the Restore And Manage Media tab.

4. Right-click the backup job file, and then click Delete Catalog.

5. Click the Close button.

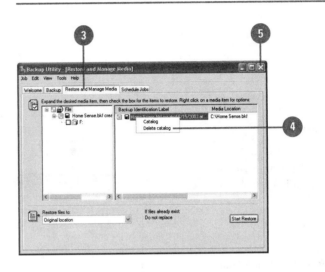

Did You Know?

You can delete the backup file using My Computer. Click the Start button, click My Computer, locate the backup file, select it, press Delete, and then click Yes to confirm.

Changing Backup Options

Backup provides additional options to customize the backup process on your computer. You can select options to estimate the number of files and size of the backup or restore, verify data after the backup completes, back up to a mounted drive, such as a mapped network drive, and show alert messages. These options are available on the General tab on the Options dialog box.

Set Backup Options

1. Click the Start button, point to All Programs, point to Accessories, point to System Tools, and then click Backup.

2. Click Advanced Mode, if necessary.

3. Click the Tools menu, and then click Options.

4. Click the General tab.

5. Select the check boxes with the options you want.

   TROUBLE? *If you are not sure about the options, click the Help button, and then click the option.*

6. Click OK.

Creating an Automated System Recovery Disk

In the event of a major system failure in which you cannot start your Windows XP computer, you could lose important data and waste a lot of time trying to fix your computer. To avoid these disastrous results and prepare for possible problems in the future, you can use the Automated System Recovery Preparation Wizard to help you create a backup of your system files and an Automated System Recovery (ASR) disk to restore your system. The Backup program backs up your system files then asks you to insert a disk to complete the ASR process. The ASR disk doesn't back up your personal data files, so it is a good idea to use the Backup Wizard in addition to creating a separate backup of your personal data files so they can be restored, too. To recover from a system failure using Automated System Recovery, insert the original Windows XP installation CD into your CD drive, restart your computer. (If prompted to press a key in order to start the computer from CD, press the appropriate key.) Next press F2 when prompted during the text-only mode section of setup, insert the ASR floppy disk when prompted, and then follow the on-screen instructions.

Create an ASR Disk

1. Click the Start button, point to All Programs, point to Accessories, point to System Tools, and then click Backup.

2. Click Advanced Mode, and then insert a floppy disk in the Floppy disk drive.

3. Click the Automated System Recovery Wizard button.

4. Read the wizard welcome, and then click Next.

5. Select a backup type (if available).

6. Type a backup name and location (a tape or network location), and then click Next.

7. Click Finish.

See Also

See "Restoring Computer Settings" on page 392 for information on restoring your computer system.

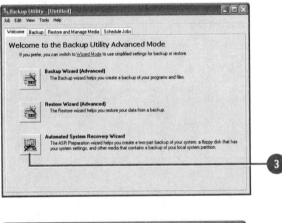

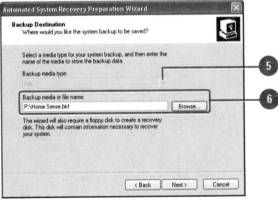

Administering Your Computer

Introduction

If you have purchased a computer and set it up in your home, you are that computer's administrator. Computers on a network in a company or an institution, such as at a university, are called clients. The clients are managed by one or more system or network administrators, who have the task of ensuring that the network and its services are reliable, fast, and secure. Although most network administration takes place on the server (host, as described in earlier chapters), clients must also be administered. Windows XP includes administrative tools that make it easy to ensure that client computers are operating as they should.

You use the administrative tools to track and view the activity on your computer. You set up criteria for gathering event information, then Windows automatically gathers that information for you. In the event of a problem, you can then view that data to help you find and fix the problem.

When you open an administrative tool, the window uses a two-pane view that is similar to Windows Explorer. The hierarchy of tools in the left pane of the window is called a **console tree**, and each main category of tools is called a **node**. The nodes in the console tree allow you to manage and monitor system events and performance, and make adjustments as necessary.

Exploring Windows Administrative Tools

Windows XP offers a set of administrative tools that help you administer your computer and ensure it operates smoothly. The Administrative Tools window, opened from the Control Panel, provides tools that allow you to configure administrative settings for local and remote computers. If you are working on a shared or network computer, you might need to be logged on as a computer administrator or as a member of the Administrators group in order to view or modify some properties or perform some tasks with the administrative tools. You can open User Accounts in the Control Panel to check which account is currently in use or to check with your system administrator to determine whether you have the necessary access privileges. Many Windows XP users won't ever have to open the Administrative Tools window, but computers on a network will probably require administrative support.

View Administrative Tools

1. Click the Start button, and then click Control Panel.

2. Double-click the Administrative Tools icon in Classic view.

3. When you're done, click the Close button.

Did You Know?

You can access administrative tools from the Start menu. Right-click the Start button, click Properties, click the Start Menu tab, click Customize, click the Advanced tab, scroll down the list, click the Display On The All Programs Menu And The Start Menu option, and then click OK twice.

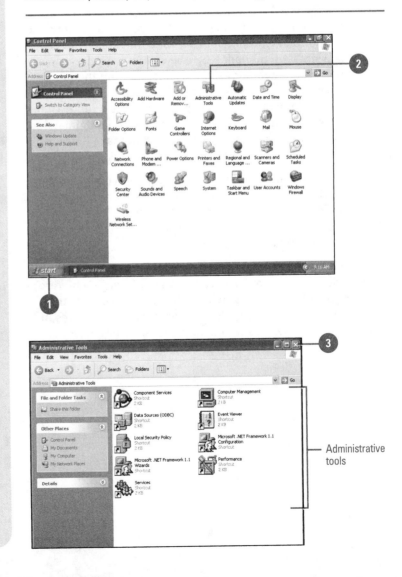

Administrative tools

Monitoring Activity with Event Viewer

Every time you start Windows, an event-logging service notes any unusual event that occurs, such as a failed logon, the installation of a new driver for a hardware device, the failure of a device or service to start, or a network interruption. For some critical events, such as when your disk is full, a warning message appears on your screen. Most events, however, don't require immediate attention, so Windows logs them in an event log file that you can view using the Event Viewer tool. Event Viewer maintains three logs: System, for events logged by Windows operating system components; Security, for security and audit events (such as who logged on); and Application, for program events. When you are troubleshooting problems on your computer, you can use the Event Viewer logs to monitor what activity took place.

Monitor Activities

1. Click the Start button, and then click Control Panel.

2. Double-click the Administrative Tools icon in Classic view.

3. Double-click the Event Viewer icon.

4. Click the log (Application, Security, or System) in which you want to monitor events.

5. Double-click an event.

6. Click the Up Arrow button or the Down Arrow button to display other events.

7. Click OK.

8. When you're done, click the Close button.

Managing an Event Log

Event logs grow in size as you work on your computer, but Event Viewer provides tools that help you view just the information you need and store the information you want to save for later. For example, you can apply a **filter** that allows you to view only events matching specified criteria, such as all events associated with a certain user. You can also search for a specific event using similar criteria. You probably don't want your active log to include events that happened long ago. With Event Viewer, you can **archive**, or save, your log periodically and then clear the archived events. Most administrators archive event logs on a regular schedule.

Filter an Event Log

1. Click the Start button, and then click Control Panel.

2. Double-click the Administrative Tools icon in Classic view.

3. Double-click the Event Viewer icon, and then click the event log you want to filter events.

4. Click the View menu, and then click Filter.

5. Select the event type check boxes in which you want to filter.

6. Specify filter information by specific value.

7. Select filter options by date.

8. Click OK.

9. When you're done, click the Close button.

> **Did You Know?**
>
> *You can open the log file from the Event Viewer.* Click the Action menu, click Open Log File, select the log file, and then click Open.

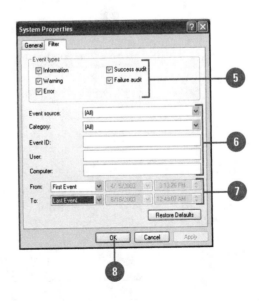

Find an Event

1. Click the Start button, and then click Control Panel.

2. Double-click the Administrative Tools icon in Classic view.

3. Double-click the Event Viewer icon, and then click the event log in which you want to find events.

4. Click the View menu, and then click Find.

5. Select the event type check boxes you want to find.

6. Specify find information for a specific value.

7. Click Find Next, and then click Yes, if prompted, to continue.

8. Click Close.

9. When you're done, click the Close button.

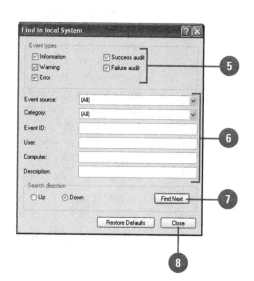

Save an Event Log

1. Click the Start button, and then click Control Panel.

2. Double-click the Administrative Tools icon in Classic view.

3. Double-click the Event Viewer icon.

4. Right-click the log you want to save, and then click Save Log File As.

5. Select a folder, and then type a name for the log file.

6. Click Save.

7. When you're done, click the Close button.

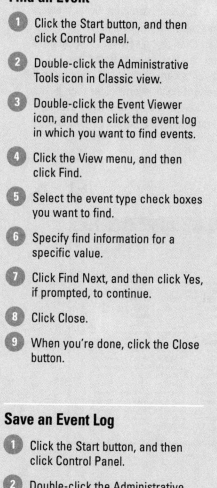

17

Changing Log Settings

You can control how any log in the Event Viewer collects data by defining a maximum log size (the default is 512K) and instructing Event Viewer how to handle an event log that has reached its maximum size. Only users with administrative rights can change log settings. In addition to specifying a maximum log size, you can also choose from three log options when the log is full: new events can automatically overwrite the oldest events, new events can overwrite only events older than a specified number of days, or Event Viewer will not overwrite events, in which case you must manually clear a full log before it can resume logging events.

Change Log Settings

1. Click the Start button, and then click Control Panel.

2. Double-click the Administrative Tools icon in Classic view.

3. Double-click the Event Viewer icon.

4. Click the log (Application, Security, or System) in which you want to change settings.

5. Click the Properties button on the toolbar.

6. Click the General tab.

7. Specify the maximum log size.

8. Select an option when the maximum size is reached.

9. Click OK.

10. When you're done, click the Close button.

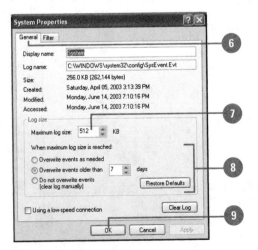

Creating a Performance Chart

On a daily basis, your system generates a variety of performance data, such as your computer's memory or processor use, or the amount of congestion on a device. As the system administrator, you can use the Performance tool to create charts from the data that enable you to observe how a computer's processes behave over time. The types of performance data you monitor and record are called **performance objects**. Each performance object has a set of **counters** associated with it that provide numeric information. The Performance tool charts the numeric data gathered from the counters and provides graphical tools to make it easier to analyze and track the performance of your computer. Performance charts include statistics about each counter you select, but unless you know how your system should perform, these statistics might not be very meaningful. For this reason, administrators create baseline charts, charts made when the computer or network is running at a normal level. When there are problems, the administrator can create another performance chart that can be compared to the baseline chart.

Create a Performance Chart

1. Click the Start button, and then click Control Panel.

2. Double-click the Administrative Tools icon in Classic view.

3. Double-click the Performance icon.

4. Click the Add button on the System Monitor toolbar.

5. Click the Performance Object list arrow, and then select an object.

6. Click the counter you want.

7. Click Add. You can continue to add other counters.

8. Click Close.

9. To delete a counter, click the counter, and then click the Delete button on the System Monitor toolbar.

10. When you're done, click the Close button.

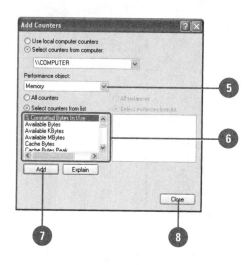

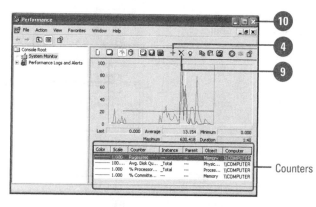

Counters

17

Setting Up an Alert

In addition to creating performance charts, you can use the Performance window to create user alerts. An **alert** is a warning that is generated when a counter value exceeds or falls short of a threshold value you have specified. When an alert condition is met, the date and time of the event are recorded in the Application log, which you can view from the Event Viewer. For example, you can set the % User Time alert to monitor the percentage of elapsed time the computer spends running programs. Some programs require more processing time than others, which can slow down your computer. The %User Time alert can let you know if your programs are using too many resources and slowing down your computer. Your system can record up to 1,000 alert events, after which the oldest events are discarded as new events occur.

Set Up an Alert

1. Click the Start button, and then click Control Panel.

2. Double-click the Administrative Tools icon in Classic view.

3. Double-click the Performance icon.

4. Click the Performance Logs And Alerts icon.

5. Click Alerts.

6. Click the Action menu, and then click New Alert Settings.

7. Type an alert name, and then click OK.

8. Click Add.

9. Click the Performance Object list arrow, and then select an object.

10. Click the counter you want.

11. Click Add.

12. Click Close.

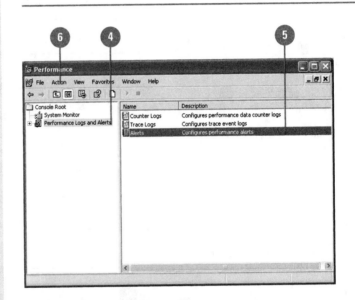

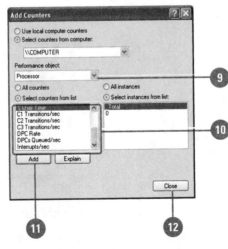

13 Click the Alert When The Value Is list arrow, and then select an option.

14 Type a value, if necessary.

15 Click OK.

16 To delete an alert, right-click the alert icon, click Delete, and then click OK.

17 When you're done, click the Close button.

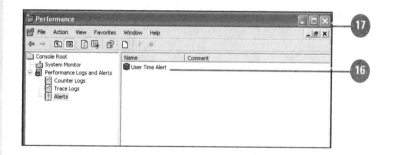

For Your Information

Using Alert Actions and Schedules

The Action tab in the selected alert's Properties dialog box allows you to specify what action you want to take when your system triggers an alert. By default, the system logs an entry in the application event log when it triggers an alert. You can also specify that the system send a message to the network administrator, that performance data be collected, or that a specific program be run. To run a program, click the Browse button, specify the program path, and then click OK. You can also schedule alerts using the Schedule tab in the selected alert's dialog box. Your system will scan for an alert at the times or intervals you specify.

Monitoring Local Security Settings

Using Windows XP Professional, you can view and monitor local security settings with the Local Security Settings tool to ensure that computer users are adhering to the organization's security policies. For example, you can set user account and password options to require computer users to create complex passwords of a specific length and change them on a regular basis. A **complex password** contains characters from at least three of the four following categories: uppercase (A through Z), lowercase (a through z), numbers (0 through 9), and nonalphanumeric (!, $, *, etc.). In addition to setting security options, you can also **monitor**, or **audit**, the success or failure of security related events, such as account logon and logoff activities, user account changes, and program launches. When an event that you have chosen to audit is triggered, it appears in the Event Viewer in the Security node.

Change Password Policies

1 Click the Start button, and then click Control Panel.

2 Double-click the Administrative Tools icon in Classic view.

3 Double-click the Local Security Policy icon.

4 Click the plus sign (+) next to Account Policies.

5 Click the Password Policy folder.

6 Double-click the policy you want to change.

7 Change the policy setting.

8 Click OK.

You can continue to change other password policies.

9 When you're done, click the Close button.

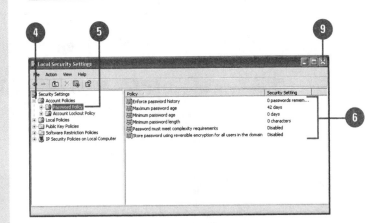

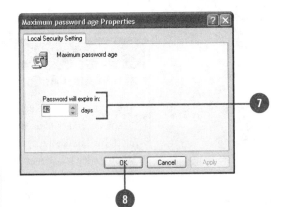

Audit Policies

① Click the Start button, and then click Control Panel.

② Double-click the Administrative Tools icon in Classic view.

③ Double-click the Local Security Policy icon.

④ Click the plus sign (+) next to Local Policies.

⑤ Click the Audit Policy folder.

⑥ Double-click the audit policy you want to change.

⑦ Select the Success and/or Failure check box.

⑧ Click OK.

You can continue to change other audit policies.

⑨ When you're done, click the Close button.

Viewing Computer Management Tools

Computer Management consolidates administrative tools, such as Event Viewer and Performance, into a single window that you can use to manage a local or remote computer. The three nodes in the Computer Management window (System Tools, Storage, and Services and Applications) allow you to manage and monitor system events and performance and to perform disk-related tasks. Each node contains **snap-in tools**, which come in two types: standalone or extension. Standalone snap-ins are independent tools, while extension snap-ins are add-ons to current snap-ins. The selected tool appears in the right pane, and you can use the toolbars and menus that appear to take appropriate action with the tool.

View Management Tools

1. Click the Start button, and then click Control Panel.

2. Double-click the Administrative Tools icon in Classic view.

3. Double-click the Computer Management icon.

    TIMESAVER *To open Computer Management, right-click My Computer on the Start menu, and then click Manage.*

4. Click a plus sign (+) next to the category you want to view.

5. Click the item you want to view.

6. Double-click the item you want to change, adjust the setting, and then click OK.

    You can continue to change other items.

7. When you're done, click the Close button.

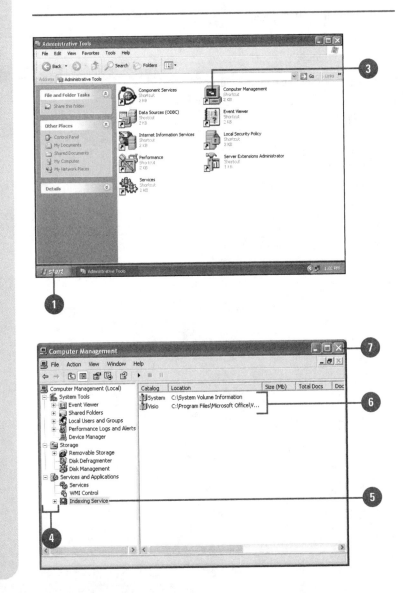

Managing Disks

The Storage node in the Computer Management window provides you with tools, such as Disk Defragmenter and Disk Management, to help you manage your disks. The Disk Management tool is a graphical tool for managing disks that allows you to partition unallocated portions of your disks into volumes. A **volume** is a fixed amount of storage on a disk. A single disk can contain more than one volume, or a volume can span part of one or more disks. Each volume on a disk is assigned its own drive letter, which is why the term volume is often synonymous with the term drive. Thus, the same physical disk might contain two volumes. Each volume can use a different file system, so you might have a single disk partitioned into two volumes, each with its own file system. You might partition a single hard disk in two different ways: first, with a single NTFS volume, and second, with one NTFS volume and one FAT volume, which can be helpful if you have a computer with two operating systems, Windows 98 on the FAT volume and Windows XP on the NTFS volume.

View Disk Settings

1 Click the Start button, and then click Control Panel.

2 Double-click the Administrative Tools icon in Classic view.

3 Double-click the Computer Management icon.

TIMESAVER *To open Computer Management, right-click My Computer on the Start menu, and then click Manage.*

4 Click a plus sign (+) next to Storage.

5 Click Disk Management.

The volumes on your computer display in the right pane.

6 Click the drive you want to modify.

7 Click the Action menu, point to All Tasks, and then click a command, such as Format, Change Drive Letter And Paths, Mark Partition As Active, or Delete Partition.

8 When you're done, click the Close button.

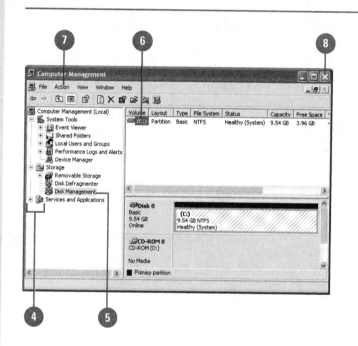

17

Managing Local Users and Groups

In Windows XP Professional, you can manage the access privileges and permissions of local user and group accounts. A local user account is an individual account with a unique set of permissions, while a group account is a collection of individual accounts with the same set of permissions. You can change local user and group accounts in the Computer Management window using the Local Users And Groups tool. This security feature limits individual users and groups from accessing and deleting files, using programs such as Backup, or making accidental or intentional system-wide changes. You can create or modify a user account, disable or activate a user account, identify members of groups, and add or delete members to and from groups.

Manage Local Users and Groups

1. Click the Start button, and then click Control Panel.

2. Double-click the Administrative Tools icon in Classic view.

3. Double-click the Computer Management icon.

4. Click Local Users And Groups, and then double-click Users.

5. Click the plus sign (+) next to Local Users And Groups.

6. Click the Users or Groups folder.

7. Double-click the account you want to change.

8. Change the settings you want; add members if requested.

9. Click OK.

   You can continue to change other settings.

10. When you're done, click the Close button.

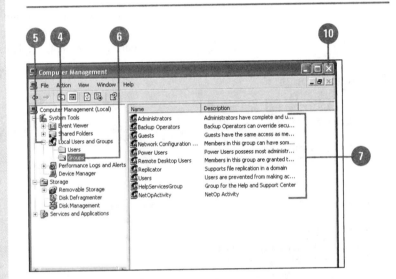

Viewing and Saving System Information

If you are having problems with Windows XP or a program installed on your computer and can't figure out what to do, you can use System Information to locate valuable information for a support technician. For most people, the information in System Information is difficult to understand. However, if a support technician asks you for information about your system, you know where to find it. After you find the information, you can save and send it to the support technician.

View and Save System Information

1. Click the Start button, point to All Programs, point to Accessories, point to System Tools, and then click System Information.

2. Click System Summary to view the main information about your system.

3. Click a plus sign (+) to view a system area.

4. Click the item you want to view.

5. Click the File menu, and then click Save.

6. Select a folder.

7. Type a name for the file.

8. Click Save.

9. When you're done, click the Close button.

Did You Know?

You can run Net Diagnostics and System Restore from System Information. Click the Tools menu, and then click Net Diagnostics or System Restore.

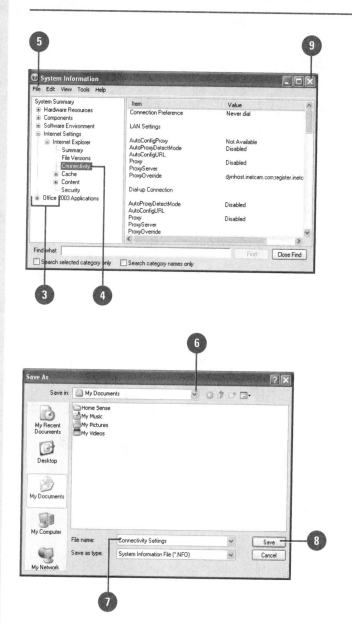

Changing Registry Settings

Windows XP manages all its internal settings with a database called the **Registry**. If you are an administrator or seasoned veteran of Windows and know what you want to change in the Registry, you can fix a problem with your system or a program, or you can enhance the functionality of Windows.

Edit the Registry

1. Click the Start button, and then click Run.

2. Type **regedt32**.

3. Click OK.

4. Click the plus sign (+) next to the function you want to display.

5. Click the folder with the item you want to change.

6. Double-click the item you want to change, Change the setting, and then click OK.

   You can continue to change other items.

7. When you're done, click the Close button.

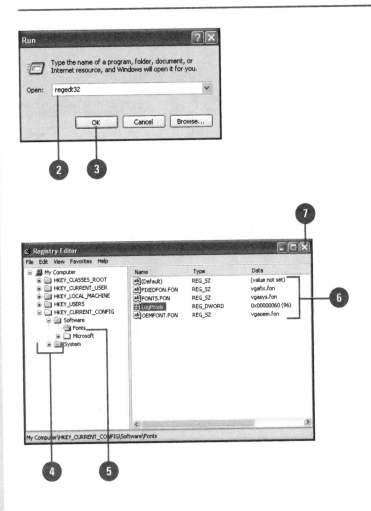

Appendix

Introduction

If you're upgrading to Windows XP from a previous version of Windows, this appendix describes how to prepare and install Windows XP. The temptation is to insert the Windows XP CD and start the installation, but you can avoid problems by making sure your computer is ready for Windows XP. Before you install Windows XP, you need to check your computer hardware and software and make several setup decisions that relate to your computer. The Windows XP Setup Wizard walks you through the installation process.

Microsoft is continually updating and enhancing Windows XP. Instead of releasing multiple updates individually, periodically Microsoft releases an update, known as a **Service Pack (SP)**, which provides all-in-one access to the most up-to-date drivers, tools, enhancements, and other critical updates (which were formally referred to as hotfixes). Service packs as well as individual updates are available free for download and installation over the Internet using the Windows Update web site. The latest service pack for Windows XP is Service Pack 2 (SP2), which dramatically improves security over the Internet or a network.

If you purchased a new computer that came with Windows XP already installed on it, you can use the Transfer Files And Setting Wizard to transfer the files and customized settings from your old computer to your new one.

Preparing to Install Windows XP

The Windows XP Setup Wizard (New!) guides you through many of the choices you need to make, but there are some decisions and actions you need to make before you start the wizard. To ensure a successful installation, do the following:

Make sure your hardware components meet the minimum requirements. Your computer hardware needs to meet the following minimum hardware requirements: 300 megahertz (MHz) Pentium or higher microprocessor or equivalent recommended (233 MHz minimum); 128 MB of RAM recommended (64 MB minimum); 1.5 GB of free space on hard disk; Super VGA (800 x 600) or higher resolution video adapter and monitor, keyboard, mouse or compatible pointing device; and CD-ROM or DVD drive. It's also important to make sure your computer's BIOS (Basic Input/Output System) is compatible with Windows XP; contact the manufacturer of the computer or the BIOS for the information. Beyond the basic requirements, some software and hardware services, such as Internet access, networking, instant messaging, voice and video conferencing, and sound playback, call for you to meet additional requirements; see Windows XP documentation for specific details.

Make sure your hardware and software are compatible. The Windows XP Setup Wizard automatically checks your hardware and software and reports any potential conflicts, but it is always a good idea to determine whether your computer hardware is compatible before you start the wizard. You can view the Hardware Compatibility List (HCL) at the Microsoft web site at www.microsoft.com/hcl/.

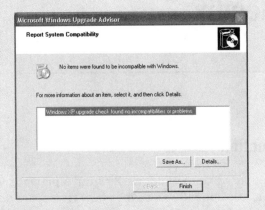

Make sure you have required network information. If you are connecting to a network, you need the following information from your network administrator: name of your computer, name of the workgroup or domain, and a TCP/IP address if your network doesn't use a DHCP (Dynamic Host Configuration Protocol) server. If you are not sure whether you are connecting to a workgroup or a domain, select the workgroup option. You can always connect to a domain after you install Windows XP Professional.

Determine whether you want to perform an upgrade or install a new copy of Windows XP. After you start the Windows XP Setup Wizard, you need to decide whether to upgrade your current operating system or to perform an entirely new installation, known as a **clean install**. A clean install includes completely erasing your hard drive and reformatting it with a new file system (either NTFS or FAT), which eliminates incompatibilities and makes your system run better. See Chapter 14, *"Maintaining Your Computer,"* for more information about file systems. Before you perform a clean install, you need to backup your files and settings on a CD, removable, or network drive before you begin. After a clean install you still need to re-install all of your programs. To perform a clean install, you also need the Full Edition of Windows XP, which is more expensive than the Upgrade version. You can upgrade from Windows 98, 98 SE, and Me to Windows XP Home Edition or Professional, and you can upgrade only from Windows 2000 Professional and Windows NT 4.0 Workstation to Windows Professional, but not to the Home Edition. Windows 98, 98 SE, and Me users can uninstall Windows XP, but this capability is not available to Windows NT 4.0 and Windows 2000 upgraders. Windows 95 and Windows NT 3.51 or earlier are not supported for upgrading, so those users will need to perform a clean install.

Back up your files in case you need to restore your current operating system. If you're upgrading from an earlier version of Windows or performing a clean install, you should back up your current files so you can correct any problems that might arise during the installation. You can back up files to a removable disk, a CD-R or CD-RW drive, a tape drive, or another computer on your network. See Chapter 16, *"Backing Up Your Computer,"* for more information.

Make sure you have the required product key information. On the back of the Windows XP CD-ROM packaging is a unique 25-character product key, such as KFEPC-12345-MHORY-12345-IROFE, that you need to enter during the Windows XP Setup Wizard installation to complete the process. Keep the product key in

a safe place, and do not share it with others. The unique product key allows you to activate and use Windows. Product activation and product registration are not the same. Product activation is required and ensures that each Windows product is not installed on more than the limited number of computers allowed in the software's end user license agreement. Activation is completely anonymous and requires no personal identification information to complete. To complete the activation process, you enter a unique 25-character product key during the Windows XP Setup Wizard installation process or when using the Activate Windows program located on the Start menu. You have a 30-day grace period in which to activate your Windows product installation. If the grace period expires and you have not completed activation, all features will stop working except the product activation feature. During the activation process, you can also register your copy of Windows XP. Product registration is not required, but completing the process ensures that you receive product update and support information from Microsoft.

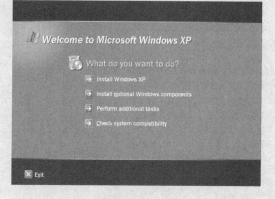

Installing Windows XP

The Windows XP Setup Wizard (**New!**) guides you step-by-step through the process of installing Windows XP. When the installation is finished, you are ready to log on to Windows XP. Be aware that your computer restarts several times during the installation process. Depending on the type of installation you need to perform, either upgrade or clean, you start the Windows XP Setup Wizard in different ways. If you perform an upgrade or clean install on a Windows version, you simply start your computer and insert the Windows XP installation CD to start the Windows XP Setup Wizard. However, if you perform a clean install on a nonsupported operating system or a blank hard disk, you need to start your computer by inserting the Windows XP installation CD into the CD-ROM drive, which starts the Windows XP Setup Wizard. A clean install requires you to select additional options as you step through the wizard, but the steps are basically the same.

Install Windows XP

 Insert the Windows XP CD into your CD-ROM drive, and then start your computer.

The Welcome screen appears.

 Click Install Windows XP.

 Click the Installation Type list arrow, select an installation type, and then click Next.

 Click the I Accept This Agreement option, and then click Next.

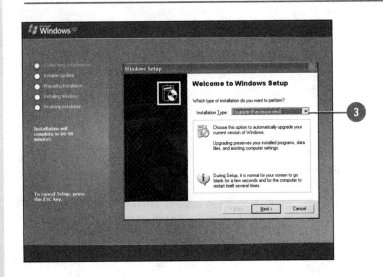

Did You Know?

You can clean up your old installation to save space. Click the Start button, point to All Programs, point to Accessories, point to System Tools, click Disk Cleanup, select the check box next to your old Windows version, and then click OK.

5 Type the 25-character product key, and then click Next.

6 Click the Show Me Hardware Issues And A Limited Set Of Software Issues (Recommended) option, click Next to display an upgrade report screen if issues arise, resolve any issues as directed, and then click Next, if necessary.

7 Click the Yes, Download The Updated Setup Files (Recommended) option, and then click Next.

8 Select a network type, and then click Next, if necessary.

9 When the Welcome to Microsoft Windows setup screen appears, click Next to activate Windows, click an activation option, and then click Next.

10 If you want, click a registration option, click Next, and then complete the registration.

11 If you want, click the Get Online With MSN option, click Next, and then complete the process.

12 Enter other user names to share the computer, and then click Next.

13 Assign account passwords and customize each user's desktop settings, and then click Next.

14 Click Finish.

The Welcome screen appears.

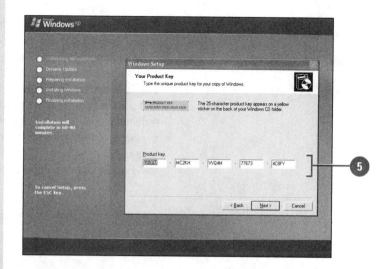

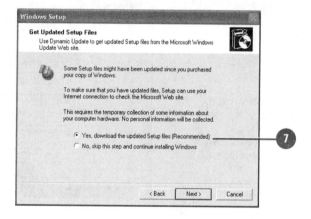

Updating to Windows XP Service Pack 2

If you have any version of Windows XP (except the 64-Bit one) you should update Windows XP to Service Pack 2, which provides critical security enhancements to protect your computer from harmful attacks over the Internet (NewSP2). With the enhanced Windows Update web site, Microsoft makes it easy to securely download and install this important update over the Internet. After you complete the installation, turn on Automatic Updates to help you keep your computer up-to-date and secure. If you're experiencing problems with the service pack and need to reinstall it again, you can uninstall (or remove) it from your computer using Add Or Remove Programs in the Control Panel (NewSP2).

Download and Install Windows XP Service Pack 2

1. Click the Start button, point to All Programs, and then click Windows Update.

   Windows connects to the Internet.

2. If prompted to install Windows Update software, click Yes.

3. Click Express Install, and then wait for the update scan to complete.

   If your computer qualifies, Service Pack 2 is automatically selected.

4. Click Install.

5. Review the End User License Agreement, and then click I Accept.

   Windows Update downloads Service Pack 2, starts the installation, and then begins the Setup Wizard to help you install it.

6. Click Next in the Welcome to Windows XP Service Pack 2 Setup Wizard to start the installation.

   While updating your computer, Windows checks your system for compatibility and archives files in case of removal later.

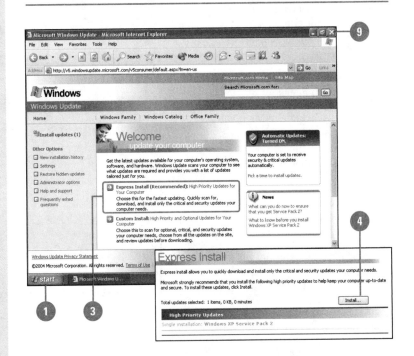

For Your Information

Preparing for Service Pack 2

Before you download and install Service Pack 2, it's important to (1) backup your personal files to make sure they are safe in case of a problem and create an Automated System Recovery (ASR); see Chapter 16, "Backing Up Your Computer"; (2) log on to your computer with an administrator account; see "Switching Users" on page 20; (3) make sure all other users are logged off; (4) get the latest critical Windows updates (not SP2); and (5) close all programs.

7 Wait for the updates to be installed on your computer, and then complete the Setup Wizard.

8 If prompted, click OK to restart your computer, and then turn on Automatic Updates.

9 Click the Close button in your browser as needed.

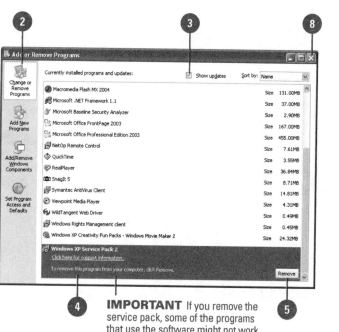

Uninstall Windows XP Service Pack 2

1 Click the Start button, click Control Panel, and then double-click the Add Or Remove Programs icon in Classic view.

2 Click Change Or Remove Programs.

3 Select the Show Updates check box.

4 Click Windows XP Service Pack 2.

5 Click Remove.

6 Click Yes to confirm the removal, and then follow the instructions.

7 When it's done, click OK.

8 Click the Close button.

See Also

If you encounter a problem after removing a Windows service pack, see "Restoring Computer Settings" on page 392 for information on restoring Windows to a previous state using the System Restore Wizard.

IMPORTANT If you remove the service pack, some of the programs that use the software might not work correctly.

Transferring Files and Settings from Another Computer

Instead of trying to re-create Windows settings manually from an old computer on a new Windows XP computer, you can use the Files and Settings Transfer Wizard (New!). If you are connected to a computer over a network or a direct cable connection and want to transfer files and settings from that computer to your new Windows XP computer, you can use the Files and Settings Transfer Wizard to transfer settings for Windows, such as folder and taskbar options, desktop and display properties, and Internet Explorer browser and Outlook Express mail setup options, and files or entire folders, such as My Documents and Favorites.

Prepare the Old Computer

1. Insert the Windows XP CD into your CD-ROM drive, and then start your computer.

   The Welcome screen appears.

2. Click Perform Additional Tasks.

3. Click Transfer File And Settings, and then click Next.

4. Click the Old Computer option, and then click Next.

5. Click the option for the way you want to transfer the files and settings, select a disk or network drive if necessary, and then click Next.

   TROUBLE? *The network option is available only when both computers are connected to a network and using the Files And Settings Transfer Wizard.*

6. Click an option to specify the type of information you want to transfer, and then click Next.

7. Click Finish.

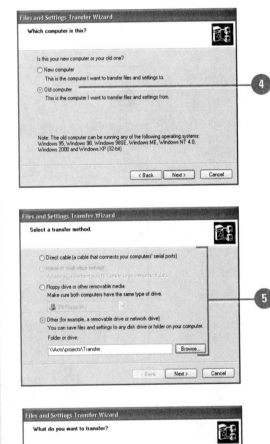

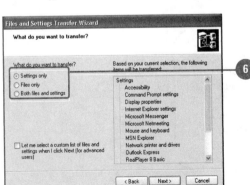

Transfer Files and Settings to the New Computer

1 Click the Start button, point to All Programs, point to Accessories, point to System Tools, and then click Files And Settings Transfer Wizard.

2 Click Next.

3 Click the New Computer option, and then click Next.

4 Click the I Don't Need The Wizard Disk option, and then click Next.

5 Click an option to specify the location of the files and settings, and then click Next.

6 Click Finish, and then click Yes to log off Windows.

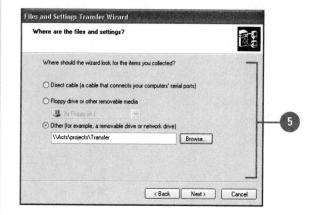

Files and Settings Transfer Wizard

Which computer is this?

Is this your new computer or your old one?

○ New computer
This is the computer I want to transfer files and settings to.

○ Old computer
This is the computer I want to transfer files and settings from.

Note: The old computer can be running any of the following operating systems: Windows 95, Windows 98, Windows 98SE, Windows ME, Windows NT 4.0, Windows 2000 and Windows XP (32-bit)

[< Back] [Next >] [Cancel]

Files and Settings Transfer Wizard

Where are the files and settings?

Where should the wizard look for the items you collected?

○ Direct cable (a cable that connects your computers' serial ports)

○ Floppy drive or other removable media
  3½ Floppy (A:)

○ Other (for example, a removable drive or network drive)
  \\Acts\projects\Transfer   [Browse...]

[< Back] [Next >] [Cancel]

Having Fun with PowerToys

Microsoft Windows XP provides additional programs you can download from the Web. The PowerToys Fun pack (**New!**) includes a video screen saver, desktop wallpaper changer, and much more. Before you can use the PowerToys fun pack, you need to download it from the Web and install it. When new programs are developed, the PowerToys fun pack gets updates, so check the Microsoft Web site from time to time for the latest power toys.

Download and Install PowerToys

1. Open your Web browser.

2. Go to *www.microsoft.com*.

3. Search for Windows XP PowerToys.

4. Download the PowerToys file, and save it to your hard disk, and then double-click it to install it.

5. Follow the wizard instructions to complete the installation.

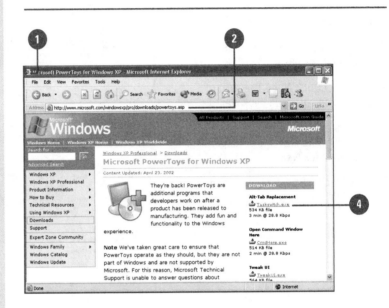

Troubleshooting

Index

i

A

deleting e-mail, 160-161
diverting e-mail to folders, 162-163
draft messages, working on, 159
Find People dialog box, 146
folders for messages, 158-159
forwarding e-mail, 155
help in, 143
identity, adding, 165
importing and exporting information with, 174
Inbox on starting, 143
maintenance options, changing, 161
managing messages, 158-159
message flags, 154
new accounts, adding, 164
reading e-mail, 154
recovering deleted e-mail, 160
replying to e-mail, 155
rules for incoming e-mail, 162-163
saving files in message, 157
selecting contact names, 151
sending e-mail, 150-151
signatures on message, 152
sorting messages, 159
spell-checking in, 151
starting, 142-143
Start page, viewing, 146
stationery for e-mail, creating, 152-153
switching identities, 165
Web browser, starting from, 143
window, viewing, 147
See also Address Book; newsgroups

P

page order for printing, 356
pagers, Windows Messenger sending messages to, 196-197
Page Setup dialog box
changing, 28
for Web pages, 133
Paint program, 27, 199
background designs, creating, 220
drawing and editing pictures in, 200-203
Toolbox, 200-201
paper
for photos, 218

printing options, 356
paragraphs
indents and tabs, setting, 33-34
parallel ports, 347
parity for modems, changing, 408
partitioning disks into volumes, 451
Password Reset disk, creating, 288
passwords
case-sensitivity of, 6
complex passwords, 448
Content Advisor password, changing, 302
for dial-up connections, 323
domain networks, changing administrator password on, 287
files, protecting, 290
in FTP (File Transfer Protocol) site address, 137
for Internet connections, 114
network, starting Windows XP on, 7
for offline Web pages, 126, 128
for Outlook Express e-mail accounts, 164
policies, changing, 448
for power schemes, 412
for private folders, 291
for remote computers, 338
resetting, 288
on switching users, 20
on synchronizing Web pages, 126
for VPN (Virtual Private Network) connection, 325
See also user accounts
pasting
command, Paste, 64
for embedding and linking, 39-40
with Whiteboard, 189
pausing
fax, outgoing, 365
printing job, 352-353
peer-to-peer networking, 313
people on Web, searching for, 131
performance charts, 445
performance of computer, improving, 389
Performance window
alerts, creating, 446-447
Computer Management with, 450
permissions
backup permissions, 423